Communication for Development

Communication for Development

A Practical Handbook

John Tuckey

BLOOMSBURY ACADEMIC
LONDON • NEW YORK • OXFORD • NEW DELHI • SYDNEY

BLOOMSBURY ACADEMIC
Bloomsbury Publishing Plc
50 Bedford Square, London, WC1B 3DP, UK
1385 Broadway, New York, NY 10018, USA
29 Earlsfort Terrace, Dublin 2, Ireland

BLOOMSBURY, BLOOMSBURY ACADEMIC and the Diana logo
are trademarks of Bloomsbury Publishing Plc

First published in Great Britain 2022

Cover design: ianrossdesigner.com
Cover image: Ruth Akulu in Kampala, Uganda, 2019.
(© Badru Katumba/AFP/Getty Images)

A catalogue record for this book is available from the British Library.

A catalog record for this book is available from the Library of Congress.

ISBN: HB: 978-1-7845-3819-4
         PB: 978-1-7845-3820-0
         ePDF: 978-0-7556-3792-8
         eBook: 978-0-7556-3791-1

Typeset by Integra Software Services Pvt. Ltd.
Printed and bound in Great Britain

To find out more about our authors and books visit www.bloomsbury.com
and sign up for our newsletters.

Contents

Section 4   Empowerment and engagement

Section 5   Communication for behaviour and social change

Section 6   Training plans and materials

Journalism

Drama

Illustrations

Figures

Tables

Acknowledgements

My sincere gratitude goes to those who helped with comments and reviews in the development, writing and publication of this book: Dr Michael Brophy, Emma Gremley, Sulakshana Gupta, Nicola Harford, Judy Houston, Mwendalubi Maumbi, Karen Merkel, Zuhur Fauzi Noah, Becky Palmstrom and Keith Ricketts.

Thanks also go to Dawn Chapman for all her support and to her and Margaret Gaskin for their painstaking work on the text, to Dr Michael Brophy, Mohammed Gaas, Naomi Goldsmith, Nicola Harford and Liz Mundler for their great help with the Glossary.

Finally, the book is dedicated, with my very sincere gratitude, to those who it has been a great pleasure to have worked with, who have taught me so much and whose responses to my training have given me the confidence to attempt writing it: Burhan Mohamed Abdi, Sehra Mohammed Abdilahi, Rica Abueva, Alsanosi Adam, Said Ali Mohamed Afrah, Daniel Realkuy Awad B Akec, Liza Altar, Jean Rose Baduria, Jessa Cabonegro, Cheerily Cabrera, Bul John Deng, Adan Dule, June Paulette Eclipse, Jeina Evance, Kenyi Evans, Nicola Franco, Mohammed Gaas, Bill Germinal, Clarita Golan, Ahmed Isse Gutale, Barbara Hambaba, Hamdi Abdulahi Hassan, Diana Hatilima, Hodan Yassin Ibrahim, Laurence Ingabire, Nicole Isimbi, Winnie Jaguru, Zarghuna Kargar, Kululu Elgebana Kuku, Angelo Kuri, Margaret Lawrence, Ahmed Ali Mahed, Mwendalubi Maumbi, Kojo McPherson, Mohannad Mergani, Abdillahi Jama Mohammed, Victor Moola, Akapelwa Mushinga Wa Mooto, Sibeso Mulenga, Mazuba Mwinga, Nalucha Nganga, Diana Njeru, Zuhur Fauzi Noah, Farah Omar Nur, Alfred Opana, Rahma Mohamed Said, Nadia Umutoni and Abukar Haaji Mohamed Yussuf.

Introduction

In 2015, Claudia Evers, the Ebola emergency coordinator in Guinea for Médecins Sans Frontières (MSF), said that the charity had gone in completely the wrong direction in trying to tackle a huge epidemic of the Ebola virus in West Africa the year before.

> We advocated for an increase in beds for too long, and everyone listened to MSF. Instead of asking for more beds we should have asked for more sensitisation activities. In the first nine months, if people had been given proper messages, all this could have been prevented.[1]

In that crisis, more than 28,000 people were infected, with more than 11,000 dead, according to the World Health Organisation.[2] What Ms Evers said was that proper communication would have stopped the devastating outbreak at an early stage, saving thousands of lives. This admission by MSF shows how important communication is in development, how its value is underestimated and how to do it is not well understood. The aim of this book is to show people, working in all fields of development, the value of communication and effective ways of doing it.

The book focuses on mass communication – mainly broadcasting (which includes social media) because of cost-effectiveness. When asked, people almost always prefer face-to-face communication, but that requires a large effort in social mobilization (for volunteers) or is expensive. One way or another, it is a huge consumer of resources.

It is true to say that, now, some people in the field recognize communication as an important part of the international aid effort, because information is as valuable to people in the Global South as material help. Those who use it have ambitious aims: to change behaviours, to save lives, to end corruption to improve livelihoods – overall, to have real impact on the lives of those they are trying to help. This book is a thoroughly practical guide to the specialist, innovative production techniques and formats needed for communication for development broadcast projects. It is based on my own experience of what works and on research into successful projects from all over the world.

This book is aimed at fellow professionals in the field and at students in media and in development, who will carry our work forward.

The book is not about the lobbying and fundraising communications of international development agencies with the wider world but about their communication with the populations that they are trying to help. Neither is this book an academic study aimed at identifying and presenting best practice. It is a practical guide that discusses communication for development projects on the ground, and which presents, in detail, ways in which these have been carried out. The book presents ways that have worked – which are not necessarily the ideal ways in which projects could be carried out. In some cases, it looks at projects whose failures present lessons to be learned.

Important note

It is not expected that many readers will read the whole of this book. It is assumed that most readers will read Section One and then go to the section that covers the field they plan to develop a project in, whether that is in emergency humanitarian response, distance learning, empowerment and engagement or social and behaviour change.

Disclaimer

I was directly involved in some projects discussed in this book. Therefore, my accounts may not be completely dispassionate. However, I feel that the insights I can bring from this in-depth involvement justify their inclusion.

The projects are, in chronological order:

Somalia Distance Education Literacy Project, Africa Educational Trust/BBC Media Action

Afghan Lifeline Project, BBC Media Action

Gama Cuulu, Southern Province, Zambia, Media Support Partnerships for Centers for Disease Control

Fala Mwa Lilangu, Western Province, Zambia, Media Support Partnerships for Centers for Disease Control

Somalia Livestock Livelihoods Project, BBC Media Action

Beled Taki hou Taki!, a radio serial drama in South Sudan, Free Voice

Small-scale Agriculture and Natural Resource Management, Horn Relief

Somalia Lifeline, BBC Media Action

Somalia Strengthening Radio Stations, BBC Media Action

Nolosha iyo Qaanunka, BBC Media Action

Sudan Election Mentorship, Fojo Institute at the University of Linnaeus and International Media Support

Dareemo, a mother and child health drama in Somalia, BBC Media Action/UNICEF

Life in Lulu, a mother and child health drama in South Sudan, BBC Media Action

Internews Humanitarian Radio Service, The Philippines, known as *Radyo Bakdaw*

Sakwe, a drama promoting empowerment for teenage girls, Girl Effect Rwanda

Itetero, a children's television programme, The Rwanda Broadcasting Agency and UNICEF

Section One

Issues for all communication for development projects

An overview of communication for development

Communication for development is the use of the media to promote economic growth and to relieve suffering as part of the overall international aid effort. Usually it uses broadcasting – at least as one element – and it is broadcasting *for* those it aims to help, not *about* them.

The concept of communication for development has five strands.

- Communication can make a huge, positive impact on development in countries of the Global South, both in everyday life and in crises brought on by disasters and conflict.
- Broadcasting information that people can use to improve their lives, and even to save lives, is as valuable as the distribution of material aid.
- Intelligently designed communication can bring about long-term, sustainable change in knowledge, attitudes and behaviour with positive developmental outcomes.
- Communication interventions build self-help, self-reliance and self-confidence, in contrast to the dependency culture that long-term material aid can so often create, which can be destructive, as shown in the report *Time to Listen*[1] and elsewhere.
- In humanitarian crises, as well as all of the above, communication can be an important part of the provision of psychosocial support.

A key question when an organization is considering using communication for development is whether there is evidence that it can be effective. Here are four examples of projects, one from each of the areas covered by this book, which suggest that it can be.

Humanitarian response

Internews is an international media for development organization. In 2007, there was heavy fighting in Darfur, a region of Sudan. In response, Internews established Radio Sila, a dedicated humanitarian community station, in the town of Goz Beida in neighbouring Chad, about 70 kilometres from the border with Darfur. The station was designed to serve the needs of three different communities living in the area. There were refugees who had fled the fighting in Darfur, internally displaced people from fighting farther north in Chad and the resident population. There can often be tensions, and even conflict, between resident populations and refugees or other displaced people. In a report by Internews in 2013, listeners to the station attributed significant improvements in intercommunal relations between the three groups in part, at least, to Radio Sila. An earlier audience survey report, in 2009, showed that some of the health communication had had significant impact, with very high percentages of listeners reporting they had heard information on fistula, on female genital mutilation and on girls' education, for example. More than that, UNHCR reported actual behaviour change, with a 21 per cent increase in births in hospital, and the agency attributed this, in part, to the radio station.[2] UNICEF reported that 86 per cent of people who brought their children for vaccination cited the radio as the source of information.[3]

Distance education

At the end of a year-long course in the Somalia Distance Education Literacy Project, run by the Africa Educational Trust with BBC Media Action, 88 per cent of learners passed a functional literacy exam. (From, *Effective Literacy Practice*, an ongoing database by the United Nations Educational, Scientific and Cultural Organisation (UNESCO)'s Institute for Lifelong Learning.[4]) The project had a large radio component.

Empowerment

BBC Media Action's *Somalia Strengthening Radio Stations* was shown, in BBC Media Action's own research, to have had some impact on improving the quality of journalism at the stations participating in the project:

> BBC Media Action's EC-funded project in Somalia led to the realisation of clear editorial processes for some stations, use of appropriate sources for news programmes, and improvements to journalists' understanding and observance of journalistic skills.[5]

Behaviour change

Miguel Sabido, at the time vice president for Research at Televisa, a major television company in Mexico, was one of the pioneers of communication for development. He started off using television serial drama. His second series was called *Acompáñame*, produced in 1977, and focused on family planning. The series ran for nine months, and the Mexican government's national population council recorded significant increases on previous years[6] in requests for information on, and in volunteering for, family planning. There were also significant increases in the take-up of contraception and in enrolment at family planning clinics.

In each of these four cases, the media element contributed to wider development goals. In helping to establish a more stable situation by reducing tensions between the different communities, Radio Sila also made the delivery of other humanitarian assistance easier and more efficient, while enhancing the health initiatives of both UNHCR and UNICEF. The Somalia Distance Education Literacy Project's impact through teaching many thousands of people literacy contributed to the overall aim of reducing poverty – case studies in the UNESCO report cited show direct impact on learners' incomes – and literacy gives access to, for example, vital health information. From 1977 onwards, Miguel Sabido's dramas have had a direct impact on enhancing the outcomes of the government of Mexico's and other organizations' health initiatives.

Change is central to communication for development

Communication for development sets out to help individuals and communities in countries of the Global South to help themselves in a wide range of fields, including health, education, livelihoods, peacebuilding, disaster relief and governance. Crucially, it tries to have an impact by bringing about change.

The kinds of change that communication for development can achieve include the following.

- Someone who could have died will live. This may be because they and their family have learned good hygiene practices; as a refugee, they have learned not to pick up cluster bombs to sell as scrap metal; a child has avoided catching malaria because her mother has learned how to protect her; or for hundreds of other reasons.
- A family is richer because its breadwinner has learned how to run his or her business better or has learned a skill that earns money.
- A generation of children grows up better educated – and, therefore, with more opportunities to be richer and healthier, with healthier families – because their teachers have themselves been trained by distance learning, perhaps over the radio or through interactive learning on the internet.

Communication and activities on the ground

It is common for communication work to be carried out in parallel with related activities on the ground. Indeed, one of the purposes of this book is to explain to organizations working on the ground in the Global South how to use communication to enhance the impact of their existing work.

The relationship between communication and activities on the ground can be in a number of different forms.

At one end of the spectrum, activities on the ground are the major part of the work, and the role of communication is largely to inform the community being served about the activity: for example, where an organization is distributing food aid, and broadcasting is used to let the community know when and where distributions are going to happen and who is eligible to receive the aid.

However, this would be one-way communication, a practice this book does not support, and it would be much better to use the channel of communication for dialogue. (See Two-way communication, below.)

At the other end of the spectrum, the relationship between broadcasting and activities on the ground is where the broadcasting is the major activity, and activities on the ground are set up to reinforce the broadcasts' intentions.

Here are two examples of this kind of relationship in actual projects.

- A travelling theatre group visits different communities to reinforce the behaviour change intention of a radio serial drama designed to combat HIV, through face-to-face exploration and discussion of some of the issues involved.
- Learning groups are established so that the participants can listen as a group to a series of programmes on improving livelihoods from livestock, and then carry out practical exercises together, under the guidance of a facilitator, to reinforce the learning from the programmes.

Alternatively, communication for development projects can be part of a larger, on-the-ground, initiative, without the close tie-in between the broadcasting and on the ground activities of the last two examples.

From 2012 to 2013, for instance, a BBC Media Action radio serial drama in Somalia, called *Dareemo*, was designed to bring about healthier hygiene behaviour. It was funded by UNICEF and was a part of their wider WASH (Water, Sanitation and Hygiene) programme on the ground. While the drama covered the same themes as the WASH programme, the only direct link was that it promoted the uses of oral rehydration salts with zinc, which UNICEF was distributing in Somalia through social marketing.

The livestock project mentioned above was, again, carried out by BBC Media Action in Somalia, from 2005 until 2008. The broadcasting and closely associated learning groups were part of a much wider programme of livestock livelihoods work, funded by the European Commission (EC), and carried out by a number of different non-governmental organizations (NGOs). The BBC Media Action team worked in cooperation with some of these, on an ad hoc basis. One example was with Vetaid, a UK-based NGO, which taught a milk hygiene and marketing course, but only in a very limited geographical area. The BBC Media Action team worked with Vetaid to adapt the course for radio, and broadcast it in five-minute sections over a period of weeks, bringing the course to many more people, enhancing the impact of Vetaid's original work, and of the whole European Commission programme.

Thus, communication for development work is often done in coordination with work on the ground, but the relationship is highly flexible. Many aid organizations, including UN bodies, are increasingly recognizing that a media component can be important in improving the impact of any aid project.

Cost-effectiveness

A key aspect of communication for development is that it can be very cost-effective for a number of reasons, including these.

- If a project is about persuading its audience to change to healthier behaviours, then journalists, laptops and transmitters are cheaper than drugs, doctors and hospitals or premature deaths.
- Communication projects can provide opportunities for communities to find their own solutions to problems, which are almost always cheaper than solutions that need to be found by international development agency bureaucracies.

The Somalia Distance Education Literacy Project, mentioned above, provided broadcasts, print materials and facilitators, but left it to communities to arrange accommodation for classes. In most cases the solution was a school classroom left vacant after the children had gone home.

Again, in 2013, after Typhoon Haiyan had devastated parts of the Philippines, a community radio station was set up in the small town of Guiuan, which very actively encouraged listeners to send in texts for any reason they chose. A woman with a disability, who lived on one of the islands off Guiuan, asked if anyone had a wheelchair she could have, as hers had been destroyed by the typhoon. Soon after this text had been broadcast, a man appeared at the station with a wheelchair that had belonged to his mother. The radio station staff took it to the island.[7] This was clearly much cheaper than if a humanitarian agency had been involved in the bureaucracy of procuring a wheelchair, organizing its transport and accounting for the expenditure.

Two-way communication

As will be seen in a number of projects discussed in this book, it is now accepted, and is a major emphasis, in communication for development work, that the communication is two way. That is, communication for development is not just a matter of a development organization or a broadcaster giving out information but there must be mechanisms in place for the audience to communicate with the organization or broadcaster and, crucially, for the organization or broadcaster to respond to that communication. Where it is appropriate, a broadcaster can facilitate two-way communication between international development agencies and the communities they are trying to serve.

There are many reasons why two-way or participatory communication is held to be important. They include the following.

- Communication is a human right, as set out in Article 19 of the Universal Declaration of Human Rights (UDHR). This means, for example, that in a situation where agencies are trying to meet the needs of a community overwhelmed by a disaster, the agencies need to respect all of the communities' human rights, including the right to communication, that is, two-way communication, not just one-way information giving.

- Without two-way communication, there can be huge gulfs of misunderstanding between international development organizations and the populations they are trying to help. This has become especially apparent in humanitarian crises. International organizations move into a territory they are not familiar with following a disaster, but their well-intentioned actions are ineffective or, worse, sometimes even create conflict. However, the need for two-way communication applies in any situation, and particularly where an international organization with international staff is working in a country that is not their own. The organizations do not understand the population's culture, and the population do not understand the working processes and thinking of the organizations. As has been said, these gulfs of understanding can have very serious consequences, including violence.
- Two-way communication through the media can help different populations involved in an aid effort – such as host populations and refugee populations – to understand one another better, again helping to avoid conflict, as the example of Radio Sila (above) shows.
- Two-way communication, especially through the media, can also help populations hold those with power – including aid agencies and government – to account.

In summary, it is imperative that organizations listen to the communities they are trying to help. That means, agencies need to facilitate two-way communication, listen to what the communities are saying and respond to what they are hearing. Media can be an effective channel for facilitating this process.

Because of its particular importance in humanitarian work, the issue of two-way communication and how to make it work will be dealt with in much more detail in the section on communication in humanitarian crises (see Chapter 15).

Communication for development in a changing communications world

Driven by technological change, the whole world of communications is changing rapidly, as mobile and digital technology spreads in countries in the Global South. As well as increasing access to a much wider range of media content for consumers, it is changing patterns of content production and distribution.

In the past, access to the means of producing and distributing media content – radio and television studios and printing presses – was strictly limited. Now, though, mobile phones allow anyone to produce video, audio, still images and written content, and the internet allows them to distribute it. Mobile technology allows for different distribution routes from the traditional media. During an Ebola virus epidemic in West Africa in 2014, a video called *Ebola: A Poem for the Living* was distributed from phone to phone by Bluetooth, for example.[8]

The 'digital divide'

For anyone involved in communication for development, social media and mobile technology are immensely valuable, particularly for establishing two-way communication and for providing development organizations and broadcasters with important insights into audience reaction and change. However, people working in this field need to be aware that the so-called 'digital divide' – separating those with access to the new communication technologies and those without – has not gone away. It does not look as if it is going to do so in the near future. The barriers to access are poverty, issues of language and literacy, age and disability. There are also power relationships within different societies, so that, in general, women have far less access than men, for example. In many ways, this divide reinforces the marginalization of people who are already marginalized.

The media landscape

Those working in crises caused by conflict need to be aware that both traditional media and social media can be, in effect, theatres of conflict themselves. Radio and television stations are often suborned by rival sides in war or civil conflicts, and social media can be virtual battlegrounds between different sides in warfare or between criminals and legitimate organizations. For example, Facebook pages from agencies supporting refugees, and designed to help refugees, are mimicked by criminals aiming to exploit refugees.

It is partly because of this that research is so important before embarking on a communication for development project. With research, an organization can better understand the situation a project would take them into. They can make an informed judgement on the preparations that need to be made, or, even, on whether the organization has the capacity to go ahead. Even in non-contentious situations, it is important that organizations working in communication for development (or planning to) carry out research. Through research, an organization can better understand the information and communication needs of different groups among the intended audiences. It can better understand what is often called 'the media landscape', that is the pattern of media outlets, their audiences, their nature and affiliations in the country or territory where the work is to be done. From this, an organization can work out whether their plans would be a good fit in that context, or if another organization is already doing something similar.

This does not necessarily mean original research on the ground. It may be that other organizations, such as governments, have already carried out needs assessments, and there may be media landscape guides to many countries produced by international organizations. Media landscapes can change quickly, and it is important to use the most up-to-date guide available.

Communication for development in the wider media context

What is set out here is an overview of the relationship between communication for development broadcasting and more mainstream media. The issues are dealt with in greater depth in the relevant chapters of each of the four remaining sections of this book.

Can a news organization be involved in communication for development?

There is an argument that a mainstream news broadcaster, particularly a public service broadcaster, should not be involved in communication for development, on the impartiality principle. In other words, since communication for development has an intention to move its audience in a particular direction, it cannot be impartial or balanced. There are two counter-arguments to this view.

The first is that public service broadcasters often have an education brief, an obligation to educate their audiences, and there is nothing in communication for development that would fall outside an education brief. Like communication for development, education is a process of change and change in specific directions. If a child emerged from five years of schooling exactly the same as she or he went into that schooling, there would be widespread dissatisfaction.

The second argument, which applies particularly to factual broadcasting as opposed to drama, for example, is that communication for development needs balance just as much as any news coverage. The notion that it is about giving out messages which represent only one point of view – that of change in the direction the broadcaster sees as positive – is now widely seen as invalid and ineffective. Communication for development programming needs to balance voices in favour of change with voices opposed to that change. Why this is so is discussed in Section Five on communication for behaviour and social change. The point being made here is that there is no contradiction between the principles of public service broadcasting and those of communication for development.

The same is true of each of the other of the five main principles of journalism: accuracy, objectivity and fairness. (See Chapter 3 for a fuller discussion of these five principles.) In some ways, these three are even more important in communication for development than they are in mainstream reporting. If a project is asking people to change aspects of their lives, that is hardly likely to happen if the audience perceive that the material is not accurate, and if they perceive that those making the programmes are allowing their personal prejudices into the material, or that they are being unfair. There needs to be a strong sense of trust between audiences and programme makers.

Equally, communication for development broadcasting needs to have the same production values as news and current affairs, to get the attention of the audience. There needs to be stories, that are well told, with tension and drama, and imaginative, engaging formats.

Where communication for development differs from news and current affairs

In spite of the similarities, there are important differences between these two fields. Communication for development has these characteristics.

- It has defined outcomes, which are based on identified need and can be evaluated.

- It does not present people, and especially its own audiences, as helpless or passive victims, but as active participants.
- It strives to be memorable, where news is forgettable.
- It needs to get through to people who may not want to hear what it has to say.

There is also a difference of priorities between the two fields among the six standard journalistic questions: What? Where? When? Who? How? and Why? In news, the first four are prioritized, and the last two are only included if there is the time or space for them. In communication for development, it is the last two – the How? and the Why? – that have priority. (For a fuller discussion of these standard questions, see Chapter 7.)

To take an example, which might be in a broadcast series designed to change behaviour so that more mothers survive childbirth and more babies survive the early months of life. If an item is about a man who took his wife, when she was in labour, 30 km to a hospital on a bicycle, then audience members who might find themselves faced with the same challenge in future are going to find how and why he did it far more useful than who the man is or where and when it happened.

Relations with local mainstream media

Experience and research suggest there are important issues that need to be considered by any organization – and especially an international organization – operating (or thinking of operating) in the field of communication for development.

Different organizations in the field of international development often take very different views of local media in the places they are working, and of the relationship they should have with them.

The positive approach

Some organizations foster good relations with local media and work hard to get positive results with them. They often develop projects designed to involve local media and try to strengthen their capacity, while at the same time delivering wider development goals.

The suspicious approach

Other organizations, though, do not trust local media or are defensive towards them, and try to keep any contact to a minimum. They base these attitudes on what are, in some places, genuine problems with local media.

In some countries, corruption in the media is very common. Unpaid or poorly paid journalists will take a particular angle on a story, or fabricate a story, in return for payment to further the interest of the person paying. Broadcasting stations are often established to further the interests of their owners, whether those interests are commercial, political or religious. (This is often not local corruption and distortion but is funded by Western interests. Africa, for example, has many radio stations funded by Western evangelicals keen to promote their brand of Christianity.) Finally, poorly trained journalists get a story wrong, which, particularly in areas of conflict, can have disastrous consequences, even death.

The sidelining approach

Against this, there are documented cases where well-organized and well-intentioned local media have been sidelined by aid organizations, souring relations. For example, immediately after a severe earthquake in Haiti in 2010, local radio stations performed very well, providing effective support for the population, including saving lives. However, when the international aid agencies arrived, these stations were largely ignored by them, and their potential as effective communication partners was wasted.[9] (This case is discussed at length in Chapter 15.)

The independent approach

For some organizations, the preferred solution is to set up their own stations in the country. This is the approach that led to the establishment of Radio Sila, by the media for development organization Internews, discussed earlier. The case for this approach is that it ensures local populations get accurate and impartial information on which they can base important decisions in their lives. At the same time, the capacity of the overall local media world is increased by adding well-trained journalists to the local pool of talent.

It is, of course, easier to use social media than to set up a broadcasting station. However, an organization needs to have thorough research evidence showing that all sections of its target audience have ready access to social media. It needs to have adequate safeguarding in place to be able to detect any attempts to hijack or fake its social media material. The organization also needs to know how to get such hijacked material taken down.

Buying airtime

If, however, an organization decides not to take the independent approach, and chooses to work with existing local media instead, there is a key question: Should an aid-funded organization pay local media – radio or television stations – to broadcast work they have commissioned or produced?

A principle reason for aid-funded organizations not to buy air-time is that it can undermine the enterprise of a local station, the way that it meets the needs of its audience and the development of its staff. So, for example, a local radio station may broadcast a popular phone-in programme, researched and hosted by the station's staff, in which local people air their views and raise concerns over important local issues with local government. An international, aid-funded organization asks to buy that slot, to broadcast a children's educational programme produced in another country. They need that particular time slot because that is when children are in class. The station's management accept the children's programme, because they will make more money from it than they can from their own phone-in. In this example, the result would be that local staff are put out of work, and an important local need is no longer met.

Against that is the argument that most local radio stations in countries in the Global South are commercial, working on shoestring budgets, and well-funded international organizations should not ask them to become charities and broadcast material for free.

The necessity for research

For organizations thinking of using broadcast communication as part of their development work, the key measure to take before taking any decisions is, as has already been mentioned, to research up-to-date information on the media landscape in the territory or country in question.

Addressing diverse audiences

Many communication for development projects are, by their nature, aimed at specific audiences. However, there are others which need to address much broader audiences: a radio station established to support a community caught up in a humanitarian emergency, for example, or where a series of programmes is aimed at a wide section of a population.

For example, from 2005 to 2008 BBC Media Action ran a project aimed at improving the livelihoods of people working in the livestock sector in Somalia. This is a huge industry, which includes people from rich international traders to those in the poorest sections of the community, like women selling milk on the street.

Different sections of the audience for either of these projects will have different information and communication needs, arising from issues of occupation, gender, power relationships, wealth and poverty, age and disability. It is, therefore, important that any organization involved in such communication projects, either for development or in a humanitarian context, should have as clear an understanding as they can of what these different needs are if the communication is to reach and serve the needs of the different sections of the audience. Again, research will be necessary.

Before any communication for development project, it is usual practice to carry out thorough and well-planned formative research. This needs to be designed to find out the following.

- What levels of understanding there are among the different target audiences on the issues that the project aims to address.
- What barriers there are to change.
- What positives there are that the initiative can build on to encourage change.
- What the different communication and information needs of different groups are.

If the broadcasting is a drama, then characters can be devised with whom different groups among the audience will identify, and storylines can be worked out for those characters that will address the communication and information needs of the group who identify with the characters.

If the broadcasting is factual, then different interviewees, representing the different groups, will appear in the programmes, and those interviews will explore the communication and information needs of the associated groups among the audience.

This approach will be dealt with in greater depth in the chapters on communication for behaviour change.

Reaching populations in crisis

However, in humanitarian crises there is not the time for, nor normally would it be practical to carry out, carefully designed and thorough formative research. Instead, a rapid communication and information needs assessment is usually carried out, often as part of a wider needs assessment looking at practical and material needs as well. There are several published sets of assessment questions – including those developed by the Communicating with Disaster-Affected Communities Network (CDACN), such as the CDAC Network Suite of Common Needs Assessment Tools[10] – which ask the researcher, at the outset, to identify the gender, age and any disability of the interviewee. In this way, analysis of the findings can show the different needs of different groups, and those needs can be addressed in communication. Normally, again, this would be done by using appropriate interviewees. Even without a needs assessment, it is important that communication in a humanitarian crisis reflects all of the affected groups in its choice of interviewees.

'Inclusivity' – the active pursuit of involving often-marginalized groups (like the old and those with disabilities) – is a high priority in development and humanitarian work. Standards of inclusivity apply as much to communication as to any other activities in these fields.[11]

Communication for children

As in mainstream broadcasting, it is generally recognized in communication for development that the needs of children can best be met with separate programming aimed specifically at them. Increasingly, it is being seen that this kind of programming should not just be *for* children but *by* children. As long ago as 1999, BBC Media Action, for example, trained refugee Kosovar children as reporters, and UNICEF has championed child reporters for many years, particularly on issues of children's rights.

Meeting the language needs of audiences

The choice of the language or languages to be used in communication is extremely important. This might appear obvious, but, as will be seen later, there have been some terrible errors made, largely when the choice of language has been based on assumption and not research.

Assessing language use

The issue needs to be considered very carefully at the planning stage. For example, if there is a lingua franca, is it understood by the whole population? There may well be groups – especially in rural areas – who do not use it at all. If there is no lingua franca, how is one to choose which local language or languages to use? This is particularly an issue in Africa, where, in some countries, there are eighty or more languages spoken. Seen from the outside, it is easy to make mistakes over language. For example, in South Sudan, where the website Ethnologue identifies sixty-nine indigenous languages,[12] Arabic is one of the official languages and may appear to be a lingua franca. However, spoken Arabic varies so widely across the country that one Arabic speaker may well not understand another Arabic speaker. There is a north-south divide in the country. A dialect called Juba Arabic – a mix of indigenous languages, Swahili and Arabic – is spoken relatively widely across the south. In the north of the country, a dialect often known as Simple Arabic – related to Sudanese Arabic – is quite widely spoken. It is, apparently, very difficult for a speaker of one of these dialects to understand the other dialect.

Using a wrong language is useless

It is, therefore, important to assess language use. Organizations are becoming increasingly aware of this, but, still, and especially in the haste of an emergency humanitarian response, 'getting the information out' in whatever language sometimes appears to be the priority, when, of course, if the language is not understood by the audience, no information is going anywhere.

In a report on communications during a huge epidemic of the Ebola virus in West Africa in 2014 and 2015, the organization Translators Without Borders (TWB) highlighted the problems there were in the choice of languages used to communicate humanitarian, life-saving information. TWB reported that most material issued by aid agencies was in English, when, for example, only 13 per cent of women in Sierra Leone understand English.[13] In the end, TWB translated material into thirty languages.[14]

This all means that no assumptions can be made about the choice of language or languages in communication for development. At an early stage, research is necessary so that the project team have a clear grasp of languages understood in the territory concerned, and measures can be put in place to handle the editorial processes which will be needed to ensure the correct languages can be used.

The structure of this book

This book is divided into four areas of communication for development: humanitarian assistance; distance learning; empowerment, governance and human rights; and behaviour and social change. It is divided up this way, rather than, say, by the subject of the programming – health communication or livelihoods, for example – because the methodology of communication is different between these four areas, and that is the book's focus. There is, of course, overlap between these areas – a distance learning project can include elements of behaviour change methodology, for example – but, overall, the methodologies are sufficiently different to justify the book's approach.

This book's approach to communication for development

The key concepts

Messaging or stories?

There are, essentially, two different approaches in communication for development. The first can be characterized as 'messaging', that is giving out pieces of clear, unvarnished, straightforward and tightly focused information. The second approach is through stories, usually stories of role models, that is people or characters who audience members identify with and whose example they are inclined to follow.

There are circumstances where a simple, clear message might be effective: for example, a warning that going back into a damaged building after an earthquake is very risky. However, overall, while the messaging approach may appear to be the more obviously effective, that is probably not the case – and there are many reasons why. In 2004, Doe Mayer made the case against what she called 'heavy-handed messages'.[1] She was discussing fiction but she points out that the argument applies to any forms of messaging.

Perhaps the clearest and most familiar of all messages is the 'Smoking Kills' message on cigarette packets across the world. It is hard to imagine a starker, clearer message, yet it is thought that there are 1 billion smokers in the world, and that 31 per cent of men smoke.[2] If messages work, is it not likely that the number of smokers would be reduced to a small hardcore and that no one would start smoking?

The problems with messages

The following example highlights some of the problems with messaging.

A piece of information that is very common in communication for development health projects is: 'Breastfeed your baby exclusively for the first six months' (that is do not give the baby water, formula milk or any kind of solid food). Presenting this information as a message ignores many aspects of the change it is asking for. The idea of not giving a baby water is simply counter-intuitive. In some societies, there are strong cultural attitudes against exclusive breastfeeding: for example, the idea that babies cannot digest colostrum – the milk the mother produces immediately after giving birth – or that a mother cannot give milk for the first few days after giving birth.

Among some groups in South Sudan, there is a ritual known as *cibir*, usually conducted seven days after birth, in which the baby is given a piece of soft food: how the baby reacts shows whether the mother has been faithful or not. It is extremely hard for a mother to argue against the baby being put through this, because she is likely to be seen as having something to hide. If a young mother, especially if she is not educated, faces barriers like these, she needs negotiating skills. There will be other people who will have a strong influence over how the baby is treated, and the mother needs to persuade them to accept the idea of exclusive breastfeeding. A role model can be shown encountering these various barriers to change, and either overcoming them or avoiding them. For example, while a role-model young mother can be shown learning how to negotiate with her elders, it would be extremely difficult to explain this process through messages. The role model can be either a real individual who comes from the specific society and culture or a character in a drama or story, created by writers from the society and culture.

Messaging versus action and consequence in drama

When discussing drama, there is a separate argument. One school of thought, put forward, for example, by Esta de Fossard in *How to Write a Radio Serial Drama for Social Development. A Script Writer's Manual*,[3] is that an entertaining drama is created and the relevant messages are embedded in it, being spoken by one character to another. The storylines are not directly related to the messages.

Research suggests that this approach can have impact. However, it does underuse the immense power drama can have as a communication tool. Drama is action and consequences, not messages. Drama is best at showing characters in action, not characters delivering messages to each other. Characters can be shown pursuing different courses of action, and the audience can see the consequences of those courses of action. Instead of one character saying to another, 'You know you must wash your hands after using the latrine, don't you?' in the middle of a drama that is largely about something else, a child can be shown dying because her mother does not wash her hands. That is the brutal, nasty reality, and showing it is treating the audience as adults. So, the use of drama as a vehicle for messaging is a failure to fully exploit a powerful communication tool.

That the action and consequence approach works is shown by research on the impact of the BBC Media Action's *Tiraarka Qoyska*, in Somalia, from 2012 to 2013. Each weekly radio programme included an episode from a serial drama called *Dareemo*, and a discussion. In the drama, some babies died as a result of poor hygiene practices, and research undertaken after the drama had been transmitted showed that these tragic storylines had particular impact on behaviour change.

> A large majority of listeners reported that they had learned new things from *Tiraarka Qoyska* that they otherwise would not have known and, as a result, changed some of their daily habits. These audience members demonstrated improved knowledge of health issues and better practices. This was particularly true in the prevention and treatment of illness in children. Indeed, the elements

of the programme that made the strongest impression on listeners were drama storylines in which babies died from preventable illnesses. These stories are directly linked with the types of behaviours in which listeners have demonstrated better results than nonlisteners.[4]

Of course, it is important to have positive role models, and, in this case, it was mothers whose babies had died who went on to model healthy behaviour change.

Experts

Who are the best experts in communication for development projects? To stay with health programming, whose voices should be heard: doctors, or people the audience associate with more? Some would argue that voices need to be authoritative, and, on health issues, doctors are authoritative and so, their voices should predominate.

To pursue the case of communication for healthier breastfeeding practices. A doctor could, of course, explain the value of colostrum as the ideal food for a baby in the first days of life. There is, though, the question of how a doctor would explain that. Many doctors are far more interested in communicating their education – particularly in their use of language – than in communicating information that is useful to the audience. A midwife might well be a better choice, and she or he is more likely to use language readily understood by the audience.

The bigger point, however, is that most of the barriers to healthier behaviour in this area are not medical but are social or cultural. It is much less likely that a doctor, coming from the educated middle class, would have experienced those social and cultural barriers in anything like the same way (if at all) that an uneducated young mother had. The approach that this book takes is that a much better expert, in this case, would be someone who has, themselves, overcome those social and cultural barriers. In the example, that would be an uneducated mother who managed to exclusively breastfeed her baby for the first six months of its life. Of course, it is likely to be much harder for a production team to find such a person, though it is by no means impossible. (One of the advantages of using fiction or drama is that a plausible character, based on real experience, can be created who can fulfil this role.)

Discussion and learning

It has long been established from research into education (e.g. *Language and Learning* by James Britton[5]) that talk is essential to learning and that learning becomes embedded and internalized through talk and not just through listening. It follows, therefore, that a key aim of communication for development is to promote discussion among its audiences. This is an issue that runs through a number of parts of this chapter, especially the sections on complexity and unpredictability, and on including conflicting opinions.

This section looks at one strategy that can be used in drama and factual programmes, which is ending an episode or a programme with a personal dilemma, one that is not resolved until the following episode or programme in the series.

The idea of the cliffhanger – where a situation in a drama is left unresolved at the end of an episode in order to persuade the audience to listen to or view the next episode – is very commonly used in serial dramas, and this is a development of that idea. In this strategy, a character in a drama, or a real-life interviewee in a factual programme, is faced with a dilemma, and that dilemma is left unresolved at the end of the programme. The intention is not just to encourage the audience to tune in for the next episode or programme but to encourage members of the audience to talk to each other about what they think is going to happen. If the dilemma is on one of the key topics of the project, then it is likely to encourage discussion of that topic, furthering learning. Normally, the dilemma will be resolved in the next episode or programme in the series.

A dilemma might be, for example, a wife who wants to practise child spacing – using a birth control method – but fears her husband's reaction even to talking about it. On the one hand, she faces the risks of getting pregnant yet again; on the other, she risks divorce or worse. What is she going to do?

Complexity and unpredictability

When using drama in communication for development, another area to look at is complexity, multiple layers and unpredictability. For most people in the West, when thinking about the films, stories or plays they want to watch or read, they do not want neatly tied-up endings or one-dimensional simplicity. They want unpredictable endings, or unpredictable routes to predictable endings, and multi-layered complexity. Yet, so often, drama in communication for development is not like this – it is simple, obvious, predictable and one-dimensional.

Doe Mayer argues, in her article,[6] that no one likes the predictable, the simple, where everything is set out with total clarity. Audiences like ambiguity and things happening at different levels; almost all Western drama has sub-text, where there is another meaning beneath the words that are actually said, for instance.

Yet when drama is made to promote development in poor countries, it often seems as if audiences are expected to only want simplicity, clarity and endings with everything explained, as if they will not be able to learn from the complex and unpredictable.

As Doe Mayer explains, not only are more complex stories more engaging and engrossing, they are far more likely to promote discussion:

> I am arguing for... drama that is less formulaic and predictable. We can and should create layered, provocative stories that will encourage the all-important dialogue we want to generate. Let's have more complexity, more creativity and more conversations.[7]

One counter=argument to this one is that complexity is fine for an educated audience in the West but it would not work in countries in the Global South, with an audience with little or no education. What would they know about multiple layers, complexity, unpredictability? Apart from the patronizing attitude in this argument, Figure 2.1 provides one example of evidence that this is not true.

Figure 2.1 *A khuta, or bread-basket, from Sudan, showing multi-layering, complexity and unpredictability*

Figure 2.1 is a photograph of a *khuta*, a shallow bowl-shaped tray made of papyrus and used for *kisra*, soft, wafer-thin bread often eaten in Sudan and South Sudan. *Khutas* are common utensils, and this one is not an exceptional example. It was probably made by an illiterate woman, in South Sudan or in the Darfur region of Sudan. Such a woman would be part of the target audience of communication for development projects.

Obviously, the *khuta* is a piece of decorative art, yet here it is being used as evidence in support of an argument about drama. One of the themes of this book is the need for those in communication for development to listen to their audience. There are different ways of listening, and one is to ask what the artefacts produced by the audience can say. What does this *khuta* say about the qualities Doe Mayer is asking for in drama. It is multi-layered. The big, bold circles are overlaid with this much lighter pattern of curved, radiating threads. It is complex, with several different patterns of symmetry – the outer ring is symmetrical in itself, and reflects the different symmetry of the lighter, third ring. It is unpredictable. The patterning of the second ring is wholly unpredictable. It is a changing pattern: sometimes mirror images of the third ring, but not always, and, even when it is, the reflection is different. There are the three 'bouncing back' patterns, and then one which bounces back in the opposite direction. So, the maker of this *khuta* certainly understands multiple layers, complexity and unpredictability.

Conflicting opinions

Although it may appear odd and time-wasting, it is very important that a communication for development project does not just present the case in support of the change the project is intending to bring about. It needs to include opinions that have no knowledge of that case, or are opposed to it. So, to pursue the breastfeeding example, on the issue of starting breastfeeding within the first hour after birth, balanced air-time needs to be given both to voices that are in favour of early breastfeeding and those who think it is not possible, or not necessary. There are several strong reasons for this.

- What may appear, on the surface, a simple issue can be a far more complex social and cultural matter, as the example of exclusive breastfeeding shows. It is, therefore, important that the social and cultural issues are fully explored, not least so that a dramatic character or a real-life interviewee can be seen negotiating their way through those issues to get to behaviour change. If these barriers are ignored, the chances of successful behaviour change are diminished, perhaps severely.
- It is important that a communication project addresses people in the audience who are opposed to the change the project is promoting, as they are the ones in the greatest need of change, and they are far more likely to listen to, or view communication in which their opinions are represented. If there are only voices in support of the change, it is unlikely that they will engage. As long as they keep listening or viewing, there is the possibility that they will start on a process of change, but, obviously, if they are not engaged, there is little chance they will change.
- It is important that communication for development promotes discussion among members of its audience. Clearly, communication material which only contains voices from one side of the argument is very much less likely to promote discussion than material which includes conflicting opinions.
- Humans are fascinated by conflict (see the chapters on drama for a full discussion of this claim). Any broadcasting needs to be engaging if it is going to attract an audience, and broadcasting without any conflict in it is unlikely to be engaging.
- Any communication for development project – especially one that is run and funded by international organizations – needs to see itself in the wider context of local media and governance. One of the basic rules of good journalism is fairness and balance, giving both sides of an argument, for example. Any broadcasting that does not follow this rule can be seen as one-sided. If an international organization makes one-sided broadcasts, that could well be taken as justification for one-sided broadcasting in a political context by an authoritarian government or by media serving particular political or economic interests.

Step by step

Particularly in behaviour change communication, the audience should be offered, where possible, a step-by-step approach, so that instead of being expected to make a large change in one move, they are shown small steps towards change. This is especially important where those being addressed are the poor and relatively powerless, as self-motivated change is much more difficult if an individual has relatively little control over her or his own life. There are, essentially, two reasons for this approach.

The first reason concerns self-efficacy. Self-efficacy is a concept developed by Albert Bandura, of Stanford University,[8] and it is widely accepted in behaviour change communication. In this context it means that for someone to change their behaviour, they need to have the belief that they can make the change. It is obviously easier to make a small change than a large one, and, if an individual succeeds in making one small change, that will give them more self-efficacy to go on to further change, so that, over time and a series of small changes, their self-efficacy is likely to be significantly enhanced, making further change easier.

An example of how this can work in practice is from *Life in Lulu*, a BBC Media Action mother and baby health radio drama in South Sudan. A young mother who has learned the need for exclusive breastfeeding for the first six months of a baby's life, which includes not giving water, is about to give birth. She is going to be attended by her mother-in-law, who is a traditionalist, and thinks a baby should be given water. The young mother, instead of trying to persuade her mother-in-law of the need for six months' exclusive breastfeeding, chooses the much easier task of persuading her not to give the baby any water in the first hour. The mother believes that, after the first hour, she will be in charge of the baby, and so can prevent any water being given, but she is not certain she will be in charge immediately after the birth. So, a suggestion is being given to prospective mothers who are listening of a small step they can take, which will protect the baby, and is very much easier than trying to persuade those around her of the need for exclusive breastfeeding for six months.

The second reason for a step-by-step approach is that people learn by doing, by taking action. It is much easier for someone, especially someone who is largely powerless (as, to follow the example just given, young mothers often are), to take a small action. Then they learn from both the process and from seeing the result of that action, and, from that learning, take further action.

In essence, this step-by-step approach can make change manageable and, in some cases, can make it possible, when otherwise it would not be.

Knowledge, attitude, behaviour

Alongside a step-by-step approach, this book takes the approach that communication for development needs to understand and acknowledge the sequence of change. In order to achieve behaviour change, it is necessary, first, to have a change of knowledge, followed by a change of attitude and then a change of behaviour. Someone is not going to change their behaviour unless they first know why they should change, how they can change and that they are able to change. Even with that knowledge, there is unlikely to be any behaviour change unless there is first a change of attitude. There could be, for example, an attitude of fatalism – 'what happens will happen, whatever I do' – which would largely prevent any effort at change. This attitude would need to alter to one of the person believing they can change themselves, and benefit from the change, for any behaviour change to occur. Communication for development therefore needs to follow that sequence of changing knowledge, changing attitudes, changing behaviour.

A participatory approach

As the idea of two-way communication implies, an essential part of the approach this book takes is that participation by the audience in programmes can make a big contribution to the success of a communication for development project.

Participation means that programming can keep much more closely in tune with the perceptions, understanding and needs of the audience. It means that the language being used is completely comprehensible for the audience, and that the production team can have a much clearer grasp of the priorities of the audience. As members of the audience participate in the programmes over a period of time, audiences can see or hear people like themselves learning and changing over time, and they are more likely to understand the change is relevant to them and to have more confidence that they can achieve the same change. As has been said earlier, the experience and expertise of some audience members can often be more relevant than that of professional experts.

Participation can take a number of forms.

- A significant proportion of interviewees in a recorded factual programme are audience members.
- Members of organized listening groups regularly report back to the programme on their activities.
- Members of the audience are long-term participants in learning activities featured in the programmes.
- Sections of the programmes are led by audience priorities, as expressed in texts, emails, social media messages, calls or as recorded by reporters in the field.
- There is a phone-in element in the communication, for example, after each episode of a drama.

All of these are discussed in greater detail in the chapters on producing different types of programme.

Long form and long term

What follows from the use of stories rather than messages, the focus on achieving change and the step-by-step approach is that this book is largely about the production of material which is both long form and long term. That is, it mainly looks at programmes of fifteen minutes to thirty minutes duration, with programmes organized into long-term series, sometimes lasting years. The principal reason for this approach is that change – especially change on the scale some projects envisage – takes time. It takes a process of accumulation of information, and a slow process of change of attitude and of behaviour.

Training agendas and materials

Suggested agendas and materials for training in topics relevant to this chapter can be found in Section Six:

Module J1: An exploration of how people learn

3

The principles and ethics of communication for development

Like any development work, communication for development work needs to be carried out within a tight framework of principles and standards.

Thus, communication for development needs to comply with the following.

- established and codified ethical standards of all aid and humanitarian work, as set out, for example, in the *Core Humanitarian Standard on Quality and Accountability*[1] (See Chapter 15.)
- the principle of 'Do no harm'
- the need to protect the privacy of those it is trying to help
- the need to maintain the safety of staff and those it is trying to help
- the need to ensure maximum effectiveness and value for money, and to be able to prove it
- the need to be accountable to those it is trying to help
- the need to contribute to the building of institutional knowledge of what works and what does not

There is one further standard in addition to these, which applies if the project involves journalism:

- the ethics of journalism

This chapter looks at each of these in turn, to see how they apply to the specifics of communication and the measures that need to be taken to ensure that communication for development work follows these principles and meets the standards required.

Established and codified ethical standards

There are several codes of standards that apply specifically to humanitarian action but which also form useful guides to standards in all development work. They include, *The Sphere Handbook – Humanitarian Charter and Minimum Standards in Humanitarian Response*[2] *The Good Enough Guide: Impact Measurement and Accountability in*

Emergencies[3] and, as previously mentioned, *The Core Humanitarian Standard on Quality and Accountability.*[4]

This last guide includes two standards for communication, which are cited and discussed in the context of two-way communication in Chapter 15.

The principle of 'Do no harm'

Again, this is primarily a humanitarian standard but, self-evidently, should apply to all development work. It is an absolutely basic minimum standard. Of course, while one would hope that no one working in communication for development would deliberately set out to do harm, it is very easy for there to be unintended harmful consequences of any media work.

Understanding audience perceptions

In the past, serious harm has resulted simply from a lack of understanding of an audience's perceptions on the part of aid agencies, so that their communication did not address the real issues. In the Caribbean country of Haiti, there was a cholera epidemic following a catastrophic earthquake in 2010. To begin with, however, the reaction to the international agencies' attempts to deal with the epidemic was, from many Haitians, hostile. Treatment centres were firebombed and personnel were attacked. It was only when the Haitian Red Cross conducted participatory research that they discovered what was behind this hostility. They found out that many Haitians regarded the cholera outbreak not as a disease but as a foreign conspiracy to kill them.[5]

Once they were able to understand these perceptions, and the fear which fuelled them, the Haitian Red Cross could react. They trained their staff to address these perceptions and fears directly. Only then did the humanitarian effort to prevent cholera begin to be effective. This is a strong example of the harm that can be done when there is a failure to communicate, stemming from a failure to listen.

Inadequate research

The Ebola virus epidemic that was mainly focused in the West African countries of Sierra Leone, Liberia and Guinea in 2014 and 2015 has already been mentioned (see Chapter 1). Then, the failure to understand the communication needs of the populations was largely to do with language, though there was also a literacy problem as much of the material initially produced was written, when less than half the population in these three countries could read.[6] The *Translators Without Borders* report shows the consequences of this communication failure:

> Information in the wrong language can lead to serious misconceptions on how to contract the disease and how to treat the disease. As mentioned by one aid worker 'in the Ebola epidemic, rumours and misinformation were rampant and fuelled

the spread of Ebola'. In a survey published in late August, UNICEF found that in Sierra Leone, 30% believed Ebola was transmitted via mosquitoes and another 30% believed it was an airborne disease. Moreover, four out of ten respondents (42%) believed hot salt-water baths are an effective cure.[7]

In other words, inadequate research into the population's communication needs meant that more people died than could have been the case. This finding, taken alongside the admission by Médecins Sans Frontières, referred to at the beginning of this book, and the communication failure in that epidemic looks very harmful indeed.

The need for research

The main measure that can be taken to avoid causing this kind of harm is thorough research into the target population's communication and information needs, including levels of literacy and languages spoken. A number of communication and information needs assessment questionnaires and guides have been published. (See Chapter 13.)

Research into the target audience's perceptions, knowledge, attitudes and behaviour – usually called formative research – is important in helping to avoid harm but is also crucial because any communication for development project needs to start where the audience's understanding is, so that audiences become engaged and can then be helped on a learning journey. Starting from an antagonistic or unwittingly patronizing point of view, for example, is less likely to be successful, as it will alienate many in the audience.

In a humanitarian crisis, when the speed of a response is a priority, it is unlikely there will be time, at the earliest stages, for detailed research of this kind, as has been said. A few broad-brush questions will be the best that is possible. However, as the situation stabilizes, then for the avoidance of harm, agencies do need to get a much better understanding of the population's perceptions, as the examples given illustrate. While these two examples in Haiti and West Africa may be of particularly serious harm, there is a lot of evidence of lower-key harm done in humanitarian crises, as is explored in greater depth in Section Two, on communication as part of the humanitarian response.

Inaccurate reporting

Two further areas in which harm can be caused, especially in conflict situations, are inaccurate reporting and hate speech. These areas are significant where a communication for development project includes some element of news reporting. (This is where the ethics of journalism play a vital role in preventing harm.) Many projects will not, but it is an important area of development work. For example, people – especially the displaced – in areas of actual or potential conflict need accurate information on what is happening around them so that they can make informed decisions.

It is easy to envisage how harm could be done by inaccurate reporting. For example, if a news item reporting an attack by one armed group on another is broadcast, it could provoke a revenge attack in which people are killed. If it is then discovered that the original report was wrong, and no attack had taken place, the inaccurate reporting might well have caused deaths.

Hate speech

The impact of broadcast hate speech in the Rwanda genocide in 1994 has been well documented. An estimate has been made that 10 per cent of the violence was caused by *Radio Télévision Libre des Mille Collines*[8] broadcasting propaganda against one community.

Any communication for development project must, of course, avoid being used as a medium for hate speech. This could be perpetrated either by staff members or by other contributors, including callers in phone-in programmes. Hate speech could go undetected, where broadcasting is in a language not understood by a project's senior management. It could arise simply from the unacknowledged prejudice of the broadcasters. A project also needs to ensure that any partner station broadcasting the project's material does not also broadcast hate speech. The authority of the project's material could be used to lend authority to the hate speech.

Broadly, to avoid doing harm through inaccurate reporting or hate speech, projects need to provide:

- thorough recruitment procedures
- robust training in journalistic values and, specifically, in the dangers of hate speech
- a code of conduct for staff and for partner stations
- robust editorial control, involving the monitoring of the project's own output and that of partner stations, by trusted individuals who understand the broadcast language
- thorough training for phone-in hosts and, where possible, pre-vetting of callers and a broadcast delay device, so that callers who start using hate speech can be cut off before they are broadcast

Relations with local media

A further area where there is risk of doing harm is in the relationship between a communication for development project and local media. There is a risk of harm resulting from the financial power of an internationally funded project, when the project buys air time from local stations. (See Chapter 9 for a full discussion of this issue.) There is the further risk of harm in international projects recruiting the most skilled and talented local staff, through higher wages, and thus denuding local media of that skill and talent.

A key mitigating measure which is often taken is that, at the proposal stage, a significant media capacity-building element is included in a project and budgeted for, even if that is not the major purpose of the project. In this way, a project's presence can enrich the whole local media landscape.

Favouring one section of a community

Another possible source of harm is circumstances where a project's support for one part of a community could be perceived as causing harm to another. Clearly, projects should be even-handed, offering equal support to all sections of a community. But what about those circumstances where this is not possible?

One example of this arose in a project which has already been mentioned: BBC Media Action's *Somalia Livestock Livelihoods Project*, which ran from 2005 to 2008. One section of the radio programmes broadcast prevailing prices for livestock in different markets across Somalia. This was in the interests of transparency, so that pastoralists and other livestock owners could know if they were being offered a fair price or not. Up to that time, the brokers in the markets had been keen to keep the details of each individual deal private, going to the length of indicating the price they were offering not in words but using their fingers on the palm of the seller's hand, after putting a shawl over both hands, so that the deal was not visible. While pastoralists welcomed the broadcasting of prices, market brokers did not, unsurprisingly. However, the decision to continue broadcasting prices was made on the basis that it was in the interest of transparency, and offered all concerned a level playing field, and it only disadvantaged those brokers who tried to exploit the ignorance or naivety of different sellers.

Clearly, any decision that causes harm or perceived harm to one section of a community needs to be weighed very carefully, and must be made on grounds that can be publicly defended. In this case, it was on the grounds of fairness, transparency and reducing the exploitation of the very poor.

The need to protect the privacy of those it is trying to help

This is a principle that applies to all development work. With regard to communication, there are two main areas of risk:

- in gathering data for needs assessments
- in audience members accessing communication material

With electronic devices, like tablets, increasingly being used to make needs assessments, and the data increasingly being stored electronically, there is an increasing risk of personal information from respondents being inadvertently published or hacked.

Any organization involved in communication for development work should take all necessary measures to ensure online security.

When a communication for development project is concerned with a sensitive issue, like HIV, audience members who are accessing the material should not have their privacy put at risk when doing so, through their search history, perhaps, or because they could be seen or heard accessing the material. When material is broadcast on mass media, like television or radio, and is of interest to a wide spectrum of the population, there is unlikely to be a problem. However, if the material needs to be accessed online, and is likely to be of particular interest to those who are, say, HIV+, to follow the example, then accessing it may risk the privacy of the user.

Local consultation with service providers and with focus groups of potential audience members on feasible and culturally appropriate measures to mitigate the risk should come up with information to be included with the material, warning users of the risk and explaining how to mitigate it.

The need to maintain the safety of staff and those the communication for development project is trying to help

Risks for staff

This is clearly a responsibility of any employer, but there are aspects of it that are specific to communication work, particularly in conflict situations, and if a project is employing journalists.

There are many countries where journalists are at high risk, for a range of reasons, as reported by *The Reporters without Borders World Press Freedom Index.*[9] At an early stage in the planning of a communication for development project, an assessment should be made of the risk posed to journalists and other media workers in the territory being considered. *The Reporters without Borders World Press Freedom Index* is a useful source of information for this. If there is a risk, then measures for mitigating it need to be planned, which would normally include hostile environment and security training, security measures at premises and evacuation plans. Consultation with media organizations already working in the territory would normally be helpful in assessing risk and different mitigation measures.

In conflict situations, media can often become one of the theatres of war, with local media particularly – though by no means exclusively – at risk, as conflicting parties attempt to suborn them, to take them over or to destroy them. Again, the risk of this needs to be carefully assessed, and mitigating measures planned. These would include monitoring of the project's output, and that of partner organizations, for evidence of individual journalists being suborned.

Risks for audiences

Audiences can be put at risk, again particularly in conflict situations. In some circumstances, simply accessing a communication for development project's output – such as listening to a radio programme – could put audiences at risk.

There are situations in the world where to be identified as someone who is part of a stigmatized group – such as the HIV+, or as a health worker – can put individuals at severe risk. Such situations can arise where territory is under the control of a group violently opposed to gays or what they regard as 'Western' medicine, for example. In some communication for development projects, health workers are involved in distributing communication material, through, for example, Bluetooth, from mobile to mobile. However, this is a way through which they can be identified to people who are hostile to them, potentially putting them at severe risk. Similarly, if communication material is specifically targeted at the HIV+, for example, and individuals are seen accessing it, by such a method then they, too, are at risk of physical attack.

Mitigating risk

This is not a reason to avoid running a communication for development project in territory under this kind of hostile control. Those populations are in just as much need as any others. However, consultation with security advisors and with the personnel concerned, if they are workers, and with focus groups of potential users, held remotely if necessary, should lead to a body of mitigating measures.

If there is a social media element to a project, audiences can be put at severe risk by criminals or parties involved in the conflict mimicking the intervention's pages, to distribute fraudulent or misleading information. For example, high-profile organizations attempting to help migrants as they tried to get to Europe in a crisis in 2016 reported that both criminal people smugglers and factions involved in the Syria conflict frequently mimicked their Facebook pages. In this way, fraudulent information or propaganda appeared with the apparent endorsement of the organization mimicked.

The only measure that can be taken against this is for organizations to monitor social media for such fraudulent material, and get it closed down as quickly as possible by service providers.

The need to ensure maximum effectiveness and value for money, and to be able to prove it

This is another principle that ought to be applied in all aid-funded work, whatever the source. This book takes the term 'value for money' at its face value, although, of course, it has itself been devalued by being used as a euphemism, particularly by governments.

Research

As has been said, the ultimate effectiveness and efficiency of a communication for development project begins with effective research, if possible, reinforced by observation. That is, does observation of conditions on the ground match answers given in individual interviews and focus groups, or from literature?

Any communication for development project has to be designed to meet an identified need or identified needs among a population. Most often, the identification of the need or needs to be addressed is not a decision taken at practitioner level. Often, donors themselves have identified a need they want agencies to address, or inter-governmental and non-governmental organizations have a specified mandate to address particular needs.

However, this is often 'broad brush' identification and research is still needed to identify which specific needs are most pressing, or which needs, when met, will have the widest impact, in the specific context the project is intended for.

If an organization is already working in the field, and is looking to enhance the impact of its work with the addition of a communication element, then these detailed needs will have been identified, and the only question left for the organization is how a communication intervention can be most effective.

Research is also required to identify what change will meet the chosen need or needs. For example, if a significant proportion of babies are dying in the first six months of their lives, and the cause is unhealthy feeding practices, then the need is for those practices to be changed towards healthier ones, like exclusive breastfeeding. Another example might be: if a significant number of girls are leaving school before they have finished their education, a project needs to try to change behaviour among parents, by changing their perception of the value of education, so that more girls stay at school.

Target audience

Once a need and change have been identified from research, the next step for making a communication for development project effective is to identify the target audience or audiences, which, again, will need research. The target audiences will be the groups in the community who most need to make the change that the project is trying to achieve, and who have the power to make the change.

It is a vital principle that project teams must establish whether the potential audience can make the change they are asking for. So, in the examples given, while the final decision on exclusive breastfeeding will be made by the mother herself, in many communities she may well not have the power, on her own, to make the change. So, while mothers-to-be will be one of the target audiences, others who have influence over the decision will also need to be target audiences. These might be the older generation of women, who, as mothers, mothers-in-law or as traditional birth attendants, may have a strong influence over the young mother's decisions. In the example of girls leaving school early, in many communities the girls themselves may have very little say in the choice, which will be made by their fathers. So, it would be the fathers who are the target audience. Research also needs to be done on whether the target audience have the material means to make the choice. In the example of exclusive breastfeeding, the answer will be that, in the vast majority of cases, young mothers will be able to breastfeed. However, in the example of girls continuing in education, families may not be able to afford to keep their daughters at school, and need to get them married for the dowry. (If this is the case, a wider project, beyond the communication for development component, could offer cash payments to overcome this barrier.)

The choice of platform

The choice of the platform or platforms to use – radio, television, short message service (SMS) or other mobile technology, social media, the internet – needs to be made entirely on the basis of research into the target audiences' access and preferences, following the principle of 'People before platforms'. (This issue is explored in detail in Chapter 9.)

Structure

Communication for development programmes are very often in series broadcast or distributed over a period of time, because change often takes time. If an audience is being asked to change, especially if it is a change that requires the overcoming of difficult barriers, then it is not going to happen in one day, or from one programme. So, a series of programmes is needed, and, if a series is to be as effective as possible, it needs to have an organized structure. If the chosen medium is a drama, the structure will be built round a storyline or storylines in which role-model characters go through processes of change. If the series is a factual or a 'reality' format, the structure will be a series of topics that the audience need to understand in order to bring about change, organized into a chronological order dictated by the process of change. This chronological order can be worked out by judging which topic the audience need to understand before they can understand the next, and so on. It may be that for some series, there is no particular order.

Production

It sometimes seems that there is a widespread belief that if communication is in some way beneficial or educational, then it is all right to bore an audience in its delivery. However, if communication for development is to be effective, audiences need to be engaged through high production values, which can be achieved by paying attention to issues that have been discussed in earlier chapters. That is, series should include storytelling with conflict and tension, engaging characters or real-life role models, location recording, and, where possible, debate and argument.

Monitoring and evaluation

As with any aid work, it is important that the production and delivery processes of a communication for development project are carefully monitored to ensure they are working effectively and efficiently. In particular, impact needs to be evaluated, so that changes can be made to maximize it, as necessary. Though it should be noted that, in behaviour change communication, there may be no impact visible for a considerable period of time. For example, 2015 research into a BBC Media Action weekly radio serial drama in Somalia showed no impact until about Episode 35. However, after that, the impact was strong.[10] It is reasonably obvious why this would be the case. In behaviour change dramas, characters do not start showing behaviour change from the beginning of the drama, and the positive consequences of behaviour change may not start to show until a long way into the drama.

The impact research will provide the proof of offering value for money.

Accountability

A communication for development project has two principal accountabilities: to the target audience and to the donors.

Normally, donors will explain how they want a project's accountability to them to be exercised, and it will usually be financial reporting and evaluation of impact reporting.

Accountability to the project's target audience essentially means listening to them and acting on what they say. As has already been shown in this book, failures to listen can have disastrous results. A project should, therefore, do the following.

- Set up an effective and efficient feedback mechanism, which all sectors of the audience have access to.
- Repeatedly invite the audience to provide feedback.
- Build the feedback into the project's output.

Routes for receiving comments

The nature of the feedback mechanism will depend on research into the technology the target audience have access to, at the time of the project's start. After a disaster, for example, the population may all have mobile phones, but if there is no electricity, as often happens, those phones will rapidly become useless.

The options are: a dedicated phone hotline, whose number is widely distributed and frequently broadcast, and is set up to be free of change to callers; use of SMS (text), again to a publicized number, and free to senders; social media to a publicized page; phone-in programmes; face to face; or, and this is most likely, a mix of some or all of these options.

Phone hotline

The advantage of a phone hotline is that it is proper dialogue, in which the project's contact can get clarification of callers' comments. Against that, it is an expensive option, as there will need to be dedicated staff to take calls. This will be especially true if the hotline is open all the time, and, if it is not, it will be necessary to publicize opening hours as well as the number.

SMS

Texting has a substantial advantage over a hotline, as texts can be received at any time, and there does not have to be staff there all the time to receive them. There is the disadvantage that, if a text's meaning is not clear, it is much more difficult to seek clarification.

Social media

A social media page has the advantage that comments are public, so that there can be dialogue between members of the audience as well as between the project and members of the audience. The project can judge, for example, from other audience members' responses to a comment, how far the comment is supported or not. A huge disadvantage is the digital divide. A project will need to know who, among its audience, has access to the internet via smartphone or other route.

Phone-in or contact programmes

These are live programmes, that is, programmes which are broadcast when the presenter and a panel or an audience are in the studio, for members of the audience not in the studio to call on the phone or to send messages to by other means. So, there is a strong element of dialogue, between the project and its audience members, and between audience members in the studio and those calling in. Such a programme can provide a lively forum. A disadvantage is that such programmes are time-limited, so that the number of callers is limited.

Normally, such programmes would be on topics the project wants to communicate to the audience, but there is no reason why one could not be about the project itself, to get feedback on it.

Face to face

Having a dedicated team who go out to have face-to-face dialogue with a broad cross-section of a project's audience is likely to be very expensive, and a complex operation to manage.

However, there are instances where face-to-face feedback could be relatively cheap and easy to obtain. Any communication for development project is going to have some people who go out into the population. In every project, there will be researchers who meet the audience in the evaluation of impact. In a journalism-based project, there will also be journalists who work within the population. As part of their jobs, these people could gather feedback.

A project may have an outreach or reinforcement element built into it. This could be public meetings, established audience learning groups, or travelling theatre, for example. If it has, then such an element obviously offers opportunities for gathering feedback.

A further face-to-face feedback mechanism is dependent on the choice of where the project is based. (This is an issue which is addressed at greater length in Section Two, Humanitarian Communication.) If a project is based at the heart of a population centre, and it is made clear that visitors are welcome, then that is an effective mechanism for receiving feedback.

There is also a case for having at least a small dedicated face-to-face team. If research has shown that there are sectors of the audience who do not have access to either mobile or digital technology, then it is justified to budget for a face-to-face team, specifically to seek feedback from these sectors.

Managing feedback

An essential element of a feedback mechanism is a reliable logging process, to ensure that all feedback is recorded and a response made. The more routes there are for feedback, the greater the demands on this process, and the greater the risk of missing some feedback. For example, if the only route is by SMS to a single mobile phone, all the information that needs to be logged will be on that phone. However, if there is also a social media page and journalists and researchers are coming back with face-to-face feedback, a more capable logging process will be needed to capture all that information. So, it is important to balance the number of feedback routes with the capacity of the logging process. In other words, the more feedback routes, the more expensive the logging process.

Encouraging feedback

It is important to let your audience know frequently that they can give you feedback, and the routes they can use. It is useful, too, to reinforce the information with a short account of an earlier piece of feedback, how the audience member got the feedback to the project and how the project responded to the feedback.

Responding to feedback

It is important to respond to feedback as quickly as possible. The response should not just be with a message back to the audience member who gave the feedback. The project should explain – or, better, show – how it has changed in response to the feedback.

It is also useful, without being too bureaucratic, for a project to have an agreement on what level of response and in what circumstances individual staff members can respond to feedback on their own initiative.

In general, once feedback has been evaluated and a response decided and implemented, the feedback and the response should be reported publicly in the project's output.

In order to maintain a regular dialogue between the audience and the project, there should be a regular slot in the output for this element of the work.

Other advantages of listening to the audience

Maintaining two-way communication with the audience through a feedback mechanism is also likely to be an effective safeguard, covering many aspects of issues discussed in this chapter, especially under the 'Do no harm' and the value for money principles. Through it, for example, managers could get early warning of hate speech being broadcast, and it should provide valuable evidence of project impact or a lack of it.

Pre-planning

What will be apparent is that listening to the audience is not something which can be considered once a project is up and running. It needs to be fully thought through and budgeted for at the proposal stage. Indeed, some donors demand an accountability mechanism is included in all proposals for funding.

The building of institutional knowledge of what works and what does not

This book argues that it is a matter of ethics that any organization involved in communication for development has in place an effective knowledge management system. This system should not only assemble an archive of project evaluations and relevant academic research but also make findings readily available to proposal writers and project managers, in particular. The aim is that an organization, as it carries out more communication for development projects, assembles a library of evaluations of these projects. To make findings readily accessible, an honest digest of evaluation findings which summarizes which projects or elements of projects were successful and which were not, should also be produced and regularly updated. Or, there could be a number of digests specializing in different kinds of work the organization carries out. The digest or digests would be guidance to the development of future projects, building on past success and avoiding past failure.

It is certainly possible to do this. I wrote a very simple example of such a digest for BBC Media Action (then the BBC World Service Trust) in 2004, focused on humanitarian communication in displacement crises. The digest drew on evidence from earlier projects for refugees, internally displaced people and host communities in West Africa, Kosovo and Albania, and in Afghanistan and Pakistan. It did prove helpful for the development of proposals for subsequent humanitarian projects.

The need for the development of institutional knowledge is related both to the value for money principle and the principle of accountability to those people the organization is trying to help. If an organization does not have such a digest, it risks repeating past failures. That means it risks not delivering value for money, and letting down the people it is trying to help, when, with a proper procedure in place, both of those risks could have been avoided. So, it is unethical not to have a mechanism for developing institutional knowledge.

There is, however, a problem with delivering effective institutional knowledge. This is that project evaluations which admit a project, or part of it, failed appear to be rare. It may be that communication for development organizations are exceptionally successful, but, given that many communication for development projects have innovative elements, or are being carried out in difficult circumstances, it seems unlikely that all projects work well. I once evaluated a project as a serious failure in 2004. (That was an unusual circumstance, in that the evaluation was commissioned by the broadcaster of the project material, and not by the organization running the project.)

So, it seems likely that projects do fail, yet evaluations rarely report that. Why is that?

Project evaluations are either conducted by in-house research departments or by independent organizations specially commissioned for each evaluation. For in-house research departments, their researchers' livelihoods depend on the organization continuing to be successful in winning funding. So there is little incentive to evaluate one of the organization's projects a failure. Similarly, if an independent research organization finds a project they have been commissioned to evaluate has failed, how likely is it that they will be commissioned again by the organization whose project they have judged a failure? This remains an issue for investigation and reform.

The ethics of journalism

This section is a development of what has been said in Chapter 1.

Ethical standards in journalism vary widely from one organization to another. However, in communication for development, organizations need to adopt the highest standards. In purely practical terms, unless a project earns the trust of its audience, any communication with them is pointless. They need to be able to trust information given to them, if they are going to change their lives on the basis of it. In humanitarian situations, the audience needs information that is reliable enough for them to base sometimes big decisions on, for example, whether to cross a border or not. Whether the information is correct can be a matter of life or death.

The highest standards of journalism have five requirements:

Accuracy

A journalist has to get the facts right, which means checking everything. It means having two original sources, if at all possible, the people directly involved or people who actually saw the event or events, and avoiding second-hand sources. Where expertise is needed, the journalist must make sure the interviewee is, indeed, qualified and competent. She or he must ask the source of any statistical claim, so that they can check it themselves. They also need to check facts, names and locations.

A journalist needs to listen carefully to a source. Even if someone claims to have seen an event, it may not be true. If what they say has little detail, then it is likely they are not telling the truth.

Accuracy in the use of language is vital. In particular, adjectives should be avoided in giving information, as they can carry value judgements.

Finally, if, in spite of everyone's best efforts, a mistake does go out, it must be corrected as quickly as possible.

Objectivity

In communication for development, a journalist needs to be objective, and keep their own feelings and opinions out of their work. It is easy to be unconsciously biased in the choice of interviewees. A journalist needs to ask themselves if they have feelings or opinions on the topic, and, if they do, they need to take great care to keep those feelings and opinions out of the story.

Fairness

This means being fair both in how a story is presented and how contributors are treated. The journalist needs to approach the story fairly, without making their own judgements about it. Again, it requires being careful in the use of language, avoiding judgemental adjectives. The journalist has to give all the information the contributor needs to know about what the item is for, what they are doing in it and whether it will be broadcast live or recorded and edited.

Balance

Where there are two or more sides to an argument, all sides should, over time, be given equal coverage and time on air or in writing. If one contributor has said something about another person who has not been interviewed, the other person should be offered the right of reply. If a person or an organization has been invited for interview, but has not taken up the opportunity, that should be said or written in the item.

Impartiality

A journalist should not show an opinion on the subject of a discussion or debate but allow all relevant sides to express theirs. And, again, this includes using neutral rather than judgemental terms.

Recruiting production teams for communication for development projects

This chapter sets out an approach to recruiting teams for the practical elements of a communication for development project, and discusses the factors behind that approach. It explains two recruitment methodologies. The first is a detailed procedure for recruiting an experienced team and the second for recruiting an inexperienced team. This second methodology is less detailed and will require the use of a number of the training modules set out in Section Six, both for recruitment and training.

The approach and rationale

Most individuals and organizations involved in communication for development projects would take it for granted that usual practice is to recruit local teams for the writing and production of broadcast material, rather than recruiting an international team to do the work. There are very strong arguments for this approach, a fundamental ethical one and a number of practical ones.

The ethical case

This argument for employing local teams is straightforward. Aid money is allocated to promote development in countries in the Global South. So, ethically, as much of it as possible should be spent in the country in question, and not simply recycled back to the countries it came from, through fees to international staff.

This is not to suggest that no international staff are employed. There is often need for skills that, at present, only international staff possess. (That situation, though, is changing.)

The practical case

While a local team may not have the skills for, say, writing and producing a broadcast serial drama – and substantial capacity building may be necessary – they will bring other knowledge and skills that are crucial to the effectiveness of a communication for development project.

Language

This book has given a lot of emphasis to the need to address audiences in the most appropriate language or languages, so writers or journalists must be fluent in the broadcast language. Further, it is important that the writing team are local, living in the country or territory where the project is taking place. This is because language can change quickly. An experienced writer, for example, who is a native speaker might be found outside of the country, but, if they have been living abroad for a few years, there is a risk their language will not be up to the minute, and audiences are likely to notice.

Cultural knowledge

This is indispensable. For example, during the development of a radio serial drama in Somalia, a serious error was only avoided by the cultural knowledge of the writing team. Somalia is a deeply divided country, with three politically and socially distinct regions. One of the key criteria for the drama was to have characters from all of the three regions, to make it acceptable throughout the country. Originally, the chosen setting of the drama was to be a village. However, the writing team pointed out that, in reality, people from all three regions would not be living together in a village, and the best alternative would be that the setting was changed to a displacement camp. There were many camps in Somalia at that time, as people fled conflict and drought, and there would have been people from all three regions in them. In all likelihood, if that change had not been made, the entire basis of the drama would have appeared implausible to the audience, undermining its credibility in every other regard, including its behaviour change aims.

Equally, many communication for development projects deal with highly sensitive issues. Projects aiming to combat HIV, for example, often face huge cultural sensitivities. Without the cultural expertise of a local team, successfully negotiating those sensitivities would be very difficult, if not impossible.

The cultural expertise needs to be embedded in the production team, and not just brought in occasionally from outside. Cultural issues arise constantly and, without the expertise being on hand, they are very likely to be missed altogether. It should be said that calling in particular cultural expertise from outside the project is also important, as will be discussed in the next chapter.

Contacts

Particularly for factual programmes, a local team will have contacts that would probably never be available to an international team. A vivid example of this was in a project in South Sudan in 2012. Armed cattle raiding is common in some parts of the country, and one of the local journalists working on the project recorded an interview with a young cattle raider. It was very moving, with the man described being shot and badly injured on a raid and only just escaping with his life. The team said it would have been impossible for an outsider to have got that interview.

The need for a culturally specific team

It is widely understood, but, again, it is worth emphasizing, that cultural boundaries do not necessarily correspond with political boundaries. In 2009, Media Support Partnerships were already producing a radio serial drama aiming to change behaviour with regard to HIV, in Southern Province, Zambia. That year, they launched a similar drama in Western Province. However, launching the new drama was not simply a matter of translating the existing scripts written in the language of Southern Province, Tonga, and re-recording them in Lozi, the language of Western Province. When the storylines were examined by a Lozi-speaking team, they saw that one of the six storylines, each built round a main character, did not reflect the culture of Lozi-speaking people, at all. So, a new main character and storyline had to be developed. Further, the village life of Lozi speakers works within a framework of annual migration. Entire villages move from the plains to the higher ground to the East, as the River Zambesi's annual flooding inundates the whole area of the plains. In contrast, Tonga speakers' village life is sedentary. All of the storylines had to be adapted to take account of this migration. Even after these changes, more minor aspects of all the other storylines had to be modified to better reflect Lozi speakers' lifestyle and culture.

Core team role outlines

This section gives brief outlines of the roles commonly identified for the production of factual, discussion or reality material on the one hand, and drama on the other.

The section is looking just at the core production team that is involved in making the material for broadcast and distribution through digital and mobile technology for a communication for development project. There will normally be other people involved, in management, finance, administration and reporting to donors, for example, and, if there are on-the-ground activities associated with the broadcasting, there will be outreach workers and learning group facilitators. Many projects will have a research team, carrying out monitoring and evaluation.

A factual, discussion or reality programme production team

Editor

This is normally a senior position, responsible for major decisions, including programme format and project curriculum. The role will often incorporate other management duties, including financial responsibility, especially in smaller projects. The editor will be ultimately responsible for the output, including ethical standards and compliance with the law, and will have the final sign-off responsibility for output before it is broadcast.

This role is often carried out by the project manager, though sometimes a specialist editorial consultant will be employed while the management and financial role will be carried out by a project manager.

Producer

In radio and television, the producer has hands-on responsibility for the output, managing the production team, briefing the reporters on their specific tasks for a programme and monitoring their work. In many productions, though, the producer will not have a team of reporters, and will, by themselves, research interviewees, record interviews, edit the recorded material and either brief the presenter and edit their script or notes, or, often enough, be the presenter, as well.

Reporter

This is the on-the-ground journalist who researches potential interviewees, prepares, conducts and records interviews and edits them into packages, or who goes out to find stories and writes them up for broadcast.

A reporter working on a communication for development project could be working in considerably different situations and with different kinds of output. On the one hand, a great deal of communication for development broadcasting is 'built' programming, that is programmes that are recorded, not live, made up of edited sections of interviews, and linked by a presenter reading a script. This kind of programming is common in communication for development, because information needs to be carefully considered and structured, to have the impact required. On the other hand, the project could be a community radio station, working with a community affected by a humanitarian crisis, helping communities hold those in power to account or providing trustworthy news where no other sources are reliable. Most of the output from a community station will be live, including interviews and discussions, with small, built packages embedded in the live broadcasting, rather than being in long-form pre-recorded programmes.

However, the skills needed will be much the same.

Researcher

This is someone who does the basic groundwork of finding contributors to programmes, whether interviewees or panel members or locations for filming. If they are looking for contributors, normally, they will be given a brief on the kind of person required – that is the knowledge or experience the producer wants to explore, or a particular profession. They either do web searches or, physically, go out to find such people, using their local knowledge. When looking for locations, again, they will be briefed on what the producer wants, in terms of looks and accessibility. They will use Google Street Views, if available. If an interior is required, they will do a web search. Or they will go out and take photographs, using their local knowledge. In either case, they then brief the producer on the options they have found.

A drama production team

Serial drama, more usually called soap opera, or just soap, is a very popular drama form, on television and radio. It involves the unending, interwoven stories of the daily lives of a group of characters, broadcast in weekly or daily episodes. This is a format which is used extensively in communication for development. In both media it demands specialist skills, in production/direction, writing and in technical areas.

(The team outlined here is for audio drama, so includes the core team directly related to the writing and production of the drama. For television, there would be additional roles, including set and costume designers and camera operators.)

A serial drama team is often divided into two teams: a writing team and a production team. The writing team usually develop the drama at the beginning of the project, and develop storylines and write the scripts as the drama goes on. The production team will record the scripts with the actors and then finalize the episodes.

Editor/producer

In communication for development, the editor will be responsible for facilitating major decisions, especially those made by the writing team. The editor will usually lead the development of the drama, guiding the writing team in the development of characters, the drama's universe and the storylines. The editor will have the final sign-off responsibility for output before it is broadcast, and will be ultimately responsible for the output, including ethical standards and compliance with the law. The editor will also be involved in the casting.

Producer/director

In a communication for development context, a radio drama producer will also be the director, and will normally be the person who realizes the drama from the scripts the writers have written. That is, the producer will cast the drama, will rehearse the actors, direct the drama for recording and then either mix the drama with music and sound effects, or direct the mix as it is done by an audio drama technician. She or he is responsible for meeting deadlines for the delivery of the recorded episodes, which need to be of the right quality and duration.

Head writer

The head writer plays a major role in the development of the drama, working with the editor and the writing team. She or he organizes, leads and monitors the work of the writing team, and is responsible for meeting the deadlines for the delivery of the scripts, which need to be of the right quality and duration, and to follow the agreed storylines.

Writer

The writers work with the editor and head writer to develop the characters, the universe and the storylines of a drama. They then follow the character profiles and the storylines in writing the episode scripts.

Audio drama technician

An audio drama technician has the same skills as any other audio technician – that is able to record voices at the correct level for broadcast, free from distortion and extraneous noise, and to edit audio, using one of the many audio editing software programmes that there are, quickly and accurately. However, for audio drama, additional knowledge and skills are needed, particularly in understanding the positioning and movement of actors, and in recording, storing and using sound effects.

The correct identification of the core team

It is very important to identify who is in this core team, and exactly what their roles are. This may appear obvious, but communication for development projects can vary enormously, depending, for example, on the intended outcome or outcomes or on the range of materials required. There have been projects where, because of the cultural and geographical spread of voices required in the broadcasts, for example, reporters from partner local radio stations have been heavily involved in gathering material. They clearly are a part of the core production team, even though they are employed by organizations other than the lead organization, but it is possible they could be missed as part of the core. A major reason for the correct identification of this core team is to ensure they all receive the training required for them to be an effective part of the team. If some members of this core have not received the training, there can be serious consequences for the entire project.

Another group who need to be identified as part of this core are, in dramas, the cast of actors. Actors can, for a variety of reasons, cause severe logistical problems. If possible, it is useful for the cast, in addition to technical training, to receive training in the aims and methodology of the project, so that they feel a part of it and identify with it. (The issues involved in managing a cast are discussed fully in Chapter 29.)

Factors affecting the make-up of a core team

The exact make-up of a production team will vary significantly, depending on the characteristics of the project design:

- the medium being used
- the format of programmes
- external social factors that make demands on who is in the team
- the nature of the broadcasting mechanism, for example, whether it is a community radio station wholly owned by the production organization, an international broadcaster or air-time allocated on a partner station

Alternative recruitment procedures

As has been discussed in the section 'Do no harm', in Chapter 3, in some countries in the Global South, people with the skill sets asked for in the job descriptions set out in the Addendum to this chapter are likely to be very rare, and already employed by local media or other communication for development organizations. In these circumstances, a project design should consider adopting not just a role of delivering the communication for development work but also a role of capacity building to widen the pool of skilled reporters and drama professionals available, by recruiting individuals with no journalism or drama skills or experience, but with appropriate qualifications and aptitudes, and training them. Of course, this element needs to be considered, and budgeted for, at the project proposal stage, so that the necessary time frame and resources are in place.

A decision on which recruitment route to follow would be best based on a reasonably thorough understanding of the media landscape of the country or territory in which the project is based. An assessment through secondary sources, like media guides, will be helpful, but, if possible, an on-the-ground assessment of skill levels and availability should be undertaken.

Recruiting an experienced production team

This is a procedure that can be ethical as long as there is a reasonable body of talented and experienced people, who can be recruited without damage to existing local media, as discussed above.

This process would be based on using the relevant job descriptions given in the Addendum to this chapter, and would involve the familiar procedures of advertising for applicants, applicants completing applications, shortlisting and interviewing, alongside relevant practical tests.

The job descriptions given in the Addendum are for recruiting people who already have some experience and/or qualification in the particular role.

Recruiting an inexperienced team

As discussed above, this is the alternative route of recruiting people who have no skills or experience in the particular role but who have the appropriate aptitudes and capacities. These recruits would then need capacity building to enable them to be effective in the role. This second route may need to be followed if an assessment of the indigenous media shows that taking experienced personnel out of it may cause damage.

It is, however, likely that, for a substantial period of time, a team recruited in this way will need the support and supervision of either a local professional experienced in a relevant editorial role or an international professional with that experience.

This procedure will be based on the selection workshop process, as set out in the following training modules in Section Six:

Module J2: A selection workshop procedure for factual communication
Module D1: A selection workshop for a serial drama project

After recruitment, there will need to be substantial capacity building, based on the relevant training modules set out in Section Six.

The selection workshop

The heart of this recruitment procedure is the selection workshop.

A selection workshop is often five days long, and it might appear a cumbersome and expensive method for recruitment but, given how important it is to the outcomes of the project to select the most appropriate staff available, it has often been thought worth the effort and money.

In this procedure, the job advertisement needs to focus on provable personal attributes and educational qualifications, as here.

Advert: Selection and Training Workshop for Radio Journalists
(Brief description of the organization and the project)

[Name of organization] is planning to train new radio reporters. Candidates will be shortlisted from their applications. All shortlisted candidates will be invited to a five-day training workshop, after which four will be chosen, according to the selection criteria. All participants who successfully complete the workshop will receive a certificate.

[Name of organization] is not looking for existing media professionals, and, if you are already working as a journalist/drama professional in any capacity, please do not apply.

Successful candidates will:

- have successfully completed secondary school
- have a strong willingness to learn
- be able to plan, organize and carry out work on their own and deliver on time
- be able to work well as part of a team
- be able to give and receive criticism
- have a good understanding of the news agenda and be well-informed about events
- have language skills appropriate to the audience and to the organization's working language

The selection workshop process

For a selection workshop there is, normally, a shortlisting process, based, as usual, on experience, qualifications and an application statement. At the beginning of the selection workshop, candidates are given a clear statement of the criteria on which they are going to be assessed. The candidates are then taken through a series of sessions in which they are given a brief training in the different skills required, and, after each session, they are given a task that should demonstrate their learning in the session. Each candidate is marked on their performance of the task. Throughout they are given a daily mark on overarching approaches and attitudes they display in the workshop, like teamworking, giving and receiving constructive criticism, discipline and concentration. At the end of the workshop, the marks given in both categories are totalled, and the candidates who achieved the highest marks are given the jobs.

The sessions are led by a facilitator or a team of facilitators, and the marks can be awarded either by the workshop leader or by the team of facilitators or by an external observer or observers. There may well be a need for specialists in the assessment team. For example, if the workshop is being led by an international facilitator who is not a native speaker of the broadcast language, there is very likely to be a need for high-level language specialists to judge the quality of the writing in that language.

Of course, the selection process needs to abide by any legal requirements in force in the country, the recruitment policies of the organization and the donor, if there is one, and principles of equality and diversity.

The criteria set, and the content of the training sessions as well as the design of the tasks, will all be determined by the basic requirements of the work and the nature of the project and of the organization. They may well be based on the requirements set out in the job descriptions in the Addendum to this chapter.

One of the key aspects of the design of these sessions is that, while candidates will be assessed on their first attempts at each task, there is then a mechanism in place so that any mistakes in the first attempt are corrected. It is important to have this in place, as many of the tasks build on earlier tasks and so, if earlier mistakes are not corrected, they will have a cumulatively negative impact on the marks awarded for subsequent tasks, and, if this was the case, the process would not be assessing correctly the learning at each stage.

Chapter 4 Addendum

Detailed job descriptions

This addendum sets out example job descriptions which organizations can adapt to their particular needs, rather than a comprehensive set of job descriptions covering all possible roles in communication for development.

The job descriptions given here cover the core production roles. They just give the core duties commonly assigned to each role and the skills usually required. They do not go into further detail, as they are designed to be used by organizations that are introducing a communication for development component to their existing work, and that will already have human resources procedures and formats, into which these descriptions can be incorporated.

A factual, discussion or reality programme production team

Editor/Team Leader/Project Manager

Responsibilities

To deliver the project to have the maximum impact in the outcomes set out in the proposal, on schedule and to budget

To have editorial control of the project, ensuring all outputs are engaging, follow coherent communication for development methodologies and conform to internationally accepted ethical standards

To have managerial control of the project, making sure that all production procedures are effective and efficient and conform to best development practice and internationally accepted ethical standards

To ensure that training is consistent and coherent, that research is production orientated, and that both contribute to improving output standards and impact

To ensure that the project conforms to the requirements of contracts and legislation

To manage the project budget

To maintain and manage the relationship/s with the donor/s

To keep under review the project work plan, to ensure it is meeting project priorities

To set up and be involved in the design of effective monitoring arrangements to review outputs and make sure there is effective response to findings

To establish and maintain a high level of two-way communication with the target populations, and to respond to feedback effectively

To maintain contact with other projects where there are connections of aims, content or methodology to make mutually beneficial partnership arrangements and to avoid duplication`

To maintain the relationship with the parent organization, including making sure that lessons learned are contributed to institutional knowledge

To be responsible for the safety and security of staff and contributors involved in production, including anticipating potentially dangerous situations and having in place mitigating measures

To provide regular management and financial reports as required

Skills, knowledge and experience

Strong understanding of the role and methodologies of communication for development

Strong experience of an editorial role in broadcasting

Experience of senior project management (including the management of large budgets and donor reporting) in a Global South context

Relevant academic qualifications

Good experience of managing diverse teams

An understanding of international journalistic and ethical standards

Ability to work on own and with strong time management skills

Ability to balance different priorities in a demanding work schedule, without losing sight of overall strategy

Excellent personal communication skills

Factual/Discussion/Reality Programme Producer

Responsibilities

To produce engaging radio/television factual/discussion/reality programmes of the required length and by the due deadline, which meet the editorial and development aims of the project and to the highest production values, with a team of reporters

To apply the principles of communication for development at every stage of production

To be editorially responsible for the content, making sure it meets the specified aims of each individual programme, within the overall aims of the project, as agreed with the editor, and that it meets the appropriate ethical standards

To manage the programmes budget

To develop a production schedule, for the radio/television factual/discussion/reality programmes, ensuring deadlines can be met within the available budget, and with a contingency fund to allow for flexibility when circumstances or priorities change

To be in overall charge of the production of the programmes, either selecting interviewees, conducting interviews, editing the material and writing and recording scripts yourself or briefing reporters to do this and monitoring their work, present the programmes yourself or brief a presenter and monitor her or his work

To be in overall charge of the production of the recorded discussion programmes, selecting panel members, commissioning other material needed, chairing the discussions or briefing a presenter to do this and monitoring their work

To be studio producer during live broadcasts: back-timing, screening and selecting phone calls, monitoring calls and the discussion to keep them within ethical and legal confines

To ensure that programmes maintain effective two-way communication with the communities they are intended to serve, adjusting output as needed

To be involved in the design and running of monitoring and evaluation and respond to regular feedback sessions

To ensure agreed safety and security procedures are followed, for staff and contributors

Skills, knowledge and experience

Experience of live/recorded radio/television factual/discussion/reality programme production

Strong experience of managing a broadcasting team

An understanding of international journalistic and ethical standards

Strong understanding of the role and methodologies of communication in development

Ability to work on own and with strong time management skills

Ability to balance different priorities in a demanding work schedule, without losing sight of overall strategy

Excellent interpersonal, communication and influencing skills

Good working knowledge of computer packages, including Word, Excel, PowerPoint and audio/video editing software

Excellent written and spoken skills in the appropriate language/s

Reporter

Responsibilities

To research and record high quality interviews and to edit them into accurate and engaging reports and packages, following the brief you will have been given, of the required length and by the due deadline.

Skills, knowledge and experience

An understanding of the ethics of journalism
Able to conduct yourself ethically and professionally at all times when carrying out this work
Able to follow a brief
Able to find appropriate interviewees
Able to develop appropriate questions
Able to interview effectively, following your agenda and not that of the interviewee
Be diplomatically persistent in interviewing
Able to edit audio and/or video quickly and accurately
Combine strong judgement in editing material with good scriptwriting skills to tell a story clearly and engagingly
Demonstrate strong microphone and/or camera presentation skills
Able to work on your own and as part of a team, as required

Researcher

Responsibilities

To follow your producer's brief in finding people and/or places for making television/ radio programmes or material for distribution by digital and mobile technology, and deliver the options you have found by the deadline set, with a detailed brief on each option.

Skills, knowledge and experience

Excellent local knowledge
Able to work on their own initiative
Able to work in a team
Able to follow instructions precisely
Able to meet deadlines
Be confident, persuasive and easy with people

A drama production team

Editor

Responsibilities

To realize the radio serial drama on time, to budget and to the maximum impact in the project's development aims
To lead the team of writers in the development of a set of compelling characters, based on formative research and following the principles of a well-established behaviour change methodology, and of a credible universe

To facilitate the development of entertaining and compelling storylines, following behaviour change methodology

To oversee the subsequent writing and production processes to make the drama as engaging and understandable as possible for the target audiences

To monitor all recruitment processes, including the casting, to ensure that all outcomes maximize the impact of the drama in delivering the project's aims, and that recruitment follows internationally accepted ethical standards and is in compliance with employment legislation, including legislation on child labour

To provide capacity-building – either by themselves or by a commissioned facilitator – as needed for all staff to maximize the impact of the drama

To monitor the creation of a production schedule and its implementation

To monitor the scriptwriting process, ensuring scripts are compelling and entertaining, while using behaviour change methodology effectively

To sign off scripts for production

To monitor the attendance of actors for rehearsals and recordings, and support the producer/director in putting in place robust measures to ensure cast compliance and attendance

To monitor the rehearsal process, ensuring the cast develop a thorough grasp of their characters, and of the individual situations the characters are placed in, so that the listener can be fully engaged, while the procedure keeps to the production schedule

To monitor the recording process to ensure that it is efficient and effective, so that voice, sound effects and actors' movements all contribute to the listeners' understanding of the drama. To ensure that measures are in place to check that all voices are fully audible on the most basic radios or mobile phones used by listeners

To monitor the mix, ensuring all sound effects are included and are at a balance with the voices, that all voices are fully audible on the most basic radios or mobile phones used by listeners, and that any music is used to maximum effect

To manage the radio serial drama budget, including quarterly forecasting and cost control

To ensure that the production team work closely with the writers in rehearsals and recordings to ensure intended meaning is conveyed to the listener

To sign off recorded episodes as being of a sufficient standard for broadcast or other delivery

To oversee monitoring arrangements for reviewing the audience reactions to the drama and to lead in organizing effective responses to all findings

To monitor the working of two-way communication with the target populations

To be responsible for the safety and security of staff involved in production, including anticipating potentially dangerous situations and having in place mitigating measures

To provide regular management and financial reports as required

Skills, knowledge and experience

Strong experience of writing or directing behaviour change serial drama
Experience of staff management
An understanding of ethical and legal employment standards

Strong understanding of the role and methodologies of drama in communication for development

Ability to work on own and with strong time management skills.

Ability to balance different priorities in a work schedule, without losing sight of overall strategy

Experience in team leading

Excellent interpersonal, communication and influencing skills

Good working knowledge of computer packages including Word, Excel, PowerPoint

Excellent written and spoken skills in the appropriate language/s

Radio Drama Producer/Director

Responsibilities

To realize the radio serial drama on time, to budget, and to the maximum impact in the project's development aims

To conduct casting following internationally accepted ethical standards and in compliance with employment legislation, including legislation on child labour

To provide cast training in radio acting, as necessary

To follow a rehearsal process that ensures actors fully understand their characters and all aspects of the situations those characters are in

To employ effective direction that makes sure that all means available – voices, sound effects, music and movement – are used to make the drama as engaging and understandable as possible for the target audiences

With the head writer, to create a production schedule, to follow it strictly and to keep it under review in case of changed priorities or situations

To organize a system for calling actors for rehearsals and recordings, and to put in place robust measures to ensure cast compliance and attendance

To either conduct the mix or direct it, ensuring all sound effects are included and are at a balance with the voices, that all voices are fully audible on the most basic radios or mobile phones used by listeners, and that any music is used to maximum effect

To manage the radio serial drama budget, including quarterly forecasting and cost control

To work closely with the writing team to ensure scripts are readily producible and do not make excessive demands on production resources

To deliver fully mixed episodes of the correct duration on time

With the head writer to set up and be involved in the design of effective monitoring arrangements to review the drama and make sure there is effective response to findings

To establish and maintain a high level of two-way communication with the target populations, and to respond to feedback effectively

To be responsible for the safety and security of staff involved in production, including anticipating potentially dangerous situations and having in place mitigating measures

To provide regular management and financial reports as required

Skills, Knowledge and Experience

Experience of radio drama or stage production
Experience of managing actors
An understanding of ethical and legal employment standards
Strong understanding of the role and methodologies of drama in communication for development
Ability to work on own and with strong time management skills.
Ability to balance different priorities in a work schedule, without losing sight of overall strategy
Experience in team working
Excellent interpersonal, communication and influencing skills
Good working knowledge of computer packages including Word, Excel, PowerPoint
Excellent written and spoken skills in the appropriate language/s

Audio Drama Technician

Responsibilities

To record all drama, in the studio and externally, to the highest possible quality and at the correct level, while ensuring that all voices are fully audible on the most basic radios or mobile phones used by listeners
To advise the drama producer/director on the best technical options available to make the drama communicate most effectively with the audience
To advise the drama producer/director on any technical misconceptions he or she holds, and any technical errors or omissions he or she is making
To seamlessly edit the drama, under the direction of the producer/director, quickly and efficiently
To conduct the mix, under the direction of the drama producer/director, ensuring all sound effects are included and are at a balance with the voices and that all voices are fully audible on the most basic radios or mobile phones used by listeners, and that any music is used to maximum effect
To record and edit, to the highest quality, all required pre-recorded sound effects
To archive all pre-recorded sound effects, which allows for rapid identification and retrieval of required effects
When recording in the field, to follow all required safety and security procedures

Skills, knowledge and experience

Experience of radio recording and mixing for broadcast
Technical recording, editing and multi-channel mixing skills using Adobe Audition or similar software
Understanding of the characteristics of different audio file formats and their use in production
Experience of team working
Communication and influencing skills at a personal level

Excellent written and spoken skills in the appropriate language/s

Ability to hear extraneous noises during recording (like pops, distortion and rustles) and to take appropriate action to prevent them

Competence in recording sound effects on a portable recorder

Ability to archive sound effects so they can easily be retrieved

Willingness to record sound effects at any time of the day or night, in any weather

Head Drama Writer

Responsibilities

To lead a writing team in all aspects of the creation of a radio serial drama for development

In conjunction with the project team, create and develop characters and storylines using formative research and designed to meet the behaviour change objectives of the project

To co-ordinate storylines across the drama and create an episode-by-episode structure

To devise and write engaging scenes that will work on radio and have impact

To lead the writing team in producing compelling scripts which follow agreed character profiles and storylines, and the agreed methodology, and which make the maximum use of voices, sound effects and movement, to the required duration and on schedule

To seek appropriate external advice and information in the development of storylines and episodes, as needed

To be editorially responsible for the scripts

To carry out a due share of the scriptwriting

To manage the writing team, keeping the work on schedule, managing small issues, and involving project management in larger ones

With the drama producer/director to set up and be involved in the design of effective monitoring arrangements to review the drama and make sure there is effective response to findings

To establish and maintain a high level of two-way communication with the target populations, and to respond to feedback effectively

To be responsible for the safety and security of staff involved in writing, particularly when undertaking research in the field, including anticipating potentially dangerous situations and having in place mitigating measures

To provide regular management and financial reports as required

To establish a character bible and make sure it is kept fully up to date

Skills, knowledge and experience

Experience of radio drama writing

Experience of managing a small team

Strong understanding of the role and methodologies of drama in communication for development

Ability to work on own and with strong time management skills. Ability to balance different priorities in a demanding work schedule, without losing sight of overall strategy

Experience in team working
Excellent interpersonal, communication and influencing skills
Good working knowledge of computer packages including Word, Excel, PowerPoint
Excellent written and spoken skills in the appropriate language/s

Drama Writer

Responsibilities

To be part of a writing team in the creation of a radio serial drama for development
In conjunction with the project team, help to create and develop characters and storylines using formative research and designed to meet the behaviour change objectives of the project
Help to co-ordinate storylines across the drama and create an episode-by-episode structure
Devising and writing engaging scenes that will work on radio and have impact and which make the maximum use of voices, sound effects and movement, to the required duration and on schedule
To seek appropriate external advice and information in the development of storylines and episodes, as needed
To carry out a due share of the scriptwriting
To keep work on schedule
With the drama producer and head writer to be involved in the design of effective monitoring arrangements to review the drama and make sure there is effective response to findings
To take part in maintaining a high level of two-way communication with the target populations, and to respond to feedback effectively
To follow measures to maintain the safety and security of staff involved in writing, particularly when undertaking research in the field, including anticipating potentially dangerous situations and having in place mitigating measures
To contribute to the maintenance of the character bible

Skills, knowledge and experience

Experience of radio drama writing
Strong understanding of the role and methodologies of drama in communication in development
Ability to work on own and with strong time management skills. Able to balance different priorities in a demanding work schedule, without losing sight of overall strategy
Experience in team working
Excellent interpersonal, communication and influencing skills
Good working knowledge of computer packages including Word, Excel, PowerPoint
Excellent written and spoken skills in the appropriate language/s

5

Consultation

As with any development project, a communication for development project needs substantial consultation with different individuals, groups and organizations, to ensure that:

- the information given is accurate and sound
- the communication is culturally appropriate, especially in ensuring that any behaviour change portrayed is culturally acceptable
- the communication is harmonized with other, related projects in the field, to maximize the impact of each, and avoid clashes and confusion
- the principle of 'Do no harm' is upheld

Consultation mechanisms

There are different mechanisms for consultation, with advantages and disadvantages, but two which are commonly used are sometimes called the Technical Advisory Panel and the Local Advisory Panel.

The Technical Advisory Panel

This is normally a panel that overarches the whole project, and is formed of donors, government (see below) and international and local staff of international organizations, whose expertise is in the main topics of the project, whether the topic is health, livelihoods, peacebuilding or whatever. Panel members know the development change that is being sought, though they may not know the local and regional nuances of trying to bring the change about. They try to ensure that the broadcasting project is aligned with other projects in the same area and covering similar themes, and that it is able to reinforce on-the-ground activities by these organizations.

It has already been said that audiences should not be asked to do things they cannot do, because any materials they would need are not available or affordable. Another function of the Technical Advisory Panel is to check that any materials needed to carry out activities promoted by the broadcasting are available and affordable. For example, in a child health project, the broadcaster can check if oral rehydration salts and zinc are widely available and affordable, before the communication for development project encourages their use.

Involvement of government

The panel would normally include representatives of national and local government, so that the communication project is aligned, as far as possible, with government policy, and so that the communication project can reinforce government activities on the same theme, on the ground. For example, if there is to be a government-led vaccination campaign, and vaccination is a theme of the communication for development project, the project can prepare the ground for the campaign. It could broadcast discussions on the effectiveness of vaccination, by challenging rumours that there is a hidden agenda of harm in vaccination campaigns. It could discuss and challenge other barriers to vaccination, as well as simply let the audience know that the campaign is taking place, and when vaccinators will be where.

The Local Advisory Panel

This will be formed largely of local government, local cultural experts and local staff of international non-governmental organizations (INGOs) and national non-governmental organizations (NGOs). Essentially, it includes commentators who have local and cultural knowledge. They can advise the communication for development project on issues of culture, ensuring that the project is appropriate and in line with local culture, or, where it is trying to challenge aspects of the culture, that it does so in a way that is culturally acceptable.

For example, in 2009, a team was making a behaviour change radio serial drama about HIV, in Western Zambia. In that part of the country, there was a practice known as 'sexual cleansing'. After a man had died, his widow had sex with another man, apparently to confuse the husband's spirit to prevent it from haunting the widow. In a country with high rates of HIV infection, this was clearly a risky practice.

On consultation, it was found that there was another version of the cleansing ritual, which was used much less. This version involved the widow in wrapping herself in a cloth, and then, while bathing in the river, discarding the cloth and allowing it to float off downstream.

With this knowledge, the writing team of the drama were able to construct a storyline in which a man assigned to sexually cleanse a widow learns of the risk of HIV. He refuses to carry out the sexual cleansing, encouraging the widow to use the alternative ritual.

Another radio serial drama team, in South Sudan, faced a different cultural issue. In some cultures in South Sudan, there is a ceremony known as *cibir*. As previously mentioned, a baby, at seven days old, is given a piece of food, apparently as a test of the mother's fidelity. Again, this is risky behaviour. There is a strong possibility the baby will contract an infection and get diarrhoea, which can be fatal. In this case, there was no alternative ritual, but the drama team did not think they could challenge *cibir* without offering an acceptable alternative.

A local panel was assembled to explore the possibilities. It was explained that a young mother in the drama wanted to prevent *cibir* being carried out on her newborn baby. The writing team, however, did not know what alternative the character could suggest. There was considerable discussion of how strong this ritual was. As an illustration of its strength, it was revealed that, if a child from this culture is born in another country, and does not go through *cibir*, they have to go through it the first time they visit South Sudan. This applies even if they are adult by then.

One of the experts suggested that the mother in the drama could propose that *cibir* is postponed until after the baby is weaned at six months old. He thought that would be culturally acceptable, as evidenced by the acceptability of adults undergoing it. The panel agreed, and that was the storyline that was broadcast.

Working with the panels

For these reasons, communication for development projects often have these two advisory panels, made up of local and international experts on the technical aspects of the project and local experts on cultural issues. The panel meets every few months and reviews key documents – storylines, for example, if the project is a drama, or, say, the behaviour change curriculum, if it is factual – and a selection of the output. They might also be called on when specialist advice is needed on a particular programme item or story, as in the examples given.

Preparation

While most consultation exercises run smoothly, that is not always the case. However, careful research and preparation for the consultation exercise will help to avoid many of the problems that consultation can throw up. At its worst, a consultation can fall into an almost endless round of wrangling between different parties, consuming time and energy, or it can lead to energy- and morale-sapping hostility.

Primarily, problems can arise from two sources: where there are organizations that are covering the same area of activity, and are rivals for resources; and where organizations regard the media with suspicion or even hostility – based on real or imagined difficulties with the media or in fear of the media – and they do not welcome any media intervention.

Rivalry

An example, based on real events, of a problem arising from rival organizations, might be where an INGO is running a project designed to strengthen journalism which includes support for a journalists' organization. There are several organizations that claim to represent journalists. Normally, all such organizations would be invited to take part in the consultation panel. However, the panel could become a forum for these organizations to campaign against each other for resources from the INGO, which could paralyse the consultation process, and absorb a lot of project time for the INGO.

Suspicion or fear of the media

The second source of potential problems is suspicion of, or hostility towards, the media. The poor relations between international organizations and local media in Haiti in 2010 have already been mentioned (see Chapter 1). In 2016, one large international organization advertised for bids to deliver communication training for its staff. In the terms of reference, the organization asked for training 'in the management of pressure from journalists', rather than in positive engagement with the media. This reflects an attitude that the media are somehow 'other'.

In this context, it is not difficult for organizations to see a communication for development project that uses mass media as part of that 'other', 'the media'. If they are invited to take part in the project's consultation process, they can use it to try to divert or undermine the project.

To give an illustration of how bad consultation can be, I once found myself, at the initial consultation meeting with a project's partners, sitting in a single chair on one side of the room, facing a line of ten people sitting behind a long table on the other side of the room. A lesson to learn from this is, make sure all consultation meetings take place on your own project's territory, not someone else's, or, at least, somewhere you can arrange the furniture.

Mitigating the risk of bad consultation

Two measures to try to prevent bad consultations are research and explanation.

Research

In the example of the INGO and journalists' organizations, prior to the establishment of a consultation panel, research among journalists on which organizations they actually belong to would tell the INGO which of the organizations truly represent most journalists. Then, only those with large memberships – or even the one with the largest membership – would be included on the panel.

A communication for development project can also research attitudes towards it among organizations that might be invited to be part of an advisory panel, before assembling the panel. While a project should be prepared to face and answer informed criticism, it needs to avoid getting embroiled in wrangling with suspicious or hostile organizations through its consultation processes, because it diverts staff from their intended work and saps energy and morale.

Explanation

A second line of approach might be the diplomatic, starting with a clear explanation of the role of media in development (something which is, generally, not well understood in aid organizations) and the specific aims and methods of the particular communication project. This approach is not guaranteed. In a situation, for example, where an organization feels it has something to hide or where an organization feels it has been unreasonably or even harmfully handled by sections of the media, the organization is unlikely to welcome having journalists anywhere near its activities. An explanation of the kind proposed is unlikely to have much effect.

Keeping control of the consultation process

It is important for a communication for development organization to keep control of its consultation process, by choosing which organizations it wishes to have represented on its advisory panel, by setting the agenda and by chairing panel meetings. To reiterate, this does not mean the organization should not be willing to face criticism but that it should not allow its consultation process to become subject to other organizations' or even individuals' agendas.

Even after these preparations, a communication for development project would be wise to be ready for adverse responses in its consultation process, and to have measures in place to deal with them. Sometimes, these can come as a surprise. For example, in the first meeting of an advisory panel for a communication project in Somalia, a great deal of time was taken up as government representatives objected to the term 'non-state actors' in the project's title, believing it was designed to exclude themselves.

Alternatives to regular panels

There are alternatives to having a regular advisory panel, including one-to-one consultation and ad hoc panels assembled to discuss specific issues. Both of these are more time-consuming than regular panel meetings.

One-to-one consultation

This is very time-consuming, and means that ideas are not bounced off other individuals and organizations, which can be important, especially in the development of solutions to problems. However, it does avoid a whole panel being caught up in wrangling or rivalry on the part of other panel members, and it is wise to, at least, start a consultation process with a series of one-to-one meetings to carry out the preparations outlined above.

One-off, ad hoc panels

These are also time-consuming, because each one needs to start with a substantial explanation of the project and its intentions and methods, whereas, with a regular panel, that explanation is only needed at the outset. However, such panels can be useful where there is a specific issue that needs a solution. For example, during storyline development for a serial drama, individuals or panels can be invited in, at short notice, without the need for a formal agenda, to gain information and ideas on how to solve a problem.

Summing up

Consultation is essential and can be very helpful, as shown in the two drama examples, of sexual cleansing and avoiding giving food to a newborn. However, careful preparation and organization is necessary.

- Research organizations that are potential panel members before setting up a panel.
- Ensure all consultations are on the project's territory, or, at least, somewhere the project can arrange the furniture.
- Ensure the project chairs the consultation meetings.

Of course, the ultimate consultation is with the communities and populations that a project is aiming to help, and this is dealt with, at greater length, in Chapter 15 on two-way communication.

6

Factual programmes, drama and reality

Once the decision has been taken to do a communication for development project, or to add a communication for development element to an existing project, the next step is to decide on the basic format. Broadly, there are three formats in common use in communication for development broadcasting. These are: *factual programmes* (magazine or discussion), *serial drama* and different *reality* formats. (One area where there is a wider range of formats is in humanitarian broadcasting, where the need for urgency and the need to use immediately available resources can affect the choice of format, which includes one-off, short-form material.) Often, a combination of formats is used, for example, a serial drama followed by a discussion programme.

There is also the decision on whether the broadcasting will be live or recorded. Normally, programmes are recorded, because of the need for sensitivity, accuracy and clarity. Live programmes are riskier, though they will often have recorded material in them. The real exceptions are phone-in programmes, which need to be live, and humanitarian programming is often live because it can depend so much on interaction with the audience.

This chapter considers the pros and cons of each format and of a combination, including the ease or difficulty of production, cost, facilities needed and risks. It considers the strengths and weaknesses of each format and their appropriateness for different kinds of project.

Factual programmes

Factual programmes in this field are usually either in a 'magazine' format or are discussion programmes or a combination of the two. A magazine programme is one that consists of a number of items on different topics, linked by a presenter. A discussion programme has a panel of up to about four guests, representing different viewpoints and experience, who discuss questions put to them by the chair, or by members of the audience. This can be an audience in the studio or viewing or listening to the broadcast. The viewing or listening audience either call in with questions or send questions by SMS or social media. Sometimes, a magazine programme will have a discussion as one of its items. One reason that these are the main formats used in communication for development is that there are different sections of the audience whose needs have to be addressed. Different items can address different parts of the audience. If the programme was about only one topic throughout, it would only address one part of the audience, and would thus alienate the rest of the audience. When a factual programme follows a drama, it will normally be about topics raised in the drama.

It is possible, in communication for development, to make programmes that are largely discussion; however, they will still need some factual input, some information, because any change in the audience starts with a change of knowledge, and knowledge cannot change without information. That information could come from an interview at the beginning of the programme, which then becomes the basis of the discussion, or from the knowledge and experience of the discussion panel members, or both.

Where factual and discussion programmes in communication for development differ from those in similar formats in the West is that they tend to focus on a narrower range of topics, and they follow a structured syllabus, rather than dealing with topical issues. Factual programmes can be about almost any subject associated with development, including a range of health issues, livelihoods, the importance of education or good governance, for example.

Drama

In the context of communication for development, drama, whether on television or radio, will normally be serial drama, that is with the same set of characters following a number of storylines that continue episode after episode. As has been said, this is the familiar format, in the West, of the soap opera. Communication for development dramas, again, tend to have a narrow focus on one area of behaviour, such as mother and baby health. Dramas cover a wide range of different topics, including a range of health topics, peacebuilding, agriculture or natural forest habitat protection, as genuine examples.

Reality

Reality television is a huge genre, with a wide variety of formats and purposes. BBC Media Action, in particular, has been using different versions of it for many years. They have used it in the past to combat HIV, for example, and, in Chapter 10, there is a discussion of *Amrai Pari*, a reality television series BBC Media Action made to help communities in Bangladesh become more resilient in the face of the climate crisis. In particular, the reality genre can show people overcoming challenges or being spurred on by being challenged. What the genre can do is to set up an artificial situation in which a participant faces a real challenge. For example, in a BBC Media Action show in India, a young wife was set the challenge of asking her husband to start using condoms. However, instead of doing it for real, she had to try it with a life-size puppet, which, being funny, gave her the chance to try it in a relaxed atmosphere.[1] The genre can also work in audio. One audio format I have used, in Somalia and in the Philippines, is a short-form adaptation of the business makeover genre (see Chapter 7), and another I used in the Philippines is, essentially, a humanitarian version of the home makeover show. (See Chapter 17 and Figure 17.1.)

These last two examples were short-form reality formats used in combination with factual formats, which is, perhaps, a good way of using the advantages of each genre.

The advantages and disadvantages of each basic format

The advantages of factual programmes

- Factual programmes can feature people the audience identify with, talking about their real experience, which can both explain to the audience how change is made and help to give them the self-confidence to believe they can do the same.
- They can include the drama of a news story, with conflict and tension, which helps engage audiences and keeps them listening or viewing.
- They can provide immediately useable information – for example, farming programmes can have a weather forecast and a market prices slot, or health programmes can include information on places and dates of vaccination projects, alongside longer-term educational or behaviour change material.
- They can incorporate a discussion element, as a panel of individuals with different views and experience talk about a topic, which helps to promote discussion among the audience. Discussion among the audience, as has been said in Chapter 2, and will be seen in Chapters 25 and 26, is an important factor in both learning and in behaviour change.
- In distance learning, factual programmes can effectively be used to set up practical education activities for associated learning groups, either with parallel print material or just with spoken instructions.
- Factual programmes are much better than drama in explaining. In a drama, when one character is telling another one how to do something – perhaps how to prevent soil erosion – while the listener or viewer is overhearing the advice, it sounds very stilted and artificial, and is not drama.
- It is much easier to have interaction with the audience in factual programmes than in drama or reality programmes, as phone calls, texts and messages on social media can easily be woven into the programme's fabric, and they can be live, allowing for much faster interaction, as in phone-in programmes, for example.
- Factual programmes are far more flexible, both in content and structure, than either dramas or reality programmes, which means they can react much better to changing circumstances and topical events, and, crucially, to feedback and suggestions from the audience.
- Factual programmes can incorporate items using reality formats, for example, challenges, which have the advantage of showing participants undergoing long-term change. (See below and Chapter 7.)
- These programmes are relatively cheap to produce, in comparison with dramas, because production teams are smaller, and programmes can be made with relatively limited facilities, as they do not need the space required for drama, the cast, nor the complicated mixing.

- In most countries and contexts, there are already journalists who could make behaviour change factual programmes. They might need extra training, but it would be much less than is required to do a good drama. It is, therefore, likely to be quicker and easier to launch a factual series than a drama for behaviour change. It is probably also true to say that, for the long-term future of the staff trained, journalism skills are likely to be more transferable than drama skills.

The disadvantages of factual programmes

- As will be seen in Chapters 26 and 27, communication for behaviour change usually requires long-term role modelling, showing characters going through a behaviour change process to be effective. In factual programmes, it is possible to have real people being the long-term role models for behaviour change, as they themselves try to change and are interviewed regularly on their progress. However, the outcomes of such an effort are very unpredictable: the individuals may or may not succeed in changing and the dropout rate can be high. For this function, drama is a significantly safer and more predictable option.
- A key difference between factual programmes and dramas is that factual programmes 'tell'; that is, they describe and explain the issues they are dealing with, whereas dramas 'show'. In dramas, for example, audiences can hear or see characters going through a process of behaviour change, and they can hear or see characters facing up to the consequences of their actions. In factual programmes the process or the facing up is explained and described, so that factual programmes are more detached and cerebral, while dramas are more involving and emotional.

Factual formats: A summary

- Factual programmes are the better choice when audiences need practical information for distance learning, especially where there are learning groups carrying out practical lessons on the ground; in humanitarian crises; and for programming for political engagement. Some behaviour change can be brought about by information only, usually where it does not involve complex cultural issues or issues of identity, and factual programmes can make it happen.
- Factual programming is the stronger option for broadcasting in humanitarian situations, with the need to respond – sometimes rapidly – to changing circumstances, to have strong interaction with the audience and to provide practical information. However, short video dramas and animations have been used to convey information in humanitarian crises, successfully.

The advantages of drama

- Drama can bring about strong emotional engagement, which tends to make it more memorable. Audiences can get very involved in dramas, and where they often cannot identify the source of any information they have received from a factual programme, they can often recall characters and storylines from dramas. Emotional engagement can be a very powerful driver of change. (See Chapter 27.)

- Drama can take audiences on methodically worked-out, long-term journeys of behaviour change. In behaviour change communication, the aim is to take the audience on a journey of change, led by a role model, and going step by step. The role model needs to be seen tackling specific, identified problems: how a young mother can make sure no one gives her baby water while she is at work, for example, or how someone can intervene to stop violence without themselves being killed or injured. Even if a production team can find a real person who has done this, the story can only be told in retrospect. It can, as has already been discussed, only be described and explained, not lived and experienced. Drama is the only format that can do this. It is very difficult to find real-life examples of role models as they go through change, and difficult to manage, if they can be found.
- Drama *shows* characters making change, rather than change being explained and described. That is, drama shows; it does not tell. For some behaviour change, especially involving overcoming relatively complex barriers, showing is more effective than describing and explaining, as it is more direct.
- Drama can show the consequences of a particular course of action, even if the consequences are death. No one can do that in factual or reality programmes.
- An important characteristic of drama is that it can use humour, when factual programmes rarely can. This is particularly important because it is part of the reason dramas can address sensitive issues that would be difficult or impossible in a factual programme. Humour can help to defuse sensitivity. Reality formats can do this, but, without a script, whether the outcome is funny or not is unpredictable.

The disadvantages of drama

- The main disadvantage is that drama is more expensive than either factual or reality programming. Drama needs more people, because of the cast, and better facilities.
- Drama takes significantly more time to produce, with the need to develop effective characters and complex storylines, to record with a large number of people. For audio there is the need to mix voices and sound effects, and for television it is substantially more complex.

Drama: A summary

- Drama is by far the strongest format for bringing about behaviour change, as it can show characters negotiating socially and culturally complex journeys of change, while being emotionally engaging and able to show the most serious consequences of certain courses of action.
- Drama is weak for giving practical information, and to use it for that is an expensive misuse of the format.

- Because drama shows, while factual programming describes and explains, a combination of drama and factual programming can be very effective, as it allows for topics to be explored from two different perspectives. However, this is the most expensive option of all.

The advantages of reality formats

- Situations can be set up in which real people face challenges. This is much simpler than trying to find interviewees for factual programming, who have or are facing specific challenges, and, for some audiences, the fact that these are real people facing real challenges might be more convincing than scripted drama.
- If the same people return for each programme, then change over time can be shown. This is almost impossible in factual programming. It can, of course, be done in drama, but a reality format would be much cheaper.
- Like drama, reality formats can show people changing, rather than describing and explaining change, as factual programming has to do. This can make the impact much more immediate.
- Reality offer produces huge flexibility, with a very wide range of formats, which can be adapted to all kinds of topics and circumstances.

The disadvantages of reality formats

- One of the central appealing features of competitive reality formats is the aggression, even brutality, with which losers are ejected from the show. The anticipation for the audience of which participant is going to be ejected keeps them watching. However, in communication for development, such a format cannot be used, since it would breach ethics.
- While reality shows can promote long-term identification between an audience and participants, they cannot have the emotional engagement of drama.
- Reality formats sometimes provoke cynicism, as audiences suspect manipulation of participants, and even scripting of supposedly 'real' dialogue. Clearly, in a communication for development context, producers need to avoid anything similar, as it would, in all likelihood, entirely negate any development impact intended.

Reality formats: A summary

- Reality formats have great flexibility, allowing for gripping competition and conflict, and humour. They can offer long-term engagement between audiences and participants and can show role models in action.
- Against that, they are not as strong as factual programming in giving practical information. While the uncertainty of outcomes can be a big strength of reality formats, it does mean that they are not strong for behaviour change, where methodically worked-out storylines have great strength. Attempts to remove the uncertainty of outcomes in these formats are very likely to provoke cynicism in audiences.

7

Producing factual programmes in communication for development

Factual programmes are used in all of the different fields of communication for development discussed in this book: humanitarian, distance learning, empowerment and behaviour change. There are differences between the requirements of programming in the four fields, but there is a core production technique that can be used in all of them.

A key difference between mainstream factual programmes and those for communication for development is that those for the development field are built around identified needs in the target audiences. The needs are identified from the formative research.

(One item in a programme or even a whole programme is not going to meet a need completely, and it is most likely that it will be done over time.)

One approach to making a factual magazine programme

In this suggested approach, the process of developing an item has six stages. These are as set out in Table 7.1, which has been used in a number of different broadcast series, including series for distance learning, for empowerment and for behaviour change.

Strand: Topic:

Table 7.1 A grid for developing a factual package to meet an audience need

1. What is the identified need that this package is helping to meet?	
2. What change can the audience make to meet this need?	
3. Which part of the audience needs to make this change?	
4. What kind of change does the target audience need? A change of knowledge, attitude or behaviour?	

| 5. Does the target audience have access to the resources to make this change? | Yes/No:
If the answer is No, stop and research a different change.
If the answer is Yes, explain the answer. |
| 6. List the points of information the audience need to make this change. | Against each point, or set of points, list who the information would best come from. |

Stage 1 is to identify a need the project must address. Normally, this will have been worked out in advance in some kind of curricular structure spanning the whole series. (See Chapter 21 for developing a curriculum for distance learning and Chapter 30 for developing a curriculum for behaviour and social change.)

Stage 2 is to work out one of the changes that the target audience have to make to help meet the identified need.

Again, in most series, this will also come from the series curriculum. For example, in a series on the need to alleviate poverty, a part of that is the need to earn more money. For part of the audience, a change might be of improving marketing in a small business. An early item on this might be the need to understand better hygiene is a factor that can improve sales in food and drink businesses. So, the change is acquiring the knowledge that hygiene matters, and the knowledge of how to improve hygiene.

Stage 3 is to identify the part of the audience who need to make this change. In the example given, it would be small business owners, and especially those in the food and drink business.

Stage 4 is to research what kind of change is asked for: one of knowledge, attitude or behaviour. This information is needed as it affects the crucial answer to the next question, and the choice of journalistic sources for the item.

In the example, the change is one of knowledge: that better hygiene is a factor in better sales, and of learning ways to improve hygiene.

There is now the crucial Stage 5, which is research into whether the target audience has the material resources to make the change. That is, if a certain level of wealth is required to make the change, or if a particular product is required, do this target audience have the money needed or is the product available to the target audience? It would be a waste of time and energy to ask the audience to do something they simply cannot do, and it would damage the credibility of the communication.

Stage 6 involves two tasks: identifying the broad information points needed by the target audience to be motivated and able to make the change, and where that information is going to come from. In other words, who is the journalist going to interview and what questions are going to be asked.

So this grid is an analytical tool, to help take the journalist from the original identified need to the practicalities of the choice of interviewees and what to ask them.

A completed grid for the example just discussed might be as shown in Table 7.2.

Strand: Increasing personal income. Topic: Better hygiene is better marketing

Table 7.2 A completed factual package development grid, showing the analytical steps taken

1. What is the identified need that this package is helping to meet?	For better marketing to increase sales
2. What change can the audience make to meet this need?	Learn how improved hygiene is better marketing in food and drink businesses
3. Which part of the audience needs to make this change?	Owners of very small food and drink businesses
4. What kind of change does the target audience need? A change of knowledge, attitude or behaviour?	Knowledge
5. Does the target audience have access to the resources to make this change?	Yes/No: Yes If the answer is No, stop and research a different change. If the answer is Yes, explain the answer. Since the change is one of knowledge, the only material resource needed is access to the broadcast material

6. List the points of information the audience need to make this change:
a) Taking the example of the milk business:
   i) Plastic jerrycans are not hygienic containers for transporting milk, as they cannot be adequately cleaned, and are a deterrent to customers
   ii) Milk containers, like metal churns, which can be thoroughly cleaned and which are visible to customers, improve sales
b) Examples from other food and drink businesses of simple changes for visibly better hygiene which improves sales
	Against each point, or set of points, list who the information would best come from.
	A street milk seller who witnesses how dirty the inside of a plastic jerrycan is, even after it has been cleaned, when it has been opened up by the journalist or a hygienist
	A street milk seller who has changed from using plastic jerrycans to metal churns or traditional containers
	An informed customer whose choices of where to shop are based on hygiene standards

The next item in the same series might address the need to invest in order to gain improved sales through better visible hygiene, and the change would be taking measures to acquire capital for that investment. There might be a number of programme items on meeting this need – budgeting and saving or microfinance, for example – but here is a grid on one option (see Table 7.3).

Strand: Increasing personal income. Topic: Acquiring capital for better marketing

Table 7.3 A second completed factual package development grid, showing the analytical steps taken

1. What is the identified need which this package is helping to meet?	More capital to buy more hygienic equipment
2. What change can the audience make to meet this need?	Negotiating the creation of a traditional credit union
3. Which part of the audience needs to make this change?	Owners of very small food and drink businesses

4. What kind of change does the target audience need? A change of knowledge, attitude or behaviour?	Knowledge on how traditional credit unions work Behaviour, specifically negotiation skills for establishing a traditional credit union
5. Does the target audience have access to the resources to make this change?	Yes/No: Yes If the answer is No, stop and research a different change. If the answer is Yes, explain the answer. Since part of the change is one of knowledge, the only material resource needed is access to the broadcast material. The resources needed to acquire negotiating skills are role-model demonstrations, which will be in the programme, and opportunities for practice. If the individual audience member is in an organized learning group, that will provide a structured opportunity for practice, or an individual listener can practise within her or his family or other social group.
6. List the points of information the audience need to make this change: a) How traditional credit unions work. b) Negotiating skills for setting up a traditional credit union.	Against each point, or set of points, list who the information would best come from. Members of longstanding existing credit unions. Someone who has set up a traditional credit union. Witnesses to this setting up. Someone who is in the process of trying to set one up.

The universal application of this approach

The process just set out for the development of broadcast items promoting learning and change can be an effective basis for almost any communication for development project, using whatever is the most appropriate medium for communication with the target population. In distance learning, in empowerment and in behaviour change, these small items can be set within an established framework. In distance learning, there will be a curriculum, of varying flexibility. In empowerment, there will be a structure for bringing the disempowered into a political process. Even if the broadcasting is reporting a justice process, there will be a structure to help the population bring that justice process into a political and peacebuilding process. A behaviour change project will want to take different parts of the audience through different long-term trajectories of change.

The one field where there is not, at least at the early stages, going to be such a structure to fit broadcast items into is in broadcasting in a humanitarian response. In the early stages of a humanitarian crisis, the overwhelming need is for a broadcaster to be very nimble in response to rapidly and unpredictably changing circumstances. The item development process suggested above will still be valuable, but items will need to be developed to meet changing needs and not be part of a prearranged structure. At the later stages of a humanitarian crisis response, distance learning and empowerment curricula may well become relevant.

Magazine programmes

This focus on relatively short programme items is based on the assumption that most built factual programmes in a development context will be magazine programmes, as that is the format that is likely to be most commonly used. A magazine programme is one in which there are several items, perhaps five or six in a thirty-minute programme, each on a different topic, and in a range of different formats. They can be broadcast live – that is the presenter and guests, if there are any, are in the studio and are being broadcast as they speak – or they can be pre-recorded. Even if the programme is live, many of the items in it will be pre-recorded.

Addressing the needs of different parts of the audience

Because there is a number of items on different topics, while all of the programme should be interesting for the whole of the audience, different items can be made to be highly relevant to different parts of the audience.

For example, a series on livestock had different strands addressing different parts of the sector. A strand is a large topic which runs for many weeks, broken down into small, weekly items. In this series, different strands were aimed at livestock owners, livestock exporters, women who sold milk on the street and the very poor, with items on economic opportunities in the sector that would earn at least some money. And a series aimed at reducing mortality rates in babies up to six months old had different strands aimed at mothers-to-be, husbands and older women who had strong influence over how a newborn was cared for.

Interviewing for programmes in a development context

There are normally thought to be six standard journalism questions: What (happened)? Where (did it happen)? When (did it happen)? Who (was involved)? Why (did it happen)? How (did it happen)? Journalism courses say that the last two are the least necessary and can be left out if time constraints demand it. However, in a development context programme, saying what happened is important, but saying where and when it happened and who was involved can be kept to an absolute minimum, because what really matters is how the person or people involved did whatever it was, and why it was done.

Formats

The different items in a built programme, or those interspersed in a long live programme, on, say, a community station dedicated to humanitarian broadcasting, should be in a variety of formats. The choice will depend on the function of each item. Varying formats helps to avoid the programme being monotonous and helps the listener understand that the programme has moved on to a new topic.

The formats that can be used are the same as in mainstream magazine programmes, though there are a few which would not normally be used in mainstream programming, because of their educational intent.

The one-to-one interview

The most basic format is the one-to-one interview, with the interviewee answering questions put by a reporter or the programme's presenter. In a development context, this format can be used for role modelling, as an interviewee explains why and how he or she has changed behaviour, or, for example, has earned more money by adopting a new business practice.

In a humanitarian context, the format can be used to hold an agency or government to account. This might be complaints from the crisis-affected population being put to a representative or an individual official or a representative being challenged with evidence of corruption gathered in an investigation.

Another variation of the one-to-one interview is when questions from the audience are put to a subject specialist. The questions will have been gathered from social media, texts or recorded by reporters when they are out in the field, over a period of time. They are grouped under headings. Each week, or more frequently than that, a different subject specialist is brought in, to provide answers to the questions collected under the heading relevant to his or her specialization.

One advantage of this format is that it is audience-led, and so is part of two-way communication.

The report

For this format a journalist researches a topic and records interviews, but then writes the story for a single voice, including quotes from, and paraphrases of, the interviews.

The format's main advantage is that the story can be told very succinctly. It is a format used quite often in news, because it can be written to any given duration. It can overcome technical problems – for example, if the interviews were recorded over a poor quality line and would be hard for an audience to understand. If some of the interviews were recorded in a language many in the audience do not understand, doing a report avoids the cumbersome and time-consuming process of voicing-over a translation.

The monologue

This format is used, usually, when an interviewee is telling a very personal story or describing something personal and emotional. While some monologues are recorded as such, many are recorded as interviews. The journalist will phrase the questions in ways that will not prompt answer forms of speech. The questions will often be put in forms like, 'Tell me about what happened when you reached the border.' The questions will then be edited out, to form an uninterrupted flow of speech.

The advantage of this format is that it increases the sense of intimacy between speaker and audience, with no sense of an intermediary.

Small discussions

Typically involving up to three people and the presenter or reporter, these can be useful for exploring topics where there are conflicting views or different perspectives, but also where ordinary people are teasing out the implications of an issue for themselves. This format has been used, for example, for discussing the value of giving birth in a health facility rather than at home. In this case, the panel might be a midwife who favours health-facility birth, a mother who has had all of her children at home and a first-time mother-to-be.

The same basic format has been used, as another example, in a series exploring a proposed new constitution that included guaranteeing certain human rights. The format brought together a human rights specialist with three ordinary citizens with an average level of education. Each discussion took one article on rights in the proposed constitution. The specialist explained the article to the group, and then there was a discussion of its implications for ordinary people, focusing on its impact on people's day-to-day lives.

Formats of this kind, bringing together expertise and the people affected, bring the issue into the perspective of the population. If these items had been a one-to-one interview with a specialist, it could easily have been pitched at a level listeners could not understand or in a language they could not engage with.

The continuing challenge

In this format, in the past, three people have been brought together on a long-term basis to provide role models for money management. The format has been used in a number of different contexts, but, essentially, it involves bringing together an experienced advisor with two learners. The learners are individuals who need to learn how to budget, save and invest. In a development context, they are trying to improve their livelihoods. In a humanitarian crisis context, they are trying to rebuild their livelihoods. In either case, very small amounts of money are in question.

This format does require long-term commitment by the participants, and producers need to put in place the arrangements needed for this to work, which may involve small remunerations for the participants. Two small-business people are brought together with a financial advisor. In the first session, the advisor asks the participants about their current financial situation and discusses the need for saving in order to invest and so build a better future livelihood. Having heard what the participants have to say, the advisor sets them a challenge for the following week: to come up with a budget that will produce a small amount to be saved.

The following week the participants explain how well they have met the challenge, and the advisor sets them a new challenge for the week after that. The process goes on, taking the participants on a real-time journey of budgeting and saving, and, when it becomes possible, making decisions about investing the money saved in something that will expand or restore the business.

The broadcast package

This is the most sophisticated and difficult format to produce. A package is an item of up to about seven minutes long. It is based on a number of interviews, up to about four, representing different experience of, or opinion on, the topic in question. The interviews are edited tightly into succinct segments, and the whole is usually linked by a reporter's script. The art of a package is that the edited clips are organized into an order so that they tell the story or make the point almost on their own, and the script links them together to make the meaning clear. However, in the best packages, every link also provides information.

On location

An item for television will almost always be recorded on or broadcast live from a location: it is visually more interesting than a studio setting, and the interviewee can use elements of the location to illustrate what he or she is talking about. It may be less obvious but it is valuable practice, in making radio programme items, to record on location, too.

The soundscape of a location gives a sense of immediacy and is, in itself, more ear-catching than the deadness of a studio. When a radio interviewee is in a place where they can talk about what they can see – for example a farmer at a place where he or she is part of an effort to reverse environmental degradation – they can often be much more articulate and can discuss details of what they are doing more easily. If the interviewee is carrying out a relevant activity and talking about it at the same time, that usually makes for strong radio.

However, when recording for radio on location, it is important that the journalist makes sure that at least two minutes of the background sound of each location used is recorded without any voices. This sound is known as wildtrack, and can then be used in editing and mixing to make fades, so that the background sound does not appear or disappear abruptly.

Assembling a programme

Once the items have been created, they can be included in any overall structure. In a humanitarian context, for example, they might be in an hour-long programme, interspersed with music and text messages from the audience. However, in a development context, they are more likely to be organized into a tightly built programme. When this is the case, the structure that makes them into a coherent programme is the presenter's script. Here is a possible briefing for a typical script for a magazine programme for communication for development.

A presenter's script brief for a magazine programme

The menu and menu clips

The menu is essential for drawing the audience in, and keeping them attentive, so it needs to be created carefully. It is a short list of the items that are going to be in the programme, usually illustrated with very short clips from different items, linked by a short script. The links should create intrigue and tension. There should be two or three clips in each menu.

- A clip is not needed for every item in the programme.
- One clip should always be from the most appealing item in the programme.
- A menu clip should be between ten and twenty seconds long.
- A menu clip should be the second best line in the item (the item must always be better than the menu).

Presenter links

Once the audience has been drawn in by the menu, the presenter's script has to keep them engaged. This means that the links the presenter reads between items need to create tension, perhaps to ask a question the item answers, or set up a mystery the item resolves. Tension is created by the temporary withholding of information. This will help make the audience want to listen to or see the item.

To write an effective link, taking the following steps may be useful.

- Identify the crucial issue in the item you are introducing.
- Create tension about that issue, by suggesting that the item is going to provide some kind of answer to the crucial issue.
- Do not tell the whole story in the link, nor say what the answer the item is about to offer is.
- Be personal in talking to individual members of the audience, trying to make the issue relevant to their life.

To give the idea, here is a link as originally written for an item in a programme on hygiene, for displaced people.

> Hand washing has huge benefits for the individual and the whole family. It is essential for hands to be washed. It is especially important for displaced people to understand the importance of hand washing.

This is all right, as a factual link, but it does not identify the crucial issue, nor create a tension that makes the audience want to hear the package. The crucial issue in the package is that thousands of children die of diseases like diarrhoea and cholera, and the simple measure of handwashing can prevent many of these deaths. Nor is this link personal.

So, using the crucial issue, creating tension and being personal, the link could be,

Every year, thousands of displaced children die of diseases like cholera and diarrhoea, yet there is a very simple measure that can prevent your child becoming one more victim.

Cues for pre-recorded items

A cue is a piece of information written in a script to identify a recorded item, which is going to be part of the broadcast programme. It is a key issue in writing the presenter's script to show the production team, very clearly, which recorded item goes where in the programme. It is easy to mix up different items and it is important that they are accurately identified in the script. It is also vital that everyone, but especially the presenter, knows when the item is about to end, so they are ready to continue the presenter's script. Every item will be a software file, and each needs to be identified in the script with the following information:

- the filename in the script which should be exactly the same as the one in the software
- the In-cue, which is the first few words spoken in the item
- the Out-cue, which is the last few words spoken in the item
- the duration, which is the exact length of the item in minutes and seconds

So, each item should be written in the script in this format:

Filename:

IN:

OUT:

DUR:

A suggested presenter checklist

This is a list of all the items that could go into the presenter's script for a magazine programme.

Introductory music

Presenter: Introduction – this usually includes the name of the series, the presenter's name, what the programme, overall, is about and, sometimes, who it is aimed at

Link to menu clip 1

Menu clip 1

Presenter: Link to menu clip 2

Menu clip 2

Presenter: Link to menu clip 3

Menu clip 3

Presenter: Summary of other items in the programme Link to first item

Pre-recorded item 1

Presenter: Back announcement for Item 1 – this will include a credit for the reporter and a brief reflection on the item

Music sting

Presenter: Series and broadcaster identifier Link to audience participation slot, with information on how to contact the programme or station

Pre-recorded item 2: Messages from audience and appropriate responses

Presenter: Announcement of the topic for the next programme, request for questions or comments, including SMS number, email address and social media page. Reminder that the contact details will be given again at the end of the programme

Music sting

Presenter: Link to item 3

Pre-recorded item 3

Presenter: Back announcement for Item 3 – this will include a credit for the reporter and a brief reflection on the item

Music sting

Presenter: Series and broadcaster identification Link to item 4

Pre-recorded item 4

Presenter: Back announcement for Item 4 – this will include a credit for the reporter and a brief reflection on the item Link to item 5

Pre-recorded item 5

Presenter: Back announcement for Item 5 – this will include a credit for the reporter and a brief reflection on the item

Music sting

Presenter: Series and broadcaster identification Link to item 6

Presenter: Back announcement for Item 6 – this will include a credit for the reporter and a brief reflection on the item Closing announcement: including an invitation to call, all possible contact details

Music

8

The project production handbook

A production handbook is a document that needs to be tailor-made to match the needs of each different communication for development project. It contains all of the information on the project that the production team needs, and it includes sections that are aide-memoires to the training the team has received. A copy should be on the desk or laptop of every member of the team, for quick and easy reference. This chapter looks at the reasons for having a handbook, and what kind of information should be in it.

A production handbook is something that is common to all communication for development projects, but the details of content will vary significantly from one kind of project to another. For those details, see the later relevant chapters on the production of different kinds of communication.

The production handbook provides production teams – or, in the case of a drama, the writing and production teams – with the essential information they need for all the production processes, all in one document.

It can also be an introduction to the project for any new members of a writing or production team, giving them the essential information they need to quickly understand how the production process works, and how to carry out their jobs. It is not, though, a substitute for training. It is more an aide-memoire following training.

The handbook can also be a yardstick for an editor, setting a standard against which scripts and programmes can be evaluated. For example, if the handbook contains a summary of the methodology being used in a drama or factual programming, the editor can readily check if a script or programme is following that methodology.

A production handbook needs to be updated regularly. This is partly because a project evolves over time. For example, in a behaviour change drama, main characters who are role models for change will reach the end of their change storylines, when they will become more minor characters, and different characters will become role models. Furthermore, administrative details will change: for example, workplans are not normally longer than one year, and need to be updated each year.

The content of a drama production handbook

Typically, the handbook for a serial drama aiming to bring about behaviour and social change would contain the following sections. (The content of each section will depend on how the information in Chapters 27, 28 and 29 has been applied to the individual project.)

Project purpose and rationale

This would be an explanation of the project purpose and rationale, covering the overall aim of the project, who the target audience or audiences are and the rationale for the choices made and the specific behaviour change objectives. This section would go on to cover the project context the drama is in, such as whether there is an associated factual or discussion programme, what reinforcement or learning activities there are on the ground or the role of any partner organizations.

Drama methodology

This would be a brief explanation of the methodology, and how it has been realized in the individual project, in the choice of behaviour change objectives, the role-modelling characters that have been developed and how the methodology plays out in the storylines.

This would be followed by a list of the main characters who are role-modelling behaviour change, and the behaviour change objective their storyline is taking them to.

The project structure

This would be a brief explanation of the staff structure, with key responsibilities and reporting lines. It would not contain detailed job descriptions, as concision is important in a production handbook.

The basics of good television or radio drama writing

This section would be an aide-memoire to the training the team have previously received. For an editor, it would be, in effect, a checklist of what should be found in a well-written scene in a television or radio drama.

The summary in the handbook should accurately follow the training the team has received, so that there is no confusion. It is likely to cover both what makes good drama and what makes good drama for the particular medium – that is, the characteristics of scenes that make them effective and readily understandable on that medium. It is also likely to cover the mutual reinforcement that can exist between the principles of good drama and the behaviour change methodology.

The writing process

Again, this section should be an aide-memoire, after the teams have been taken through the process in training or on the job. It should set out the stages of the writing process – character development, the development of behaviour change storylines, etc. – and identify who works on each stage. It may be, for instance, that the earlier stages, like character development, are done by both the writing and production teams working together, along with some external support, like people with good, practical local knowledge of the subject areas, and external expertise in behaviour change drama, while the later stages, like scene synopses and dialogue, are done by the writing team alone.

The section should also contain guidance on what considerations have to be brought in at each stage. So, for example, behaviour change principles need to be applied at the initial, long storyline stage, but, once the long storylines have been shaped by those principles, thereafter the principles of good drama writing become the most important.

The Character Bible

The Character Bible is a record of what happens to each character in the drama, and it needs to be updated after every episode has been written. It is used by the writers to check what has happened to each character in the scenes before the one they are currently writing.

The concept and practice of the Character Bible should have been introduced in the writing team's training, and this section of the production handbook is a reminder to them of what information needs to be recorded in the document, and in what form, so that entries are consistent, and the updating can be done as efficiently as possible.

Stages of production

This section of the production handbook is an aide-memoire for the production team, to reinforce what they learned in their training. Again, it sets out all the key stages of the production process, what is involved in each stage, and identifies who is responsible for each stage.

The workplan

In any activity where a number of people are working on different elements of a project, and in which all the elements have to be brought together into a whole by a tight deadline, it is essential there is a detailed workplan so that each individual knows exactly what they have got to complete and when.

The content of a production handbook for factual programme-making

If the project's output is a daily or weekly recorded factual programme, with associated activities on the ground, then a production handbook might contain the following sections.

Project purpose and rationale

This would be an explanation of the project purpose and rationale, covering the overall aim of the project, who the target audience or audiences are and the rationale for the choices made, the specific behaviour change objectives and the project context the programme is in, such as whether there is an associated drama, what reinforcement or learning activities there are on the ground or the role of any partner organizations.

The methodology or methodologies

In a factual magazine programme, different items may be driven by different methodologies, and, of course, there will be large differences between programmes for distance learning, for political engagement, for humanitarian assistance and for behaviour change. However, in some projects, there may be a mix of the methodologies behind each of these approaches in the same programme. For example, a distance learning programme may have a slot that uses the role-modelling approach of behaviour change communication, while humanitarian broadcasting could well contain items following the methodologies of all of the other three approaches. If the production team have to hand a brief explanation of the different methodologies underlying different programme slots, they are likely to find it much easier to produce appropriate material. So, this section of a handbook would be a brief explanation of the methodology by which the information given to the audience is to positively affect development. Again, the team should have received training, so that this section is an aide-memoire.

The structure of the overall course

This section would not be in every factual programme production handbook, as not all projects using factual programming will follow a structured course. It is very unlikely, for example, at least in the early stages after a crisis, that humanitarian broadcasting would follow any pre-set structure, as it would be responding to the changing needs of its target populations; and a project promoting political engagement following a conflict by reporting on a war crimes trial would follow the events in court. However, for distance learning and behaviour change, in order for effective learning and change to take place, the audience need to be taken, step by step, through some kind of course. Therefore, the programmes need to be within a long-term structure, based on a step-by-step breakdown of each topic.

This section of the handbook will normally be a table, showing the structure of the programming over a year or more.

The programme design

This section of the handbook sets out the structure of different items – each often with a different format – in a programme and explains the rationale for the choice of items and their formats.

Activities development guidance

This section is most likely to be in the handbook for a distance learning project, though some political engagement projects may have learning groups. When a series of programmes has associated learning groups, there will be activities for the groups to undertake, after the end of the programme, and, often, the instructions for these activities will be given in the programmes. This section of the handbook would offer guidance to the production team on how to devise and develop these activities.

Package development

A package is a report, between three and seven minutes long, using clips from interviews with two or more people, linked by the reporter reading a script. In training, reporters should have been taken through the whole procedure of making packages, and this section of the handbook is an aide-memoire, setting out the process of making a package.

Finding the right interviewees

The quality of a factual programme depends heavily on how appropriate interviewees are to the topics in question and the audience. This section is an aide-memoire for reporters and producers on researching and finding the best interviewees and working out questions that will elicit the most appropriate answers to meet audience need.

Chairing a discussion

If the programme either is a discussion programme or includes a discussion section, then the handbook needs to have guidance on: how to choose discussion panel members, so that they represent a broad range of opinion and experience; how to prepare questions that will elicit the best responses from the panel; and how to control the broadcast.

Presenter's script guidance

This section would break down the presenter's linking script into all the different sections needed: the introduction, the menu of the items that are to be in the programme, links between different items and the close, which may include activity instructions. It will give guidance on what needs to be said in each section.

Editorial guidance

This is binding guidance on the programme's content, on what can and cannot be said in programmes, so that the production team comply with the law in whichever territory the programmes are broadcast, and with the principles of ethical journalism. These standards may be set by the project itself, by the broadcaster or by the organization running the project. The production team should have been thoroughly trained in complying with these standards, and this section is a reminder both of the standards themselves and the importance of complying with them.

Stages of production

This section would set out all the key stages of the production process and what is involved in each stage, and would identify who is responsible for each stage, again, as an aide-memoire.

The workplan

In any activity where a number of people are working on different elements of a project, and in which all the elements have to be brought together into a whole by a tight deadline, it is essential there is a detailed workplan so that each individual knows exactly what they have got to complete and when.

9

Project choices

Researching the rules

Before writing a proposal for a communication for development project, the framework within which the media operates in the chosen country or countries needs to be thoroughly understood.

In most countries, the media, and broadcasting in particular, are a sensitive area, and it is important to understand the legal, political and commercial framework within which the media operates, to assess whether the planned project is going to be feasible, any risks there might be and any measures that might need to be taken to ensure the project can work effectively.

The following are useful sources.

- As already mentioned in Chapter 3, *The World Press Freedom Index*, published annually by Reporters Without Borders, ranks countries by levels of press freedom and is very useful for assessing risks that may be faced.
- The BBC News website carries country profiles, which include brief overviews of the media landscape and the political and commercial framework.
- UNDP's *Human Development Reports* have, for example, basic information on internet access by gender.
- The CIA World Factbook contains country profiles.
- More detailed information, both on the context for the media and on individual media outlets, can be found in the *Media and Telecoms Landscape Guides*, which can be downloaded as pdf files from: http://www.cdacnetwork.org/tools-and-resources/i/20140613150126-ndeiz. However, only twenty-one countries are covered by these guides.

It is not wise to assume that the context for the media can be judged by a country's image. For example, to compare the context in two countries as things stood in 2018: South Sudan was unstable, with ongoing conflict and widespread poverty, while the Philippines had a stable democracy, was a relatively prosperous middle-income country and was a tourist destination. Yet, in *The World Press Freedom Index* for 2018 the Philippines, at 133rd in the world, was only ten ranks above South Sudan.

A reminder: It is important to find the most up-to-date information available, as media landscapes and contexts can change quickly.

Research on the actual context in which the media operate in a particular country, and not just the media laws which apply there, matters. Some countries have laws guaranteeing press freedom, but other forces are at work – like national security organizations, local politicians or local militias – which restrict freedom of expression.

The choice of platforms

As has been said in Chapter 3, the choice of a platform or platforms a communication for development project can use depends on the target audiences' access and preferences. These need to be well researched, especially to establish the access women have to different platforms. However, in most contexts in the Global South, there is still (and it is likely to remain the same into the foreseeable future), the need for broadcasting, either on television or on radio. Radio is especially important for reaching the rural poor and marginalized groups in many countries.

In 2016, the UK NGO The C4D Network developed the dictum 'People before Platforms'. An organization needs to base its choice of communication platform or platforms on the needs and preferences of the people it is trying to communicate with. A media landscape guide is likely to give much of this information, though, of course, on-the-ground research will be more reliable. In on-the-ground research, these needs and preferences can be understood by, for example, asking what technology different sections of the audience have access to and which communication routes – including broadcasters – they prefer and, significantly, they trust. If a project chooses to broadcast its output on a radio station that few people listen to, then that output is not going to be heard, and, therefore, it will have little impact. If a project chooses to broadcast its output on a station audiences do not trust, then it is running the risk that the output will be tainted by audiences' opinions of the whole station.

The decision on the means of dissemination is an important one for a project, based on careful consideration of certain questions.

- Is the project going to set up its own broadcasting station, or use broadcasting partners?
- Are there obvious and simple choices of partner: for example, is the project part of, or associated with, an organization that either is a broadcaster or has its own broadcaster?
- If it is going to use broadcasting partners, who are those partners going to be and what is the nature of the partnership going to be?
- How can the project be sure it is following the principle of 'Do no harm'?
- What mechanisms is the project going to put in place to ensure there is two-way communication with the audience?
- Are some sections of the intended audience going to need other media than mainstream broadcasting? If so, what platforms are going to be used?

Gender, age and disability

The choice of platforms is best made while bearing in mind the 'digital divide', as discussed in Chapter 1, and the fact that different parts of the audience are likely to have different levels of access, even to radio. If on-the-ground research questionnaires are going to be used, they need to be designed to pick up this information, so that the data they provide can be analysed according to gender, age and disability. (This is often referred to as the disaggregation of data according to gender, age and disability.)

Age and Disability Capacity (ADCAP) published a set of minimum standards for inclusion in humanitarian assistance, in 2015, which is also a useful guide for any communication for development project. There are two standards that apply particularly to communication: Standards 4 and 5.[1]

Platforms and complex change

Some platforms may restrict the nature of the communication possible. As discussed in Chapter 2, this book focuses on long-form and long-term communication, because change takes time, and audience members need to know both what change is going to be beneficial and how to bring about that change, which can be complex. Any organization should be very careful to evaluate the complexity of the change they are asking their audience to make, before using short videos on social media to try to bring that change. For example, in 2013, UNFPA in Nigeria launched a campaign to encourage young people always to carry and use condoms, called *No Hoodie, No Honey* (Nigerian slang for 'No condom, no sex').[2] At the campaign's heart were two video animations for distribution on social media, each 2.5 minutes long. One was on why girls should carry condoms, and the second on how girls can negotiate their use. The videos were stylish and well produced. However, UNFPA recognized that two short videos were not enough to help girls overcome the barriers they face in carrying condoms and in trying to negotiate their use. Built around the videos was a discussion via social media, mainly Twitter, and, more importantly, a network of trained peer-to-peer facilitators, who ran training sessions using the videos, which included a role-play session on negotiating condom use. So, although there was the social media element, the main channel of communication was face to face, a channel that can only ever reach a limited number of people. UNFPA's research in 2016 showed that 350 educators had reached only 5,000 people. The video animations themselves reached relatively small numbers, the first being seen by just over 6,000 and the second by just over 3,000. To indicate how relatively small these numbers are, the Twitter discussion reached more than 8 million people.[3] Given that only a tiny minority of participants in the discussion had seen the videos or been in a face-to-face session, it is hard to say the discussion had been well informed. A serial drama, for example, could show a character role-playing the negotiation, and reach far more people. However, if a change is relatively simple and compelling, short videos on social media can work.

While it is obviously not possible to draw any overall lessons from just a single example, this example of *No Hoodie, No Honey* does illustrate some further key questions that should be asked when choosing platforms.

- What numbers of people can be reached by the use of a particular format, in this example, video, on a particular platform, in this example, social media?
- How appropriate is face-to-face communication when it can reach only limited numbers?

The future

There will, of course, be new platforms appearing, and, the more platforms, the more opportunities for communication for development practitioners to create innovative material and formats to communicate better. However, the access and preferences of all of a project's target audience must be the deciding factor in which platforms are chosen.

A project's dedicated broadcasting station

A major consideration at the proposal stage may be to ask if either the situation or the nature of the proposed project justifies setting up the project's own broadcasting station. Some media for development organizations do this routinely. This is a large part of the work of the media for development agencies, US-based Internews and Switzerland-based Fondation Hirondelle. The Dutch NGO Free Press Unlimited also occasionally does it, when necessary. In the case of Fondation Hirondelle, it often sets up and runs stations for the United Nations, like Radio Okapi in the Democratic Republic of Congo.

Typically, this is done in order to provide populations with reliable information that they can use to make informed decisions, but where they either do not have access to any reliable information or even to any information at all, often in conflict situations or humanitarian crises. (Much of this work involves straightforward journalism to international standards, and so does not come within the remit of this book.)

A snapshot of just one country, South Sudan, in 2016, can give an overview of this kind of project and the contexts for it. Internews runs Eye Radio – a national broadcaster – and a network of community radio stations. Fondation Hirondelle originally set up Radio Miraya, a national broadcaster, for the United Nations Mission in South Sudan (UNMISS), though it withdrew from the operation in 2014. Free Press Unlimited established Radio Tamazuj after South Sudan's independence in 2011, specifically to broadcast in the disputed border region between Sudan and South Sudan. The context for this is that there are many radio stations in South Sudan, but few are independent and reliable. There is South Sudan Radio, comprising a national broadcaster and a network of local stations, but it is run by the government and is not independent. The Catholic Church is a major player, with nine stations, and there are numerous local private and other faith-based stations. It is in this context – of stations that are often poorly resourced and have agendas – that INGOs and the UN see a need for independent stations.

The other context in which setting up a station is likely is after a humanitarian disaster, in which existing broadcasting capacity has been destroyed or put out of action. There are organizations that are set up to respond very quickly in these circumstances, like First Response Radio and UNESCO's 'Radio in a Box'. This kind of station is discussed fully in the section on humanitarian communication.

Having broadcasting partners

Outside the circumstances of conflict or humanitarian crisis, it is unlikely that creating a broadcasting station would be justified, and so an organization setting up a communication for development project will need to select a broadcasting partner or partners, assuming that broadcasting on radio and/or television are part of the choice of platforms.

Choosing the partner stations is an extremely important decision. Apart from the audience's perception of the stations, as already discussed, an unreliable station can damage or even destroy a project's impact. For example, if a station misses out some episodes of a carefully structured behaviour change serial drama, or broadcasts the episodes in the wrong order, the drama becomes incomprehensible. If the relationship is more than just a broadcasting one, and the station's staff are involved in gathering material, for example, poorly trained or overstretched staff may record inappropriate material or even falsify material.

The structure of the working relationship

Setting out how the relationship with a broadcasting partner or partners is going to work is something that should be done before the proposal is finalized, if possible, so that everyone can be sure the funding is available for the relationship to be handled properly.

Buying airtime

The nature of the arrangements between a communication for development project and broadcasting partners can vary substantially. At its most basic, the project buys airtime from the broadcaster, provides the completed programmes to them and they are broadcast.

This is common practice, even among experienced media for development organizations, especially smaller ones with limited capacity-building resources. For an organization that is new to communication for development, it may well be the only viable option, though the organization needs to ensure that ethical principles and the principle of 'Do no harm', set out in Chapter 3, are observed.

Building capacity

However, there are some organizations that, as a matter of principle, will not pay local stations to broadcast their material, especially among the larger media for development INGOs, and there is a case for a different kind of relationship between an organization making communication for development materials and a broadcaster, which is much more a partnership than a simple commercial deal.

Partly, this case is based on ethics and on the principle of 'Do no harm.' Additionally, however, the case is made in an article by Alison Campbell of Internews, published in April 2015, on the relationship between humanitarian agencies and local broadcasters during an Ebola epidemic in Sierra Leone, Guinea and Liberia, which started in 2014. She points out that just buying airtime on local media for transmitting messages, without any other relationship between the humanitarian agencies and the local media, actually limited the effectiveness of the communication effort.[4] Campbell argues that building the capacity of local media and involving them in establishing two-way communication with the affected populations would have enormously increased impact.

Campbell's article also reinforces the case against messaging, as set out in Chapter 2, because, in the Ebola crisis, simple messages did not deal with vital issues in sufficient depth, and did not take into account helping the audience overcome the barriers to the behaviour change being asked for.

Campbell's proposed model is for the humanitarian agencies to build the capacity of local broadcasters so that their journalists can run interactive discussion programmes, including phone-ins. These would explore in greater depth the content of the agencies' messages, and address the barriers to carrying out the requested behaviour change that members of the audience report. The benefit for the local stations would be that their staff could make better and more appealing programmes on other topics, as well as on Ebola. Further, they would be an active part of the campaign to stop the Ebola epidemic, instead of being bystanders, marginalized by the humanitarian agencies. Ultimately, these staff would remain as a legacy left after the humanitarian agencies have withdrawn, to be part of an indigenous response to future crises.

Integrated partnership

In communication for development projects, outside of a humanitarian response, there have been many different partnerships between organizations using communication for development and broadcasters, each designed for different circumstances and different outcomes.

In South Sudan, in 2013, BBC Media Action partnered with the Catholic Radio Network's nine radio stations across the country, for a project designed to reduce illness and mortality among mothers and babies under six months old. Among other elements, there was a weekly thirty-minute radio magazine programme. For the production of this element, a strong and integrated partnership was put into place. The BBC Media Action production team – comprised completely of South Sudan nationals and based in South Sudan's capital, Juba – recorded some of the material used in the programmes. However, a significant proportion was recorded by staff from the different Catholic Radio Network's stations, following detailed briefs given to them by the BBC Media Action team. That material was edited and packaged by the team in Juba. This arrangement did throw up some problems, but, in the end, it was mutually beneficial.

For the Catholic Radio Network, selected members of their staff were provided with capacity-building and day-to-day experience over a long period of time, in making high-quality, behaviour change programmes. For BBC Media Action, the benefit was that they had a much wider range of voices from different regions of the very diverse country. The programmes were broadcast by the Catholic Radio Network, in English and Juba Arabic, a dialect widely spoken across South Sudan.

Selecting broadcasting partners

Whatever the structure of the partnership, as has been discussed, the selection of local broadcasting partners is crucial. The extent and difficulty of this task will vary significantly from one country to another, depending on the number of radio and television stations, the quality and editorial independence of those stations, patterns of ownership of stations, the political stability of the country or region and the breadth of the target audiences.

There are, however, certain overarching criteria that can guide the choice.

- The target audience's access to the different stations available. This can be found from the research into the audiences, if necessary, backed up by a simple survey of where each station's signal can be heard or seen.
- Related to the first criterion, the reach of the stations is important, that is, the number of people who can view or listen to each particular station. This will be a matter of the location of the station, the power of its transmitter, the spread of broadcast relay stations and, in the case of radio, the frequency used for transmissions. Most local radio stations, for example, will use FM transmitters, which give a clear signal but have limited range (typically a radius of less than 100 km). If the station uses FM relay stations, which rebroadcast the signal in other areas, this will significantly increase the reach. Medium-wave transmitters have a much greater reach, though at a lower quality. Short-wave signals – often used by international broadcasters like the BBC World Service – can be received across very large areas, of thousands of square kilometres, but at fairly poor quality. Many local stations also broadcast on the internet, but, of course, how useful that is will depend entirely on the target audiences' access to the internet.
- It is important to remember that it is not the overall reach that a station may have, but, rather, its reach among target audiences. With most FM stations based in urban areas, if an organization's target audiences are rural people, for example, FM stations may not be useful.
- A further factor in making the choice of partner is the listening or viewing preferences expressed by different parts of the target audience, in response to research questions. Broadcasting programmes on stations that are already popular with the target audiences is going to make it much more likely that they will be heard or seen by the people they are designed for.
- The stations selected need to broadcast in the language or languages spoken by the target audiences.

Once the field has been narrowed down from judging the available broadcasters against these criteria, there are further detailed criteria.

Most of this information will need to come from the stations themselves, and it is often useful to invite selected stations to apply to be partners. Quite apart from anything else, the quality of the application will show the level of commitment of the station to the idea of the partnership.

The following criteria can be in the application questionnaire, backed up by interviews with staff, observation at the station and by researchers listening to or viewing the station's output.

- The sustainability of the station itself is crucial. It needs to be well established, with a good chance of a long-term future. The longevity of the station, evidence of income and observation of resources at the station are key indicators.
- If training is to be provided as part of the partnership, the sustainability of the learning after the end of the project is important. The station needs to have a feasible plan for maintaining what has been learned from the capacity building and other benefits of the partnership after the end of the project. Staffing needs to be stable and long term, so that there is a good chance that staff receiving training will be the same throughout the project period, and are likely to remain beyond the project period.
- For most communication for development projects, a partner station needs to have editorial independence from its owners or funders. However, in situations where such independence is rare or non-existent, a judgement will need to be made on the impact of the station's partisanship on the project's achievement of its aims.
- Staff need to be educated.
- A station needs to be able to demonstrate a track record in responsible journalism, showing some balance in coverage, accuracy in reporting and evidence-based stories.
- A station that can show some understanding of its audience, preferably based on research, and has some element of two-way communication with its audience at least starts with a base from which a proper communication for development project can be established.
- A commitment on the part of management and staff to the project, beyond the commercial, would be helpful, where the partnership goes beyond the commercial.
- Management need to be happy to enter a formal partnership agreement with binding commitments from both sides.
- If a station is receiving support from any other project, a judgement needs to be made as to whether that might, in any way, harm the project.

On the basis of these criteria a communication for development project can run a selection process. The core of this would be an application form that shortlisted stations would be asked to complete. The answers given should be further researched by observation at the station, and monitoring of its output and key parts of its audience.

A final agreement will need to include binding commitments to meet the project's broadcasting and, if included, training requirements, with effective measures in place to hold the stations to account in the event of a breach of the agreement.

There is one further selection criterion, depending on the circumstances in the country or territory. The most likely source of this information is local UN officials.

- The station is in an area where the security situation will allow organization personnel (facilitators or broadcast monitors, for example) to visit regularly, and where there is no threat to the station itself. (When an armed group take over an area, they are very likely to take over any broadcasting stations in the area.)

Section Two

Humanitarian communication

Introduction

This section of the book is aimed at two different audiences. On the one hand, it is for media organizations that perceive a need to involve themselves in the humanitarian response to a specific disaster or conflict, or to be more widely ready to be involved in humanitarian responses as and when they occur in one country, a region or throughout the world. On the other hand, it is for people working in the humanitarian field – either in a large international organization, a local NGO or the private sector – who see the need to improve their communication with the communities they are trying to help and improve the effectiveness and transparency of their accountability to those communities. These are people who want to do this via the media, either working with existing media or setting up their own media project.

It makes sense to address both audiences simultaneously for two reasons. First, there are significant overlaps in information needed, and second, a number of reports on the response to some disasters have revealed a substantial gap in understanding between these groups. Reports have included one on Haiti in 2010,[1] and two already cited on the Ebola epidemic in West Africa, which started in 2014. One of these was by Translators Without Borders,[2] the other by Internews.[3] So it is worthwhile to address the two together. What this does mean, however, is that there will be parts where the material will be information that one or other audience will already know.

A note on terminology. There is an argument that the term 'natural disaster' is not appropriate, on the grounds that disasters are not natural. The basis of this argument is that a powerful natural event – like an earthquake or a typhoon – is only a disaster when it affects vulnerable communities who do not have the resources to protect themselves or to recover. Therefore, such disasters are products of social, political and economic factors rather than natural ones. However, in this section of the book, the term 'natural disaster' is used, so that such events are distinguished from disasters created by conflict. It is necessary to distinguish between the two because, in some regards, the response of, and challenges to, the humanitarian broadcaster will be different, depending on the cause of the disaster.

The rationale of humanitarian communication

The role of humanitarian communication can be summarized as, 'To help populations change what can be changed, and cope with what cannot be changed'. The original concept of using broadcasting in humanitarian and conflict crises was that information is aid; that is, communication is as important to humans as food and safe drinking water. The introduction to a humanitarian broadcasting handbook, written in 2004, started with:

> Recent emergencies have shown that, in addition to food, water and shelter, people who are displaced have a great need for information. This might include how to prepare for travel (if there is time); the availability of shelter; where to go for food and water; how to maintain health while travelling and while living in refugee camps; avoiding dangers such as landmines or unexploded ordnance; ways of making a living and of improving conditions in camps; how to protect children; how to handle relationships; and how to protect the environment in and around camps.[1]

Two-way communication

The concept of 'Information is aid' is still valuable but, more recently, another dimension to humanitarian broadcasting has been added: the establishment of two-way communication. As has been said, several important reports have shown the damaging consequences when agencies fail to listen. So, now, too, there is the necessity for humanitarian agencies and other organizations trying to help populations affected by disaster or conflict to listen to and communicate with those populations and to be accountable to them. Some donors now make it a condition of their funding that agencies hold themselves accountable in this way.

Changing the aid relationship

This change has come about because, in the past, the relationship between agencies and affected communities was entirely supply-led. That is, the suppliers – the humanitarian actors – decided every aspect of the relationship. There is a huge power imbalance in this arrangement, and it could lead to inappropriate aid being delivered at inappropriate times, perceptions of unfairness and discrimination among the population, corruption, inefficiency and even conflict. (This issue is covered at greater depth in Chapter 15.)

Promoting communication between communities

Affected communities find it extremely useful to be able to communicate with each other. Broadcast and social media can facilitate communication between populations and agencies (including holding agencies to account), and between communities that are otherwise isolated from each other as a consequence of disaster or conflict.

Another important communication that is needed when populations are displaced by disaster or conflict is that between the displaced communities and the communities whose territory they have come into, often known as 'host communities'. When broadcast media can facilitate this communication, it can have real impact in reducing tension and preventing conflict.

Achieving the full potential of the media

Although this is the potential for what humanitarian communication can achieve, reports suggest that it rarely achieves all of the aspects of this potential. In some projects, it has achieved one part of the potential, in another project, another part, and so on. A key reason for this is that – as has been shown above in the discussion of the use of media in the West Africa Ebola epidemic of 2014 – humanitarian actors often do not understand how to use media effectively, and, as will be discussed in Chapter 15, the relationship between the agencies and, especially, local media can be poor. These are issues this book attempts to address.

So, for example, humanitarian agencies often prefer to be held accountable through their own call centres than through the media. One report suggests call centres appear to be used relatively little, in general, and do not serve the needs of the most vulnerable.[2] They are certainly more expensive than the media, and there is less transparency in the accountability, as it is conducted on a medium controlled by the agency, rather than in a public forum.

What can humanitarian communication achieve?

The aims of any humanitarian communication project need to be determined by the circumstances and nature of the crisis, and its impact on the communities it has affected.

In an emergency response, and using the categorization of the phases of a response, more fully explained in Chapter 17, these aims can include the following.

In the relief and early recovery phases

- To provide information which saves lives, by helping the population to limit the spread of disease and to limit the risk of injury
- To give the population the information they need to make informed choices after a natural disaster or during a conflict
- To provide respite

In the recovery and rehabilitation phases

- To provide information to support populations affected by conflict in resettlement or repatriation
- After a natural disaster, to provide practical information to help a population rebuild their lives and livelihoods

In all phases

- To help provide psychosocial support for affected communities
- To provide channels of communication between communities, to facilitate mutual support, re-establish disrupted social support networks, or create new ones, with many outcomes, including the reestablishment or creation of social institutions, like schools
- To facilitate communicating with communities, that is, listening to affected communities to understand their priorities, complaints and suggestions and publicizing them, and providing a channel for affected communities to hold authorities and humanitarian agencies to account
- To promote an understanding of the technical, social, economic and political skills of affected communities, especially of those displaced in conflict, so that they can be used and built on in recovery, rehabilitation and rebuilding
- Where there is displacement, to communicate with host communities the situation of the displaced, and facilitate communication between displaced communities and host communities to ease intercommunal tensions

Outside of an emergency response

- To provide information and education to help communities in disaster-prone areas be better prepared for and more resilient to disasters
- To provide information and education to help communities facing slow-onset disasters take steps to be more resilient to them, or even to reverse some disasters like environmental degradation and desertification

This may appear an ambitious list of aims, but, as the next chapter shows, many of these aims are not only achievable by communication but can be delivered in a highly cost-effective manner.

The relief and early recovery phases

Providing information to save lives

The provision of information of use to people affected by conflict or natural disaster is, perhaps, the most obvious role for humanitarian communication.

The kind of information is likely to be different depending on whether the crisis has caused people to be displaced, as conflicts very often do, or not. Displacement situations, especially when caused by conflict, are very much more complex, and affected people are likely to need much more information.

Natural disasters

In the aftermath of a natural disaster, when communities have either not been displaced or are displaced locally to emergency shelter, the initial information they are going to need is likely to include: maintaining good health, that is, hygiene, in changed circumstances, how to treat contaminated water; where and when relief supplies are to be distributed; avoiding further injury by reducing risk, after an earthquake, for example, warnings that entering damaged buildings is dangerous. During an epidemic, when, again, there is no displacement, information on how to avoid infection, what to do if someone in the family or area becomes infected, the care an infected person needs and where medical attention can be found is essential.

Conflict

In conflict, information needs are greater, and situations can be far more complex. Affected communities need the same kind of information on maintaining health and on food distributions. However, the information on maintaining health is more complicated, as they need information on maintaining health while travelling, as well as at the destination. Different localities may throw up different health threats. For example, a population who grew up in a malaria-free location, and so have no immunity, may be displaced to a malarial area, where they will be very vulnerable.

People on the move are vulnerable to a range of other threats, from armed groups, from people smugglers and traffickers or from unexploded ordnance and landmines. Affected populations need information on safe routes for escape, and the location of places where help and shelter are available. (It should be said here that careful research is needed as to whether broadcasting this information could be harmful, because people aiming to exploit or harm the displaced may make use of it to help them carry out their intentions.)

Broadcasting as a major component in information-giving

The value of this kind of information would appear self-evident, and broadcasting in these circumstances has clear advantages over the only other transmission methods available, which are face to face and the distribution of printed material.

- It is more cost-effective, unless the face-to-face communicators are volunteers.
- Its reach is likely to be greater.
- It does not put communicators or materials distributors at risk, and, in the case of an epidemic, it avoids the possibility of communicators both being at risk and of being a disease transmission route themselves.
- Unlike print material, radio is accessible to the illiterate and those with sight impairment.

That said, however, all available routes of distribution of such vital information need to be used.

Providing information for informed choices

In many humanitarian crises, a high priority for information for affected populations is what has happened and is happening in their area. This may include answers to the following questions.

- What is the extent of the crisis?
- How many are dead?
- How badly damaged is infrastructure?
- What measures are being taken by government, the humanitarian response and others?
- What is the likely timescale for the arrival of help and for recovery?

In this case, broadcasting has the added advantage of immediacy, so that developments can be reported almost as soon as they happen. This information is important for psychosocial support and for people to make informed decisions.

Countering rumours and misinformation

A key role of humanitarian communication is challenging rumours. Rumours can be disturbing or, worse, can lead to bad decisions on the part of affected people.

Displaced people on the move sometimes need to make extremely important decisions. They may face the choice of crossing a border, with the change of legal status from being internally displaced but still a citizen to becoming a refugee, or of taking a sea-crossing. For such decisions they need all the information they can get on the options and the risks involved in the different choices. A final role of broadcasting in conflict circumstances is to counter misinformation, whether that is unfounded rumour or is deliberate and designed to mislead the displaced, by criminal gangs, for example.

In circumstances like these, broadcasting has clear advantages over other information channels. People within conflict areas are not easy to meet by face-to-face communicators without those communicators being put at high risk, and people on the move are hard to find. So, broadcasting is a very valuable information channel for them, and it is uniquely placed to meet these information needs quickly and in multiple languages, so that affected people can take steps to protect themselves and to make informed decisions.

Again, however, all available routes of distribution of such vital information need to be used.

Providing respite

Playing music, comedy or reading out personal messages sent in by the audience, for example, can help to establish a certain level of normality, as well as helping rebuild social networks and providing reassurance.

The recovery and rehabilitation phases

Once populations affected by disaster or displaced by conflict are settled in accommodation – which may be temporary – and are receiving humanitarian aid, or are able to meet their own needs, then communication can help in rehabilitation or rebuilding of infrastructure and livelihoods, or in improving life in displacement camps. The next chapter will show how a small community radio station could help members of a community in the Philippines both rebuild devastated livelihoods and rebuild their homes to be more typhoon-resistant, after Typhoon Haiyan in 2013. Communication can help improve life in displacement camps largely through social mobilization and establishment of social networks. For example, broadcasting, or, say, cheap tablets preloaded with appropriate material, can provide emergency education for children, which can become a strong focus for adults and bring a sense of hope as it is building for the future.

In the rehabilitation phase, broadcasting can provide information on options for the displaced, so that they can make informed choices about repatriation or resettlement.

All phases

The role of communication in psychosocial support

Psychosocial support is designed to foster resilience among communities and individuals affected by disaster or conflict. It aims at easing the resumption of normal life, facilitating affected people's participation in their convalescence and preventing potentially long-term consequences of traumatic situations.

Humanitarian communication can provide psychosocial support to its audiences, and, in fact, many of the communication activities already described are important for psychosocial support. According to *Psychological First Aid: Guide for Field Workers*,[3] published by the World Health Organisation (WHO),

> P[sychological] F[irst] A[id] involves factors that seem to be most helpful to people's long-term recovery (according to various studies and the consensus of many crisis helpers). These include:
>   feeling safe, connected to others, calm and hopeful;
>   having access to social, physical and emotional support;
>   and feeling able to help themselves, as individuals and communities[4]

Feeling safe, connected to others, calm and hopeful

By providing information and education for rehabilitation and rebuilding, and, particularly in providing emergency education for children, humanitarian communication is providing strong hope for the future. In broadcasting information which counters rumours of impending threats, it can help communities and individuals feel safe and calm.

Having access to social, physical and emotional support

In facilitating family reunification and communication between communities, as well as broadcasting personal greetings and messages between individuals, a humanitarian broadcaster is helping audience members gain access to social and emotional support, and to feel connected to others.

Feeling able to help themselves, as individuals and communities

When a humanitarian broadcaster broadcasts information which helps individuals and communities make informed decisions for themselves, when it broadcasts information and education to help individuals rebuild for themselves and when it provides education to enable collective action, it is clearly supporting communities in feeling able to help themselves. These functions are described in the section on responses to slow-onset disasters, also above.

Psychosocial support for children

Children's needs for psychosocial support are met in different ways from adults' needs. Although it is a specialist training manual for teachers, UNICEF's *The Psychosocial Care and Protection of Children in Emergencies: Teacher Training Manual*[5] has useful information on the kind of programming that a humanitarian broadcaster could transmit for the psychosocial support of children, if that is not being provided on the ground in functioning schools. There is a handout which lists activities for the psychosocial support of children.[6] Of these, broadcasting can directly provide: music and singing; storytelling, encouraging children to work out endings before they are broadcast; and instructions for making toys out of scrap materials. A humanitarian communication project can organize activities, like story writing competitions and encouraging children to devise their own dramas for broadcast.

Communication between communities

In the aftermath of a number of disasters, it has been shown that a local radio station can play a vital role in family reunification. If the station receives messages, in whatever form, from members of the community, it can put out calls to family members who have become disconnected. It can help families within the affected area find each other, help family members in communities outside the affected area or, if the station broadcasts on the internet, in the diaspora, get in touch with relatives inside the affected area.

As is shown in the next chapter, facilitating communication between communities can lead to communities finding their own solutions to problems, rather than relying on humanitarian agencies. This has the added advantage of helping to re-establish self-help and self-esteem, which is vital psychosocial support, as just discussed.

A radio station can become a social focus, especially if it organizes social events itself. It can also be a channel for motivated individuals to reach out to others in the community to join in a collective enterprise, whether that is, for example, building latrines or establishing a school. It could even be putting together a case to a humanitarian agency for a reallocation of resources to projects which are the community's priorities. In doing this, the station is helping to re-establish social networks, or in the case of displacement, establish new social networks.

Communicating with communities or community engagement

While two-way communication is important in all communication for development work, its importance in humanitarian crises has been shown in many reports, as is discussed in Chapters 11 and 15. A failure to listen to and communicate with disaster- and conflict-affected communities has caused social tension and even exacerbated conflict. An understanding on the part of humanitarian actors of the priorities, needs, suggestions and complaints of affected communities, and action taken in response, is vital to efficient and effective delivery of humanitarian aid. As is shown in the next chapter, media can be a very effective channel for facilitating this communication.

Understanding the knowledge and skills available among the affected communities

Particularly in displacement crises, where populations may be outside of their normal social milieu, the knowledge and skills individuals may have are likely to go unnoticed, unless a specific effort is made to find them. Broadcast communication can be an effective method of bringing people with particular skills forward.

Using existing skills among affected populations is good in promoting self-esteem, and, therefore is good psychosocial support, but is also highly efficient. Humanitarian agencies are keen that schools are established quickly, as they give the whole community a focus and hope for the future. They also help to protect children from different kinds of exploitation and harm. Establishing a school is clearly going to be easier and quicker if teachers are identified among the affected population. The principle applies to a large range of skills.

Communicating with host communities

When people are displaced or become refugees, there will almost certainly be 'host' communities. The displaced may be in camps close to existing settlements or may come to live within existing communities. Very often there is tension between the displaced and hosts, caused, for example, by a perception among host communities that the displaced have access to aid and resources which they, themselves, do not. Sometimes, host communities perceive that displaced people are taking livelihood opportunities away from them. Host communities and the displaced have different cultural expectations. Or, displaced people cause environmental harm, by cutting firewood, for example, which adversely affects the host community.

Broadcast communication can help to ease tensions by showing that host communities and the displaced have equal access to resources, for example, or by host communities learning about the plight of the displaced. Displaced communities can learn about the cultural expectations of the hosts, and about behaviour which is causing resentment among the host populations. This has already been discussed with the example of Internews' *Radio Sila*, in Chad. (See Chapter 1.)

Outside of an emergency response

Information and education in the face of slow-onset disasters

Practical immediate measures

Slow-onset disasters are drought, environmental degradation, desertification and the climate crisis. They can become much more complex when they either cause or contribute to conflict. Some analysts have, for example, suggested that increasing desertification was one of the causes of the conflict in the Sudanese region of Darfur, which started in 2003.

Even where there is no conflict, slow-onset disasters often cause major displacement crises, with, for example, large movements of impoverished rural populations into towns.

Communication can clearly play an important role in warning communities who are likely to be affected of a forthcoming drought, so that they can prepare, as far as possible, or, in the case of nomadic communities, they can migrate to unaffected or less affected areas, or to areas where there are functioning boreholes. It can also provide preparedness education for communities, for example, in water-conservation methods.

Longer-term measures

However, humanitarian communication can perform a much more valuable role in preventing, mitigating and even reversing environmental degradation and desertification, where these are caused by human activity, as they are in many cases. This has taken the form of mobilizing communities to stop the cutting down of trees for charcoal production, which is a major factor in environmental degradation, and, particularly, in soil erosion, in many semi-arid and arid areas, like Somalia.

It can, though, be much more ambitious than this. In 2008, for example, a Somali NGO called Horn Relief had two of its training manuals – on natural resource management and on small-scale agriculture – adapted into radio series to be broadcast on local stations. The first of these was strongly focused on water conservation and on soil conservation and restoration. The aim was for the broadcasts to be used, particularly, by facilitated learning groups, and included relatively ambitious projects. In most of Somalia, rivers only flow while it is raining, and for a short time after the rain stops. Normally, the water rushes down the dry river beds, eroding the banks and disappearing into the sea. One of Horn Relief's aims was to use radio to teach communities to build check dams. These slow the water flow, reducing soil erosion and allowing more water to penetrate the ground for agriculture.

Information and education for preparedness

The ultimate slow-onset disaster is, of course, the climate crisis. Humanitarian communication can play an important role in helping communities increase their resilience to climate change. In 2015, BBC Media Action published research on its reality television programme, *Amrai Pari*,[7] which is broadcast in Bangladesh. The research showed that the programmes had achieved some of their key aims. Essentially, the series showed examples of successful resilience building among communities who are at risk from the climate crisis. The research showed that 'some individuals replicated resilience-enhancing techniques they had seen on the programme'.[8] More importantly, the programmes motivated some communities, even one which already enjoyed a high level of cooperation, to improve their cooperation and get other players involved to carry out larger projects.

> Often community members were unsure how they could overcome top-down power structures. Sometimes they felt that they required support from local NGOs and leaders; especially for larger projects such as building a dam. The programme can use its reality TV format to showcase how communities garner the support of influential stakeholders and tackle resilience projects together.[9]

This example illustrates that communication can motivate and teach communities to undertake practical measures to be better prepared for different kinds of disaster. As will be seen in Chapter 17, radio was one part of a campaign to teach householders how to rebuild their houses to be more typhoon-resistant, after Typhoon Haiyan devastated areas of the Philippines in 2013.

Of course, disaster preparedness cannot be solely the responsibility of vulnerable communities, and the international community, national and local government need to play large roles in it, by stockpiling emergency supplies and building effective storm shelters, for example, but part of the rationale for humanitarian communication is its capacity to help communities be better prepared themselves.

An overview of humanitarian communication

This chapter sets out the basics of what humanitarian communication has been able to show it can achieve. It concentrates on one humanitarian crisis – the disaster created in parts of the Philippines by the Category 5 typhoon, Haiyan, which made landfall on the island of Samar on 8 November 2013 – and on one communication project created in response.

As a reminder of what was said in the last chapter, the kind of information humanitarian communication provides changes according to the phase of the disaster response. Normally, four phases are identified. (The humanitarian definitions of these phases are given in Chapter 17.)

Communication and the phases of a disaster response

The relief phase

Immediately after the disaster, humanitarian communication will concentrate on life-saving information and gathering information to help assess the needs of the affected communities.

The early recovery phase

The focus will be on information for survival, that is, where and when relief supplies are being distributed, where shelter is available and how to maintain health in very changed circumstances.

The recovery phase

The focus of humanitarian communication will move to information on reopening of schools, re-establishment of utilities and ways of making the best of emergency shelter, as well as listening to the communities' responses and suggestions for the humanitarian effort.

The rebuilding phase

In the case of a natural disaster – or the camp settlement phase in the case of populations being displaced – then communication moves to providing practical information on re-establishing livelihoods and permanent shelter and children's education, for example.

Humanitarian agencies' accountability mechanisms

There have been several references in this book so far to reports that show how a failure to listen on the part of humanitarian actors can be very counter-productive. One of these reports is Plan International's *Who's Listening? Accountability to Affected People in the Haiyan Response.*[1] This report was on the humanitarian response to the disaster caused by the super typhoon Haiyan. The impact of the typhoon had been very severe, particularly on the towns of Guiuan and Tacloban. Every building in Guiuan was damaged or destroyed, and hundreds died there, while in Tacloban, many thousands died.

The report is significant in that it shows that many humanitarian organizations thought, after the humanitarian response was over, that for the first time in any disaster their accountability mechanisms had worked well. However, the report shows that the mechanisms had not worked well, and the agencies had failed to detect the deleterious consequences of some of their procedures. Food distribution particularly had been a problem, where, for example, different households were assessed on various criteria as to who should receive food aid.

> While varying the amount of assistance a household received according to family size was regarded as fair, as long as most households were assisted, socio-economic targeting between households, targeting by livelihood group, and geographic targeting were regarded as highly unfair, especially if it meant some people got nothing. The former approach – of assisting all households, according to household size – was adopted by the Tzu Chi Foundation, the Taiwanese Buddhist philanthropic organisation, which was by far the most popular organisation with local communities in the Haiyan response in Tacloban. The approach of targeting by socio-economic status/vulnerability, geographically, or by livelihood group was practiced by the majority of humanitarian agencies. The inappropriateness of targeting was raised by one focus group after another in our fieldwork, as a major issue striking deep into the heart of Filipino culture where neighbours are regarded as extended family and people's sense of dignity is defined by their status in the community. Targeting and selective relief distributions triggered status anxiety and a deep sense of shame amongst those excluded. Our research uncovered social divisiveness, competitiveness, and conflict arising within close-knit communities as a result of agencies' targeting practices.[2]

The agencies did not pick this problem up, partly because of the nature of their accountability mechanisms, largely using SMS call centres or phone call centres.

> For example, humanitarian agencies felt they were more accessible for feedback than local people experienced, and were not always sufficiently alert to the social and cultural factors that inhibited communication. Agencies tended to favour

more formal and technological approaches to AAP [Accountability to Affected Populations], focusing particularly on feedback mechanisms, while affected people strongly favoured face-to-face and more human forms of interaction.[3]

The report continues:

> the perspectives of affected people in the Haiyan response provide a reminder of the essence of AAP. At a minimum, it is about two-way communication, about a conversation. For affected people, it is about being seen and heard by humanitarian responders, and it is about engaging in dialogue: face-to-face communication is what really counts to affected people. At its more expansive, AAP is about building relationships with affected communities by spending substantial time in those communities to understand them and to find out their needs and priorities.[4]

An accountability alternative

However, it is expensive and time-consuming for agencies' staff to spend a lot of time doing this, however desirable it might be. An alternative, which this report did not look at, is for accountability to be channelled through local media, especially community radio stations. Here, there can be more 'human forms of interaction', and information is mediated by local journalists who understand the culture.

In the Haiyan response, there was an example of a community radio station that did, to some extent, perform this role.

The *Who's Listening?* report makes a brief mention of two stations:

> our research indicates that most community members did not approach local media outlets to raise concerns, although the few that did received high profile, and journalists at both Radio Abante and Radyo Bakdaw, for example, sought out specific agencies to respond, on air, to concerns being raised.[5]

Radio Abante was originally set up by the INGO First Response Radio in Tacloban, and Radyo Bakdaw was set up by international media NGO Internews in Guiuan. Guiuan had had only one radio station before Haiyan, and that was completely destroyed by the typhoon. The population in the town and surrounding villages and islands had no access to television, as the electricity supply had also been destroyed.

Radyo Bakdaw will be discussed throughout this section of the book, as I had first-hand knowledge of it, though it should be borne in mind that it was operating in a relatively unusual situation, in that there was no competition throughout its life, and it was in a fairly small and relatively tight-knit community.

Beyond the brief reference in *Who's Listening?* Radyo Bakdaw is considered as something of a model for the role of a local station in humanitarian response in the case study by the Communicating with Disaster Affected Communities (CDAC) Network. The CDAC Network is an organization of members including most of the major players in the humanitarian field, including the United Nations Office for the Coordination of

Humanitarian Affairs (UNOCHA or OCHA), the United Nations High Commissioner for Refugees (UNHCR), UNICEF and the International Organisation for Migration (IOM).[6]

The case study refers to an incident involving a generator, as an example of holding to account. At the end of the Radyo Bakdaw project, in March 2014, the production team wrote up some of their achievements, and one of the accounts expands substantially on the generator incident. In the Philippines, the lowest level of local government is the *barangay*, at very local community level, and the chief official is the *barangay* captain. After the typhoon, the captain of one *barangay* in the Guiuan area asked an international NGO operating in the district for help, and, as the community had identified it as a particular need, requested a small generator for recharging phones. The INGO sent the generator, addressing it, to make sure it arrived, personally to the *barangay* captain. Once the generator had arrived, the captain claimed it had been sent for her personal use, as it had been addressed to her, and not for the community. In spite of members of the community making representations to her, she was adamant and would not allow community access to the machine.

The community knew Radyo Bakdaw and approached the station for help. The station's journalists called the INGO in Tacloban and recorded an interview with the regional director, who confirmed the generator was for community use. The station invited the *barangay* captain to come in for an interview, live on air. She agreed and, at first, on air, maintained her position that the generator was for her personal use. The presenter then played her the recording of the interview with the INGO regional director. She had to concede she was wrong, and shortly afterwards the generator was put into the public hall, for use by all of the community.

This is an important element of accountability to affected communities: to challenge corruption and ensure that aid gets to the people who are supposed to get it. In this case, it improved the effectiveness of the humanitarian response by making sure this happened.

The CDAC Network case study shows that this is just one example of how the station acted as a conduit for the community to give feedback to the humanitarian agencies and government and to ask them questions, and, at the same time, operate as an on-air forum for holding the agencies and government to account.

A second example given in the case study is in ameliorating community mistrust. There was tension between local government and the community when the content of the food packages, distributed from the agencies through local government, changed. The community suspected corruption. The station was able to dispel the tension by getting the agency concerned to go on air and explain that it had changed the contents, and why it had done so, exonerating local government from the accusations.

So, the station established effective and transparent dialogue between the affected communities and the humanitarian responders. As the case study explains, one woman said that the radio station was the first place people turned to when they had a problem.

An issue of trust

An important factor in the station being able to play this role was that it was trusted by all sides, according to the case study. (The issue of trust between humanitarian responders and the media is problematic but is very important, and is addressed later in this section.)

One reason, not mentioned in the case study but which I witnessed, for this commonality of trust was the make-up of the station's team. It was largely Filipino, drawn from the local area. So, it was made up of people who had shared the experience of the typhoon and were sharing the aftermath – living under tarpaulins, separated from families – with the community. There was a four-person international team as well. Partly because of this make-up, the station's team could engage in dialogue, and be trusted, in both directions. It could be said that the interface between the international responders and the community was within the station's team, and dialogue across that interface was continuous, all day, every day.

As the case study explains, it was the international team leader who took community concerns to the humanitarian responders and got them to speak on air. It is important to point out that, although it worked closely with the international humanitarian agencies, the radio station was independent and neutral. This is both ethical and is needed to maintain the trust of an audience.

This is just a single example of media facilitating two-way communication in a humanitarian crisis. How it was done at Radyo Bakdaw and in other projects will be explored more fully in Chapter 15.

Figure 11.1 *The whole operation of Radyo Bakdaw had to be accommodated in one room, which served as the office as well as the studio*

Cost-effectiveness

Radyo Bakdaw also provided other vital functions of humanitarian communication, as described later in this chapter, and is useful in showing the breadth of what can be achieved at relatively low cost. The station was funded by the UK Government's Department for International Development. A review of DfID's role after Haiyan, by the UK Government's Independent Commission for Aid Impact, said that Radyo Bakdaw was a 'thoughtful and cost-effective niche programme... [which] led to disproportionately positive impacts'.[7]

Communication between communities

Another vital need that communities affected by disaster or conflict have is for communication between communities, and media can, at least partly, meet this need. This is especially important in the relief phase when other communication channels are not working, because, for example, mobile phone masts have been destroyed or because a lack of electricity means phones cannot be charged. The CDAC Network case study briefly explains the role that Radyo Bakdaw had in facilitating communication between communities, but the stories the production team wrote describe some examples much more fully.

Reuniting families

Family reunification is a desperate need after a disaster. Typhoon Haiyan mainly affected the eastern islands of Samar and Leyte, and most of the rest of the Philippines were not directly affected by it, although people living on other islands had relatives and friends in the devastated area. Two months after the typhoon, a woman living on Panay Island had not been in touch with her sister and brother-in-law in Guiuan. She saw the text number for Radyo Bakdaw on television and immediately sent a text appealing for her relatives to get in touch. Just ten minutes after the message had been read out on air, the brother-in-law arrived at the radio station and was able to use the station's phone. According to a report by UNOCHA, in only three months of operation, Radyo Bakdaw supported forty-four instances of family reunification.[8]

Helping a community find its own solutions

Guiuan is a coastal town, and there are several low-lying islands off it, which were very badly hit by Haiyan. Soon after the station had gone on air, the team received a text from one of the islands, from a wheelchair user whose chair had been destroyed when the house collapsed, asking if anyone could help. The station repeatedly broadcast the message, and, after about a week, a man called the station to say he had a wheelchair that had belonged to his mother. When no one else was available, some of the station team took the wheelchair to the island themselves. A community finding its own solution. In a later report, Internews said that broadcasting this story led to a further six listeners texting to say they had lost their wheelchairs in the typhoon. When only one of these got a replacement from another community member, Radyo Bakdaw called in Handicap International.[9] This is a good example of the role the broadcast media can play in helping disaster-affected communities communicate with each other. It also shows the role communication can play in helping to shape a humanitarian response to better meet the needs of the affected population as a result of communication with the community.

Changing the response as the situation changes

In terms of providing information that listeners could use, in the relief phase, the station gave out information on issues like aid distributions, the clear-up operation and maintaining health. Later, though, as the crisis moved into the recovery and rehabilitation phases, it added more detailed and long-form broadcasting on four themes: livelihoods, shelter, psychosocial support and programmes for children.

Wherever possible, this specialist programming was designed to support humanitarian agencies' work on the ground and aimed to be highly practical. For example, part of each weekly shelter-themed programme was closely linked to the IOM's Build Back Better campaign, which encouraged householders to rebuild their homes in ways that would make them more resistant to future typhoons. (How these specialist programmes were designed and produced will be discussed in detail in Chapter 17.)

Psychosocial support

While the station had dedicated broadcasting slots for psychosocial support, in fact a lot of its output provided this kind of support. Radyo Bakdaw was, primarily, a music station, so that all of its news and humanitarian broadcasting was punctuated with music. Many of the text messages it received and broadcast were interpersonal messages, between individuals. These elements provided respite for the station's listeners and a sense of normality returning.

Challenging rumours

As already mentioned, a more specifically psychosocial role that communication can play in humanitarian crises is the challenging of rumours, which can cause fear and distress, and create social tensions.

Rumours are very common in humanitarian crises. In the case of Guiuan, in early January 2014, before most homes had been repaired, and many people were living in tents or under tarpaulins, a tropical cyclone sat over the region for many days, creating winds that were strong enough to tear tents apart and pull tarpaulins away, and heavy rain. A rumour started and spread quickly that a second typhoon was on its way. As the CDAC Network case study says, Radyo Bakdaw had broadcast weather forecasts since its beginning, but, during this period, someone from the Philippines national weather service was in the station almost every day, challenging this rumour.

One night, the weather was so bad that humanitarian agencies evacuated people living along the shore to concrete buildings further inland. On her own initiative, the presenter on Radyo Bakdaw read the weather forecast every ten minutes, in between playing music. This was in response to texts she was receiving, which were repeating the rumour that a second typhoon was approaching. Then, the station began to receive texts asking the presenter to keep the station on air beyond its usual shut-down time. Listeners were scared, and were finding the station reassuring and comforting. There was no other broadcaster in the area.

As the station's humanitarian journalism facilitator, I was at the station at the time, and the presenter and I discussed what she should do. She decided to keep on air for an extra hour, from 9 to 10 pm, in spite of the discomfort, as the station itself was leaking quite badly.

This is an example, on the ground, of what can be done to successfully challenge a rumour: present credible information to counter the rumour, and keep presenting it. (Information from the Philippines weather service was credible, because they had accurately forecast Typhoon Haiyan.) The fact listeners wanted the station to stay on air is evidence that the strategy worked.

In 2017, the CDAC Network published a guide on handling rumour, called *Rumour Has It*.[10]

This chapter, in concentrating on one radio station, has given an overview of the multiple roles communication can achieve in humanitarian crises. How these roles are fulfilled will be discussed in the following chapters.

Communication in the context of the relief effort

In most large-scale humanitarian emergencies where the government of the country concerned does not have sufficient capacity to handle the necessary response, that response is led and coordinated by United Nations agencies mandated to do the work, like UNOCHA, UNHCR and the IOM. The response also usually involves several large international organizations that are also specialists in this field, like the different Red Cross/Red Crescent agencies. Increasingly, however, other organizations, including the private sector and local and regional NGOs and volunteer organizations, are involving themselves, often working outside the UN-coordinated system. However, the major players are the agencies within the UN-coordinated response.

It has to be remembered that the first responders are almost always local, either established in preparation for a disaster or just present at the scene. Any organization intending to use communication as part of the humanitarian response should try to make itself aware of as many of these different players as possible, so that they can support as much of the response as they can and, where necessary, contribute to transparency and accountability across the response.

It appears clear that a better understanding between humanitarian agencies and media is needed if media are to achieve their potential in improving the overall effectiveness of the humanitarian response, as outlined in the previous chapter. This means close coordination and communication between the agencies and the media. That does not mean the media hand over editorial control to any relief agency, nor that the station or stations become the mouthpiece of the humanitarian response. Individual agencies should be invited to speak on air but, as discussed in the last chapter, the station needs to remain neutral.

What this does mean is that an effective working relationship based on mutual trust between the station and the agencies needs to be established, which has to be a two-way process.

For the station, this means a number of things (each of these points will be expanded on later in the chapter):

- familiarizing themselves with the way the humanitarian agencies organize their work, especially the 'cluster' approach, and, if possible, participating in some of the most appropriate clusters
- joining the Communicating with Communities (or Community Engagement) Working Group, if there is one, or, if there is not, participating in setting one up

- explaining the role of humanitarian communication, if the humanitarian agencies' teams are not familiar with it and with the role of media in communicating with communities
- having high journalistic standards, particularly of accuracy, and of fairness and balance, so that the agencies know that any stories about them will be truthful and they will be treated fairly by the station
- playing a positive role in helping the agencies get out to the communities the information they want the communities to understand, though it is up to the station to decide the best ways to edit and package the information which meet the audience's needs
- facilitating two-way communication with communities, so that feedback and suggestions from the communities are referred to the relevant agency, and the agencies and others can be held to account

A station and the clusters

The cluster approach was established by the Inter-Agency Standing Committee (IASC) in 2006. (The IASC is a body set up by the United Nations in 1992 which brings together UN and non-UN organizations involved in the humanitarian system.) It divides the work of a humanitarian response into eleven clusters, such as nutrition, protection, shelter and health, and each cluster brings together all of the agencies involved in work under that heading. Each cluster is under the leadership of an agency assigned by the IASC – for example, the assigned lead agency for protection is UNHCR, and for nutrition, it is UNICEF. There are six defined core functions of the clusters, but, very broadly, the purpose of the cluster approach is to coordinate the work of different agencies in the cluster, and between clusters, so that the humanitarian response is as effective and efficient as possible.

The cluster approach is fully explained in the *Cluster Coordination Reference Module*, published by the Inter-Agency Standing Committee (IASC).[1]

This module sets out the minimum commitments required from an organization for participation in a cluster. Any communication organization ought to be able to meet these commitments relatively easily.

The commitments are flexible and are not meant to be exclusive, and one of the commitments is that translation will be provided, as necessary, so that staff of a local radio station involved in the humanitarian effort, for example, should be able to participate in cluster meetings.

A member of the communication team should attend cluster meetings, so that they understand the priorities of the humanitarian response. They can put forward positive ideas about how the broadcaster can help deliver those priorities, where editorially appropriate. An explanation of what the station is doing, overall, can help to build trust. Also, a broadcaster should advocate for the needs of the community, as identified through their contact with the community. However, the broadcaster needs to remain neutral, and not become an advocate for the work of the cluster.

A humanitarian station and the Community Engagement Working Group

A Communicating with Communities (or Community Engagement) Working Group usually consists of the individuals in different organizations who are responsible for communication with the affected communities or for their organization's accountability to them. Therefore, any television or radio station engaged in humanitarian communication should be in the working group. The group's function is to ensure that communication and accountability work is coordinated, to avoid duplication and confusion, and to advocate for communication with communities among the clusters. (The rationale for, and implementation of, communicating with communities is discussed fully in Chapter 15. It should be noted that the term is often shortened to CwC, and there are several alternative names for it, of which community engagement is the most common. For other terms, see the Glossary.)

Advocacy with the agencies

It can sometimes appear that humanitarian agencies have a rather narrow view of what broadcast media can achieve in terms of contributing to a humanitarian response, and particularly of the contribution local media can make. In Haiti in 2010, for example, the agencies did not recognize the huge contribution that local radio stations had made in the hours and days immediately after the earthquake, and shut local media out from their own communication.

Against that, UNOCHA has urged agencies to include information and communication needs in their needs assessments of disaster-affected communities. In the Philippines after Typhoon Haiyan in 2013, for example, the United Nations Population Fund (UNFPA) supported another local humanitarian radio station, Radyo Abante in Tacloban, the most badly affected town.

A humanitarian broadcaster may well need to explain what they are intending to do and have to set out the potential of humanitarian communication, as summarized at the end of the previous chapter. On the basis of that potential, the case should be put for coordination and cooperation between the clusters and the broadcaster, and for including the broadcaster in both the shared needs assessment and in the cluster plans to enhance the impact of the overall humanitarian response.

It is equally likely that the new players coming into the humanitarian response, including private sector organizations and voluntary groups, will have less understanding of the potential role of media in a humanitarian response, and advocacy is likely to be needed to persuade them to cooperate with humanitarian broadcasters. It is also true that some new players, like the Tzu Chi Foundation, mentioned in the *Who's Listening?* report and cited in the last chapter, may be better at communicating with communities, and humanitarian broadcasters could well look to them to learn.

High journalistic standards

High journalistic standards are crucial to the credibility of a humanitarian broadcaster, both with the humanitarian world but also with the communities. Any proposal for either working with existing local media or setting up a new station is very likely going to need to include a substantial capacity-building element. Even if there are existing journalists of the required standard, they are unlikely to understand humanitarian communication, unless thorough preparations for humanitarian crises have been made. *Module J4: Humanitarian communication*, in Section Six, provides training plans and materials.

Getting agencies' information out

A humanitarian broadcasting station may well need to approach the agencies to show how they can help get information out to the affected population. In particular, the station will need to show how it can use innovative formats for this role. (This happened at Radyo Bakdaw, in the Philippines, with the IOM's Build Back Better campaign. See Chapter 17.) If a humanitarian communication project is working properly, its positive impact on the humanitarian response must become clear as the response goes on, improving their relationship with the humanitarian agencies.

Facilitating two-way communication and accountability

A humanitarian station's team can show their competence and reliability in their expertise in gathering and reporting back to the agencies feedback on the humanitarian response from the communities. Having established a level of trust in their professionalism, the team can start to hold agencies and government to account, so helping the agencies achieve their commitments to accountability to affected populations.

The initiative can come from the humanitarian agencies

For staff in humanitarian agencies who want to cooperate with the humanitarian media – whether international specialists or local stations – to facilitate communication with the communities, there are several things they need to do.

The clusters and individual agencies have information that they want to get out to the communities, but handing over simple messages is unlikely to be the most effective way of doing it, as discussed in Chapter 2. It would be much better for them to work with the broadcasters to package the information in more effective ways. If the broadcaster is a station run by an international communication for development organization, this is unlikely to be a problem but, if the stations are local media, then a longer-term approach may be needed.

- On arrival in the country, research what local media have done and are doing as part of a humanitarian response.
- Explore what gaps in the humanitarian response local media can help to fill.
- If not already done, read the previous chapter on what humanitarian media can and has achieved.
- Where appropriate, and where no other organization is doing it, support capacity building for the local media in humanitarian communication.
- Where appropriate, help to facilitate local media participation in the clusters.
- If not already done, read Chapters 2, 10, 12, 17, 18, 19, to understand the role of information in a humanitarian response and prioritize its dissemination in the most useful formats, while understanding the weaknesses of messaging.

The value of humanitarian agencies engaging with local media

Unless very effective preparedness measures have been put in place, there is almost always a gap between the outbreak of a humanitarian crisis – whether caused by conflict or disaster – and the arrival of the international humanitarian response. In that gap, as has been said, there is always a local response, not as well organized and resourced as the international response but there nevertheless, and, often, local media are involved.

As already mentioned, one of the best documented responses by local media was that in Haiti in 2010, when a huge earthquake struck the capital, Port-au-Prince. A number of local radio stations spontaneously took on a humanitarian role, with one in particular, Signal FM, performing several of the functions described in the previous chapter, including saving lives, family reunification and broadcasting health and safety information.[2] However, when the international humanitarian response arrived, many of these stations were largely ignored and, in fact, excluded from the humanitarian response.[3] (This example is discussed more fully in Chapter 15.)

Clearly, if there are local radio stations that can meet the criteria set out in the section of Chapter 9 on choosing broadcasting partners, initiatives like these could be built on, with partnerships and capacity building, to fulfil the roles described in the last chapter. It is probably more efficient to use existing local stations with established audiences than to bring in an international organization to set up a station from scratch. It also means that, when the humanitarian response is withdrawn, the local stations will remain but with staff trained and experienced in humanitarian communication, as preparedness for any future humanitarian crisis (and for the reasons set out in the discussion of the Internews article in Chapter 9).

Local media could bring to an international humanitarian response knowledge of languages and culture and of their community, which, if used, could save some of the problems that have been revealed in earlier responses. (The discussion in Chapter 11, on the report *Who's Listening*, shows that humanitarian agencies did not have as good a grasp of Filipino culture as they thought they had.) Again, if there are stations that meet the criteria set out in Chapter 9, or could do that with capacity building, then they could form valuable interfaces between the international response and the affected communities.

If there is a station, or are stations, that can meet Chapter 9's criteria, they could be facilitated into participation in the clusters – by facilitating access to agency premises, and addressing language issues, for example – where they could offer valuable insights into the communities and bring feedback from them.

The information and communication needs assessment

One key area where coordination between the clusters and a humanitarian broadcaster is needed is in the assessment of the needs of affected communities following a sudden-onset disaster or displacement crisis caused by conflict. This assessment is known as the Multi-Cluster/Sector Initial Rapid Assessment (MIRA).[4] The IASC recommends that it is coordinated across all the clusters or sectors so that it can be as complete and consistent as possible. It also avoids affected communities repeatedly being asked questions by different agencies.

The MIRA is carried out so that a joint humanitarian strategy can be worked out and resources mobilised. It consists of two components: a secondary data assessment, based on available literature, which should be completed in the first seventy-two hours after a disaster; and a primary data assessment, based on interviews with the affected communities, which should be completed within two weeks.

Any humanitarian communication organization that is involved in the response should be part of the development and conduct of the MIRA, so that there is a thorough assessment of the information and communication needs of the affected communities.

A key part of this is getting information and communication needs questions on the investigation form, which will be used for the primary assessment and, if possible, getting a member of the communication team as part of the primary assessment team.

A practical guide to an information and communication needs assessment is provided in the next chapter.

The information and communication needs assessment

The needs of populations affected by a disaster or by conflict for both information and communication are almost always huge, and an effective intervention to meet those needs can have impact in saving lives, reducing injury and disease, as has been discussed earlier. However, the nature of any intervention, or even whether an outside intervention is necessary, can only be decided on a needs assessment.

The Multi-Cluster/Sector Initial Rapid Assessment

In most sudden-onset humanitarian crises, the UN agencies' country team conducts a Multi-Cluster/Sector Initial Rapid Assessment (MIRA), to assess the humanitarian needs of the affected population. However, the IASC guidance says that not all the information needs of humanitarian responders can be met by the MIRA,[1] and that what is included needs to be negotiated. So, any organization considering a communication intervention can negotiate to try to get the affected population's information and communication needs included in the MIRA, if there is one. (As already said, in 2012, UNOCHA urged humanitarian agencies to include information and communication needs in the overall needs assessment in disasters as a matter of routine.[2] It is possible, therefore, that the questions a humanitarian broadcaster needs will already be in the assessment. It is important, though, to check.)

According to the IASC guidance, updated in 2015, a MIRA consists of three days' research into secondary information sources, followed by two weeks' on-the-ground research and report writing. (These first phases are, in turn, followed by a further two weeks' harmonizing sector assessments and five months' monitoring, to create a new overview.)[3]

An information and communication needs assessment is likely to follow the same pattern, of desk-based research into secondary and web sources, followed by an on-the-ground assessment. It does not make any difference whether it is part of a MIRA or has to be conducted independently by the organization thinking of running a communication project.

An information and communication rapid needs assessment

Overall, from the secondary and primary sources, an information and communication rapid needs assessment primarily has to investigate the affected populations' access to broadcasting and other communication and the factors affecting access. It needs to find out the following.

- What were the population's preferred and trusted sources of information before the crisis, and which are still available, if any?
- Are there sources of information that are not trusted and, if so, why?
- Are there groups among the population, or areas, that are particularly affected by a lack of access?
- What are the population's immediate information needs?

Of course, in any crisis of this kind, the speed of intervention is vital, as many lives are often lost in the hours and days immediately after the crisis starts, and the earliest possible intervention reduces deaths, distress and ill-health.

The desk-based research

The first stage of an information and communication needs assessment is largely through secondary data, that is, a literature search of the media landscape. This should be followed by a monitoring of primary sources that can be remotely accessed, which would include broadcast stations identified in the literature which are also on the web, and social media.

The key questions the desk-based search should answer are the following.

- Is there a need for a humanitarian communication project?
- Are there existing, indigenous media that are capable of providing the affected population with the information and support they need and of conducting communicating with communities? (The example of Haiti in 2010 proves this is perfectly possible.[4])

Are there functioning broadcasters and what are they doing?

A desk search of the media landscape, as discussed in Chapter 9, should show the broadcasting stations that existed before the disaster or conflict outbreak. Since many stations, even at community level, have websites and broadcast their output over them, a search for those stations should show which are still functioning. With translation, it should be possible to determine the nature of their broadcasting, to discover if they are broadcasting humanitarian information and facilitating communicating with communities.

If there are no functioning stations in some or all of the affected areas, then, clearly, an intervention should be undertaken.

If there are functioning stations, but they are not carrying out humanitarian communication very well or not at all, further investigation of them should become part of the primary sources assessment.

Local, independent journalist associations will also have information on the stations still operational, and their standards.

However, it is likely that not all of the broadcasting stations in the affected areas will also broadcast on the internet, and they may need to be assessed on the ground in the primary source assessment.

Can the affected population communicate?

There are other elements of humanitarian communication projects that include communicating with communities and which can be assessed from a desk-based search.

- Does the affected population have the resources to listen to broadcasting?
- Does it have the resources to respond to it?
- Are mobile phone networks functioning in the affected areas, and can the population buy airtime?
- Is electricity available for charging phones, and for televisions and radios?

It may be possible to find at least partial answers to these questions from news sources – information given out by the government concerned, and humanitarian organizations already on the ground will also produce assessment reports.

There are, too, private sector sources. Mobile phone companies operating in the area will have a wealth of information about the disaster's impact on the network, and on the numbers of calls and text messages being sent and received in the affected areas. Utility companies will be able to provide information on which areas have power and which do not.

A social media search

A search of social media could provide further evidence for the desk-based assessment. People affected by a disaster or conflict use social media to appeal for assistance, and these appeals can help humanitarians understand where a response is needed, and, to some extent, what the response should contain. More specifically, for an information and communication needs assessment, for example, a local or national radio station's social media pages might show that they are carrying out effective two-way communication (though any assessment of social media needs to take into account the digital divide, as discussed in Chapters 1 and 9, and not be taken as evidence that all parts, or even a majority of the affected communities, are engaged in the communication).

Big data

A further secondary source is so-called big data. This comes from three sources: from individuals using communication technology; from governments, who gather it from surveys and censuses and from their tax systems; and from private companies, who can gather it from, for example, what people spend their money on, and where and when.

The scale of big data can be daunting. However, information from it can be accessed for assessments. Increasingly, governments – including some in Africa – are putting their data online. Crowdsourcing can also be used. This is a process in which volunteers from all over the world analyse data to produce useable information. An organization of such volunteers, the Standby Task Force, has been used to help humanitarian organizations in many recent crises, and it is now part of the Digital Humanitarian Network, a network of networks specifically aimed at humanitarian work.[5]

To show how valuable big data can be, the OCHA study, *Humanitarianism in the Network Age*,[6] gives an example from Haiti in 2012:

> A July 2012 study demonstrated that real-time monitoring of Twitter messages in Haiti could have predicted the October/November 2010 cholera outbreaks two weeks earlier than they were detected.[7] Anonymised data, shared by Digicel, demonstrated that population movements in response to the cholera outbreak began prior to official detection of the outbreak.[8] Deaths from cholera are preventable and outbreaks are more easily dealt with in their early stages. This means there was a lost opportunity to save lives.[9]

A consideration in the use of big data is protection of individual's information, as set out in Chapter 3 on the ethics of humanitarian communication. If an organization publishes information or analysis of information drawn from big data, it needs to be checked to make sure that no individual can be identified, even by implication, from the evidence.

What is the nature of the humanitarian crisis?

An analysis of news media should provide the information on whether there is a displacement crisis or not. In many natural disasters, there is not. Populations made homeless often find, or are provided with, shelter within their communities. Conflict often causes displacement.

If there is a displacement crisis, then a humanitarian communication project will probably need to provide broadcasting and two-way communication for the host community, as well as the directly affected populations. Any host communities will need to be included in an information and communication needs assessment. (See Chapter 19 for the rationale for broadcasting to, and communicating with, host communities.)

Is a humanitarian communication intervention feasible politically?

In some countries the media is a highly politicized field, and there may be no exception for humanitarian communication. In conflict situations, this can mean that, as discussed in Chapter 3, the media is virtually a theatre of war. In that case, a significant part of an organization's energy and resources needs to be devoted to protecting their media, either in protecting their staff or in protecting premises or in dealing with hijacking of their social media output. Even in humanitarian disaster responses, the political environment can pose threats to humanitarian communication, especially where it involves holding those with power to account.

The search of secondary sources should include a study of the political context and any threats that might pose to humanitarian communication. The security and future of any local staff who are to be employed are of special consideration. If a station runs into political trouble, then that could adversely affect future employment possibilities for any local staff employed at the station, or worse.

By assessing any such threats, an organization can look at ways of mitigating the threat and of their capacity to deal with such threats, including building mitigation and protection measures into their proposals to donors.

It may be, for example, that the broadcasting partner could be an international station or a station based in a neighbouring country – as long as it already has, or can gain, a good audience in the affected country – since that reduces risk as there are no vulnerable premises on the ground, and reporters can move in and out of the affected country, or can keep a very low profile, thus reducing their vulnerability.

To take an example, in 2002, BBC Media Action carried out the Afghan Lifeline Project, broadcasting daily programmes for populations displaced by the war that started in Afghanistan in 2001. The programmes were broadcast on the BBC's Dari and Pashto Services, with the production team based in Peshawar, in Pakistan and in London, UK. These services already had very high listenership figures in and around Afghanistan. Most of the production team, and all of the production premises, were, therefore, outside the war zone, and far less vulnerable to the conflict. Reporters were able to move across the border into Afghanistan, for brief periods, to record material, and then return to the relative security of Peshawar. Much of the material could also be recorded among recent refugees who had arrived in countries neighbouring Afghanistan.

Avoiding errors

Information from almost any source is potentially unreliable, and if inaccurate information is used in a humanitarian assessment, there can be serious consequences. News, in the speed it is gathered, can be inaccurate, and its focus on drama can lead to the loss of a sense of perspective. Governments have agendas and may want to exaggerate the level of destruction or to play it down, or, worse, in conflicts, they may indulge in misinformation campaigns. Humanitarian agencies have misunderstood humanitarian crises in the recent past. As mentioned in the introduction to this book, early assessments of the response needed to the Ebola virus outbreak in West Africa in 2014 were mistaken.

On big data, UNOCHA gives this warning:

As the automated extraction of data from big open-data systems becomes incorporated into humanitarian response, the risk of compound error grows and humanitarian organizations need to be on constant guard. If the basic data is wrong, decisions based on the analysis of that data will reflect those errors and can lead to incorrect results.[10]

Using as many sources as possible for the desk-based research, with discrepancies identified and investigated, to identify a population's information and communication needs, is likely to limit the risk of errors.

Information from social media needs to be regarded with particular scepticism because of the digital divide. The poor and vulnerable – those in most need of humanitarian help – will often be excluded from social media and, even, from mobile technology.

One purpose of the primary sources assessment is to check what the desk-based research has given.

What should be done with the desk-based assessment?

The first action to take is to share it with anyone who wants to see it. In their 2013 report, UNOCHA recommended that humanitarian agencies:

> Recognize that sharing information is a core task and part of the mandate of international humanitarian organizations. Define how information will be used in emergencies and how it will be shared with communities, Governments and other partners.
>
> Share data collected and generated by humanitarian organizations (surveys, assessments, reports) on open platforms for anyone to use and review, particularly where this can fill gaps in national data.[11]

Apart from its overall contribution to the shared knowledge on the humanitarian crisis, this measure has the advantage of allowing others to review the material, adding a further stage of verification.

If the desk-based assessment suggests a humanitarian communication intervention is needed, then the primary sources team will need to use it to inform their research on the ground.

The desk-based assessment is likely to be used to develop a proposal to donors for a communication project. Alternatively, it can also inform the development of a humanitarian communication strategy, in conjunction with other agencies involved in the humanitarian response. Such a strategy could address the following.

- How can the affected population's access to communication, and any hardware provision needed (mobile phone chargers, mobile phones, etc.) be rapidly restored?
- What measures are needed to restore broadcasting, if any?
- What information does the population need to save lives and mitigate risk of disease, malnutrition and further injury, and what channels and formats are going to be used to convey it?

- Are agencies prepared to use broadcast media to meet, at least part of, their accountability to affected populations and communicating with communities commitments, or are they going to use other mechanisms, like call centres?
- If the crisis involves extensive displacement of populations, how are the information and communication needs of a host community or communities going to be met? (A particularly significant issue here is whether the host communities and the displaced speak the same language.)

If this route – the development of a humanitarian communication strategy – is taken, the desk-based assessment and the communication strategy would also be used as the basis for a proposal for an intervention to put to donors. The proposal can be refined once the findings of the primary sources are analysed and published.

The primary sources information and communication needs assessment

If the desk-based assessment suggests that it is viable for the organization to carry out a stand-alone humanitarian communication project as part of the humanitarian response, or a wider humanitarian communication strategy, then the next step is the primary sources assessment.

There are useful materials available for conducting a primary sources assessment. There is the *Assessing Information & Communications Needs: A Quick and Easy Guide*, published by the CDAC Network and The Assessment Capacities Project (ACAPS).[12]

This booklet is aimed at workers in humanitarian organizations and has five key questions for inclusion in the rapid needs assessment, as well as advice on observation, to see what communication infrastructure is still intact (for example, looking for standing transmission towers, and using a radio to find stations that are still broadcasting).

The primary sources information and communication needs assessment is carried out on the ground in the affected area, and it usually consists of three areas of enquiry: an assessment of the media situation, an assessment of the humanitarian responders in the area and their capacity to take part in communicating with the affected communities and an assessment of the affected populations' information and communication needs and preferences.

An assessment of the media situation

The assessment of the media situation is to establish, definitively, which broadcasting stations are on air in the affected region, if any. It discovers what infrastructure remains or can be rapidly rehabilitated for a new emergency broadcasting station. It asks whether any of the surviving stations are appropriate partners for a humanitarian communication intervention.

So, the assessment team need to visit any surviving stations to find out what they have done since the disaster and what they are doing in support of the affected population. They need to assess how a humanitarian communication intervention can support and build on what is already happening, if the stations are appropriate as partners.

The team also assess if any local stations which are off air as a result of the crisis can be brought back into action and how long such rehabilitation is likely to take. (Whether this is a useful strategy and which stations are to be helped will depend, largely, on the population's priorities, as expressed in responses to the rapid assessment information and communication questions. If, for example, a station that is widely popular and trusted can be rehabilitated, that station would have priority over a less popular or less trusted station.)

An assessment of the humanitarian responders

The team assess the humanitarian agencies already operating on the ground. As has been said, information to save lives, keep disease and injury to a minimum and reduce risk is vital in the early stages of a humanitarian response. Ideally, it should come from the agencies that are operating in the area, as they will have in-depth knowledge of the situation. However, as Translators Without Borders reported in 2015,[13] sometimes these agencies have not had the capacity to give out this information for broadcasting. The rapid assessment needs to establish whether the agencies in the area do have the capacity and will to do this. Perhaps the easiest and most reliable assessment method is simply to ask them for the information. If the information is provided, that is very satisfactory; if it is not, then other sources need to be assessed.

A second key issue to be assessed is the agencies' capacity and flexibility in response to two-way communicating with communities.

- Will they be willing to respond on air to messages – complaints, feedback and suggestions – coming from the affected communities?
- Do they have the capacity and flexibility to change their activities in response to messages coming from the affected communities?

As has been discussed earlier, humanitarian agencies now have commitments to be accountable to the populations they are trying to help. The rapid assessment needs to determine whether the agencies active in the emergency response are willing to have, at least in part, this commitment met via humanitarian broadcast communication.

An assessment of the affected populations' information and communication needs and preferences

As has been discussed above, the CDAC Network's *Assessing Information & Communications Needs: A Quick and Easy Guide* contains a comprehensive set of questions for affected populations, the answers to which will provide a great deal of useful information for shaping a communication response.

Standards 4 and 5 of the *Age and Disability Capacity* (ADCAP) set of minimum standards for humanitarian work should be applied to these assessments, especially, the second – greater depth – one, to ensure the inclusion of the most vulnerable groups in the populations. These are referred to in Chapter 9.

The response to the primary sources needs assessment

Once the assessment has been completed and analysed, it can be used to revise and refine the stand-alone broadcasting proposal or the humanitarian communication strategy proposal.

In particular, a final decision is needed on the broadcasting channel or channels. The options are likely to be the following:

- the creation of a new, emergency station, if there are no existing local stations on air or which can be rapidly rehabilitated, and no national or international broadcaster available, which is popular and appropriate to the population's needs
- the formation of a communication partnership, if there are trusted and popular stations still on air – which meet the criteria set out in Chapter 9, on choosing a broadcasting partner – or that can be quickly rehabilitated
- the formation of a communication partnership with a national or international broadcaster, if there is one that is popular and trusted, and adequate means of communicating with communities can be established

The revised strategy may be used to refine any proposal to be put to donors.

The second assessment

It is common practice to undertake a second, more detailed and thorough, assessment through primary sources, to be carried out after the initial rapid assessment.

There is a much more detailed suite of tools for such an assessment, which was developed in 2014 by three of the largest media for development organizations: BBC Media Action, Internews and International Media Support (IMS), under the auspices of the CDAC Network.[14]

The materials are a suite of four documents:

A Guidance Note on Using the CDAC Network Common Communication Needs Assessment Tools
Questionnaire for Use with Affected Population
Humanitarian Responder Questionnaire
Media Station Profile Questionnaire

Given the huge experience of these organizations, it would appear sensible for anyone conducting a second assessment, at least, to use these documents as the basis of that assessment.

14

Recruiting and training a local team for emergency communication

Recruitment

When the decision has been taken to set up a new radio station and the funding has been provided, the first task is to find premises and then to recruit a communication team. If the desk-based research or the community questionnaires show that there had been a radio station or stations, the quickest way to find a team would be to track down the former staff of the station, probably through the local authorities.

If this cannot be done, then a call will need to go out, probably through the local authorities or through the rapid assessment questionnaire. If this call does not give results, then a selection workshop will need to be organized, as described in *Training Module J2: A selection workshop procedure for factual communication.*

Of course, once the station is on air, it can broadcast adverts for further staff needs.

A communication team

The size of a team in a humanitarian radio station will depend on a number of factors, particularly the broadcasting hours and the nature of the broadcasting. If a station is largely broadcasting music, it will need significantly fewer staff than one that is news heavy.

Radyo Bakdaw, Internews' community station in the Philippines after Typhoon Haiyan in November 2013, eventually had what might appear a large staff, with around twenty Filipinos and five international staff (one of whom worked elsewhere as well as at the station). Of these, seven were regularly on air, and the others were technicians, drivers and administrative staff. The station also had an audience research team, of four, led by an international. In spite of the size of the staff, the UK government's independent aid assessment unit judged that the station had delivered good value for money (see Chapter 11).

However, four of the international staff and eight of the Filipino staff did not join the station until after it had been on air for two months. At the outset, there had been one international team leader, the seven on-air staff, an administrator, the technicians and drivers.

In comparison, Radio Sila, Internews' station in Eastern Chad (discussed often, but particularly see Chapter 19), seems to have had a journalism staff of about nine.

Changing roles with changing output

At Radyo Bakdaw, staff members performed a number of different roles, and those roles changed over time as the station developed its humanitarian output. It is not being suggested this is a model of best practice, but it is an example of some roles that appear to be important. It also shows how a station, starting with few trained journalists, was able to develop its reporting to meet much better the information and communication needs of its community. The station did this in a relatively short time.

Of the seven broadcasting members of staff, most had been disc jockeys at the only radio station that existed in Guiuan before Typhoon Haiyan. (The typhoon had completely destroyed that station.) Only two of these staff had had any journalism experience. So, while the station went on air the staff received intense journalism training, so that they could go out and find local stories, augmenting the station's mix of music and listeners' text messages with original and relevant news.

When I arrived, as the international humanitarian journalism facilitator, two months after the station had gone on air, the disaster had moved into the rehabilitation phase, but the team were exhausted from being on air and being trained. The decision was taken that training would be restricted to the introduction of humanitarian item formats, with training being for the realization of those formats. (It also has to be remembered that the Filipino staff were having to deal with the fact that their own homes had been devastated and, in some cases, they had lost friends or relatives.)

That said, within two weeks, four new themed humanitarian programmes were introduced, covering livelihoods, shelter, psychosocial support and a children's programme, to join the existing health programme. New story researchers were recruited, each allocated to one of the themes, while the existing on-air staff and one administrator took on new roles, in addition to their existing roles, as producers of these themed programmes.

Maintaining the core format

However, the bulk of the station's airtime was still music and personal messages, largely sent by SMS. It is worth pointing out that this mix is not confined to middle-income countries like the Philippines. According to the Infoasaid *Chad Media and Telecoms Landscape Guide*, Radio Absoun, another of Internews' humanitarian stations in Chad, broadcast programmes with a very similar format, and they were among their most popular programmes.[1]

In this way, the station was able to meet specifically identified humanitarian needs.

A range of staff provides unique access

There was one role played by one of the researchers which has echoes in other humanitarian projects. This particular researcher came from a different background from the rest of the staff. While they were graduates and undergraduates, she came from among the fishing community. This was a large group in Guiuan, and one of the worse hits. The vast majority of the small wooden boats they used were destroyed by the typhoon. In addition, a storm surge which passed over the town was reported to have washed sewage back out into the inshore waters, killing the fish. Her background gave this researcher unique access to this community, so that it was much easier for the station to understand and address their needs.

Radio Sila had reporters who were residents in each of the refugee camps in the region, and, again, they offered unique access, which would not have been available to outsiders.[2] In the BBC Media Action Somalia Lifeline programmes in 2009, there were two reporters who were residents of the towns of Garowe and Galkayo. These towns were of particular significance at that time. One of the main topics of the programmes was migration, as there was a large traffic of Somalis and others, fleeing conflict, to the port of Bossaso, on the Gulf of Aden, from which they could get boats to take them to refuge in Yemen. There were, of course, risks in taking this route, as boats would sometimes sink, or captains would force migrants to leave the boats while they were still far from the Yemeni shore, so that they could get away from Yemeni coastguard vessels. The town of Garowe was on the route of most would-be migrants and so unique insights into their outlook and motivation could be obtained by the reporter there. Galkayo was a conflict zone, in a three-way battle for control, and, again, the resident reporter could get unique access to people caught up in the conflict, a major part of the intended audience.

Managing feedback

At Radyo Bakdaw, a second staff member with a role specific to humanitarian communication was one who logged the text messages that the station received from listeners, which were relevant to the humanitarian response. It was by having this almost full-time job that the station could feed back community members' comments, suggestions and questions to the relevant humanitarian agencies, which were then invited to respond. It was this mechanism that allowed the station to be part of the overall communicating with communities' effort, and to the agencies' accountability agenda.

So, this is an account of how one humanitarian station managed to get on air quickly, and subsequently developed its staff to deliver a more comprehensive humanitarian service. It illustrates that, since getting the station on air is the highest priority, it can go on air before the team are fully trained, and training can continue while the station is broadcasting.

Training priorities

It is useful to determine what the minimum skills set needed is at each stage of the station's development, and to do that, it is necessary to set priorities for the station's activities at each stage, based on the assessment of communities' information and communication needs. These might be the following, with each stage adding new activities to those in the earlier stages.

Stage 1, the first days of broadcasting

The station would do the following:

- provide psychosocial support through respite, largely music and personal messages
- give information to help save lives, limit disease and injury, and limit risk
- facilitate communication between communities, particularly for family reunification

The team's skill set needed to deliver this would be:

- adequate microphone skills, to be able to present with clarity and confidence
- an understanding of the rationale and ethics of humanitarian communication
- the ability to conduct straightforward on-air interviews to fill out the basic information
- basic research skills to verify family identities and to find appropriate interviewees
- ability to give basic news on what has happened and is happening in the area

Stage 2, as soon as possible

The station would do the following:

- give basic news on what has happened and is happening in the area, including: the impact of the disaster or conflict; the activities of the humanitarian response; and any remaining threats and the options individuals and families have, with enough information for them to make informed decisions
- offer specialist health programming, answering questions from the communities and giving advice for different stages of the recovery

The team would need these additional skills:

- understanding the need for accuracy in journalism and how to achieve it
- basic journalism skills to be able to tell a story on air, and to frame questions to get from interviewees the information communities need
- the ability to confidently control an interview to keep the interviewee on track

Stage 3

The station would do the following:

- hold government and humanitarian agencies to account, on behalf of the affected communities
- feed back suggestions from the communities to government and the humanitarian agencies for the humanitarian response to better meet the needs of the communities

The team would need these additional skills:

- a strong grasp of the ethics of journalism in a humanitarian context
- basic investigative journalism skills to develop a case to put to government or agencies
- confidence in politely but firmly and persistently interviewing to get responses to complaints coming from the communities

Stage 4, in parallel with the beginning of the rehabilitation phase

The station would do the following:

- provide accessible and engaging specialist humanitarian programming for rehabilitation and rebuilding after a disaster, and for consolidation after displacement, covering livelihoods, shelter and more sophisticated and targeted psychosocial support
- offer specialist programming for children

The team would need these additional skills:

- ability to use different formats for better engagement
- audio editing and package-making skills
- research skills to find role models
- skills in broadcasting for children, and in interviewing children

A broadcasting structure

If a station is going to be on air for many hours each day, seven days a week, it is almost certainly not going to be possible to have the presentation fully scripted in advance, and it would not be desirable to do that, for a number of reasons. For new presenters, writing a script would pose significant challenges, even assuming they can type efficiently: for example, how could they work out the timing accurately? If the radio station is receiving texts or social media messages from the community, many of those will be personal, audio greetings cards, and the radio station will not need to do more than simply broadcast them. It is important that they are broadcast soon after they have been received, so that there is a sense of engagement and immediacy for the listener. (They certainly cannot be stored up for broadcast the following day, because they will lose their topicality and will be an additional management problem.) It is, therefore, much better for them to be read out on air immediately after receipt, and then deleted, to prevent repeating the broadcast. (For other messages, which concern the humanitarian response, issues of governance or rehabilitation and rebuilding and family reunification, there needs to be a system of storage and classification, so that they can be grouped and followed up, as discussed in Chapter 3.) Obviously, if a significant part of the presenter's talk is handling listeners' personal messages, then scripting is not possible.

However, it will be of enormous value to inexperienced presenters if there is a structure within which they can work. This would be a pattern in which to broadcast different kinds of items, perhaps, for each hour of broadcasting, and would be something like the following.

News: information on the local situation, the humanitarian response, the recovery and rehabilitation effort

Song
Presenter: Back announcement for the song
    The station's identifier
    Two to three listeners' personal messages
    The station's text line number/social media page

Song
Presenter: Back announcement for the song
    Important information to save lives, limit disease and injury, and limit risk

Song
Presenter: Back announcement for the song
    Station's identifier
    Two public service announcements (news of agencies' aid distributions, job advertisements, information about public services)

Song

Song
Presenter: Back announcement for the songs
    Station's identifier
    Family reunification appeals and reports on successful reunifications
    The station's text line number/social media page

Song
Presenter: Back announcement for the songs
    Station's identifier
    Appeals for help from listeners

Song
Presenter: Back announcement for the song
    Weather forecast

Song
Presenter: Back announcement for the songs
    Two to three listeners' personal messages
    The station's text line number/social media page

Song

Presenter: Back announcement for the songs
  Interview with an agency or government on a key piece of information to save lives, limit disease and injury, and limit risk

Song

Presenter: Back announcement for the songs
  Station's identifier
  Question of the day and a listener's response to it*

Song

Presenter: Back announcement for the songs
  Two to three listeners' personal messages
  The station's text line number/social media page

Song

Presenter: Back announcement for the songs
  Station's identifier

*A question of the day can be worked out at a morning editorial meeting. It can be anything to do with how listeners are dealing with some aspect of their current situation. An example might be, 'How are you dealing with your children while there is no school for them?'

This structure is only an example, and the pattern should be determined from listening to other stations in other nearby areas, so that the new station is following a pattern that is familiar for listeners. Familiarity is important in re-establishing some sense of normality.

An understanding of the rationale and ethics of humanitarian communication

The elements of the rationale of humanitarian communication that need to be understood at this stage are:

- material being broadcast needs to be of direct, practical use to the audience
- the key reasons for communicating with affected communities

The principle ethical consideration is the need for accuracy in information being broadcast; that is, any information broadcast needs to come from a reputable source and be verified by another, independent source.

Whether the decision is taken to create a new local radio station or to work with existing local stations, when emergency broadcasting is based within the affected population, and especially when it is a community radio station, it can be very difficult to find staff with any journalistic skills or experience. In this case, it is necessary to find and train a team in basic journalism and radio skills very quickly, so that the station can be on air, offering support to the population as early as possible.

Training agendas and materials

Suggested agendas and materials for training in topics relevant to this chapter can be found in Section Six:

Module J3: Presentation training
Module J4: Humanitarian communication
Module J6: Creativity in writing for children

15

Using the media for two-way communication

The last chapter touched on how, among other functions, a community radio station can facilitate two-way communication between disaster- or conflict-affected communities and the agencies and others trying to help them. This chapter looks at this particular issue in greater depth, exploring why two-way communication matters so much. It looks at why the media are such a good conduit for that communication, for all sides, and how the media can make it happen very quickly and effectively. It explores the role media can play in involving a community in its broadcasting, and in reflecting views and information from the community back to the agencies and government. It will look at how this community involvement can help to make information from the agencies and government more accessible, as well as how the media can pick up, for example, complaints from the community about aid delivery, can follow up those complaints and feed complaints back to the agencies or government. Finally, it looks at how social media and mobile technology can link with broadcasting in this kind of two-way communication.

Why two-way communication is essential

The point that information is important to disaster- and conflict-affected communities has been made earlier in this book. However, why should hard-pressed humanitarian responders put time and effort into listening and responding to information coming back from the communities?

There are many reasons why two-way communication is essential in a humanitarian response. Some are purely practical: the efficiency of the humanitarian response is improved when communities are listened to, because it is better tailored to the needs of the communities, as logistical problems and corruption are exposed, and agencies and government are held to account, by the people they are trying to serve. Others are a mix of practical and ethical, in the light of strong evidence that agencies that are not listening to communities do not understand those communities, often resulting in aid creating tension and even conflict. Clearly, creating conflict is not the intention of aid and is counter-productive to the humanitarian effort. So, ethically, listening helps to ensure the principle of 'Do no harm' is followed.

Beyond these practicalities, there is the question of what humanitarianism is saying to the communities it is trying to help, and, indeed, to the world. Humanitarian aid is about solidarity between different groups, not gift-giving or beneficence. This means respecting the dignity of affected populations, and listening to what they have to say, is a crucial part of showing decent respect. Associated with that is respecting the human rights of affected people, and they have a right to communicate, enshrined in the Universal Declaration of Human Rights (UDHR).

Finally, it is clear from many studies that disaster- and conflict-affected communities have a powerful need to communicate, with agencies and with each other, and that many benefits flow from that communication, especially where it is between displaced and host communities. One of the major benefits is in psychosocial support.

Another way of looking at the situation and putting the case is to say that, in most walks of life, supply-led delivery, in which it is the supplier who decides what is delivered, to whom and when – most often associated with the former communist regimes – is no longer acceptable. Yet, without two-way communication, that is exactly what humanitarian aid is.

The practical consequences of listening

This is an example where listening to affected people caused a small change to a project, but that change may have made the difference between success and failure. The International Organisation for Migration (IOM) often concerns itself with helping populations affected by disaster rebuild their homes in more disaster-resistant ways. One of these projects was a one-room shelter (ORS) programme in Pakistan, in the aftermath of severe flooding in 2011.

The project involved making staged payments to householders for the building process. However, after the first 5,000 householders had received payments, the IOM listened to their feedback and found that the early payments were too small to build a proper foundation – key to flood resistance – and that, for some householders, this undermined their faith that the IOM would see through the whole building process. In response, IOM increased the payments, and the project went on to be judged a success.[1]

This is just one example, but there are many more.

Understanding communities

A little while into a cholera outbreak that followed the 2010 earthquake in Haiti, the Haitian Red Cross (HRC) held meetings with residents in camps, not intentionally to find out what they thought, and discovered that the residents saw cholera very differently from what they were being told in public service information. Indeed, the residents did not see cholera as a disease at all:

> They argued that they had lived in these conditions for years and cholera had never manifested before, therefore it must be a deliberate attempt to kill people ahead of the upcoming election. They frequently referred to the Haitian Kreyol saying 'mikob pa touye ayisyen' (Microbes don't kill Haitians). Haitians also used frameworks of colonial occupation, distrust of foreigners and past experience of disease to interpret the cholera outbreak. Participants also expressed

disappointment and mistrust of international organisations following the response to the earthquake and the fact that so many people were still living in camps nearly a year after the disaster.

From a psychosocial perspective, the HRC paper identified fear as the driving factor behind most reactions not just to cholera, but also to any of the facilities or methods being promoted as ways to prevent or cure the disease. This fear had very real consequences: cholera treatment centres were firebombed and rejected, people who were sick, had recovered or whose work brought them into contact with the disease, were stigmatised, and perceived perpetrators were attacked. The study also found that the belief that foreigners had brought the disease was undermining the credibility of foreign organisations carrying out information campaigns.[2]

This example illustrates that assumptions about community perspectives can be wrong in the extreme and that proceeding without an understanding of those perceptions can lead to conflict and harm. (It is, though, of interest, that the Haitians' perception that foreigners had introduced cholera – albeit unintentionally – was completely correct, as it is now acknowledged that the outbreak started at a UN base.[3])

Solidarity, rights and ethics

It is a long time since the term 'beneficiary' disappeared from the humanitarian vocabulary, as humanitarianism has come to be seen as based on solidarity between humans, as we help each other when one group are suffering and others can provide assistance and aid. Solidarity means mutual respect and inclusion, underpinned by a respect for human rights.

Article 19 of the UDHR states:

> Everyone has the right to freedom of opinion and expression; this right includes freedom to hold opinions without interference and to seek, receive and impart information and ideas through any media and regardless of frontiers.

Respecting this right would seem to mean helping those who have been denied it – either through natural disaster or conflict – to reclaim it, by providing the means of communication.

Seventeen Sustainable Development Goals were adopted by the UN heads of state and governments in 2015, to set the international development agenda until 2030. Goal 16 is relevant to the inclusion of disaster- and conflict-affected communities in decisions by organizations which affect them:

> Promote peaceful and inclusive societies for sustainable development, provide access to justice for all and build effective, accountable and inclusive institutions at all levels.

As has been shown, the effectiveness of a humanitarian response is improved by listening to affected communities; accountability depends, too, on listening to affected communities; and inclusivity means communicating across the spectrum of those communities.

As has been referred to in Chapter 3, there are several codes of ethics for humanitarian action, which are interlinked, and *The Core Humanitarian Standard on Quality and Accountability* sets communicating with communities firmly in the humanitarian response in Commitments 4 and 5:

> 4. Communities and people affected by crisis know their rights and entitlements, have access to information and participate in decisions that affect them.
>
> Quality Criterion: Humanitarian response is based on communication, participation and feedback.

> 5. Communities and people affected by crisis have access to safe and responsive mechanisms to handle complaints.
>
> Quality Criterion: Complaints are welcomed and addressed

The desire for communication and the support it brings

The Tsunami Coalition's *Synthesis Report* on the humanitarian response to the Indian Ocean tsunami in 2004 said:

> Surveys show that people's main concern after the initial days was to get on with their lives, and to recover as fast as possible. If not aid, they at least wanted – and deserved – reliable information about recovery plans, resources and methods to allow them take their own decisions.[4]

This quote is surprising in that it suggests that, in this situation, at least, an affected population put communication as a higher priority than material aid. It points, also, to one of the chief drivers of the desire for communication: regaining a sense of control, which, as was seen in Chapter 10, is a major part of psychosocial support.

A woman who was living in a bunkhouse – a wooden terrace of small cabins built as emergency shelters in the Philippines in 2013, after Typhoon Haiyan had destroyed or badly damaged many houses – expresses this desire for control, for an aid response shaped for the affected population's needs. She is quoted in the *CDAC Network Typhoon Haiyan Learning Review*:

> Expressing feedback would be useful not just to express problems, but if NGOs would ask what project do we really want to have, what project is needed in the bunkhouse. For example, here our problem is health, so it would be good that we can express what we really need here' (Woman, Palo Bunkhouse).[5]

Here, a failure to listen on the part of the humanitarian response left this individual frustrated and also meant that the aid response was not meeting the population's needs properly.

That there is a strong desire for communication among communities affected by disaster or conflict is shown by the simple fact that, as soon as an effective channel opens, it is used. Again, the CDAC Network Learning Review on Typhoon Haiyan reports that the Internews community radio station in Guiuan, Radyo Bakdaw (already discussed at length in Chapter 11) was sent, on average, over a thousand SMSs a day, and Radyo Abante, in Tacloban, received 40,694 SMSs between 13 January and 31 August 2014.

Finally, there is the matter of facilitating communication between communities. Again, as shown in Chapters 10 and 11, this is important for family reunification and for helping to restore mutual support between communities. There is also a commercial aspect to this kind of communication. Facilitating communication between communities means helping to restore commercial ties, thus helping to rebuild livelihoods. Information and communication are crucial parts of the economic infrastructure.

These are some compelling reasons for communicating with communities.

The means of communication

Face to face

When asked, affected communities will very often say that face-to-face communication is their preferred route. It does have the advantage that it can reach people who do not have access to other means, either because they do not have access to the hardware needed – such as a mobile phone or radio – because they have a disability or because they are illiterate.

However, face-to-face communication is expensive, unless carried out by volunteers, which is often not possible, or where agency staff meet the community anyway – for example, help desks at aid distribution points.

The media, though, can build face-to-face communication into its work, particularly if it is a local station. Community members can call at the station in person, and the case of Signal FM, a local radio station in Haiti, given below, shows how much that is valued by communities. At the same time, a station's journalists can go out into the community for face-to-face contact. If properly planned, such contact can ensure that all parts of the community are brought into the communication – so that journalists seek out sectors that would not, of their own volition, come forward – so that the communication can be truly inclusive and participatory.

Call centres

Some of the channels that often appear to be preferred by humanitarian agencies are not strictly communicating with communities. Call centres are only for communicating with individuals, and self-selected individuals, probably the more confident and articulate. Further, they are not necessarily transparent. They may well meet agencies' accountability requirements, but that is not the same as communicating with communities.

A major part of both accountability to communities and communicating with communities is response on the part of agencies or government to what they are hearing from the affected communities. This will often mean changing what they are doing, as in the example given above, of the IOM in Pakistan. To build the trust of the affected communities, that response needs to be transparent, and visible across the communities, which it cannot easily be if it is given through a call centre or even face to face.

A local radio station

When it comes to communication between communities, the media, and again, particularly a local station, are far more effective and efficient than any other communication channel. Social media can be effective in this, always allowing for the digital divide and as long as there is power to recharge phones. If a station is also broadcasting on the internet – as, for example, several were in Haiti in 2010 – then it can also provide a vital link between an affected community and a diaspora.

It is relatively easy and cost-effective for a local radio station to be a major channel for communicating with communities. This is a case study from a report on communicating with communities in Haiti after the 2010 earthquake (*Ann Kite Yo Pale (Let them speak)* by Imogen Wall and Yves Gerald Chéry, Infoasaid, 2012). A number of existing local stations took on the role. This study looks at Signal FM, which took on the role without any pre-planning or training for its staff. They had not even heard of communicating with communities and yet fulfilled many of the functions assigned to the concept within hours of the disaster. All of this happened before any of the international humanitarian response had arrived on the ground.

> For survivors of the earthquake, local radio stations became essential to survival in the days after the quake. For many, they were the only way to find out what was going on. They were also a source of entertainment, solace and community feeling – a reminder that survivors were not alone.
>
> Signal FM is one of the most important news radio stations in Port au Prince, and was also one of the few unscathed by the earthquake (all its staff also survived). Within a few hours of the quake, four staff members had arrived and began to broadcast what they had seen.
>
> The station quickly found itself turned into a spontaneous information exchange centre, with queues of listeners wanting to broadcast requests for help, names of the missing or to just tell their stories. Signal FM found ways to tell people how to handle the catastrophe. Doctors, engineers, seismologists and clergymen went on air. They told people what to do with dead bodies, where it was safe to sleep, where they could locate medicine and food, which hospitals were open, and also read lists of those confirmed dead or alive. They also relayed confirmed reports of people trapped but alive. 'We were like a phone for the country,' says station CEO, Mario Viau.
>
> One woman, Elcie Dyess, came to Signal FM on the third day after the quake to appeal for help in finding her husband, Jean François, who had been at work

at a nearby bank at the time of the quake. Listeners heard her appeal, went to the bank that had collapsed, and dug him out alive.[6] Signal FM also played an important role internationally. Their online broadcasts were listened to by many Haitians overseas; foreign embassies gave Signal FM information on how their citizens in Haiti should contact them; and many diaspora radio stations in the US, Canada and France rebroadcast Signal FM's broadcasts.[7] Haitian stations abroad also requested time on Signal FM to broadcast requests for information from diaspora Haitians looking for relatives in the affected area. Throughout this time, the only formal assistance Signal FM received was a government delivery of fuel for generators when the station ran out. As with many stations, Signal FM was at times dependent on donations and support from ordinary Haitians in order to stay on air. Listeners brought food and water to the journalists to help them continue working.[8]

A combination of channels

Successful two-way communication with communities usually uses a combination of channels, based on what channels are available and an assessment of which channels are preferred and trusted by communities. Preferred channels will vary, dependent on many factors, including culture, language, literacy and availability of certain technologies. Preferred and accessible channels will vary for communities in conflict situations, for people on the move and for those whose communication infrastructure may have been destroyed by a natural disaster. In every case, as has already been said, assessment of communities' preferences and channel use is vital.

Radio has been shown to be a very successful medium for two-way communication in humanitarian emergencies, usually when it is combined with social media, SMS or phone calls. This mechanism works by the station broadcasting a phone number and inviting listeners to send in SMSs or call, and broadcasting the names of pages on social media.

To sum up, the media, and radio in particular, are effective in communicating with communities.

- Radio is accessible in circumstances when other means are not, because it works when there is little or no electricity, and publicly placed radios – at aid distribution points, for instance – can serve when individuals do not have their own access.
- It can be up and running with life-saving information, and live phone-ins getting communities' questions answered quickly.
- A station can put voices from the community on air and can facilitate community discussions; communication between communities can hold people to account over issues raised.
- A feedback mechanism is provided for humanitarian responders categorizing messages from the community and sending them to the appropriate agency.
- Radio broadcasts can provide psychosocial support, helping people feel connected, encouraging hope and providing respite in music.

Training agendas and materials

Suggested agendas and materials for training in topics relevant to this chapter can be found in Section Six:

Module J4: Humanitarian communication

Channels for humanitarian communication

An overview of channels for humanitarian communication

A wide range of channels has been used for humanitarian communication, partly determined by what is available at the time.

There have been radio stations specifically created for a particular crisis, as was the case for two stations often discussed so far: Radio Sila in Chad and Radyo Bakdaw in the Philippines.

Existing community and commercial stations have volunteered themselves or have worked with humanitarian or media for development organizations.

National stations have been used, though it appears to be more common for international broadcasters to carry humanitarian programming. The BBC World Service, for example, has broadcast humanitarian programming on its Arabic Service for Iraq and Gaza, its Somali Service and its Pashto and Dari Services for Afghanistan.

Politics will always be a consideration in the choice of communication channels. Radio stations have, for example, been created to broadcast in specific displacement or Protection of Civilians sites. However, there can be complicated politics around broadcasting in such camps. Protection of Civilians sites are set up to protect certain groups who are at risk of attack from members of other communities. They are often within the geographical region of the conflict. So if, for example, a Protection of Civilians site is in a UN compound, the UN may not want a broadcasting station for the site. Its broadcasting could be heard outside the compound, and might exacerbate already difficult community relations. Partly in order to get round this problem, Internews used a loudspeaker system fitted to the back of a quad bike to broadcast humanitarian programmes in South Sudan.[1]

The nature of the broadcaster and the media being used

While the information and communication needs assessment – discussed in Chapter 13 – will show the target audience's preferences, and, clearly, the chosen broadcaster needs to be one the target audience listen to and trust, there will also be one further factor in choosing which type of broadcaster is required: the location and distribution of the affected populations.

Many natural disasters affect a relatively small area or areas. For example, in 2013, in spite of its size and power, Typhoon Haiyan affected only relatively small areas of the Philippines, principally the islands of Samar and Leyte, and most displacement was relatively local. However, a widespread conflict can displace populations over a very wide area. In 2001, for example, the war to remove the Taliban from power in Afghanistan displaced populations both internally and also into Pakistan and Iran.

Clearly, while the information and communication needs of the population affected by Haiyan could largely be met by a few local or community radio stations, efficiently meeting the needs of the displaced population in and around Afghanistan in 2001 required a different solution. As with many conflict zones, there were no functioning local stations, and it was not possible to set any up within Afghanistan. In this case, the solution was to work with an international broadcaster, the BBC World Service in Dari and Pashto, which, broadcasting on short wave, could reach displaced people wherever they were in the region. It was fortunate that these services were already well established and were popular and trusted by many in the affected populations.

Broadly, these are the range of broadcaster or media options available.

- A dedicated emergency community radio station is set up in order to support an affected population after a disaster or during conflict.
- An existing local or community station is prepared to give over a substantial element of its airtime to humanitarian broadcasting, working in cooperation with a communication for development humanitarian organization.
- A dedicated broadcasting slot is organized on an existing local or community broadcaster, preferably at least 30 minutes long and daily. If the five lessons for communication for development organizations, discussed in Chapter 9, have been learned, this should not just be a programme made by a humanitarian or communication for development organization which is then just broadcast in paid-for airtime, without any other involvement of the station. (The five lessons are: fully engage with local media; build capacity instead of buying airtime; be consistent in what you say, but do not broadcast oversimplified information; support communicating with communities; and help local media hold agencies and others to account.)
- A network of existing local broadcasters is prepared to carry humanitarian output, each serving a different area, perhaps alongside one or more dedicated emergency stations. This could be a communication for development organization providing capacity building to each of the stations, which are producing their own output, or a ready-made humanitarian programme distributed to all of the stations, followed by a live discussion, hosted separately by each station. The humanitarian programme could be made of material recorded by the different stations, so that different parts of a dispersed population are represented, and there is at least some level of communication between communities facilitated. There could also be other live elements, including a networked family reunification service. This could be a good alternative to a national or international broadcaster, when a displaced population is widely dispersed, with better opportunities for communicating with communities, though significantly more difficult to manage and monitor. In some

countries there are existing networks of local stations, like the Catholic Radio Network in South Sudan, and working with one of these might make management simpler.

- A dedicated slot on a national or international broadcaster is set up. Many countries have a national broadcaster, though, of course, it is vital to find out from the information and communication needs assessment if the affected populations in question can hear it, and whether they trust it. Often, supposedly national broadcasters cannot be heard in large parts of a country and, especially if a national broadcaster is seen as the mouthpiece of a government, they may not be trusted by populations.

- Social media is valuable, either alongside broadcasting, on its own, where there is good evidence many of the target audience have access, or where there is no other option. For example, during the movement of many refugees towards Europe in 2015 and 2016, The International Committee of the Red Cross (ICRC) used Facebook to communicate with them. This was partly because many of them came from relatively rich countries, especially Syria, but also because there was no other way.

Flexibility of formats

A dedicated emergency community radio station will have the greatest flexibility in the choice of formats, as the whole of its airtime will be, in different ways, dedicated to humanitarian ends. This means it will probably have a more relaxed feel, and most of its output will be live, so that formats will be very simple, especially in the weeks immediately after a disaster or displacement: one-to-one live interviews, and presenters giving vital information on, for example, aid distribution, and news that is useful to the affected populations, for example, on recovery and rebuilding after a disaster, or on the state of the conflict in a conflict.

An existing local or community station prepared to give over a substantial element of its airtime to humanitarian communication will probably be very similar.

If the broadcast output is a slot of about 30 minutes a day on a local broadcaster, then the output will need a much tighter format, with information and advice given succinctly, using pre-recorded interviews that have been edited, so that only the most important information is broadcast. It is unlikely that the slot will need to include news, as most local stations will carry their own news output, which will be relevant to a humanitarian target audience. The humanitarian slot should be followed by a live discussion, either a phone-in or with listeners texting their questions or views, so that listeners can better absorb and understand the information.

There are several international broadcasters, broadcasting in a range of languages in different parts of the world, and on different platforms, including online, television and radio. For example, as of 2019, Voice of America broadcasts in more than 40 languages, Deutsche Welle in 30, All-India Radio in 23, the BBC World Service in more than 40 and Radio France Internationale in 15. The BBC World Service has often carried humanitarian output for specific places within its international broadcasting schedules: for example, in 2014, in its Arabic service, it broadcast a twice-daily humanitarian programme for people in Gaza, which was, at the time, under attack by the Israel Defence Forces.

Of course, international broadcasters are normally run by the government of the country of origin, and have a range of intentions. It is, therefore, important to check to ensure they comply with the ethics of humanitarian communication. So, for example, if a broadcaster's key purpose is to promote a particular image of the country of origin, a humanitarian communication organization needs to consider if that is that compatible with its ethical code, and, if it is not, whether the imperative to get humanitarian broadcasting on air overrides that ethical consideration. Once again, the decision needs to be guided by the information and communication needs assessment, which should show how far the affected population watch or listen to the station and how far they trust it.

An advantage of an international broadcaster, especially in conflicts, is that its facilities, being based in a different country, will be largely unaffected by the conflict or disaster the humanitarian response is reacting to. The programmes need not be remote from the audience, however, if the content largely comes from the affected area, and if there are means for the affected population to communicate with the programme.

Podcasts

Either as an extra channel when there is an existing radio or television channel, or as a stand-alone channel, podcasting is a valuable form of internet media. If there is already a built 30-minute radio programme for a non-dedicated radio channel, it can easily be used as a podcast, either on the station's own website, or on one of the many podcasting platforms available. If there is a dedicated humanitarian station, a podcast can be assembled from the specifically humanitarian content being broadcast. One big advantage of a podcast is that, once a listener registers for the podcast, each new podcast will be automatically sent to that listener. It is vital to have a parallel channel to allow for two-way communication. Of course, humanitarian information can be posted on a platform like Facebook, usually in the form of short videos, or written and illustrated with images. An advantage of Facebook and Twitter is that they are designed for two-way, or multi-way, communication. These were the social media platforms widely in use at the time of writing, but it is very likely they will be made redundant by new platforms with greater capacities in the future.

Training agendas and materials

Suggested agendas and materials for training in topics relevant to this chapter can be found in Section 6:

Module J4: Humanitarian communication

Communication for adults directly affected by crisis

Probably more than any other kind of communication for development, humanitarian communication can be in a huge range of formats, often determined – especially in the early days and weeks of an emergency – simply by what resources are available, and which broadcasters the affected population are most likely to be able to hear and trust. A broadcasting format is the shape of the programme or broadcast item. A magazine programme, for example, is a series of items on different topics, linked by a very broad theme. In a humanitarian context, all of the items would meet different needs among the affected population. It is also likely that the items within a magazine programme will have different formats from each other: one-to-one interviews; a monologue; a package, in which there are edited clips from different interviews held together by the reporter's narrative; topical news or a short comedy skit. A discussion format will have a panel of people with different perspectives, with a chair who controls it, talking about one or more topics.

The reason for using different formats is to look at issues from different perspectives and in different ways, to fully engage the audience, and address the issues in ways that will most effectively meet the audiences' needs.

The broadcasting formats available will depend on a number of factors:

- the nature of the broadcaster and the media being used
- the skill and experience of the production team
- the nature of the content, and the stage of the emergency
- the communication needs of the overall audience and different parts of it

Two guiding principles

Directly affected populations are those who survive conflict or disaster but whose lives are disrupted, often very severely, as a direct consequence of the natural disaster or conflict; that is, their homes and livelihoods are damaged or destroyed, they are forced to leave their homes, they suffer loss of loved ones and possessions, their family and social relationships are disrupted or destroyed, they suffer injury or ill-health.

Every humanitarian crisis is different and the needs of the directly affected – including their information and communication needs that can be met by broadcasting by television, radio or social media – are different. However, there are principles guiding communication for directly affected populations, content and broadcasting formats, which are common to many circumstances. This chapter looks at the principles and content, and at format ideas.

There are two guiding principles for this kind of communication, which might be lost sight of in the urgency of a crisis, but which are important if the impact of the communication is to be maximized.

Communication for, not about, affected populations

Often, humanitarian agencies and, sometimes, affected people themselves see any kind of broadcasting as a route to addressing the wider world. So, for example, humanitarian agencies will speak about, or give reports on, their overall achievements, like quantities of food aid distributed to how many families, how many people re-housed in tents, how many children vaccinated. This information is of little value to directly affected people. It lets them know that things are being done to help them, but it is not information they can use. They need to know where and when they can pick up food aid, what they can expect to receive, what the criteria are for receiving food aid or temporary shelter, or the case for the efficacy of vaccination against rumours that it is harmful, and where children can be vaccinated.

Sometimes, directly affected people will use the opportunity of a broadcast interview to make an appeal to the outside world for assistance. If it is a specific appeal, this is useful information to feed back to humanitarian agencies, for members of a diaspora who are watching or listening and for other members of the affected population who can respond. However, if it is a general appeal, again, it is not useful information for the main audience, and broadcasters need to make sure interviewees are briefed on the purpose of the broadcasting and who it is for, so that they know they are mainly addressing people like themselves.

Use the right language or languages

The second principle is that communication is in a language or languages that the affected population can understand. The Translators Without Borders report on information dissemination during the West African Ebola epidemic in 2014, cited in Chapter 3, showed that some humanitarian agencies did not appear to understand this issue, with substantial negative impact.[1] As has been said, experience shows, too, that 'getting the information out there' is not a reason for broadcasting in a language that many in the audience do not understand. For most listeners, it is not information that is being 'got out there', it is blah, blah, blah. Sometimes, humanitarian agencies, especially if they have something important to announce, will only allow an interview in a language, usually English, which many in the audience will not understand, because they want the matter accurately represented. In this case, the broadcaster needs to explain the language situation and the need for the audience to understand.

Apart from the immediate impact of a station broadcasting irrelevant information or information in a language many in the audience cannot understand, which is wasted airtime, there is a more damaging impact. The credibility of the station among its target audience will quickly become undermined, as populations affected by crisis have better things to do than listen to irrelevant or incomprehensible broadcasting, and so are likely to quickly stop watching or listening at all.

Other key principles

Understanding the local situation

International staff need to take time to understand the local social and political situation they are working in. The Listening Project's report, *Time to Listen*, published in 2012,[2] was largely about the impact of material aid, but many of its findings apply equally to communication and information aid. The report came up with this shocking finding.

> Although people want improved security and political stability, they see that aid can worsen conflict and increase tensions among groups. Many countries where aid is given have experienced wide-scale violence, sometimes over extended periods. In every location where the Listening Project visited, people talked about the effects of international assistance on the likelihood of conflict in their areas. In all but one country, people said that international aid over time had introduced or reinforced tensions among groups and that, cumulatively, it had increased the potential for violence and/or fundamental divisions within their societies.
>
> People say that for outsiders to avoid exacerbating conflict (and, even more importantly, to recognize opportunities to support existing systems that enable cooperation and joint problem solving), aid providers must learn about local political and social dynamics. They point out that prepackaged programs and techniques developed in one context translate badly into other local realities. Where schisms exist, international actors must consult with and listen to a range of local views. People observe that current project cycles and procedures do not allocate attention, time, or resources for such consultation. They identify the urgency to distribute resources on a schedule set by donors (often 'too fast') as undermining opportunities for outsiders to understand local social and political dynamics and processes.[3]

Especially in conflict situations, there is the question of what information can be broadcast and what cannot. Decisions about this largely need to be guided by the principle of 'Do no harm'. For example, in South Sudan in 2015, large numbers of people were displaced by conflict, yet only a small percentage turned up at official displacement camps, and the UN did not know where they were, or how they got to their safe havens. It can only be surmised that many people in South Sudan, most of whom have grown up with war, have safer places they can get to. They can follow relatively safe routes to get them there. If a radio station found out where some of these places are and how to get to them, should they broadcast the information to help those who do not have it?

Clearly, to reveal this information on air would potentially put some displaced communities at risk of attack, as hostile groups could listen to the station as well.

A media refuge

A BBC World Service Trust *Handbook* on broadcasting for refugees, from 2004, suggested:

> The tone should be warm and welcoming, slower paced than the news, and without strident messages. The programmes need to be an audio refuge, showing concern and offering help for the individual listener, emphasising that this is time exclusively for them. The programme is firmly on the side of refugees. Empathy is an essential element, and so is humour.[4]

This is probably a good starting point, especially the idea of a media refuge. For the use of humour in humanitarian programmes, see below.

The broadcasting should contain a balance of practical, positive information, support and respite and relevant news, and it should help affected people regain some control over their lives, with testimony from, and portrayals of, affected people who are taking steps to regain control. Mental health professionals say that such a balance can have a powerful psychosocial impact.

Broadcasting formats should remain consistent, offering an element of predictability and stability for people whose lives are full of uncertainty. This, of course, does not mean that content should be repetitive and predictable. Also, as the situation of the affected population changes, the content of the programmes needs to change, and that may well require changes of format. If the production team or teams lack skills, they should be receiving training as the broadcasting goes on, and that should allow for more sophisticated and more engaging formats, too.

Inclusion

This principle needs to be at the heart of a humanitarian communication response, as, for example, the needs of women and men in crisis situations can often be sharply different. The information and communication needs of different groups among the affected population should have been identified by the rapid needs assessment (MIRA) and subsequent assessments (see Chapter 13 for a full discussion of these assessments). One of the most straightforward ways of ensuring these needs are met is by reporters seeking out members of different groups who are taking steps to regain control of different aspects of their lives, and getting them on air. The needs of the old, and those with disabilities, require particular attention, as they are often among the most marginalized. In a displacement crisis caused by conflict, they can be the ones left behind, quite literally, in the urgency of flight. They can even end up on the other side of a front line from the rest of their community. As mentioned before, the Age and Disability Capacity Programme (ADCAP) provides useful guidelines.[5] Children will almost certainly need special programming to meet their particular needs, and such programming can offer important psychosocial support for the adults around the children. (See Chapter 18.)

Rapid response to changing needs

The principle of rapid response to changing needs is key. Unlike many parts of a humanitarian response, communication can respond quickly and nimbly to changes in the situation of affected populations. Agility, the capacity to understand changing circumstances and to respond appropriately and quickly, is especially crucial to humanitarian communication in conflict, where situations can change rapidly and unpredictably. (See below.)

The phases of humanitarian response

In all emergencies, there is a process of change in the situation of those affected. In the aftermath of natural disasters, this tends to be reasonably predictable, and has been defined as a set of phases.

Natural disaster

1. Relief phase, immediately after the disaster: the priorities of the humanitarian response are saving lives and keeping illness and injury to a minimum, while at the same time rapidly establishing the needs of the affected communities and identifying the communities' own recovery initiatives that the response can build on.
2. Early recovery phase: the priorities for the humanitarian response are sustaining the affected communities on a day-by-day basis, with medical assistance, emergency shelter and food aid.
3. Recovery phase: affected communities have shelter, regular food supplies and clean water. The humanitarian response priorities are on re-establishing social institutions, like schools and hospitals, and such utilities as were in existence begin to be repaired.
4. Rehabilitation phase: the humanitarian priorities are focused on the rebuilding of livelihoods and the social fabric, as permanent housing begins to be rebuilt.

Conflict

It is possible to set out a similar set of phases for populations affected by conflict.

1. Attempts at reconciliation between communities are made before violence breaks out.
2. Relief phase: violence impacts and affected populations are trapped within zones of violence or are victims of violence; populations are displaced – by accident or design – and on the move. Affected populations need immediate relief aid.

3. Early recovery phase: camps are established, humanitarian aid is delivered to affected, but not displaced, populations; displaced people arrive in camps or settle elsewhere; host communities are affected.
4. Recovery phase: displacement becomes prolonged, displaced communities – either in camps or elsewhere – have shelter, food supplies and clean water, as they had prior to displacement, and children are receiving an education at least as good as that they were receiving before displacement.

However, conflict is extremely unpredictable, and situations can change enormously, very suddenly. Armed groups and military forces often use surprise as a weapon, or when tension is high and a single shooting incident, for example, can trigger a much wider battle. Such events can cause subsequent waves of displacement, so that the humanitarian response cycle has to start all over again.

Equally, life in a displacement camp or a Protection of Civilians (PoC) site does not always follow a progressive course towards settlement and calm. In some cases, living conditions in such sites and camps can deteriorate over time, so the idea of a recovery phase does not exist.

Displacement can be very prolonged. The longest displacement currently going on is that of Palestinians, many of whom have been refugees since 1948. Many conflicts are very prolonged. In South Central Somalia, there has been conflict since 1991 and, in South Sudan, conflict has continued, on and off, since 1955.

The pattern of a humanitarian response – including humanitarian communication – is far less certain in conflict situations.

Conflicts do come to an end, and so, to add to the four phases set out above, there are two further phases:

5. Reconciliation and rebuilding phase: a peace process gets under way.
6. Settlement phase: displaced communities return and resettle or take up permanent settlement elsewhere; a justice process gets under way.

For the purposes of this book, this chapter will look at humanitarian communication for the early stages of a conflict and its humanitarian consequences, which may run into a few years. The longer term, where communication plays a role in peace processes, returnee processes and justice processes, is looked at in Section 4 on Empowerment and Engagement.

Capacity building

As discussed in Chapter 9 on the five lessons learned from the Ebola crisis, capacity building for local production teams is an essential principle of humanitarian broadcasting. The range of formats proposed below does not need to be used from the start of emergency broadcasting, but can be introduced as the skill and confidence of the team in handling different formats progresses. Fortunately, it is only in the later stages of the crisis – particularly at the rebuilding stage – that the full range of formats is needed. While all of the different channels discussed in Chapter 16 will require slightly different programming formats, the basics of the programming are likely to remain much the same. For example, as explained in the last chapter, a slot on an international broadcaster is likely to be a dedicated half hour, using a magazine format of six or seven items, each with a different format. On a dedicated local radio station, short programme items will be interwoven with music and personal messages, but the items could be much the same.

A format for a 30-minute daily humanitarian magazine programme

This format is put forward as a starting point, to be adapted as the series continues and audience feedback is received. The format should be relatively easy and quick to produce and get on air, while (depending, of course, on the content) having the possibility of being high-quality and engaging. It should offer a good balance of practical, positive and useful information, support and respite. The format is highly flexible, and can be adapted rapidly as circumstances change.

(More information on the production of some items is dealt with in greater depth in Chapter 7.)

Menu

This is a list of the items in the programme, illustrated with one or two short clips of between 10 and 15 seconds each. The aim is to make the programme sound very inviting for a range of listeners (45 seconds).

Testimony

This is a slot offering psychosocial support for affected populations. It consists of a monologue or one-to-one interview with an individual from the affected population, talking about some personal, positive experience that has come out of the disaster or conflict. It should offer support by validating listeners' experience and showing their connectedness and that they are not alone. Ideally, it may encourage listeners to talk to each other about their experience (2 minutes).

If possible, interviews can be conducted in a way that makes it possible for the answers to the reporters' questions to be edited into a monologue. This can usually be done posing questions in a form starting, 'Tell me about …' rather than in an actual question form. This format helps to keep the focus on the individual and their experience. If this cannot be done, then the slot can be a one-to-one interview.

In recording the interview, the reporters need to explain that the audience are people like the interviewee and in similar circumstances, and need to help the interviewee lead the interview rather than just responding to questions.

Over time, the choice of interviewees should reflect the diversity of the affected population.

If the presenter is sharing the experience of the interviewee and the affected population, then they can comment on the testimony, but if they are not in the same situation, it is probably better not to comment.

News for affected communities

This gives reliable, up-to-date information that is of practical use to the affected population (2 minutes). It could be aid information, on distribution of food, medicines, drinking water and shelter, or on where and when medical assistance can be accessed. It could include news of imminent threats, like disease outbreaks, with the symptoms and measures that can be taken to avoid infection or to treat it if someone becomes infected. The news should include information on the changing situation in the wider context and in specific localities, especially any progress in rehabilitation and reconstruction, if appropriate. Challenging unfounded rumours with provably accurate and reliable information is a key function of this slot.

Production teams need to remember, all the time, that this is news *for* the affected population, not about them. Many news sources will want to tell a wider audience about what they are doing for the affected population, but this is not appropriate for that population themselves. They need information that is practical and of use. It is easy, especially for inexperienced reporters, to be led by such sources.

Main topic

This provides information for the affected populations that they can immediately use to improve their situation and lives; it may even save lives. If possible, the choice of topic should be led by the audience. This does not necessarily mean directly asking what topics they would like, but working out their priorities from feedback and messages sent in. The topics and format will vary widely, from a one-to-one interview with an official, after which affected communities receive aid intended for them, to items for rebuilding livelihoods, or on health issues, for example (4–6 minutes).

The content should be practical, and based on the circumstances of the affected communities. However, it is important that, if the item suggests any action on the part of members of the affected population, the production team are sure that they have the material means to carry out the action. The item is likely to be more effective if it is built around voices from the affected population.

Entertainment

This is a brief period of respite for the audience, either a song, a piece of comedy (see below), a one-off story reading or a serial reading (3–4 minutes).

There is then a series of optional slots that may be included, depending on their relevance to the circumstances of the affected population. They may feature in every programme, or alternate. Decisions on these issues will depend on the information and communication needs assessment, and on subsequent feedback and requests from the affected populations. They can also be guided by observation. For example, in the Philippines, after Typhoon Haiyan, in some areas it was clear from the widespread destruction of the extensive coconut palm plantations, and the visibility of wrecked fishing boats, that a strong emphasis on information about rebuilding and alternative livelihoods would be necessary.

Health

This gives practical information on maintaining health in new circumstances. Again, if possible, the topic should reflect priorities expressed by the audience. Again, too, the production team need to sure that the population have the material means for any health measures suggested. If, for example, the item is on the correct use of mosquito nets, then the team need to know that the affected population have nets (4 minutes).

Family reunification

This involves appeals for contacts, and, where possible, stories of successful reunifications (2 minutes).

Shelter

Information on shelter will vary significantly, depending on the situation and the stage of the humanitarian response. It may be on availability of emergency shelter materials and how best to use them, or, at a much later stage, after a natural disaster, rebuilding of permanent homes (4 minutes).

There are often other topics related to shelter, when the population is living in unfamiliar circumstances, like tents or other emergency shelter. These are particularly to do with safety, like fire risk or the safe disposal of rubbish, for example. Items could also cover economics, like comparing the purchase and running costs of different kinds of emergency lighting between solar-powered, battery-powered, candles or oil lamps, or the sustainable gathering of firewood.

Involving members of affected communities in the programmes as they attempt to tackle shelter issues has been a useful approach in the past. They are either working things out for themselves or discussing what they are doing with an expert, so that they can ask questions for clarification, and discuss particular difficulties they are facing, such as budgeting, in order to work out possible solutions (see Figure 17.1).

Livelihoods

After a natural disaster and during conflict, livelihoods are frequently destroyed, as assets are devastated and economic networks disrupted or people are forced to move away from their land, assets and economic networks (4 minutes).

Figure 17.1 *A householder repairing his house after Typhoon Haiyan talks to a Radyo Bakdaw journalist about what he is doing*

Of course, aid is often provided by the humanitarian response, but it is sometimes inadequate and does not last for ever. In addition, long-term dependency on aid can have negative impacts on confidence and self-esteem, and as the *Time to Listen* report shows, it can lead to tension and conflict.[6] Being able to earn your own living, and, therefore, to be much more in control, can have an important psychosocial impact. In communication for development, broadcasting has been shown to have a real impact on listeners' livelihoods, and it can achieve the same in humanitarian settings.

There is likely to be a considerable difference between the needs of someone displaced by conflict trying to re-establish a livelihood and someone affected by a natural disaster. A displaced person is likely to have very few existing assets, and, unless his or her economic network fled to the same place, little in the way of an economic network. However, individuals have created new livelihoods for themselves, when displaced.

Zakira was a girl from Kabul, in Afghanistan, whose family fled to Pakistan:

It is really painful to become a refugee. I can't describe it, really, I don't want to remember. We didn't have any money to rent a house so we decided to learn a skill to earn some money so that we could live a better life.

The whole family started to learn embroidery. At the beginning our pieces didn't sell well, but as we became more experienced, people began to appreciate our work in the market and many started to buy it, in fact, we could make good money out of it.

We learned this skill to make life easier and it worked. Now we have a house, which we built, and it is really wonderful. We have a much better life now. I am sure when we go back we'll make good money out of this skill.[7]

An individual affected by a natural disaster is more likely to have some assets, even if severely damaged, and an economic network that is disrupted but not destroyed. It is likely that such an individual will be looking to rebuild his or her former livelihood, when someone displaced by conflict may well be looking for an alternative livelihood. This is not always the case, though. In the Philippines, the coconut plantations destroyed by Typhoon Haiyan would take years to become productive again, and so, there, there was an urgent need for alternative livelihoods.

There are, though, other issues to do with rebuilding livelihoods that are likely to be common to both settings. For example, a key factor in rebuilding a livelihood is making the best possible use of any assets owned. So, for example, it is possible to teach money management through broadcast communication, that is, budgeting, saving and investment, even when the amounts of money are very small indeed.

A series of items on this topic is likely to be more effective if it is based round the experience of those affected, because only they know, in detail, the situation they are in, and some of them, at least, will be assessing livelihoods possibilities. External experts are going to be approaching the issues without full knowledge of the situation on the ground. The positive contributions such experts could make might be to reveal how existing assets can be exploited – for example, the economic value that can be retrieved from fallen trees in a flattened plantation. The ideal interviewees are people who have begun to make their own, new, livelihoods.

Comedy

The programmes in a number of humanitarian series have ended with a short comedy slot, with the comedy often arising from a character rejecting one of the key points made in the programme (1 minute).

The slot has been done by either a single voice or a small group of performers. It has usually followed a set formula with returning characters. These might be:

- a husband and wife, in which the husband thinks the radio is telling him nonsense
- two friends, one of whom disrupts the humanitarian response for his own ends, in different ways in each episode
- a single voice character explaining his, completely wrong, understanding of a key point in the programme

A slot of this kind can be very engaging, if it is well done. It is respite, it can give some kind of perspective on the situation – by, for example, satirizing the selfish use of humanitarian resources, or satirizing commonly held rumours, myths or prejudices. It can stimulate conversation among listeners about the point being made in the programme, which is a useful learning technique. (See Chapters 2 and 25, and *Training Module J1: An exploration of how people learn*, in Section 6, on the value of talk in learning.)

Where this format might be used

This suggested format might be on an international broadcaster, or where airtime is being taken in an arrangement with a commercial local station, where there is a dedicated time for humanitarian programming each day, every few days or each week. It could be a podcast, or individual items could be on social media.

Varying the format for other communication contexts

However, on a dedicated humanitarian station, or on a commercial station that has chosen to give a lot of airtime to humanitarian issues, the same slots can be distributed among other content, particularly music, over a longer, more relaxed period. So, for example, what has been done in the past is that a dedicated humanitarian station has had one hour every weekday with a theme of livelihoods, so that, during that hour, all the items other than music would be, in some way, related to rebuilding livelihoods. Most programmes ended with a long interview with someone related to livelihoods, either from government or from a humanitarian agency, and, from the beginning of the themed hour, listeners were asked to text in their questions for that person.

Handling emotion interviewing in a humanitarian context

Interviewing members of affected populations can be emotional for reporters and for interviewees. Reporters need to have plans for how to deal with this, probably with a strategy agreed with the editor, to protect themselves and the interviewee.

Empathy matters, but to become involved in the interviewee's emotions is probably not helpful. If an interview has been emotional, the reporter should make sure the interviewee has recovered their composure and is feeling settled. If, during the course of an interview, the interviewee starts to become upset, the reporter should ask if the interviewee wants to carry on or not, and go with their wishes.

Emotional interviews may be stock in trade for mainstream journalism but, in the context of humanitarian broadcasting, they do not serve a useful function, as the audience are likely to be all too familiar with the emotion being expressed from their own experience.

It is probably useful for reporters always to bear in mind that what they are doing is of benefit to the affected population, and use that to keep out feelings of guilt or of not helping.

Example projects: Communication to combat Covid-19

The pandemic and official reaction

The virus now known as the severe acute respiratory syndrome coronavirus 2 (SARS-CoV-2), which causes the disease called coronavirus disease 2019 (Covid-19), was first announced by the Municipal Health Commission in the Chinese city of Wuhan on 31 December 2019. In March 2020, the World Health Organisation declared that the outbreak of the disease spreading across the world was a pandemic. The first vaccines came into use in December 2020, and although treatments improved over time, in April 2021, there was no cure. By that time, the global number of deaths caused by the coronavirus passed three million.

Governments throughout the world introduced measures to slow the spread of the disease, including: handwashing; people from different households getting no closer than one or two metres away from each other and those with symptoms of the virus going into quarantine. In many countries, 'lockdowns' were introduced, that is, people had to stay at home and could only go out for a few reasons, such as work, essential shopping and exercise. Some of these 'lockdowns' lasted for months.

A survey of communication projects on Covid-19 shows that most are top-down, that is, authorities telling communities what to do, and they often reinforced the communication with laws. There are few examples of two-way communication.

Communication and the slums of the Global South

However, there is one huge group for whom no amount of top-down communication could help in the pandemic. From Brazil to India, millions of people live in 'informal settlements,' more commonly known as slums. According to a rapid study, by Pritha Venkatachalam and Niloufer Memon, published by the Bridgespan Group in July 2020, *Community Engagement to Tackle COVID-19 in the Slums of Mumbai*,[8] in India alone, 100 million people live in slums.

For slum dwellers, most of the advice or instructions given to combat Covid-19 are impossible to follow. Lack of access to reliable, clean water supplies prevents regular handwashing. High population densities and large groups sharing one household make social distancing and the quarantining of those with symptoms very difficult. Casual employment and lack of financial support mean that many slum dwellers cannot obey lockdowns, as they need to go out to work simply to stay alive. Slum dwellers have high rates of the underlying ill-health which makes them more likely to die from Covid-19.[9] As a result, slum dwelling populations have been very badly affected by the pandemic.

In a blog for the International Institute for Environment and Development, Sheela Patel, who has worked with Mumbai's slum dwellers for many years, observes that top-down advice which ignores the realities of slum dwellers' lives also has the impact of making them feel even more ignored and marginalized.[10]

What all this means is that community engagement – two-way communication – is the only route to helping slum dwellers in the pandemic.

The Bridgespan rapid study on Covid-19 in the slums of Mumbai identifies four reasons why this is the case:

- Each slum area is unique, and residents have widely different access to different resources. For example, some slum-dweller communities have very few toilets in comparison with their populations. In some, residents have access to local, regular employment while in others, people depend on casual work, and so have earned little during the pandemic.[11] These factors mean that different two-way communication between organizations providing support and communities being helped is essential. This is because, for example, different advice on behaviour change needs to be given depending on the different circumstances of communities.
- Communities are the best people to identify their different needs, and how those needs and their priorities change over time, so that appropriate support can be delivered.[12] The study points out that, during the pandemic, community needs change quickly, and the response has to be nimble and flexible. Two-way communication makes this possible.[13]
- Building trust between the community and health service providers is essential, and can only happen if support providers can identify people the community will trust. (Trust is needed, for example, to overcome unwillingness to get tested for Covid-19, or to reveal disease status, because of a fear of stigma or of losing income when in quarantine.) Only two-way communication can provide that information. Two-way communication can help build trust in many ways. In an example the Bridgespan study gives, local authority support in providing meals at the right time allowed those fasting during Ramadan to break their fasts at the correct time. The study says that this kind of caring initiative helps build trust.[14]
- Crisis-hit communities can be very resourceful in finding their own solutions. (As was discussed earlier in this section, in the example of Radyo Bakdaw, the community station set up after Typhoon Haiyan devastated parts of the Philippines.) The same is true of slum-dweller communities. The Bridgespan study gives examples of community volunteers setting up food kitchens, when their community was particularly hard hit by the pandemic. Again, as has been discussed earlier, involving communities in a crisis response brings better, more enduring solutions when they are locally owned.[15]

The Bridgespan study identifies another vital factor in an effective pandemic response, which is the provision of information in languages which are readily understood by the communities being helped.[16] (This is an issue in all humanitarian responses, as discussed in Chapters 1 and 3.) There can often be a wide range of languages spoken in slum-dweller communities, and two-way communication is essential if language needs are going to be met effectively.

Strong evidence of the success of the community engagement, or two-way communication, approach is shown in some results. This approach has enabled coordination between government, NGOs and the communities, and in one Mumbai slum-dweller community, by the end of July 2020, the number of cases of Covid-19 fell from over 2,500 to 142.

The Bridgespan Group is not alone in its view. The value of two-way communication in slums is endorsed by Slum Dwellers International (SDI), a network of community organizations of slum dwellers across thirty-two countries, which has existed since 1996. A blog – *Building Inclusive and Resilient Societies in Unpredictable Times*,[17] by Sheela Patel, a co-founder of SDI, and Deon Nel – makes many of the same points as the Bridgespan study. The writers emphasise the importance of trust, especially in challenging misinformation on the pandemic. They endorse two-way communication by giving some examples of how it works in practice. For example, they discuss the way grassroots organisations and local leaders act as channels of communication between the community and authorities, especially in targeting the right kind of support where it is most needed.

Training agendas and materials

Suggested agendas and materials for training in topics relevant to this chapter can be found in Section 6:

Module J1: An exploration of how people learn
Module J4: Humanitarian communication

Communication for children directly affected by crisis

This chapter provides detailed, practical advice and information on producing broadcast communication for children, including guidance on how to involve children in the material, as interviewers as well as interviewees, and the measures needed to safeguard any children involved.

Portraying children

… while reports of starving children or overcrowded camps for displaced persons may be dramatic, they do little to support efforts for long-term reconstruction and reconciliation. (From *The Impact of Conflict on Children* by Graca Machel, UN 1996i).[1]

It is commonplace for media coverage of humanitarian crises to focus on a child or on children, very often as helpless victims. They are not often seen as people with anything interesting to say. What children do to help in humanitarian crises is not often seen but, in such crises, children are often keeping themselves alive and healthy, are helping their siblings and, sometimes, even their parents. According to the BBC World Service, five years after the genocide in Rwanda, there were 60,000 child-headed households.[2] In the Philippines, after Typhoon Haiyan in 2013, research showed that children wanted to participate more in preparedness for future typhoons. Communication for children in humanitarian crises needs to be based on showing respect and reflecting their active participation.

Why should there be special programming for children in humanitarian emergencies?

There are several strong reasons for the media to address children as a particular group in humanitarian emergencies. These include the number of children caught up in crises; children's rights, as set out in the UN Convention on the Rights of the Child; the ethical principle of inclusion; and the positive impact on the adults around them of children engaged in constructive and educational activity.

So, in the aftermath of a disaster or in a displacement emergency, it is very important to address some programming to children. Children almost always form a high percentage (often more than half) of refugees. (In 2014, according to UNHCR, 51 per cent of all refugees in the world were children.[3]) Displaced children are extremely vulnerable, subject to more threats than adults, and their needs are significantly different from those of adults. However, making programmes for children places different demands on production teams, and involving children in programme making needs great care. As with the chapter on communication for adults affected by crisis, this chapter proposes a programme format that will enable emergency broadcasting to start quickly and to be effective from the beginning.

Rights

There are four articles of the UN Convention on the Rights of the Child (UNCRC) that humanitarian communication can help to apply in the aftermath of disasters and in conflict. In summary, they are:

- Article 12 The child's right to express their views on matters affecting them.
- Article 13 The child's right to freedom of expression, in any medium, including art.
- Article 17 The child's right to receive information and other material through the mass media, *especially those aimed at the promotion of his or her social, spiritual and moral well-being, and physical and mental health.* This article puts a significant responsibility on mass media to produce broadcasting for children in humanitarian emergencies, when a child's well-being and physical and mental health are under particular threat.
- Article 28 The child's right to education. Communication can play a significant role in providing effective education during emergencies and at later stages, when it can help children and young adults who have missed out on education because of conflict. (This chapter will cover establishing some level of education through communication in the early stages of an emergency, while the longer-term work will be discussed in the section on distance learning.)

The UNCRC is the most widely ratified of all UN conventions, and it has been ratified by all the governments in the world, except one. For the purposes of using media to support children in humanitarian crises, what the UNCRC does is provide a valuable framework for the design and delivery of broadcasting for children.

Inclusion

In a humanitarian response, all needs should be met in an equitable way, and that includes information and communication needs. Children's information and communication needs have to be addressed in ways that are quite different from the ways adults' needs are met.

Focuses adults on the future

Particularly in displacement crises, but in any humanitarian emergency, there is widespread despondency and sadness among affected populations. If children are engaged in learning activities, it can bring a focus on the future and hope to the adults around them, and this can be important psychosocial support.

Background

As has already been said, in any humanitarian crisis, children and adolescents are a large proportion of those affected, and sometimes they have been the majority. Particularly in displacement crises, support and family structures often collapse as populations flee. As a result, children and adolescents are often unaccompanied or they can find themselves in positions of responsibility for which they are wholly unprepared, and when their own development is still under way. In many crises, child-headed households become common. This can mean that the relationships that support the child's physical, emotional, moral, cognitive and social development have broken down, potentially with significant physical and psychological impacts.

Conflict and displacement

The Impact of Armed Conflict on Children[4] is a report by Graca Machel for the United Nations in 1996, and still regarded as very important more than twenty years later. Machel showed that children are not just caught up in the crossfire but are deliberately targeted. They are vulnerable to genocide, military recruitment, gender-related violence, torture and exploitation on a massive scale.

Military recruitment

Displaced children are particularly vulnerable to military recruitment, and a second UN study, ten years later, showed both how far displacement camps are targets of recruiters, and the range of motives for children and adolescents to join armed groups, from economic necessity to ideology.[5] Both boys and girls are recruited.

Economic exploitation

In times of economic hardship, caused by either conflict or natural disaster, children and adolescents can be more vulnerable to economic exploitation, in the form of sometimes hazardous child labour, or trafficking.

Health risks

Particularly when they are displaced, but also after natural disasters, children often face serious health risks. In conflict, children are particularly vulnerable to landmines and the explosive remnants of war. They are often involved in activities like collecting firewood, which takes them farther and farther afield. Bombs can often look like toys, or are just interesting-looking objects. In some cases, retreating armed forces have left enticing looking items as booby traps, to deliberately target children and adolescents.

In changed circumstances, either in conflict or after a natural disaster, disease can be a serious threat, and children are particularly vulnerable. In circumstances where there is no clean water, and sewage and rubbish disposal services are either non-existent or have broken down, disease becomes a major problem.

Thus, children and adolescents are highly vulnerable, depending on the circumstances, to exploitation, trafficking, military recruitment and transactional sex. In many conflicts, they are deliberately targeted. They are more vulnerable than adults to disease and to hazards like landmines and the explosive remnants of war, especially when they are on the move or displaced to somewhere unfamiliar.

Children in natural disasters

The impact of a natural disaster on children and adolescents is likely to be less than that of conflict and displacement. However, they may well have suffered loss – of friends, family members, home or possessions. If they were going to school before the disaster, it is very likely their education will be disrupted. Even when children are not displaced and remain in their communities, they can be more vulnerable after a disaster, as poor temporary living conditions and economic hardship can lead to child trafficking and increased levels of physical abuse. They will probably be very frightened, and fearful of the future. Being out of school does not just disrupt education but it does make children and adolescents more vulnerable. In a report published one year after the Nepal earthquake in 2015, Plan International reports that 'Children who aren't in school are at increased risk of exploitation, trafficking and child marriage.'[6]

Communication for support

These periods of disruption and increased vulnerability can be very prolonged. In the same report, Plan International says that, one year after the earthquake, no schools had been repaired or replaced, and no repair or construction work had even started. In conflicts, the periods can be far longer.

During such periods, humanitarian communication cannot claim to be able to solve all of these issues. However, it can help children and adolescents by providing psychosocial support and entertainment, help them participate in improving the lives of their communities and help them protect themselves and handle life in very changed circumstances. It can also provide learning activities and experience to partly offset the lack of schooling.

Active participation

A key factor that communication can build on is the greater participation of children and adolescents in social and adult life. Some children are forced by circumstance to participate more, to help their families economically or to take on adult responsibilities. There is also evidence that children and adolescents want to participate more. For example, in 2014 an Internews survey in the Philippines, after Typhoon Haiyan, showed that a high priority for children and adolescents was greater participation in helping families and communities be better prepared for future disasters. Initiatives like the work of Child to Child try to build on greater participation, and humanitarian communication should always try to provide motivation, structure and guidance for children to be active and participating.

Series format

All targeted humanitarian communication should be in series, if it is broadcast, and needs to be regularly at the same time, and as frequently as possible. This way it provides a strand of routine, continuity and, if possible, progress. For children, this is even more important. Educationalists and child psychologists think that children need routine in their lives, and a regular broadcast for them will provide at least an element of routine. Furthermore, a daily 15-minute broadcast that gives ideas, structure and motivation for activities could provide several hours a day of organized activity and routine for children. This could be valuable for their social and cognitive development and offer an element of protection, as children are engaged and visible and less accessible for recruiters and traffickers.

In mainstream children's broadcasting, and especially in educational broadcasting, different series are aimed at highly specific age groups, often as precise as two years: 5- to 7-year-olds, for example. This is partly to fit the demands of educational curricula but mainly because children's needs and tastes change quickly as they grow up.

In humanitarian communication, especially at the beginning, it is unlikely that such specific targeting will be feasible. The choice of age groups to address will depend on the information and communication needs assessment, which should show the predominant age groups. Initially, production teams should aim at an age range above the average age in the target audience, as younger children are more likely to listen to programmes aimed at an older age range than older children are to listen to programmes for younger ones. As time goes on, teams should aim at separate broadcasting for different age ranges.

The approach of communication for children

Programmes for children need to be child centred; that is, they need to be in the best interests of children, to be on the side of the children, and to portray things in the way children see them. This can be a problem for a team of experienced reporters and producers, who are used to making broadcasting *about* children and not *for* them. Indeed, in one training in the past, a team produced a programme for children that referred throughout to children as 'them' and 'they'. The child as victim is so much a part of the stock in trade of mainstream media reporting on humanitarian crises that it takes a substantial shift of perspective for reporters experienced in such work to portray children as proactive and positive. In so many news reports, a child is mute or crying, and, if anyone speaks, it is an adult speaking for the child.

Adult reporters need to learn how to listen to what children are saying, and programming for children should include a lot of children's voices. An alternative approach, or one that can be used in parallel with adult reporters, is to train older children to be reporters themselves. This approach has several advantages. It means that programming is, more or less, automatically child centred, that listening or viewing children are given valuable role models, and younger children are probably more likely to talk to an older child than to an adult, especially if the adult is a stranger.

Increasingly, programmes for children are being presented by children. For example, UNRWA, the UN body responsible for Palestinian refugees in the State of Palestine, Lebanon, Syria and Jordan, makes an English teaching series presented by four children who are under 10 years old, and they present it in a foreign language.

A production team working with children, either as reporters or interviewees, need to follow a strict code of conduct to avoid putting the children at risk or actually causing them harm. A suggested code of conduct is later in this chapter.

Psychosocial support for children

There is very useful information on strategies and activities for psychosocial care in *The Psychosocial Care and Protection of Children in Emergencies: Teacher Training Manual,* published by UNICEF in 2009.[7] This manual is for training teachers who are in day-to-day, face-to-face contact with children, and so it goes far beyond what broadcasting can achieve. However, some of the activities proposed below are based on those suggested in this manual, as a way of helping children with at least some support, when there is none coming from other sources. There is no suggestion that what is proposed here for broadcasting can in any way replace, or be a substitute for, psychosocial support from trained professionals.

A format for a 15-minute humanitarian children's programme

Programmes need to be highly entertaining and engaging, with lively – but not patronizing – presentation, and music is very helpful. As discussed above, they should provide stimulus and structure for activities far beyond the broadcast time.

This is a suggested format for a daily 15-minute radio or television programme for a non-dedicated station. If the broadcasting is for a dedicated humanitarian community station, then the same items could be in a much longer slot, with a lot of music in between. However, the slot would still need to be identified as one for children, so that children know this is time for them and it can become part of their routine.

Menu

This is a list of the items in the programme, illustrated with one or two short clips of between 10 and 15 seconds each. The aim is to make the programme sound very inviting for a range of listeners (45 seconds).

News for children

This is news of the local situation and the humanitarian response that has particular relevance for children. It might well include reports by child reporters on, for example, initiatives by children or for children, including those prompted by items in earlier programmes (1 minute).

Child reporters can work in groups, particularly if they are interviewing an adult. The reporters will need to be selected and trained by the production team. Such training, and the safeguarding associated with it are discussed later in this chapter.

Interactive slot

This comprises material sent to the programme in response to items in earlier programmes, which might be messages or accounts of events, or might be more extensive pieces of work sent in response to an invitation to send in material by the programme (2.5 minutes).

Entertainment slot

To keep production effort to a minimum, especially in the early stages of broadcasting, this can be a song, which is culturally appropriate – for example, from the place of origin of the displaced, if the audience are displaced. As time goes on and the production team become more skilled and are more into a routine, children should become involved. It could remain a song slot, but with children recorded requesting a particular song, and explaining why they want to hear it (2.5 minutes).

According to the UNICEF manual, singing familiar songs can be useful psychosocial support.[8] At the most basic level, the presenter can urge listening or viewing children to join in with the song as it is played. At a more complex level, the presenter could offer a set of simple movements for children to do as they sing the song, taking the children through the movements first, and then, as the song plays, reminding them what to do at each stage. The song can, of course, be played more than once in the same programme.

As production effort becomes more available, other formats could be used. These might be:

- children telling jokes
- a regular comic drama, in which the same few characters are caught up in situations like ones displaced children are, but with funny outcomes

Story

The story slot can be either just entertainment or it can be used to give important information, or, over time, there can be a mixture of both. They can be simple readings, or can have music and sound effects (3 minutes).

Stories need to be appropriate culturally and for the target age range.

If stories are used to convey information, they will probably need to be specially written, so that they reflect the realities and detail of the situation the listening children are in. Even if the story is an animal fable, for example, it would still need to reflect on the situation. Specially written stories need to be written by experienced children's writers, who are fully immersed in the same culture as the children and who understand well the situation the children are in. Topics need to be chosen on the basis of the information and communication needs assessment. It will also be necessary to look at the wider humanitarian needs assessment, so that an assessment can be made of the resources likely to be available to families, so that children are not asked to do something they have not got the resources to do.

Stories can be useful sources of psychosocial support. One aspect of this, according to UNICEF, is that 'Endings should always be happy.'[9]

A more ambitious approach suggested by UNICEF,[10] and one requiring more organization, which could be undertaken by a station that has established two-way communication with its audience, is either to leave the story unfinished and invite children to send in their own endings, or to end it and ask for alternative ways of ending the story.

> When children are asked to continue the storyline or comment and change something in a character or event, it helps them express their own ideas and emotions without feeling that they are exposing themselves. This is because they can ascribe to another (the fictitious character) emotions and feelings that, in fact, they are having.[11]

A further use of the story slot, which would build on the psychosocial support identified above, is to invite listening children to write their own stories. This could be in the structure of a competition, or it could simply be that some of the stories will be broadcast. Stimulation and motivation could be provided by broadcasting a number of stories written by children, perhaps by children of the station's staff.

Of course, inviting any written material can only be done if a significant proportion of the children are literate, and that needs to be ascertained in advance.

An alternative slot could be a piece of testimony: a child describing a positive development in his or her experience of being displaced.

The story slot can be linked to the activity slot that follows it. If, for example, the story is about older children organizing activities for younger children, then the activity slot can give instructions for how this can be done in reality.

Activity slot

This slot is designed to provide the stimulus and structure of an activity, which will take a child or a group of children an hour or more to achieve (4 minutes).

The choice of topic in the early stages after a disaster or outbreak of conflict will be driven by the humanitarian needs assessment, essentially answering the question, 'What do children need to know how to do at this stage?'

At the early stages, topics will most likely be to do with maintaining health in changed circumstances, and avoiding the risk of injury. At the next stage, activities will most likely be to do with life skills to cope with changed circumstances and to keep safer, such as being more aware of the threats posed by some adults, and how to avoid them or to take action about them, and with psychosocial support, for example, carrying out artistic activities, making toys or organizing sports. At the rebuilding stage, if schools have not been established or re-established, or, if makeshift schools have been established but lack materials and resources, activities could be a programme of emergency education (see the next section.)

Child to Child has published a wide array of activity sheets, mainly focused on health education for children, including some specific to children affected by disaster or conflict. Many of these activities can be conveyed on radio, television or via social media. (In Sierra Leone in 2014, when schools were closed in response to an Ebola epidemic, the Trust adapted their own pre-school education project – *Pikin To Pikin Tok*[12] – for radio broadcasting, which is covered in more detail in the distance learning section of this book.)

The Child-to-Child Resource Book[13] covers: *Child growth and development, Nutrition, Personal and community hygiene, Safety, Recognising and helping children with disabilities, Prevention and cure of disease, Safe lifestyles, Children in difficult circumstances* and *Living and coping with HIV and AIDS.*

For displaced children, there is *Child-to-Child and Children Living in Camps.*[14]

The format of the slot can vary. It can be a simple drama, which raises issues and poses questions, followed by instructions from the presenter on how to carry out a structured activity that will address the issues raised and help children explore the answers to the questions raised.

Another effective format is to record a group of children as they participate in an activity, preferably in a context close to that of the children listening or viewing, and then discuss what they have done and how they did it. Hearing or seeing a group of other children doing the task will give children in the audience more confidence that they can also carry it out. A slot of this kind was, for example, introduced into *Itetero*, a children's television series in Rwanda, produced by The Rwanda Broadcasting Agency and UNICEF, in 2019. (How this slot was produced is discussed in Chapter 22.)

Activities can be one-offs or a series of steps, and could be children making toys for themselves or for younger children, simple scientific experiments, health-promotion, devising a drama, being involved in agricultural activities, or older children organizing sports and other activities for younger children.

A production team should try to select children, as interviewees or reporters, who represent the range of children in the audience, that is, a range which reflects the ages and backgrounds of the children.

A possible code of conduct for teams working with children in communication

Production teams making programmes for children affected by disaster or conflict are very likely to be working with children, as interviewees, reporters, actors or storytellers, for example. Children are far more vulnerable than adults, and special care is needed when working with them.

A production team need to understand the legal situation with regard to working with children in the country, and obtain any required consents from the parents or guardians, or the school.

Any potential risks to a child or children, associated with the interview or work, should be assessed. This assessment would obviously include any risks of physical harm or risks of disease. It should also include the circumstances the child is in to assess risks of abduction or of other threats from adults, like potential retribution if they reveal certain information, or of being patronized or intimidated.

A journalist should take special care not to arouse unwanted emotion in a child. This could occur through thoughtless questioning of children who have been through distressing experiences, or clumsily asking them to look at a situation that affects them adversely but over which they have no control.

If a child becomes emotional, the interviewer should show understanding of the emotion and be sympathetic. Children should never be pressed to reveal painful details for the sake of sensation. At the end of an interview, the interviewer must make sure the child is calm and happy.

A journalist should protect themselves from any potential accusation of improper conduct by ensuring they can be seen at all times while working with children.

Children involved in interviews

In order to get the best out of an interview with a child or from a child working as a reporter, there are measures a journalist or producer can take.

Before an interview

It may seem obvious, but a journalist should make sure that the child speaks a language they themselves speak. Children often do not have even a working knowledge of an official language, for example.

Ensure child interviewees are in a position to talk freely, and will not be influenced by adults. It is a good idea to keep other adults away while you are working with children, including parents, teachers or youth workers, because they will often interrupt or try to prompt a child.

Working with groups of children can work better than with individuals, but a journalist needs to manage the discussion so that it is not dominated by some individuals, and that some members of the group are not influenced in what they say by others in the group.

Children can tend to think and talk in rather concrete ways, and they can be less good at abstract talk. So, for example, if the interview is about a particular place, then the best results may come from interviewing the child in that place; or, if it involves talking about an object, it may help to have the object there.

An interview may work better if the questions are quite concrete rather than being abstract. So, for example, rather than asking a displaced child to compare their old life at home with their new life, it may be better if the child is asked to talk through a day at home and then to talk through a day now.

Interview

Rather than going straight into an interview, which some children might find intimidating, it can be worthwhile for a journalist to ask the child or children about themselves, or do more to help the child or children become more relaxed. Journalists have been known, before interviewing a group of children, to play football with them, but less energetic games or warm-ups would have a similar effect.

Setting the scene can help. Again, a child might be intimidated by recording equipment, so describing what it is and what it does, as well as the process the journalist is following and what is going to happen during the interview may help. For children who have never heard themselves before, a journalist might record a little of the child talking and play it back.

It is even more important when interviewing children than it is with adults to avoid closed questions. Children are unlikely to take them as prompts for expansive answers.

Children are generally less articulate than adults, and find it harder to formulate their answers, so talking about the topics of the interview before recording may help a journalist to pick up hints of what the child is trying to say and, from these hints, shape the question during the actual interview to help the child express him or herself more clearly.

For the same reasons, a journalist should allow substantially more time when interviewing a child or children than when interviewing an adult. Children may well be discouraged if a journalist tries to hurry things along by interrupting or correcting them.

It is important to finish an interview session with a child or children so that they are happy and relaxed. Check that no child is frustrated because they have not been able to say what they wanted to say. A journalist could reassure the child or children that he or she has recorded what they wanted and that the children have done well. If it is possible, the journalist could repeat the reassurance to an adult who knows the child or children.

Training child reporters

While production teams or individual reporters will need to work with child reporters on formulating their questions to put to an interviewee, it is very important that the questions come from the child or children themselves. Child reporters should not be ciphers for the production team, asking the team's questions, as the whole purpose of using child reporters is so that programmes show the world from a child's perspective.

Training agendas and materials

Suggested agendas and materials for training in topics relevant to this chapter can be found in Section 6:

Module J5: Training for child journalists
Module J6: Creativity in writing for children

Communication for indirectly affected populations

Communities who are hosts to the displaced

In humanitarian crises, there are often populations who, while not being *directly* affected by the natural disaster or the conflict, are, nevertheless, affected. Most often, these will be populations living in areas displaced people or refugees come to. They are usually known in the humanitarian world as host communities.

Sometimes, a similar situation can arise after a displacement crisis has ended. In this case, it is when people who fled a crisis return home. The community who did not leave during the crisis then become, in effect, a host community to the returnees.

It has been recognized that perceived inequality of treatment between a host community and a displaced or returnee population, in which the hosts believe that the displaced or the returnees are getting a better deal than they are, can be a major cause of problems in this situation. This applies equally to communication, and any communication for the displaced should be matched by communication for hosts.

It has been shown that, especially, broadcasting displaced people talking about their experience can have a significant impact on attitudes among host communities. Broadcasting can help to promote communication between the populations, on issues where the settlement of the displaced is affecting the hosts, for example, environmental damage. It can also help bridge strong cultural differences.

This extract, from a blog written by Brigitte Sins, of International Media Support (IMS), when she was working in Sulamaniyah, in the Kurdish region of Iraq, encapsulates how much indirectly affected communities can be affected in displacement crises. (IDPs are internally displaced people, that is, people who have fled conflict or disaster, but are still within the borders of their own country.)

> After a year of a continuous influx of IDPs from other parts of Iraq into Kurdistan – as well as refugees from Syria – a change is becoming visible. The disaster affected communities are not just to be found within the refugee and IDP groups, now they are found everywhere in the society. These days, the host population is being affected: they have lost a secure and safe environment, jobs and income. The crisis has spread over the society at large.[1]

In some displacement situations, the impact on host communities can be very large. In 2016, for example, according to Amnesty International, 20 per cent of Lebanon's population were Syrian refugees.[2] In the case of Lebanon, as will be seen later, there were no tensions or conflict, but in many displacement situations there are.

Communities who are hosts to returnees

It is this group, those who are receiving people displaced from elsewhere in their own country, or refugees from other countries, who are most often referred to when speaking of host communities. However, there is another group who suffer the same kind of problems but seem to get less attention. These are populations who did not leave their country during conflict, when many others did. After the conflict is over, and a peace process is under way, those who went to other countries start to return, often after many years, assisted by UN agencies, especially UNHCR. As already said, the population who never left are, in effect, a host population to the returning former refugees, and similar tensions can arise.

The Listening Project's report *Time to Listen* came to the conclusion that, in most countries where international assistance is received, local people said that it is likely to increase social tensions and violence. One particular area is when a host community see what is or appears to be preferential treatment given to refugees, returnees or internally displaced people. 'I feel jealous. I don't know why NGOs help [the refugee village] and not our village. The refugee village has electricity; the road is better there, and here it is muddy. It makes me feel they are better than us' (male in a village next to refugee returnees, Cambodia).[3]

In 2004, in what is now South Sudan, I saw a play which was staged by Southern States Radio in the Arts Centre in Juba, the capital, and simultaneously broadcast on the radio. A ceasefire in the very long-running civil war had been declared, and people who had fled the country many years earlier began to return. The play focused on an elderly couple who were eagerly awaiting their children, who had gone to different places, including East Africa and the Persian Gulf.

As the play proceeded, the now grown-up children began to come home. All were very well dressed and carried mobile phones and laptops. Finally, one arrived with a lot of luggage, and the father said he would call the brothers of these returnees to help. Two young men in rags came on to the stage. These were the brothers who had never left. The large audience, mainly made up of those who had never left, erupted with laughter. The play clearly caught exactly how they saw themselves in comparison with the returnees. This was a piece of home-grown communication for a host community. It recognized the tensions but helped to relieve them by being very funny.

There are, then, two different kinds of host population, but both need similar approaches in media helping to support them.

Why broadcast for host communities?

If there are tensions or conflict between a host population and displaced or returnee communities, that is clearly a problem in itself, and can have serious consequences, so needs to be addressed. Communication can play an effective role in that, as will be shown later in this chapter. Just one example here is from an Internews report from 2013 on its humanitarian community radio stations in Chad.[4] It highlights a dispute over water resources between the host population and Darfurian refugees, and describes how one of the stations, Radio Sila, helped to resolve the issue.[5]

There is also a matter of equity: if communication is provided to help displaced or returnee populations through a crisis, then there ought also to be communication for host populations to help them through the crisis.

The context of communication for host populations

The situation surrounding communication for host populations can vary widely and be unpredictable. Any communication for development organization planning to address a host community's communication needs must research carefully so that they understand what the context is.

A report commissioned from the Governance and Social Development Resource Centre (GSDRC) in 2012[6] by the UK government's Department for International Development describes a number of causes of tension and conflict between displaced and host communities. There can be real or perceived inequality of provision by humanitarian agencies, for essential supplies, like water and food, and services like health and education. As the blog, by Brigitte Sins, just quoted did, this report cites evidence that refugees may affect the livelihoods and incomes of people in the host community, and that there can be competition over resources like firewood and water.

However, the GSDRC report adds the caveat that such issues can be exploited by leaders for political purposes. It also adds that there may be social and cultural divides between displaced communities and host communities, and a perception among some host communities that refugees could pose a threat, both from fighters hidden among them and from crime. The UK-based newspaper, the *Daily Express*, in April 2015, quoted the UK Member of the European Parliament (MEP), Nigel Farage, in a debate on European Union refugee policy, as saying:

> But there is a real and genuine threat. When ISIS [so-called Islamic State or Daesh, a violent extremist group in Syria and Iraq] say they want to flood our continent with half a million Islamic extremists, they mean it … Indeed I fear we face a direct threat to our civilisation if we allow large numbers of people from that war-torn region into Europe.[7]

This illustrates the point made by the GSDRC report, and the way in which politics, in this case from two sides, attempts to exacerbate and exploit divisions, in this case, between would-be host communities and refugees.

It is, however, not always the case that there are tensions between host and displaced communities. In a 2014 paper in Forced Migration Review,[8] based on research in Akkar, in northern Lebanon, Helen Mackreath reported that Syrian refugees, largely complete strangers to their hosts, had been taken into the homes of many families, largely without any expectation of any return, and that many Lebanese had lent money to refugees. This, Mackreath reported, was across all strata of Lebanese society. In some cases there was an understanding that the refugees would, at some point, repay their hosts. At the same time, the host community allowed refugees to take part in the informal economy. Mackreath points out that this is not unique, and that there was a precedent in the way that Albanians hosted Kosovar refugees in 1999.

There is no standard context surrounding communication for host communities. Tensions can be caused by real or perceived differences in humanitarian support. There can be real and serious competition between host communities and displaced people for livelihoods or resources. There can be situations where a displacement issue is so politicized that almost every other consideration is hidden. Then, there can be situations where even large influxes of displaced people are accommodated.

The aims of communication for host communities

As with any affected population, a key aim is to use broadcasting as a channel for two-way communication with humanitarian agencies and government, as discussed in Chapter 15, to give host communities a chance to express their needs and have those needs addressed, so that there is equity between the host and the displaced or returnee communities.

To promote communication and interaction between the host and the displaced or returnee communities, focus is required on:

- culturally appropriate mediation, conflict resolution and peacebuilding
- agreement on equitable use of resources, including participatory management of the environment
- mutually supportive development of livelihoods and economic co-existence, including joint enterprises
- enhancement of the quality of life of both host and displaced communities
- fostering cultural interchange between the populations
- communication to help in the integration process, if the situation comes to a point where the displacement is to become permanent

Communication with host communities aims to improve the quality of life experienced by all communities involved by equipping all with accurate knowledge by, for example, providing:

- accurate discussion of the rights of refugees and of internally displaced people, whichever is appropriate to the situation
- accurate information on the numbers of the displaced or returnees and the material support they are receiving
- descriptions of the circumstances the displaced have fled from, preferably using the voices of the displaced
- exploration of the history of displacement and assessing its impact on host communities in the past and elsewhere in the world

Challenges

Host populations will have existing and well-established media outlets, and refugees and displaced people can be an intensely political issue, as has been shown, so humanitarian communication may struggle to cut through and be heard.

Worse, the displacement of populations is often a weapon of war, and, increasingly, the media can be a theatre of war (see Chapter 3). It is, therefore, important for a humanitarian broadcaster to be vigilant that it is not, inadvertently, contributing to the conflict through its communication.

Evidence that communication for host communities works

Two contrasting examples

It has been shown that communication can play a significant role in easing tensions between host and displaced populations. This section takes two, very different, examples: the BBC World Service's *Right to Refuge* series broadcast on the English service and eight other language services, each serving different parts of the world, in 2001; and Radio Sila, one of the humanitarian radio stations in Eastern Chad, set up by Internews, an international media for development organization, between 2005 and 2006, which the INGO ran until 2012.

Right to Refuge: The reach of the global

Increasing respect and dispelling misconceptions

Right to Refuge was a major broadcasting initiative on the BBC World Service. The World Service is the international radio arm of the UK's publicly owned public service broadcaster, the British Broadcasting Corporation (BBC). It broadcasts in English for a global audience, and in a number of other languages for specific areas. *Right to Refuge* was broadcast on the global English service, and on several language services, including French for Africa, Indonesian, Pashto and Serbian. Each of the series on the different services was different, and not simply a translation, because they addressed issues specific to displacements in each region.

The evidence that the series was effective comes from quotes from listeners, in *Refugees: Emergency Broadcasting Handbook.*[9] Many of the quotes reflect that it was the voices of refugees themselves that listeners found persuasive.

> There was a lady who was interviewed, I heard the pain, the agony in her voice as she was talking and her story sounded convincing. These are realities.
>
> (Resident, Lagos, Nigeria)

> The interviews make the programmes more genuine. We heard them talk and naturally it makes you feel more sympathetic to their plight.
>
> (Resident, Lagos, Nigeria)

These quotes show that the interviews increased respect for refugees:

> It sounds convincing. They went straight to the point. They actually talked, that is exactly what it is; not a frame up, not something that is planned ... Wherever I see them, it will make me feel the pain with them and assist them in any way I can.
>
> (Resident, Lagos, Nigeria)

> For me, what touched me most is the willingness of the refugees to put all their experience behind them.
>
> (Resident, Abidjan, Côte d'Ivoire)

> Having heard these things mentioned, we will now know how to cope with refugees from other countries and how to handle them.
>
> (Resident, Lagos, Nigeria)

One quote shows that the programmes had an impact in dispelling misconceptions about the conditions refugees live in:

> I thought that the government fends for them; provides shelter, accommodation and that they are well taken care of. But from this programme, I am able to see that life is not a bed of roses even for the refugees at camp.
>
> (Resident, Lagos, Nigeria)

These programmes were made several years ago, and there was no established channel for dialogue between the radio station and host communities, but they do illustrate that such programmes, based on the voices of displaced people, can have a significant impact on the perceptions and attitudes of host communities. (At the time of these programmes, according to the BBC News website, Nigeria had a serious problem of populations internally displaced by intercommunal fighting in the centre of the country,[10] as well as hosting refugees from Sierra Leone, Liberia and Chad, according to UNHCR.[11])

Radio Sila: Small and local

Reducing violence by taking notice

Internews' Radio Sila took a quite different approach. As discussed earlier, Radio Sila was a dedicated humanitarian community station, set up in 2007, in the town of Goz Beida, the capital of the Sila region, in south eastern Chad, about 70 kilometres from the border with Darfur. Radio Sila was one of three humanitarian radio stations set up by Internews, to help meet the needs of about a quarter of a million Sudanese refugees from Darfur[12] – who had fled the war between the government of Sudan and Darfuri rebel groups – and about 100,000 Chadians who fled into the region when the fighting spilled over into Chad itself. The radio station had to serve the needs of three groups: the internally displaced Chadians, the Darfuri refugees and the local, host community.

One major advantage of the station reported by UNHCR in the Internews report was that it could reach all of these communities, while UNHCR was restricted to working in the refugee camps.[13] Before the station had been set up, the host community felt ignored by the humanitarian agencies, and there was a high level of violence against women, particularly the refugee women.

According to a report published by Internews in 2013,[14] the station performed a number of functions.

- It provided daily news, letting the refugees know what was happening in the camps and in the region.
- It helped to resolve disputes over resources, like water, through on-air discussions and explanations of how they could be shared.
- The host population learned about the cultures of both the Darfuri refugees and the Chadian internally displaced people.
- The station helped the different communities work out solutions to mutual problems, and promoted peaceful cohabitation between refugees, internally displaced people and the host community.
- It investigated and dispelled potentially dangerous and divisive rumour.
- It made a point of discussing different kinds of violence against women.
- It aired educational public service announcements on issues like the advantages of childbirth in a hospital, rather than at home.
- It carried discussion and phone-in programmes and magazine programmes on a range of topics, including the explosive remnants of war,[15] health and girls' education.[16]
- It held people in authority to account.
- It facilitated better access to services for the population.

An audience survey in 2009 identified language as a crucial issue for Radio Sila, with listeners citing it as a major draw.[17] At that time, according to Internews itself, the station broadcast in Zaghawa (a language common to Chad and Darfur), in Masalit and Fur (both Darfurian languages) and Dadjo (a local Chadian language), as well as French and Arabic. In 2012, it was reported that the station was broadcasting in four languages:[18] Masalit, Dadjo, French and Arabic.

Radio Sila attracted an audience of 70,000 people, who listened at least once a week, in 2009.[19] One advantage of looking at Radio Sila is that it had little direct competition,[20] so that, if listeners attributed achievements to it, it is likely that their attributions were correct. (If there is more than one radio station, listeners can be confused about which station they heard an item on, and can misattribute.)

In the 2013 report by Internews (see above), listeners reported that the situation in 2012 was very different from what it had been in 2006, and attributed some of the change to the radio station. Resolution of a water dispute and greater cultural understanding were attributed to the station.[21] In terms of peacebuilding, the station's manager cited an example when a rumour of intercommunal conflict had started and was growing. The station ended it by accurately reporting that the rumour had started from a job advert, and that there was nothing to the rumour.[22] In terms of holding to account, one of the reporters told of investigating a case at the university, resulting in a staff member being disciplined for sexual harassment. (See Chapter 1 for further benefits attributed to Radio Sila by audience members.)

One of the project's early directors cited the broadcasting of local voices as crucial to the appeal of Radio Sila and the other Internews humanitarian stations. He contrasted it with the top-down approach of the government stations.

Producing communication for indirectly affected communities

As with any humanitarian communication, it is important to conduct an information and communication needs assessment among the host population, either as part of a wider humanitarian and development needs assessment or as a stand-alone process. The communication then needs to be designed to meet the identified needs.

Choosing a broadcasting partner

Unless there is no existing station, and especially in more developed locations, it is probably best to choose a broadcasting partner, which should be a station that is already popular with and trusted by the host community. (This is information that should be found in the information and communication needs assessment.) This matters because, as just discussed, issues concerning refugees can be highly political, and look to become even more so. There can be, therefore, many voices competing for the attention of a host population for political ends, often strident and often with little regard for the truth. Humanitarian broadcasting attempting to bring clarity and accuracy to the issue may therefore struggle to be heard, as has been said before, so it is very important for the broadcasting to be on a popular channel.

High journalism standards and production values

High production values are essential in this kind of broadcasting, so that programmes are highly engaging and can compete with the most strident – not on the same level and with the same techniques, but with high-quality content, edited with care and thought, and with engaging presentation. It is important that all sides are represented, with plenty of voices of the host community, including those who are hostile to refugees, if that is a widely held standpoint among the population.

Very high journalistic standards, especially of accuracy, are also crucial, partly so that the broadcasting is trusted, but also because it may come under heavy scrutiny from those opposed to what it is saying, and the station needs always to be able to stand by its stories. Both the BBC and Internews are organizations that place a strong emphasis on training and high journalistic standards. Radio Sila is credited with having higher standards than other Chadian stations.[23]

Editorial judgements

In practice, what this means is that refugees who are telling their stories need to be credible. As has been said, human interest stories from displaced people or returnees can be a powerful tool in this kind of broadcasting, but such stories can be hard to verify. Any story should be corroborated by independent witnesses, if possible. However, in the chaos of flight from conflict, the chances of eye witnesses being on hand are probably slight, and it is equally unlikely that anyone fleeing, even if they have such a phone, is going to video events. However, it is important that the stories are honest because, if even only one is found not to be, that could seriously undermine the credibility of the broadcasting, especially if there is a hostile political environment.

Stories can be checked with aid agency staff who know the displaced relatively well, but at least one BBC World Service producer has found that taking time over an interview can start to reveal inconsistencies in a story.[24] Any report by a displaced person that is short on detail should be regarded with suspicion, and, similarly, any report by a member of the host community of an encounter with refugees needs to be corroborated and needs to stand up to scrutiny. In this context, as soon as there are doubts about the veracity of a story, it should be discarded.

Editorial judgements need to be made with very great care, as lives could depend on what is said, and it is essential that any tensions between a host population and a displaced or returnee one are not exacerbated by careless editorial decisions.

In both Radio Sila's output and in the BBC's *Right to Refuge*, it was the voices of those directly involved and of local people which engaged and impressed listeners, and having these voices is important for a number of reasons.

First-hand and local voices

First-hand accounts from those directly involved carry more weight than more dispassionate third-party reports. People like to hear the voices of people like themselves, and this was seen as a major attraction of Radio Sila by those managing the project. Radio Sila had refugee reporters – trained by Internews – in most of the refugee camps in the area, who could find appropriate local voices easily.

A further reason for using voices of local people is when a station is engaged in peacebuilding and conflict resolution, as Radio Sila was. The report *Time to Listen* said that people from outside come to peacebuilding with their own approaches, which can exacerbate a local situation, because it ignores or sidelines locally established approaches.

> There is a flawed impression that peacebuilding is new, coming from outside. It is as if we are presented with somebody else's framework and need to adapt it. There are local ways to do this work, and people are capable to take it into their hands. What needs to be supported by outsiders is capacity building and strengthening of communities and local governments.
>
>   (Staff of a local peace and development initiative, the Philippines[25])

All the conflict work had the same mind frame of doing dialogue. This was out of touch with what was needed on the ground. It has given conflict resolution and peacebuilding a bad name. People see it as an initiative that doesn't do what people need. Its meaning and intent have been hijacked. It's not culturally sensitive either ... A lot of peacebuilding work does not understand the local dynamics and, as a result, the intervention does not work. Conflict resolution paradigms may work for the cultures that produced them, but they don't fit here. We need to rethink it. For a while after the war, it was all about dialogue and reconstruction that was naïve. These people are from the same culture and still entered a war.

(PhD student and consultant, Lebanon[26])

Time to Listen recommends outsiders need to take time to understand, and, clearly, involving local people in the process and building on what they already do is a much sounder approach than bringing ready-made 'solutions' from outside.

Training agendas and materials

Suggested agendas and materials for training in topics relevant to this chapter can be found in Section 6:

Module J4: Humanitarian communication
Module J8: Producing a live phone-in discussion programme

Section Three

Distance learning broadcasting

An overview of distance learning broadcasting

This chapter will characterize what a distance learning project in a development context is, and will look at a number of projects to see what it can achieve, and to try to draw out some characteristics that make it effective.

While education is a right enshrined in both the Universal Declaration of Human Rights and the UN Convention on the Rights of the Child, many millions of people either have not received an adequate education or are not currently receiving one. There are myriad reasons for people, mainly women, being out of education, and for some, distance learning could offer a solution.

Distance learning using broadcasting in a development context is significantly different from other forms of distance learning. It is far less personal than distance learning using the internet, where a student sends his or her work to a distant tutor, and they have online seminars. Interaction with a teacher is more likely to be with a local teacher, and it is the broadcasts and other materials that come from a distance. Of course, the spread of social media could make distance tutoring more widely available, but the scale of the demand for basic education in many countries still makes distance tutoring unsupportable.

Who might use distance learning?

There are probably three different kinds of organization that might be interested in developing and running distance learning projects.

- NGOs who specialize in education, often alongside government education departments, may want to provide quality education for populations of adults and children who are not in formal education, or who have missed out on formal education, and are hard to reach. Children in nomadic communities, who are discussed below, are a good example, but there are also children and adults in conflict zones, or in post-conflict situations, and those caught up in pandemics, when schools are closed. Organizations like these might also want to use distance learning techniques to enhance the quality of formal education by providing educational broadcasting which comes from expertise and access to resources which classroom teachers do not have.

- NGOs who specialize in livelihoods development, often in agriculture and livestock, may want to add a training element to their existing work, or, if there already is an on-the-ground training element, they may want to reach a much wider audience.
- Communication for development NGOs, when they can see that the needs of a particular population are best met by skills development.

Of course, these different kinds of organization bring different knowledge, skills and experience. Those who specialize in a particular subject area, like agriculture, will have strong and detailed knowledge of what populations need to learn but will have little or no experience of broadcasting, while communication for development organizations with a track record in broadcasting will not have the necessary knowledge for specialist training.

To give a very specific example, Horn Relief, a specialist NGO in sustainable agriculture in north-east Somalia, has been discussed before. (See Chapter 10.) It had a great deal of expertise and experience in the subject in that area. In 2009 it had published two training handbooks for farmers and pastoralists on the subject but wanted to widen the impact to a larger population than it could reach with on-the-ground training. It approached a local radio broadcaster and got an agreement that it would produce and broadcast training programmes based on the training handbooks' content. Horn Relief then approached a small international communication for development consultancy to adapt the handbook contents into a detailed curriculum for broadcast, and to design and deliver training for the radio station's producers for them to be able to make the programmes. In contrast, a few years earlier, BBC Media Action (then The BBC World Service Trust), an international communication for development NGO, had received funding for the *Somalia Livestock Livelihoods Project*. The organization brought expertise in broadcasting and in radio-based distance learning, and had a production team with good local knowledge but relatively little expertise in the livestock sector.

For these reasons, distance learning by broadcasting projects is often carried out in partnership.

This section of the book is aimed largely at the first two kinds of organization, though there may well be material of significant value to experienced communication for development organizations, since the section is based on what has been done in distance learning broadcasting in the past, and on what has worked.

When distance learning has been used

Distance learning can be used for a wide range of subjects, in a wide range of contexts and for a wide range of learners. Normally, it is used when more formal educational approaches, in educational institutions and face to face with a teacher, are either not available or not appropriate. For example, the INGO Child to Child used distance learning by radio for its *Pikin To Pikin Tok* project in Sierra Leone to teach children literacy and numeracy, and social and life skills, in 2014, because schools were closed during an Ebola virus epidemic. (See Chapter 18.) The Africa Educational Trust's

Somali Distance Education for Literacy, Life Skills & Livelihoods, which started in 2001, used distance learning partly for cost-effectiveness and partly to have the flexibility needed when many of the learners were in conflict zones.

Some organizations have looked at the potential value of distance learning for children in nomadic communities. This is partly because schools need to have close-by, settled communities to be viable, so schools are not appropriate for scattered, mobile populations. When nomadic children have attended boarding school, it has tended to be a route for them to leave the nomadic lifestyle.[1] Nomadic culture, though, is valuable because, in arid areas, livestock production benefits from a widely scattered population. Therefore, if communities want it, it is better to educate nomadic children within their communities, rather than taking them out.

In general, it is also better for adult learners to learn while staying in their communities, where they can maintain their livelihoods. It was this factor that led to two projects teaching new livelihoods skills to use distance learning. These two projects are among those discussed in this chapter. They are BBC Media Action's *Somalia Livestock Livelihoods Project,* started in 2005, and UNESCO's *The Gobi Women's Project* in Mongolia, started in 1993.

Distance learning was defined by Hillary Perraton in 1982, as 'an educational process in which a significant proportion of the teaching is conducted by someone removed in space and/or time from the learner'.[2] Distance learning is normally structured by some kind of educational curriculum, with broadcast media, either radio or television in most contexts in the Global South, playing a significant role in its delivery. There is, though, often print material and, at least, some face-to-face teaching element. It can be used at any level from infants to university. Learners can be in more or less organized classes, or working individually. Some distance learning projects set formal tasks, which are marked, either locally or at a distance, and some include exams.

In the developed world, a lot of distance learning is done through online learning with or without personal teacher support. This material is, of course, accessible to anyone who can read the language and has internet access, which is becoming increasingly available in the Global South. However, for the poor and those affected by conflict, internet access is likely to remain limited for some years to come. A viable alternative might be, for example, to load such material onto inexpensive tablets for use in areas where there is no internet access. However sophisticated the technology, developing the content of the learning material will be similar to that for broadcast media, though, of course, the delivery will be far more interactive.

A distance learning project usually has a significantly more limited target audience than most communication for development projects. For example, it can be aimed only at learners who are registered on to a course, so that they can attend classes or be visited by a travelling teacher. This was the case in both the *Somali Distance Education for Literacy, Life Skills & Livelihoods* and *The Gobi Women's Project*. The Somali Project registered learners because they had to attend weekly classes and do a final exam, and was limited to 10,000 learners per year. The Gobi Project had a team of visiting teachers so, again, the number of learners had to be limited to 15,000.

Different distance learning projects use different combinations of media and learner organization. Some have formal classes, others informal learning groups, and some allow for individual learning via mobile phone, for example. In this chapter, I will look at the various arrangements and discuss their strengths and weaknesses.

Projects

Pikin-To-Pikin Tok

The UK-based Child to Child partnered with a local Sierra Leonean NGO, called The Pikin-to-Pikin Movement, to create an early childhood development project, in one remote area of Sierra Leone, the Kailahun District. Work started on it in 2011 and it continued until 2016. In 2014, however, an Ebola epidemic stopped all the work and so the two organizations set up this project, using, exclusively, radio. It used a local radio station to broadcast three different programmes for different age groups, covering early years education, life skills and hygiene. Major themes were encouraging children – particularly girls – to stay in education, safety, maintaining health, resilience in facing difficult circumstances, and literacy and numeracy.

Radios were distributed and the project created listening groups, each led by a trained facilitator, to encourage children to phone in to the discussion programme that followed each broadcast. In this way, the programmes encouraged interactivity, and did so by, for example, using songs and games.

The programmes had a focus on gender, trying to challenge the discriminatory attitudes to girls, whose vulnerability was sharply increased by the Ebola outbreak, because, for example, schools had closed, and girls did not have that protection any more.

Somali Distance Education for Literacy, Life Skills & Livelihoods

There was a weekly 30-minute radio programme, broadcast on the BBC Somali Service, which can be heard across the whole Somali-speaking region. The main aim was to teach literacy in Somali. The format was a magazine, with each programme carrying three items, on health, human rights and the environment, with literacy activities, following a tight curriculum, based on this content. Printed workbooks, closely coordinated with the radio programme content, allowed learners to do literacy tasks while listening and during a follow-up lesson after the programme. Teachers had printed guides, based on the programmes and the learners' workbook as well, so that they could prepare for the lessons.

Registered learners were in locally organized classes, which took place in any location available, including outdoors. Teachers were nominated by their community, and received a very basic training in using the radio programmes. They did not need to have teaching skills but did need to be literate themselves. All learners took a final exam, which was externally marked.

Somalia Livestock Livelihoods Project

A weekly 30-minute radio magazine programme was broadcast on the BBC Somali Service, as above. The project aimed at alleviating poverty by encouraging individual and collective economic development in the livestock sector across Somalia. Topics included animal health, herd management, environmental management, basic business skills and product diversification for maximizing incomes. These topics were organized into a structured curriculum, though the curriculum developed and changed over the course of the project. In addition to this distance learning core, there were items on economic opportunities in the livestock sector, and information of immediate topical use and interest, including a weather forecast and market prices around the country. There were no print materials because of low literacy levels in the livestock sector. This meant that all instructions for the group learning activities and for facilitator preparations had to be broadcast as part of the programmes.

Learners were organized into informal groups, each led by a facilitator who had received a very basic training in using the programmes. Each programme offered a range of practical learning activities for groups to pursue after the broadcasts, and each group selected which activities to do based on their different roles in the sector. These sessions were designed to be conducted outdoors. Evaluation showed that many listeners were not in a group, acting as independent learners.

The Gobi Women's Project

This was the most elaborate of the projects discussed here, and the most wide-ranging in terms of topics covered. Every week, there were two programmes broadcast nationally and one 30-minute programme broadcast on local radio in each of the districts that the project covered. The project aimed at helping nomadic women make the changes

Figure 20.1 *Interviewing a young shepherd in the field for BBC Media Action's* Somalia Livestock Livelihoods Project

to adjust from living in a rigid socialist economy to a market economy, with income generation at the project's heart. Topics included business skills, manufacturing skills to exploit animal products, farming, family planning and the law.[3] While the national programmes set out the formal teaching, the local programmes were more flexible, and were able to respond quickly to the women's expressed needs. There were extensive print materials, including booklets, information sheets and newsletters, some produced at national, and others at local, level. In addition, there were visiting teachers, who travelled extensively to meet learners in their homes, to provide support. The teachers were, in their turn, supported by a network of teacher facilitators.

The project intention was that the booklets would provide much of the education, with the radio programmes in support. (This is exactly the reverse of the Somalia literacy teaching project.) In the event, this arrangement did not always work well, with the print materials sometimes being delivered very late.[4]

There were some organized joint learning sessions, and there were district centres and more local information centres, in which learning groups were set up.

Outcomes

Pikin-To-Pikin Tok

Three months into the project, in December 2015, an evaluation was conducted by Child to Child, helped by the Overseas Development Institute, and published as a case study by The United Nations Girls Education Initiative.[5]

The project created and trained groups of child journalists to gather material for the broadcasting, two of which were all-girl groups. The majority of the child journalists were girls. The programmes were presented by a man and a woman, and girls were offered positive role models, both real and fictional. The programmes were aimed at three different age groups: 4- to 6-year-olds; 7- to 12-year-olds and 13- to 18-year-olds.

On the ground, the project set up 252 learning groups, of between 10 and 25 children. Of these groups 42 were formal while the remainder were informal. Both kinds of group had an adult facilitator, usually a local teacher. However, the difference between the kinds of group was that the facilitators of the formal groups were paid and the children received refreshments. The formal group facilitators had to hold the group sessions when there was a broadcast. The informal facilitators were not under any obligation, and there were no refreshments for the children, so it was just the facilitators' and children's interest that kept the groups functioning.

The evaluation showed that there were differences of impact between the different kinds of group.

One of the key strategies the project adopted was called 'linking learning to life'.[6] This was a strategy of encouraging children to apply what they had learned in the programme to real life, in the week following, to consolidate and reinforce the learning. Part of the role of the facilitators was to encourage this.

The formal groups showed 'markedly'[7] greater success in the results of this strategy than the informal groups. The evaluation attributes this to the chasing up of dropouts from the group by the formal facilitators, giving the groups a greater stability, and the greater level of parental support for the formal groups.

One aspect of the project that the evaluation laments is that it did not have supporting print materials, apparently because of cost.

One of the strongest draws the groups had for children was the ability to phone the live programme following each educational broadcast. The greater impact of the linking learning to life strategy in the formal groups is attributed, in part, to the greater participation in the phone-ins by children in the formal groups. Calls children made were often to tell of their own experience of the topic in the programme.

The evaluation shows that the overall impact of the project, even after only three months, was evidenced in the high levels of retention of the information broadcast and changes of behaviour, like the adoption of hand washing, as a result of listening to the programmes. Several of the in-depth interviews quoted showed evidence of concrete impact on behaviour – for example, a girl who succeeded in persuading her neighbour to go back to school after dropping out.[8]

One impact, in particular, was a marked improvement in children's self-efficacy.

> One of the major benefits seen by respondents was the increase in self-efficacy, or one's belief in one's ability to succeed in specific situations or accomplish a task, evidenced by testimonies from children and verified by peers, parents, and key informants.[9]

There were two further key factors in the impact of the project at this early stage. Participation was encouraged by the fact that listening groups were close to the children's homes, and the other that children were attending in friendship groups.[10]

On the language issue, the broadcasts were mainly in two languages, Krio and English, while some of the child journalists and callers used Kissi and Mende. This decision was based on research, which shows that a dual-language approach can have positive impact on other areas of learning, and research which shows that, when a child is learning another language, it is very important for him or her to keep their home language. This is so that they grow up fluent in at least one language.[11] The evaluation reports that there was evidence of improved dual-language abilities.[12]

Apart from the partnership between Child to Child and the Pikin-to-Pikin Movement, the project also partnered with existing social structures, like social welfare committees and school clubs, for facilities for listening groups. There was also a partnership with the radio station, so that the project's child journalists could team up with the station's professional journalists in doing their work. These arrangements were seen as 'crucial'.[13]

Somali Distance Education for Literacy, Life Skills & Livelihoods

This project was first broadcast in 2002, and the initial series lasted for a year. During that time, there were more than 10,000 learners in 351 classes across Somalia/ Somaliland. Of these learners, 88 per cent passed the final exam in literacy and numeracy. An external evaluation conducted shortly after the end of the course reported that, for most learners, the level of literacy was basic; that is, they could get the gist of a newspaper without being able to understand it in depth. However, some felt confident enough to help others in their families with their literacy. Women made up 70 per cent of learners.

The evaluation did pose the question of the value of literacy in Somali, given that there were very few texts, beyond newspapers, leaflets and shop signs, written in Somali. It came to the conclusion that it was but that the range of texts needed to be expanded. A later external evaluation, in 2007, looking at the original Level 1 series, and a newer Level 2 series, found that some learners who worked in shops or ran market stalls reported a direct impact on their incomes, simply because they could now keep records of customers who owed them money, and so avoid being exploited.

The original evaluation found that the first series had reached its target audience of young adults, especially women, who had not had an education. The later evaluation, in 2007, found that: 'All of those interviewed stated that the SOMDEL programme was the first educational opportunity they had been given.' Further, the project was designed so that education would become available to populations in conflict zones. In its first year, 4,500 learners in Mogadishu – then a site of ongoing conflict – registered for the literacy classes.

Something that this evaluation identified was that the project had generated a lot of enthusiasm among the learners. The project continued with a new intermediate Level 2 course, and repeat broadcasts of the Level 1 course, so that, by 2007, 36,000 learners had been on the courses, with a continuation of the success rate.

The evaluation in 2007 recorded these points, and the benefits the project gained from its flexibility (see below). However, the 2007 evaluation also identified some failures. The first was a failure to recruit young men into the classes, partly, at least, as a result of men seeing the project as being for women. The second called on the project to handle staff better. When the project started, the teachers had all been volunteers nominated by their communities, who received a basic training. However, as time went on, it appears that the initial enthusiasm waned, and the 2007 evaluation recommended more training and better incentives for teachers.

In 2008, a third level was added, which steered learners towards joining formal education, but the first two levels continued to be broadcast, and were made available on CDs, so that by 2010 more than 50,000 had learned basic literacy.

Somalia Livestock Livelihoods Project

This project was much shorter-lived than the Somalia literacy project, and lasted for two years. There was an end-of-project evaluation carried out by BBC Media Action's own Research and Learning section. The findings were reported in a PowerPoint presentation. These showed that the project had gained a reasonable listenership of 50 per cent who listened every week or most weeks, of the BBC Somali Service audience (at that time, the findings showed, the BBC audience was 98 per cent of the population, though it has to be said that, outside major towns, there was very little competition).

On a range of topics covered by the radio programmes – including animal disease recognition and prevention, and milk hygiene – regular listeners displayed substantially better knowledge than non-listeners. In terms of practice, the evaluation looked at one area, milk hygiene, and found that, of those who had ever listened, 30 per cent had practised three practical measures for better milk hygiene, while only 2 per cent of non-listeners had, and of those who had, 95 per cent reported a positive difference to their work.

There were similar positive results from knowledge of business skills. Perhaps most significant, since the project aimed at increasing incomes and poverty alleviation, 82 per cent of regular listeners reported an increase in income over the last two years, while only 45 per cent of non-listeners reported an increase. When asked if they thought the project had benefitted the livestock sector, a very high proportion (86–100 per cent) of those asked said it had, with a small percentage (0–8 per cent) saying it had not.

It might be questioned that this evaluation was one undertaken by BBC Media Action itself and depended significantly on self-evaluation by respondents. However, there were questions in it, which were put to respondents, which demanded specialist knowledge, and since there was, at the time, very little information available in Somalia, it is unlikely that the respondents would have learned the range of knowledge from any other source.

The Gobi Women's Project

This, again, was a relatively short-lived project, though it did have a follow-on. An independent evaluation, written in 1999, looked at the project's achievements.[14]

The evaluation shows that one of its strongest achievements was at a policy level, introducing distance learning to a country previously focused on centralized, formal education, and showing it could be successful.

There had been neither a baseline study at the outset, nor was there an evaluation of learning at the end, so there is no formal information on learning achievements. However, in terms of impact on the 15,000 learners, there was evidence that they did learn a range of income-generating skills, largely involving crafts, like saddle-making, though the evaluation says, of the overall aim: 'Though income generation was the goal, income stretching was more often achieved.'[15]

The evaluation also reports that a significant success was in changes in attitude and confidence among the learners. By the end of the project, many of the learners had learned how to help themselves and not to be dependent on others,[16] and they had acquired the confidence to state their own needs, in terms of topics they wanted to learn about, or wanted information on, which, the evaluation noted, was very different from the way they had been at the beginning of the project. There had been a literacy element but, the evaluation reports, it was not well executed and had little impact.[17]

Overall, the independent evaluation did consider that the craft skills learned and the changes in attitude and confidence made the project a success.

Characteristics of a successful distance learning project

The four projects discussed in this chapter do not represent a scientific sample of distance learning projects, and this is not an attempt at an academic definition of best practice. However, all of them were judged, in evaluations, to have had impact, and it is therefore valid to look at characteristics which they had in common that were judged to have contributed to their impact. From this analysis, it is perhaps possible to identify some characteristics which make distance learning projects successful.

A wide-ranging needs assessment

Basing the design of a project on a wide-ranging needs assessment, not only of learner-identified needs but of needs identified by civil society and government, appears to be crucial. This is identified in the evaluation of *The Gobi Women's Project*,[18] and it was an important factor in the *Somalia Livestock Livelihoods Project*. Indeed, it was the extensive needs assessment carried out in Somaliland, Puntland and south central Somalia which identified support for the livestock sector as the best route to poverty alleviation in Somalia. This assessment included discussions with civil society organizations, INGOs and government, as well as people in the livestock sector, and one of the criticisms of *The Gobi Women's Project*, is that while the needs assessment did well in finding 'learner-identified needs' it did not go wide enough in discussing needs identified by other people and organizations.[19]

Broadcasting

Of course, all of these projects were chosen for discussion because they used broadcast media. It is interesting, however, that the evaluation of *The Gobi Women's Project* particularly identified the reach and availability of radio as a factor in its success,[20] when the radio programmes had originally been thought of as a support to print materials, rather than being a crucial part of the project. The evaluation can be read as suggesting that problems with the print materials (see below) made the radio programmes more important. *The Gobi Women's Project* was carried out at a time of rapid social, political and legislative change in Mongolia, and radio's flexibility was judged an important factor: 'The media most able to respond quickly to changing circumstances were particularly valuable. Radio proved very effective in providing topical programmes.'[21]

In all of these cases, the medium was radio and, in many contexts in the Global South, radio is likely to remain important. Of course, the speed of technological development in communications means that radio could well be replaced by some kind of social media. If this happens, a big advantage would be that all materials – written, audio and video – could be delivered by the same technology. However, the basic educational approach and methodology would remain the same, irrespective of the medium.

Organized social interaction

All of the projects had an element of social interaction, in learning groups or in learning centres, and none of them was based on a structure of individual learners working separately from each other. In *The Gobi Women's Project*, the social interaction element was evaluated as having had an important impact on positive changes in the learners' levels of confidence and in their attitude. In *Pikin To Pikin Tok*, the fact that children were learning in friendship groups was seen as very important to successful learning.

Printed material

Some of these projects used print material alongside broadcasting. When this is the case, a close coordination between broadcast and print materials can be important. In the *Somali Distance Education for Literacy, Life Skills & Livelihoods* project, for example, the coordination was so close that learners could carry out writing activities in their print workbooks under the guidance of the radio programmes, while they were listening. This was achieved by the print materials being produced after the radio programmes had been made, so that they matched exactly the content of the programmes. This was not without problems in the first series, however (see below). This is an aspect of *The Gobi Women's Project* that is particularly criticized. There was a lack of coordination between the print and the radio teams, which 'resulted in poor integration of print materials with radio programmes'.[22]

Localization

The localization of projects was evaluated as a strong advantage in two different ways. In the 2002 evaluation of the first series of the *Somali Distance Education for Literacy, Life Skills & Livelihoods* project, it was assessed that the fact that classes were small and local contributed to the success of the project in reaching its target groups, in that vulnerable groups, particularly girls and women, could get to the classes in safety. Similarly, in *Pikin To Pikin Tok*, the closeness of the listening groups to the children's homes was an important factor. For *The Gobi Women's Project,* three aspects of localism were judged to have contributed to the project's success: local ownership and leadership; the scope for local creation of materials responding to local needs; and local goodwill and voluntary service.[23]

Flexibility

An evaluation of *Somali Distance Education for Literacy, Life Skills & Livelihoods,* in 2006, highlighted the importance of flexibility in its success.

> Ensuring access for disadvantaged people and achieving high retention levels has been facilitated by the flexible nature of the SOMDEL classes. Teachers are able to tape radio broadcasts, enabling classes to be run at times that are convenient for students. This has proved particularly important for women and girls.[24]

During the Level 2 course, areas of south Somalia suffered severe drought resulting in students dropping out of classes to move with their families. Similarly, drought affected four rural villages in Togdeer Region in Somaliland during the Level 1 course. However, the flexible nature of the SOMDEL programme meant that in all cases, teachers were able to move with the students and ensure the continuation of classes.[25]

Cooperation and partnerships

SOMDEL partnered with government and with local civil society organizations, as well as the operational partnership between the BBC Somali Service, BBC Media Action and the Africa Educational Trust (AET). Independent evaluation found that the partnerships worked well.[26] One factor behind this may have been AET's long-standing presence on the ground in Somalia, and the reputation of the BBC Somali Service.

Distance learning projects in development contexts can be quite complex. There needs to be subject and curriculum expertise, broadcasting production expertise and, usually, organization of learners on the ground.

Partnerships and collaboration can help:

- to provide subject expertise, and course content
- to provide or support organization of learners
- to facilitate broadcasting
- to offer production expertise
- to ensure consistency of information

For example, the way the operational partnership for the *Somali Distance Education for Literacy, Life Skills & Livelihoods* worked, was that AET provided subject expertise and teaching content, and organized groups and teachers on the ground through their existing network of offices and contacts, BBC Media Action provided radio production expertise and recruited and trained the production team, and the BBC Somali Service provided the broadcasting facility.

These partnerships were put in place at the proposal stage, but partnerships can be successfully established once a project is up and running. In many countries where there is substantial and long-term aid, there is a coordination body among the agencies, with sub-groups covering different specialist areas. For example, when BBC Media Action's *Somalia Livestock Livelihoods Project* was established in 2005, there was the overall body, The Somalia Aid Coordination Body and a sub-group, The Livestock Working Group. (This group existed because there were many organizations working in the livestock sector in Somalia because of the sector's economic significance. A UNDP report of 2002 estimated that 59 per cent of the country's population were dependent on pastoralism, in many different ways.) Through this group, BBC Media Action team were able to contact a range of INGOs working in the livestock sector.

One of these was Vetaid, with whom a very constructive partnership was made. Vetaid operated in one small area around the livestock centre of Burao. Among other activities, it ran training for people in different parts of the milk sector. Milk was, at the time, a sector that was performing poorly, so much so that many Somalis preferred to buy imported dried milk than the fresh milk available. There were a number of factors behind this, including poor hygiene procedures followed by producers and retailers, and a failure to understand the market, also on the part of producers and retailers. The training Vetaid designed and delivered helped producers and retailers improve hygiene and marketing. However, it was delivered face to face, and could only be run in the area around Burao. In a partnership between the organizations, the Vetaid milk training course was adapted for radio and broadcast as one of the strands in the BBC World Service Trust's livestock programmes, so that it reached far more people than Vetaid could: a successful example of collaboration and partnership.

Partnerships were also crucial to the success of *Pikin To Pikin Tok*, according to the evaluation. In this case, there was the central partnership of the INGO, Child to Child, which provided the educational expertise, and the local NGO, the Pikin-to-Pikin Movement, which provided local contacts and knowledge, as well as linguistic expertise. The other partners, local committees and clubs provided facilities and the radio station, journalistic expertise.

However, not all efforts at partnership are so successful and some can become time-consuming with no positive outcome. An evaluation of *The Gobi Women's Project*, for example, concluded that: 'Collaboration with other agencies brought tensions as well as benefits',[27] citing an example of the project having to work with different groups between whom there were substantial problems. It is also true that some partnerships for the *Somalia Livestock Livelihoods Project* took up considerable time and energy while offering very little benefit.

It would be difficult to successfully deliver a distance learning project without partnerships, but an organization should not commit itself to a partnership without a thorough understanding of the other party, and with very clear, agreed outcomes.

Economic benefits for participants

The adult projects discussed here all had tangible economic benefits for the participants, which could begin to impact quite quickly: the craft skills in *The Gobi Women's Project*, recovery of debt through record-keeping in the *Somali Distance Education for Literacy, Life Skills & Livelihoods*, and the achievement of fair prices through broadcasting of market prices, and the economic benefits in changing herd management in the *Somalia Livestock Livelihoods Project*.

Where and when is distance learning an effective alternative to formal education?

Essentially, it is when learners cannot, for a number of different reasons, be brought together into a formal institution on a regular basis. In the two Somalia projects, the impact of conflict, sometimes exacerbated by drought, was a major factor. In *The Gobi*

Women's Project and the *Somalia Livestock Livelihoods Project*, the learners were thinly spread over large areas, and with pressing economic and domestic duties. In *Pikin To Pikin Tok*, a highly infectious epidemic prevented formal classes.

Cost-effectiveness

There appear to be significant differences in the level of resourcing among these projects but one of them at least shows that distance education using broadcasting can be highly cost-effective. In its first year, the *Somali Distance Education for Literacy, Life Skills & Livelihoods* project had a budget of UK£140,000 (US$217,000), which meant that the total cost per successful learner was UK£14.58.

21

Producing distance learning programmes for adults

The formative research

As with any communication for development project, the first stage is the formative research to assess the precise needs of the target population, in three distinct areas:

- their educational needs within the overall subject or subjects the project intends to teach (whether that is literacy, livelihoods or a broad curriculum for children)
- their communication needs and preferences
- the barriers which are creating or have created the educational need (are these simply a lack of educational opportunities, or are they, for example, cultural or to do with attitude?)

The reasons to assess the first two of these areas are obvious: to find out what subjects, precisely, the project needs to teach and at what educational levels; and, second, to inform the choice of media (television, social media or radio, and, in the case of television and radio, the choice of stations).

The third is necessary because the reasons why the educational need exists affect how the project attempts to meet the needs. In some distance learning projects, there may be topics that are essentially behaviour and social change issues, where the need arises from something cultural or to do with attitudes and not simply a lack of knowledge. These topics have to be identified at an early stage, as they need to be approached differently from topics that can be approached with distance learning techniques.

In the *Somalia Livestock Livelihoods Project*, for example, a major topic was the size of animal herds. That is, is it better to have a large herd of, say, 100 goats, or a much smaller herd, perhaps 12? A herd of 12 will be healthier, much less expensive or time consuming to feed and care for, and will contribute to the sustainability of the environment. This topic involves behaviour and social change because the change does not just involve learning new knowledge, but a change of cultural attitude. In Somalia, at that time, a large herd was associated with social status, and to keep a large herd was to see it as a social asset rather than an economic one. To keep a small herd was to regard it as an economic asset, and to manage it in the most profitable way. In communication terms, the topic should be approached using behaviour and social change strategies, rather than distance learning strategies.

This is an important distinction to make before the formative research, so that the formative research is on the correct needs. For those topics that require behaviour and social change approaches, the formative research needs to find personal, social and cultural barriers to the change and facilitators for it, rather than just knowledge and skills needs, as an approach that specifically addresses these is more likely to work than one that does not. (See Section 5 for further information on barriers and facilitators.)

Curriculum and format

Where there is an existing curriculum

Some distance learning projects will follow an established curriculum, usually if they are in some way associated with a formal education process. If, for example, the project is designed to support those who have missed formal education at an earlier stage – such as children whose schooling was interrupted by conflict – to become equipped to enter a formal education structure in the future then it will need to follow the established school curriculum. If a project is designed to teach learners so that they can pass formal exams, then again, following the established curriculum will be necessary.

Where there is no existing curriculum

However, many distance learning projects in a development context will be about learning knowledge and skills for which there is no established curriculum; or, if a project is teaching learners a subject for which there is an established curriculum but the learners will never engage with that curriculum, then a new one can be developed that is more amenable to the approaches and strategies of distance learning by broadcasting. So, for example, in AET's *Somali Distance Education for Literacy, Life Skills & Livelihoods*, a curriculum for teaching literacy in Somali was developed that allowed for the learning to be based on journalism, because the target population's experience of radio was listening to journalism, and so the teaching could be built on an experience the learners were already very familiar with.

Where there is no existing curriculum, or where there is no link-up with formal education, then a curriculum needs to be developed, so that the learning follows a structured, step-by-step path, while the communication needs of the learners are best met.

Such a curriculum should be based on the formative research. From the research, broad topic areas should be identified, which will form the different strands in the programmes. Most distance learning projects are likely to need to address a number of broad strands.

When is a distance learning project justified?

Many distance learning projects attempt to offer a wide body of skills and knowledge, in part because even the most specialized of them is trying to address the needs of a large and diverse audience. If the potential audience is not very large, then it may be difficult to justify a distance learning approach, especially one using broadcasting. However, there are relatively small audiences whose needs and potential impact do justify such a project.

Distance learning has, for example, been used for teacher training, where a teaching force needs to learn and put into practice new and updated approaches to teaching, like child-centred learning. In most countries, the teaching force is widely dispersed and, because of the nature of the work, cannot be brought together in one place for training for any prolonged period. In addition, it is not wise to take teachers out of their workplace, as this kind of learning needs to be applied rapidly if it is going to be consolidated and in the teacher's own context. The impact of a better trained teaching force will, of course, be extensive. These factors make distance learning an appropriate methodology.

There are still many strands to such a teacher training course. There is a substantial body of theory to be absorbed and understood, including questions on what education is for and what it is trying to achieve, and on how children learn, for example. There is classroom practice and organization that are common to all subjects, and those which are specialized to particular subjects. There is different practice for different age groups. There are issues of gender and of inclusion. Much of this will be challenging for some teachers, and there will need to be an element of advocacy. So, even a specialized project is likely to include a range of different strands.

Developing a diverse curriculum where none exists

Knowledge and skills for improved livelihoods are the subject of distance learning projects, as in the examples of the *Somalia Livestock Livelihoods Project* and *The Gobi Women's Project.* Such projects are likely to be addressing diverse audiences with significantly different needs. The Somalia livestock project, for example, aimed to support everyone in the livestock sector, and they ranged from very poor milk sellers to brokers who managed livestock exports by air or by sea. By definition, a project aiming to help many people develop better livelihoods has to have diverse content. If learners all learn the same skill set to produce the same product, they would all finish up in competition with each other, while other areas of economic opportunity would not be addressed.

While addressing a diverse audience, it is important to keep all of them engaged, so, for example, it is not possible to produce single-issue programmes, as any part of the audience for whom the chosen issue is not relevant are unlikely to listen to or watch the whole programme and, subsequently, are less likely to engage with the rest of the series. It is important, as far as possible, to ensure that there is, at least, for every programme a part that is relevant to each section of the audience. For this reason, a magazine format is often chosen, so that each programme contains a variety of items, each addressing different parts of the audience, with at least one or two that appeal to the whole audience.

(Of course, a huge advantage of distributing the material on social media is that individuals in the audience, or learning groups, can select the items relevant to themselves. As ever, though, a decision to do this must be based on the communication needs assessment.)

Developing broad strands

It is good practice to divide the project's subjects into broad strands, each aimed at a different part of the audience. (These will then be broken down further, until they are each broken down into a series of small topics that can each be covered in a 5-minute long programme item.)

However, at this stage, just the broad topic strands are identified. For example, in a project promoting better livelihoods in a livestock sector, overall strands might include the following:

- animal health, that is disease identification, prevention and treatment
- herd management, that is the debate between having a large or small herd
- environmental management, which includes preventing environmental degradation by livestock and restoring degraded environments
- product diversification to maximize incomes from livestock
- how to understand and meet market demand
- business skills to help the poor and marginalized maximize their incomes

Making broad strands into a workable curriculum

A method for developing a curriculum, which has worked in past projects, is to set out a table with the strands listed vertically and the broadcast dates horizontally. (See Table 21.1.)

Table 21.1 A table for the development of a distance learning curriculum

Strand	Date Programme 1	Date Programme 2	Date Programme 3	Date Programme 4
Animal health				
Herd management				
Environmental management				
Product diversification				
Market demand				
Business skills				

This gives a format for breaking down the broad topics into smaller ones, but, in most cases, a number of levels of sub-division are needed, because of the size of the broad strands. (See Table 21.2.)

Table 21.2 An example table showing how broad topics in a distance learning project can be broken down into smaller ones for individual programmes

Strand		Date Programme 1	Date Programme 2	Date Programme 3	Date Programme 4
Animal health					
Main topic	Common diseases				
Sub-topic	Anthrax				
	Programme topic	Anthrax overview	Anthrax identification	Anthrax prevention	Anthrax treatment

In a weekly series of programmes, under this breakdown, the overall strand of animal health could run for the whole life of the project. The main topic of common animal diseases could run for several months, while each sub-topic of one disease at a time could run for one month.

Using this simple methodology allows for the creation of an organized learning curriculum, which can be for six months initially, with an assessment of the impact after a few months. The curriculum can then be extended, with any amendments needed following the assessment, for a further six months.

For some subjects, like literacy, there are well-established teaching techniques and it is advisable to employ a team of specialists in the subject to develop the on-air curriculum, in collaboration with the programme production team, as the curriculum will still need breaking down into items that will work in broadcast programmes.

Programme design and production

The design and production of programmes for a distance learning project follow the steps for the design and production of programmes for development set out in Chapter 7, except that learning activities are needed and so the programmes should include instructions for those activities. The activities can come from existing, on-the-ground training, from educational expertise fed into the curriculum development and by the production team themselves, especially where there is no external expertise in the subject. For example, when the *Somalia Livestock Livelihoods Project* (see Chapter 20) was developed, while there was educational expertise on livestock for some countries, there was very little on the particular detail of the functioning of the livestock sector in Somalia. The journalists working on the project had to go out and find information from INGOs and NGOs working on the ground, and turn that information into educational material, particularly in the design of the learning activities.

As is discussed in Chapter 2, people do not learn simply by listening, but by talking and doing. So, a distance learning project needs to set activities, from which the audience can learn. The need for learning activities affects every aspect of the design and development of programmes for distance learning projects.

Designing learning activities

Where appropriate, activities can be designed so that learners can carry them out both while listening to or watching the programme, and after the programme. However, this is not possible for some projects. In a literacy teaching project, where there are print materials, learners can complete tasks in the print materials while the programme is playing. For example, in letter formation, learners can practise writing the letters by writing over greyed-out letters in the print materials, while they listen to the sound of that letter in different words. Where activities are more practical – in livestock, for example – it is not easy to carry them out while listening to the programme. As has been discussed in Chapter 20, not all distance learning projects need print materials, but the instructions in the programme must be clear so that learners can remember them to be able to carry out the activity after the programme has finished.

Testing learning activities

The *Somalia Livestock Livelihoods Project* had organized learning groups across the country, each led by a facilitator. In a test of the learning activities technique when developing the project, two learning group facilitators listened to a programme in which there were instructions for a number of activities. These included one on how to identify the symptoms of a disease called black quarter in a goat, and a second on conducting an experiment with a plastic jerrycan to show how unhygienic they are as containers for milk. The facilitators had no written instructions.

Both facilitators remembered the instructions accurately and carried out the instructions correctly. The facilitator who carried out the animal health activity was asked if he already knew the symptoms of black quarter, and he replied that he had never heard of it, so he had carried out the activity entirely from following the spoken instructions in the programme. (See Figures 21.1 and 21.2.)

Figure 21.1 *The BBC Media Action production team in Somalia examine a plastic jerrycan's unhygienic interior, after trying out a learning activity in the* Somalia Livestock Livelihoods Project

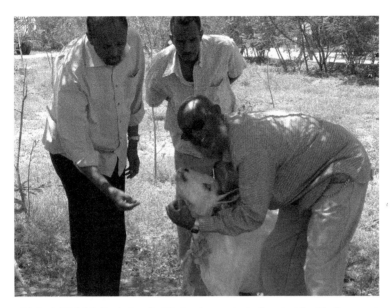

Figure 21.2 *A BBC Media Action facilitator demonstrates how to identify the symptoms of black quarter on a goat, for the* Somalia Livestock Livelihoods Project

A suggested presenter checklist

Here is a checklist of the items needed for a 30-minute distance learning programme on topics that require practical learning activities.

Introductory music
Presenter: Introduction, including a succinct explanation of the aim of and target audience for the project
        Link to menu clip 1

Menu clip 1

Presenter: Link to menu clip 2

Menu clip 2

Presenter: Link to menu clip 3

Menu clip 3

Presenter: Explains of how listeners can make the most of the activities, including the
        following:
            the activities work best for those listening in groups
            groups decide which of the activities they will do
            information on how to find and join a learning group

Journalist: Current news and information relevant to the project's topic and the programme's audiences

Presenter: Link to item 1

Pre-recorded item 1 (5 minutes)

Presenter: Back announcement to Item 1, including the activity instructions for learning from Item 1:
    a summary of the issue raised in the item
    a description of the activity and its intended learning outcome
    an example of how the activity might be carried out between the facilitator and the group

Presenter: Series and broadcaster identifier
    Link to audience participation slot, with information how to contact the programme or station

Pre-recorded item 2: Messages from audience and appropriate responses

Presenter: Announcement of the topic for the next programme, request for questions or comments, including SMS number, email address and social media page
    Reminder that the contact details will be given again at the end of the programme

Music sting

Presenter: Link to item 3

Pre-recorded item 3 (5 minutes)

Presenter: Back announcement to Item 3, including the activity instructions for learning from Item 3:
    a summary of the issue raised in the item
    a description of the activity and its intended learning outcome
    an example of how the activity might be carried out between the facilitator and the group

Music sting

Presenter: Series and broadcaster identification

Link to item 4

Pre-recorded item 4 (5 minutes)

Presenter: Back announcement to Item 4, including the activity instructions for learning from Item 4:
    a summary of the issue raised in the item
    a description of the activity and its intended learning outcome
    an example of how the activity might be carried out between the facilitator and the group

Music sting

Presenter: Series and broadcaster identification

> Advance information for group facilitators on what they will need to do to prepare for the next programme's learning session. This will include the following:
>
>> What the topics are going to be in the following programme.
>> The practical materials the facilitator needs to bring for the following programme's activities.

Presenter: A clear summary of the three learning activities described in the programme

> Closing announcement, which will include the following:
> Invites audience members to contact the programme.
> Gives all possible contact details.
> Gives information on how to find and join a learning group.

Music

The development of programme items for distance learning

This process is very similar to the factual package development process explained in Chapter 7, and a similar grid can be used, if required. The only difference is the focus on providing the motivation for carrying out the learning activity and the information needed to carry it out effectively. Once the need the item is addressing and the change necessary among learners to meet the need have been identified, it is important that the learning activity is developed early, before the rest of the package. This is because it is the activity that will guide the decisions about the content of the package.

A grid might be helpful in developing items for a distance learning programme that uses learning activities. (See Table 21.3.)

Strand: Animal health. Topic: The symptoms of black quarter disease

Table 21.3 A grid that might be helpful in developing items for a distance learning programme that uses learning activities

1. What is the identified need that this package is helping to meet?	If an animal becomes infected with black quarter disease, the owner needs to identify the disease quickly
2. What change can the audience make to meet this need?	Learn how to recognize the symptoms of black quarter disease
3. What learning activity is going to be used?	Physical practice of handling an animal to check if it has black quarter disease or not
4. Which part of the audience needs to make this change?	Livestock owners or keepers
5. What kind of change does the target audience need? A change of knowledge, attitude or behaviour?	Knowledge and behaviour

6. Does the target audience have access to the resources to make this change?	Yes/No: Yes If the answer is No, stop and research a different change. If the answer is Yes, explain the answer. The only resource needed is the animals the target audience own or look after
7. List the points of information the audience need to carry out the learning activity to make this change. The importance of detecting the presence of black quarter disease in a herd quickly, through an understanding of the disease's potential impact The symptoms of black quarter disease, which can be seen or felt on an animal	Against each point, or set of points, list who the information would best come from. A livestock owner who had a herd infected by black quarter disease but did not detect it and then witnessed its impact Someone who is familiar with the symptoms from experience, and who speaks in a way livestock owners can understand
8. List the materials needed for the learning activity. A sheep or goat	List the sources of the materials. A member of the learning group who is a livestock owner

Developing learning activities

Learning activities help audience members understand an item's learning point through discussion or practical action, or both, and make the learning point memorable. If there are no print materials to back up the broadcast instructions, activities need to be simple to explain and memorable. Any materials needed for the activity need to be readily accessible for a learning group facilitator.

Activities that are personal and encourage audience members to apply the principle discussed to their own lives are likely to have a bigger impact. As an example, in the *Somalia Livestock Livelihoods Project* one strand was on maximizing earnings from livestock, and one sub-topic was selling animal hides. A major barrier to getting a decent price for a hide was branding, the deliberate burning of parts of the animal's skin. This was done in the belief that branding could cure disease, not for identification purposes. An activity for this topic was for livestock owners to take a sample of ten animals, at random, and assess their hides. The programme item had given the difference in value between a perfect hide and a damaged one. If the animals assessed had hides that were damaged by branding, the listener was asked to work out how much money he or she had lost already.

Learning activities that are practical and can be immediately applied in the audience members' working lives are more likely to be successful, because they will be instantly reinforced by practice.

As discussed in Chapter 2, taking learners through a learning process in small steps is probably more likely to be successful, as is one which asks for small-scale experiments before making a big change. For example, in a farming project, farmers could be offered activities that involve trying out a new technique, or new plants, in a small area first, and only go on to a much larger area when the experiment proves successful.

In the production of distance learning programmes that use learning activities, it is often the practice for the production team to try each programme out with a typical learning group, to ensure that the activity instructions work properly.

It is important that the team members doing the trial simply observe what is going on, without intervening or prompting at any time. A crucial point is that production team members observe if the group do any of the activities suggested, without any prompting; that is, the observer must just wait at the end of the programme to see what happens, and not jump in with questions. The activities attempted, and how they went, should be recorded on a pro forma sheet.

If the group do not attempt any activities, then the observer needs to ask why not, and write down the answers in as much detail as possible.

Training agendas and materials

Suggested agendas and materials for training in topics relevant to this chapter can be found in Section 6:

Module J1: An exploration of how people learn
Module J10: The production of factual programmes for behaviour change

22

Producing distance learning programmes for children

While this chapter focuses on broadcasting, distance learning material for children can be provided by all kinds of means. For example, inexpensive tablets can be pre-loaded with educational material of all kinds, allowing instant interactivity. The principles, approaches and practicalities discussed in this chapter will apply to any distance learning material for children, irrespective of the medium, but the opportunity to enhance their impact through modern technology needs to be embraced wherever it is practicable.

Crucial to this chapter is the concept of 'child-centred', the necessity for programmes for children to be child-centred, and ways in which that can be done. It is imperative for programmes to address children's needs and to see the world from a child's perspective – for example, emphasizing the immediate over the long term, the doing over the thinking. (See below for a fuller discussion of children's perspectives.) At the least, programmes for children need to have children in them, and with central roles: as participants in activities, as reporters, as interviewees, as performers, as presenters. (*Module J5: Training for child journalists*, in Section 6, provides training agendas and materials.)

The most likely audience for this chapter will be individuals and organizations already involved in the education of children who want or need to use distance learning broadcasting techniques to enhance teaching and learning for children in formal education, or to provide education for children who are out of formal education for some reason.

Much of what has been discussed in Chapter 18 on producing programmes for children in humanitarian crises applies to this field of work, too.

The framework for distance learning for children

A formal curriculum

In almost every case, outside of humanitarian responses, distance learning projects for children will be within the context of formal education; that is the content will be following an established curriculum and reflect what children attending school are learning. In most cases, the content will follow the curriculum of the country the project is taking place in, unless for some reason there is no curriculum in the country. Even then, it is likely that a distance learning project will adopt a curriculum from somewhere else. Ultimately, the project will need to be preparing children for formal exams, so that they can compete on equal terms with children who are going to school.

The circumstances for distance learning for children

There are likely to be two different circumstances for a distance learning project for children. The first is when the target population of children are not attending school, either because of conflict, because of an epidemic disease that makes social interaction risky, or because the lifestyle of their communities means that they are sparsely scattered or moving frequently, as would be the case in nomadic cultures, for example.

The second circumstance is when broadcasting can enhance the quality of education. This may be because teachers lack the knowledge and skills to teach certain parts of the curriculum, because the schools do not have the resources for some subjects, or because broadcasting can bring materials that teachers do not have the time or resources to develop for themselves. This second type of broadcasting is widespread in developed countries as well as in the Global South.

A focus on children's activity and creativity

For distance learning broadcast programmes for children to make the best use of resources and to maximize impact, they need to be made with creativity and imagination. This chapter attempts to provide a range of examples of creative use of broadcasting. *Module J6: Creativity in writing for children*, in Section 6, is intended to help production teams be more creative in this field. Something for production teams to bear in mind is that their creativity should always be used to stimulate children's creativity and learning, and that should always be the focus in designing and developing programmes. Creativity does not mean extensive use of special effects, for example, which can get in the way of children's understanding of programmes, and might be demoralizing, as children judge their own work to look much less creative by comparison. This does not mean that high production values are not important – they are – but it does not mean extravagantly produced programmes.

Two characteristics are key to successful distance learning broadcasting for children: child-centredness and interactivity.

Child-centredness

This is more than just having children in the programmes: it is showing them as active, autonomous learners, and encouraging the children watching or listening to the programmes to become active, autonomous learners. It is also seeing the world from a child's perspective, that is, being immediate rather than long term, being practical and concrete rather than theoretical, doing rather than thinking, being sensuous rather than intellectual, being curious rather than set in certain ways and pushing at boundaries rather than self-limiting.

What this means for programme-making is showing children taking on challenges, solving problems through creativity, experimenting in different ways, and producing programmes that encourage children in the audience to do the same, while setting up structures for them to work within.

Interactivity

This means that child viewers or listeners are encouraged to actively respond to the programme, both while it is playing and after it has finished, so that they are not just passively watching or listening.

There are several levels of interaction that programme makers can create.

- Children watching or listening to the programme give instant spoken responses.
- Stopping points are included within the programme, so that, if it is recorded by the teacher, or distributed as an audio or video file, it can be stopped so that children can follow instructions given in the programme to carry out a learning activity.
- A simple drama in the programme has an unresolved ending, and children are invited to work out what the ending should or might be.
- Children, either on their own initiative or prompted by a teacher, replicate an activity (such as an experiment or making something) that they have seen children in the programme doing.
- Children respond to formal requests from the programme presenter to send in their own work inspired by something in the programme, and a selection of the work sent in is used in future programmes.
- The audience comment on issues raised in the programmes or comment on the programmes. Two-way communication is as important for children as for adults.

Instant spoken responses

Children watching or listening to the programme can be prompted to respond in a number of ways. The most basic is when the programme presenter asks children to respond, perhaps in a sequence of activities.

For very young children learning to count, for example, the programme will be a recording of a teacher with a group of children, as he or she is teaching them counting. A presenter will ask the children who are listening to call out the same responses as the children in the programme, as they say the numbers, and gradually build up to saying the complete sequence. There will then be a number of games and exercises to test out the absorption of the knowledge. For example, the children in the programme will say the sequence, but miss out one number, and the children viewing or listening need to call out the correct number.

Similarly, word games can be used for developing mother tongue skills, and foreign language skills.

A more subtle prompt is if there are two characters working out, for example, a maths problem, and then one of them gives the wrong answer, and the fact it is wrong is clearly signalled, probably by the other character's despairing response, and if there is then a pause, children will be inclined to shout out the right answer.

Stopping points

Where schools or less formal learning groups have internet access, programmes made with stopping points in them can be distributed that way. Where some or all do not have internet access, whether programmes are made in this format will depend in large part on the technical resources available for recording them, either in schools or for less formal learning groups. This is something that needs to be researched before any decision is made.

The mechanism in the programmes by which stopping points can be made to work is to include audio or visual signals at the points where the programme should be stopped.

The reason for doing this is that it increases the amount and range of learning activities that the programmes can deliver. If a 15-minute programme has, say, five stopping points in it, it will provide at least an hour of structured learning activity altogether.

A programme made this way can provide a sequence of, say, linked structured talk and writing activities, which can explore an issue, lead children to produce a series of small, separate pieces of work, or lead to one substantial piece of work. In the UK, programmes made this way have been used extensively to provide structured opportunities for children to use improvised drama to explore themes and issues, although this does not appear to be a teaching and learning methodology used much in the Global South.

Unresolved endings

These can provide a range of learning opportunities. Short dramas with unresolved endings could provide scenarios for children to solve maths problems. For example, in a drama scene, two children could be arguing over whether they have been given the correct change in a shop. The scene would end before the two children have come to a conclusion. Children listening or viewing are then asked to do an addition and subtraction exercise to work out if the change was correct or not.

In a similar way, unresolved drama could be used for developing language skills. A scene with hints within it of what the outcome is going to be can again end unresolved, and children viewing or listening can be given the task of writing the ending. This would be for developing listening, comprehension and narrative skills. Such a scene could also be used for developing more technical language skills – for example, summarizing skills. A drama is, again, left unresolved, and the children are asked to work out an appropriate ending, by first identifying and noting down the main points of the drama. On the basis of these points, they can write a summary of the drama.

Replicating activities

If children in the target audience see or hear a group of children on a programme doing an experiment or some other practical activity to explore a scientific issue, they may be encouraged to try the same thing themselves. If this is the specific aim of a programme, then the resources that the children in the programme use must be those available to the target audience. There is a substantial amount of material of this kind on the internet.

A more demanding approach would be for the programme to set up a structure by which children in the target audience can take the experiment demonstrated in the programme on to a next stage.

Of course, an activity children are shown doing does not have to be science-related. For example, as has been mentioned in Chapter 18, in 2019, an activity-based element was introduced into the UNICEF/Rwanda Broadcasting Agency children's television programme, *Itetero*. In one example, a small group of children aged between 5 and 10 years old were set the task of making a toy car out of wire. (Such toys are fairly common in parts of Africa.) They were given the materials, and they had the example of a wire toy car, which had been made by an adult and was quite sophisticated. Otherwise, the children were left to work things out for themselves, while the whole process was videoed. After an hour and a half, together, they had made a passable toy car. The video was edited into five segments, each up to 7 minutes long, which were slotted into the hour-long programme at intervals. The sequence ended with some still images of the materials used, and other possible materials, at the end of the programme, intended to encourage children viewing to try to do the same, after the programme.

Producing such a sequence requires considerable patience on the part of adults involved. For it to be honestly child-centred, adults cannot intervene to move the process on. In this case, for the first 45 minutes, the children were working separately, and not showing many signs of getting to make a toy car. Then, of their own volition, they began to work as a team, each making a part of the car, and sufficiently coordinated that the parts fitted together.

This sequence shows a group of children being autonomous, active and actively learning, which makes it child-centred.

Inviting children to send in work

When a programme invites children to send in work they have produced in response to the programme, it can provide a strong motivation. Of course, this does depend on there being a route for sending the material and which is readily accessible to children who are viewing or listening. If they have access to social media, or if the project has an on-the-ground presence, like visiting teachers or local centres, then it is straightforward. However, in many places and circumstances, especially where distance learning using broadcasting is needed, there will be no such route. Another condition for extending such invitations is that the project has the resources and organization to handle the material and to respond to it appropriately and quickly. A motivating response is that some of the material is used on air, and all of it is acknowledged. One model that has been used, for example, was a poetry series on radio, which broadcast poems by published poets, packaged with music and sound effects to a high level of production values. Children were invited to write their own poems in response to poems they had heard. Some of the poems sent in were then broadcast in special programmes featuring, entirely, poems written by children and sent in, and packaged with the same production values.

Training agendas and materials

Suggested agendas and materials for training in topics relevant to this chapter can be found in Section 6:

Module J5: Training for child journalists
Module J6: Creativity in writing for children

Section Four

Empowerment and engagement

An overview of communication for empowerment and engagement

Getting involved in empowerment and engagement inevitably takes an organization using communication for development into the political sphere. That very often involves risk, risk to the organization and its staff or risk of doing harm, or both. This is especially true in post-conflict situations, and projects of this kind are often in post-conflict situations. This is because donors often seek to help a new political order take hold after conflict, and see communication as an effective means of doing that. So, risk assessment and mitigation need to have a high priority in empowerment and engagement communication projects.

Projects for empowerment and engagement are funded because the spread of democracy and respect for human rights is seen as an end in itself, because mis-government and corruption are major brakes on economic development and the relief of poverty, and because successfully ending conflicts and building stability saves lives and promotes economic development.

Communication for empowerment and engagement includes, broadly:

- helping populations understand human rights – including children's rights – and bringing about greater respect for rights
- issues of good governance, that is, challenging poor administration and corruption
- helping populations understand the political process and become more effectively engaged in it
- helping give the marginalized and powerless a voice, including holding those with power to account
- post-conflict peace and justice processes, to help populations see justice done, and to help them engage with politics rather than conflict

This chapter takes six diverse example projects, to explore what can be achieved in this field and how it can be achieved, and what risks can arise and ways of mitigating them.

1. a small community radio station in Congo-Brazaville
2. a multi-platform project in Rwanda, aimed at empowering adolescent girls
3. a project in Somalia to build the engagement capacity of local media in a constitution-making process

4. capacity building in Myanmar for journalists, to help the population engage better with the new, more democratic parliament
5. help for journalists in southern Sudan, to cover elections held after the end of a fifty-year civil war
6. coverage of the trial at the International Criminal Court (ICC) of a major war leader, tailored to audiences in West Africa to help them engage with the peace process

Example projects: Empowerment

A community radio station

Radio Biso na Biso is a small community radio station in the north of Congo-Brazaville. It started broadcasting in 2009. It has a highly specific target audience, the Pygmy and Bantu forest dwellers, and its major purpose is to involve the forest dwellers in the management and protection of the forest. As a part of this, it also has a function in rebuilding Pygmy culture, which is in danger of disappearing, but which is essential to an understanding of the forest.

The station was set up through a partnership of the Tropical Forest Trust, which certificates logging companies on sustainability and environmental protection, and Congolaise Industrielle du Bois, the largest timber company in Congo. In part, Congolaise Industrielle du Bois' certification with the Tropical Forest Trust depended on the station being set up. Before the station, the forest dwellers had no involvement or say in the management of the forest, in spite of the huge impact forest management decisions could have on their lives.

This station is relatively unusual, in that it holds a company – Congolaise Industrielle du Bois – to account rather than local or national government. Indeed, the station never discusses politics.

A multi-platform project

Almost at the other end of the spectrum of empowerment initiatives is Girl Effect, which calls itself a 'creative social business', and has operated with partners in more than eighty countries. Its aim is the empowerment of adolescent girls, largely through bringing about changes in social norms – the practices, attitudes and beliefs that exist in societies – to break the old normality of many girls' lives.

The old normality includes girls having to follow pre-determined outcomes for their lives, like early marriage. Girls' lives are dominated by their parents' emphasis on protection, control and dependency, sometimes involving violence. Girl Effect aims to replace that old normality with a new normality. This new normality would give girls some control over their own lives, through employment and better safety and services for girls. Girls will have autonomy.

More ambitiously, Girl Effect aims for girls to be role models, leaders and change makers. The organization wants to empower girls through their own achievements, won by girls having ambition and stronger belief in themselves. Girl Effect wants new opportunities for girls to be established, through girls having greater knowledge, better skills and good ideas. The intention is that most of this impact will be achieved through different media and associated on-the-ground activities.

In Rwanda, for example, Girl Effect publishes a quarterly magazine, and they broadcast both a weekly radio magazine programme and a serial drama. All of these are also available on other platforms. All of these media promote behaviour and social change, largely through role models. On the ground there is a large network of girls' clubs, many of them self-started by girls themselves.

A key feature of Girl Effect's work in Rwanda is that much of the material is made by girl journalists.

Achievements

The Girl Effect website reports that 500,000 girls in Rwanda have used its media products, that is, listened to its radio magazine programme, read its magazine or listened to its radio serial drama. It goes on to say that 66 per cent of girls report that the material has strongly improved their confidence.

Example projects: Political engagement and human rights

Local media capacity building

In 2010 and 2011, BBC Media Action had a project in Somalia called *Somalia, Strengthening Radio Stations*, which involved intense training at six selected radio stations, to enable them to produce programming promoting peacebuilding, good governance and human rights. The context for this project was a new political initiative in Somalia.

After a civil war started in 1991, resulting in the overthrow of a brutal dictatorship, large areas of Somalia had been without any kind of government, and had been under the fragmented control of different warlords and, increasingly, of the Islamist group Al Shabab or different militias opposing them. In 2010, a government of national unity was formed, though with little territory under its control, and there was an internationally supported effort to create a new constitution with some kind of popular involvement in its creation so that it had at least an element of democratic legitimacy.

Achievements

BBC Media Action research on *Somalia, Strengthening Radio Stations* showed there had been some impact on the stations' journalistic output and on the understanding of the civil society organizations on working with the media.[1] A majority of those interviewed for the research said that the stations met the needs of the community.

The underlying thinking

The thinking behind this project was that, for the high-level political initiatives to have any traction at a local and community level, the local media and local civil society organizations needed to play a role in education, in making local voices heard, in fostering greater trust between populations and such local government as existed by exposing and ending corruption and creating forums for debate to foster peacebuilding.

Although there were many FM radio stations, the journalism on most of them was weak or partisan. The stations were financially fragile, so that journalists had little, if any, training, were underpaid or not paid, and the stations' equipment and technical expertise rarely allowed for quality programme making. Civil society organizations generally lacked advocacy skills and had no understanding of how to engage with the media.

The lack of regular payment for journalists meant they were extremely vulnerable to a practice known locally as *shuruur*. This involves the journalist being paid to write and broadcast a story from the angle that the organization or individual paying wants. This obviously undermines the whole basis of an independent media (though, of course, this practice is not limited to Somalia, and many media outlets in the West can be accused of a very similar practice).

Engagement with human rights

While there was a recognition that building an engaging political environment depended on an understanding of human rights, levels of education were low, illiteracy was high and no one, unless they were a returnee from another country, had had any experience of living in a rights-based political environment. The new draft constitution, which was out for public consultation, included a raft of rights clauses, which the population needed to understand if they were to make any meaningful contribution to the consultation.

The project, therefore, had a two-pronged approach to human rights. The journalists at the selected radio stations were given training in how to make broadcasting that engaged the population in the most basic education in rights, while civil society organizations who advocated for rights were given training in how to engage the media.

It is, perhaps, illuminating to understand how the approach was arrived at. According to G. N. Ray, for the Press Council of India:

> Media can play a major role in protecting and promoting human rights in the world ... The media can perform this role in different ways. It can make people aware of their rights, expose its violations and focus attention on people and areas in need of the protection of human rights and pursue their case till they achieve them.[2]

There are different approaches communication can take in a positive approach to human rights. The first is to report on human rights violations and, where possible, to pursue those violations with investigative journalism, and to expose the violators.

Another is to report on communities or individuals who are campaigning for human rights. A third is to educate communities and individuals in their human rights – best done in dialogue – so that they can recognize for themselves violations of those rights, and take any action that is possible to seek redress.

Of course, reporting such stories raises awareness among populations and communities of human rights issues that may be of relevance to themselves. This project, though, sought to educate communities and populations on human rights more systematically, so that they would gain an overall understanding of the concept of human rights, and individual human rights that apply to themselves.

Engaging audiences in a new political process

Following elections in 2015, in Myanmar, which led to a relaxation of military rule, in 2016, the international media development organization Fondation Hirondelle started a project to help the population understand the workings of the new parliament. It did this through building the capacity of journalists for reporting parliamentary processes. It ran a series of workshops with both officials of the parliament and local journalists, designed to help the local media convey the business of the parliament accurately to their audiences, and to improve the relationship between the parliament and accredited journalists. The project ran until 2018.[3]

Achievements

Fondation Hirondelle reports that they taught more than 200 journalists in their Myanmar reporting parliament project.[4] Though there does not appear to be any evidence of the impact that training had on the wider population's understanding of the workings of the new parliament.

Capacity building for election coverage

International Media Support (IMS) and The Fojo Institute of Linnaeus University also took a capacity-building approach in 2010, in an intervention in what is now South Sudan, but which was then part of Sudan and known as the Southern States, with its own autonomous, though unelected, government. In 2010, elections were held throughout Sudan, and, in the Southern States, it was the first time ever that there had been an election. The IMS/Fojo Institute project was capacity-building in election coverage for all of the major media, including the newspapers in the Southern States, Southern States Radio and Southern States Television. The radio and television stations were both controlled by the government of the Southern States, dominated by the Sudan People's Liberation Movement (SPLM), one of the parties contesting the election. The project placed an international facilitator in each of the media outlets.

This was a very complicated election, with each voter completing twelve ballot papers, as the election covered the presidencies of the North of Sudan and of the Southern States, the legislatures of the two areas, the state legislatures and the state governors. The complication was increased by the fact that some of these votes were by the party list system and some by individual names, so that on some ballot papers there were party symbols but on others there were not, all this in a country with high illiteracy rates. The individual voter had to put each ballot paper into a different box.

Throughout the election campaign, the media were monitored by the Sudan Media and Elections Consortium, and that monitoring showed little variation over the period of the campaign, with the ruling parties in each of the two areas dominating the coverage in each, and the presidential contests being the main focus of the coverage.

Achievements

The IMS/Fojo Institute election coverage project in Sudan achieved some modest success at Southern States Radio. Much of its election output was educational and non-controversial, because it was trying to prepare voters for the mechanics of the registration process and the very complicated voting system.

However, there were advances made in this broadcasting in that, for the first time, reporters went out to report on the registration process, seeing it working for themselves. On election day itself, reporters were in polling stations, phoning in their reports of how the process was working in each.

In terms of political coverage, the Sudan People's Liberation Movement (SPLM) government clearly saw the radio station as their mouthpiece. The only small advance made was that the news started to cover the other parties, in that it gave summaries of their policies as stated in their manifestos.

Engaging an audience in a post-conflict legal process

Another attempt at engaging a population in a political process was BBC Media Action's *Communicating Justice,* which reported the trial of Charles Taylor at the ICC to the populations of Liberia and Sierra Leone. Taylor was the one-time president of Liberia, who was accused of war crimes and crimes against humanity because he had supported rebels in a civil war in neighbouring Sierra Leone, in which they had committed many atrocities.

The project ran from 2009 to 2012 and had two components: one was reporting events at the trial and the other was capacity-building for local radio journalists. Two reporters at the trial made a weekly 30-minute radio programme tailored to the needs of a West African audience who had been caught up in the brutality. The programmes were translated into forty languages for broadcast on local stations across the two countries.

The capacity-building element involved four other journalists working with local radio journalists to make programmes that unpacked the proceedings at the trial for local audiences who had no knowledge of the working of any courts, let alone the ICC.

Achievements

On BBC Media Action's *Communicating Justice* project, reporting the trial of Charles Taylor at the ICC, one listener reflects on the value of Sierra Leonean reporters focusing on issues which were relevant to those affected by Charles Taylor's crimes, and seems to see a relevance to the contemporary politics in Sierra Leone.

> Without the reporters stationed over there we would have been just like the rest of the world getting one-off reports on only what interests the world media. When we listen we feel that those in authority will think about the decisions they make.[5]

The underlying thinking

This project was an example of reporting so-called transitional justice processes. In 1923, Lord Chief Justice Hewart said, 'A long line of cases shows that it is not merely of some importance but is of fundamental importance that justice should not only be done, but should manifestly and undoubtedly be seen to be done.'[6] This is often shortened to 'Justice must be done, and be seen to be done.' In other words, people must have confidence that a justice procedure is impartial and that correct procedures have been followed. It can be an important role for the media when transitional justice processes are under way, to report the processes so that populations can see that justice is being seen to be done.

Transitional justice is a process that follows the end of conflict or of an abusive dictatorship, in which people who have committed human rights violations are held to account. It can take many forms, from the accused being on trial at the ICC, to local or traditional justice or rituals, truth commissions, or the creation of memorials and museums. The purpose is to resolve past problems for a better future, as is explained in *Reporting Transitional Justice: A Handbook for Journalists*.

> By helping to address past human rights crimes, transitional justice aims to break cycles of violence and reduce the likelihood of future conflict. Ensuring that criminals are held accountable in court; that the truth about the past emerges and is documented; that the relationship between citizens and their governments is repaired; and that democratic institutions are created, are all distinct, effective, and compatible ways to address the past.[7]

One principle behind the reporting of justice processes is that populations are more likely to engage with political processes rather than resort to conflict if they feel that justice has been done, and issues resolved.

Common characteristics

The six projects discussed in this chapter were not chosen because they have characteristics in common; indeed, they were chosen to show a range of different approaches to communication for engagement and empowerment. *Radio Biso na Biso* is a small, long-term community radio station. In contrast, the Sudan election project was very short term, covering a range of media: television, radio and print, on a national scale. Girl Effect Rwanda is also on a national scale, but using a different mix of media: a radio magazine programme, a radio serial drama and print, alongside a network of community-based clubs on the ground. It also takes a brand approach, using the tools of commercial marketing, which is unusual in communication for development. *Communicating Justice*, on the trial of Charles Taylor, was international in scale, bringing a major international event to local communities. *Somalia Strengthening Radio Stations* was national in scale, but, again, trying to engage local communities. It took a training of facilitators approach. And the Fondation Hirondelle Myanmar parliament project trained journalists directly, but, again, with the intention of connecting local communities with a national political event.

One clear common characteristic is that engagement and empowerment communication projects tend to work at community level, rather than addressing a mass audience of individuals. They do this through local media or community institutions, like the Girl Effect clubs. This is because empowerment is rarely going to be an individual process, and most often involves solidarity between individuals. (Disempowerment is often the result of the destruction or enfeebling of institutions of solidarity, like trade unions.)

All of these projects involved training journalists, usually journalists who could communicate effectively with communities because of something they share with those communities. For example, the journalists in *Communicating Justice* shared language and experience with their audiences, so understood their audiences' priorities in the reporting of the trial. The journalists Girl Effect train are girls again, because of shared experience with their audience.

Finally, most of these projects were started in response to a political initiative to which the project was a response, aimed at maximizing the positive impact of the initiative. So, the Fondation Hirondelle project in Myanmar was in response to the military authorities relaxing their control and the election of a new parliament, and the IMS/Fojo project in Sudan was in response to the calling of an election, following a peace agreement. The one exception is the Girl Effect project in Rwanda. That was not a response to a specific initiative but, even there, there is an enabling environment. The government of Rwanda has a strong equality agenda, and there is little tolerance of domestic violence – one of the project's key themes – either by society or by the police.

Risks

Projects like these can involve substantial risk, as is shown by these two examples. The BBC Media Action project in Somalia in 2010 and 2011 trained four experienced journalists to be journalist mentors in each of six selected radio stations. Early in the project, one of these mentors had to flee from his home town, where he was working, when he received a phoned death threat, followed by armed men searching his house. Later, one of the radio stations involved in the project had to close because of fighting between militias.

During the IMS/Fojo project for the 2010 elections in Sudan, one international mentor and one national mentor were arrested by the security forces, and the newspaper office where another mentor was working had to close down altogether when it was threatened by an armed and angry mob.

The influence of a political dynamic on project outcomes

These two examples do not just illustrate the physical risks for staff, they also illustrate the wider risk when a communication for development project is created in response to a political initiative. What this means is that the communication for development project is tied into something much bigger than the project itself, which has a dynamic of its own. So the communication for development project is operating within a framework outside of its control, which can have a profound impact on its outcomes.

The Sudan election project illustrates just how profound that impact can be. As a result of events, one of the project's outcomes was the opposite of what was intended. The project intended to strengthen the media coverage of the election. However, the plurality of the media in southern Sudan was reduced by the closure of the newspaper, and so the overall coverage was weakened. This is not to blame the project, but events outside of its control weakened the project's outcomes.

Similarly, what were the outcomes of the Somalia project discussed in this chapter? Somalia did get a new constitution, but, for most Somalis on the ground, its impact was very little. So, in talking extensively about human rights, did the project raise expectations which were never met? If so, one of its outcomes could have been, far from engaging the population in the political process, alienating many even further from it.

What would have happened, for example, with the *Communicating Justice* project, if, after it had got its audiences in West Africa thoroughly engaged with the trial, the ICC had found Charles Taylor not guilty? If that had happened – it did not – instead of contributing to the peace process, the project could have contributed to its fracturing.

Risk mitigation and ways forward

Knowing the territory and being well prepared

These are key to handling some of the severest risks associated with these kind of projects. For example, BBC Media Action had been working in Somalia for more than ten years when the problems arose with the 2010 to 2011 project. The mentors had all received training on dealing with security problems, and the organization had in place measures so that the threatened mentor could immediately be evacuated to safety. The risk of the security situation deteriorating had been raised in the project proposal, so the closure of one of the stations over security issues did not affect the relationship with the donor.

The situation for the Sudan elections project was significantly different. The mentoring part of the project only lasted three weeks, and neither of the organizations involved – IMS and the Fojo Institute – had any long-term presence in Sudan. There was little preparedness on anyone's part, including the mentors. Yet the risks could, perhaps, have been known and addressed in advance. It was known that journalists were regularly arrested in the Southern States, and, globally, elections are often tense and sometimes violent. A preparedness plan was only put in place after the international mentor's release. However, I was the mentor arrested, and I was also at fault for a lack of foresight.

Regarding the mob and the closure of the newspaper, the international mentor (a different one) and the newspaper's staff were put at serious risk. More recently, for example, international staff working for a communication for development INGO were subjected to extremely serious violence in Juba.[8] In that attack, a local journalist was killed. With hindsight, a preparedness plan should have been in place for the mentoring project at the time of the Sudanese elections.

Security

Most international development organizations provide staff with security training for high risk deployments, but, for communication organizations involved in political engagement and empowerment more is needed. With the media increasingly becoming a theatre of war (see Chapter 3) there also needs to be preparedness plans specific to territories and projects, with, where necessary, physical security resources in place.

It is important that an organization which is not familiar with the territory does thorough research, including talking to organizations who have been on the ground for considerable periods of time, before it decides to make a short-term intervention into the politics of any country.

If the decision is to make the intervention, then there needs to be a clear guidelines for staff on how to avoid or mitigate identified risks, taking into account the likelihood of increased tension at times of important political events.

Assessing the political dynamic

However, as has been said, communication projects concerned with political engagement and empowerment face risks beyond security. In particular, the risk that a political dynamic will affect the outcomes of a communication project, rather than the other way round.

When a communication project is to be tied into a larger political initiative – like the Sudan elections or the Somalia constitution development – the organization involved needs to step back and look at the potential dynamic and environment the project will be working in. This should be done at the proposal stage. The organization needs to consider how the larger initiative's dynamic might adversely impact their own project's outcomes. Then, it needs to look at how the project can be designed to minimize any such impact.

Working with state media

Any organization working on projects to help engage populations in a political process may face the risk of appearing to endorse government control of the media. This was the risk for the Fojo/IMS project during the elections in Sudan, in placing a mentor with Southern States Radio, the government radio station. It had by far the largest audience of any of the media in the South, as it covered a significant proportion of the geographical area of the Southern States, whereas the television station and newspapers were largely confined to audiences in Juba, the capital. The newspapers could, obviously, only reach those who could read. The station was, for a very large part of the population of the Southern States, their only source of information.

That intervention could be justified on the grounds that most of the mentor's work was about the mechanisms of the election: registration and how to cast votes in each of the twelve different elections. This was with the aim of helping a population that was completely unfamiliar with elections understand the voting process. This was vital information if the population was going to be able to express their democratic voice. The work could be seen as distinct from the politics of the station.

However, there was also the intervention in getting all the political parties' manifestoes into the news. This was clearly a compromise. I was the mentor at the radio station, and the intervention was my idea, but it was an acceptance of government control of the media. Should it, therefore, not have been done?

The need for committed stakeholders

In the face of political forces, projects need both those directly involved and the politicians to have a serious stake in what the project is trying to achieve. In the Sudan election project, neither the media outlets – newspapers, radio and television stations – nor the politicians had much stake in the outcome of the project. For the media outlets, antagonising political power could have had serious consequences, as the closure of one of them showed. Of course, the media outlets would have to live with that political power long after the project had ended and gone.

In contrast, for *Radio Biso na Biso* (the community radio station in Congo-Brazaville), the organization they hold to account has a very strong stake in the outcomes of the project. Congolaise Industrielle du Bois, the logging company, is far more powerful than the small community of forest dwellers the radio station served, but their international accreditation as a responsible logging company partly depended on the success of the station and their response to what the station said on behalf of the community.

Addressing the risk of financially fragile partners

In BBC Media Action's *Somalia, Strengthening Radio Stations*, one of the factors identified by the research was the financial fragility of the stations, which made them vulnerable to journalistic and political pressure. Yet the research showed that the project's attempts to address the issue of how these stations could make themselves more financially robust had been inadequate.[9] Without being financially robust, it is hard for a media outlet to support robust journalism. Apart from Radio Hargeisa, the state broadcaster for the self-declared Republic of Somaliland, the other participating stations were all commercial. Alongside the serious journalism training, should there have been training in producing very engaging local news stories, the whole basis of local journalism – the drama and conflict of court reports, accidents, crimes, and local success stories – alongside cheap, but effective, advertising? (This is a question which is followed up in the next chapter.)

Ways forward

Perhaps, in the early stages of developing a project, organizations should assess the stakes that different actors are likely to have in the project's outcomes, and any enabling factors in the environment, and make a judgement on likely success. They could also assess if there is anything they can put into the project's design to create powerful stakes or a more enabling environment. And, to put in what needs to be done to enable participating organizations to improve their chances of continuing the project's intentions into the future. Again, all of this would start, at least, from an accurate and thorough needs assessment.

It is certainly true that organizations should assess risk, and assess their own capacity to deal with it, as well as having a sound exit strategy that can be implemented quickly.

It is, therefore, important at the earliest stage, even before seeking funding, for an organization to assess risk and to assess, in the round, the needs of the people and organizations it is intending to help for them to achieve the intended outcomes. It also needs to accurately assess if it, itself, has the experience, organization and resources to effectively support and protect its staff in carrying out their work in that environment. As has been mentioned before, the Reporters Without Borders website, the Press Freedom Index,[10] is a useful first step giving the overall situation of journalism in 180 countries in the world, and the NGO, Article 19, provides detailed information on the situation for journalists in certain countries.

Comprehensive training for staff lies at the heart of many projects of this kind in difficult environments. Production teams need to be confident and well trained, to avoid physical risk, and to avoid the risk that skilful politicians or interest groups can turn broadcasts into propaganda for themselves.

There can also be a risk that such a project raises expectations among audiences that are, ultimately, not fulfilled, damaging the audiences' faith in politics and in the media, and therefore being counterproductive.

This is not to say organizations should not undertake such projects as these in difficult countries and regions, when there is an opportunity of some chance of making a difference to intractable problems, as appeared to be the case, for example, in Somalia in 2010.

Empowerment: A voice for the poor and powerless

This chapter looks at a number of different media techniques and initiatives that either have helped, or are still helping, vulnerable groups have a public voice; or which aim to help them deal better with those in power, in whatever form that might be, including bringing to light and challenging corruption. This field is often known as communication for empowerment[1] or communication for social change.[2] The initiatives range from simple measures that can be included in programmes aimed at a particular group, to community radio stations, to specialist human rights and empowerment programming.

There are several ways in which communication for development organizations seek to empower the powerless:

- by using media to break monopolies on information
- by creating or, better still, helping, a community create a community radio station
- by supporting local media with capacity building in programme formats that can help hold those with power to account, including discussion phone-ins and investigative journalism

Using media to break monopolies on information

Information is power, and power often uses the withholding of information to control others or to enrich itself. One of the easiest ways media can help the poor and vulnerable is to break that hold on information by obtaining the information and broadcasting it themselves. A good example of this was in the BBC Media Action *Somalia Livestock Livelihoods Project,* which ran from 2004 to 2007. As we have seen, this was primarily a distance learning project, aimed at improving practice across the livestock sector in Somalia in order to increase incomes and reduce poverty. However, each weekly programme included topical information of value to all or part of the sector.

One problem poor pastoralists faced when they went to market to sell animals was that the market brokers hid their deals from public view and hearing. They told the seller what the price was by taking the seller's hand and used their fingers on his or her palm to indicate the price. Additionally, the handshake was covered by the broker's shawl. (See Figure 24.1.)

Figure 24.1 *A broker in a livestock market in Somalia shows how he keeps prices secret by indicating a deal with his fingers rather than speaking, and by covering up the deal with his shawl*

As a result, pastoralists went to market without any idea of the going price for what they wanted to sell. Journalists working on the broadcasting project researched each week and found out the prices for different animals on all of Somalia's livestock markets, and then broadcast those prices, breaking the brokers' monopoly on the information.

Creating or helping to create a community radio station

What a community station can do to help empower

A channel between the community and government

International media for development NGO Internews established a network of community radio stations in South Sudan. Internews reported that during a period of drought in Northern Bahr El Ghazal State, a group of women walked a long distance to Nhomlaau FM, which was their nearest community station. They spoke to the station's journalists about their water problem, and the story was broadcast. As a result, the State Governor had two water pumps installed in the village.[3]

Air social injustice and bring change

Mang'elete Radio is a community station in south-east Kenya. It was established in 2004 by thirty-three women's associations. In a report by the Communication for Social Change Consortium, a woman from Matangini village reported that sexual harassment and even rape had been commonplace, and was hidden under a conspiracy of silence, which women were obliged to respect. When the radio station opened, the voices of women and girls began to be heard and, as a result, the incidence of rape and incest dropped 'dramatically'.[4]

Help bring economic empowerment

In the same report, different listeners said that Mang'elete Radio had reduced poverty through a number of different strategies. Losses and theft of livestock had gone down, because it was now possible to get a loss reported on the radio station very quickly. Development issues are discussed in a language and in terms the villagers can understand, and the station addresses issues of environmental degradation.

Provide information for individuals to make informed decisions about their lives

Mang'elete Radio carries information on alcohol, drugs and HIV, and listeners have reported big changes in behaviour with regard to all of these.

Provide a forum for holding local government and others to account

Again, on the subject of Mang'elete Radio, in Kenya one respondent reported that a local politician had closed the village boreholes, so that villagers would have to buy their water from his borehole. The issue was brought up on the radio, and the politician was forced to back down.

Key factors in a successful community radio station

Strong and transparent community governance

In 2013 Internews began a process of handing over their community radio stations to the control of the communities they were in. A first step was to establish an association. The members of the association were elected at a public meeting, and each member agreed that they shared the radio station's values of 'accuracy, fairness and independence'.[5]

Location

Breeze FM is a successful commercial community radio station in the city of Chipata in Eastern Zambia. It reports that it is right in the centre of the city and that this is a characteristic it regards as important.[6]

Similarly, Radyo Bakdaw, the Internews station set up in Guiuan in the Philippines after Typhoon Haiyan in 2013 (discussed in the humanitarian section of this book), was in the middle of the town. Not only did individuals come into the station to talk but there were also notice boards outside, mainly advertising jobs. People could bring damaged radios for the station's technicians to repair and, Friday afternoons, there was a karaoke competition, which attracted large crowds. (See Figure 24.2.)

Figure 24.2 *Part of the crowd enjoying community station, Radyo Bakdaw's regular Friday afternoon karaoke competition in Guiuan, in the Philippines*

By comparison, a similar radio station in the town of Tacloban was in a building on the outskirts, and a pass was required to get into it. As a result, it could not fulfil any of the face-to-face functions of Radyo Bakdaw.

Sustainability

Financial sustainability is a major factor undermining journalistic standards in local radio stations. In 2009, at the start of local radio station training bringing staff from across what was then the Southern States of Sudan, now independent South Sudan, the participants were asked to identify the biggest problems their station faced. In every case, the answer was money.

Breeze FM is a commercial community radio station and it can, it claims, support itself with its profit ploughed back into the station. Breeze FM, however, is in Chipata, a city with a population of nearly 500,000. For community stations in small towns in poorer countries, attracting sufficient advertising revenue to maintain themselves is very difficult.

Any organization that is looking at helping a community establish a community radio station needs to carry out an audit on potential revenue and, if it does not look viable, then long-term funding, possibly from multiple sources, should be sought.

A radio station that cannot pay its journalists runs serious risks with its editorial standards.

Supporting local media with capacity building and programme formats

Capacity building in journalism

Capacity building in basic journalism, that is in the principles and ethics of journalism, the use and acknowledgement of sources and technical training in recording and editing – can help empower local communities. Through this capacity building, communities get accurate and reliable information which they can trust and use to make informed decisions.

Early failures

It is useful here to look at a brief history of capacity building for better journalism in communication for development. What used to be a fairly standard pattern was that workshops were organized in a venue away from the journalists' workplaces, and only journalists attended. The journalists, after the training, went back to their media outlets with new ideas of how to do their job. However, owners and managers, who had not attended the training, did not understand these ideas. So, they did not allow the journalists to practise their new learning. The training had, therefore, been largely pointless.

A different approach

The 2010 and 2011, BBC Media Action project called *Somalia Strengthening Radio Stations*, discussed in the last chapter, was designed to overcome this problem. It engaged managers and owners by obliging them to apply for their radio stations to join the project. It provided training for managers and owners in what their journalists were going to be taught, at the end of which they had to sign up to supporting the training and its outcomes. They also received financial training. Further, the journalists' training was based in the radio stations where they were working.

BBC Media Action's own research into the impact of the project found that:

> Interviewees reported that journalists' understanding and observance of journalistic skills (such as bearing the audience in mind when developing programming; the importance of engaging with audiences and values such as neutrality in reporting) had improved. The project also improved journalists' editing abilities and knowledge of programme editing software … For audiences, the biggest impact of the programme was that the majority reported that stations met the needs of their community.[7]

But the research found that managers and editors had not been involved enough in the training, and, by implication, did not fully grasp what changes their journalists were trying to carry out. It also found that the financial sustainability training available to managers had been inadequate.

Recommendations

Although this is only one project, some recommendations can be drawn from it.

- A project needs to be structured so that the commitment to change in journalism practice on the part of owners and managers of the media outlets involved is clearly stated. One way of achieving this is to make media outlets apply to join a training project.
- Journalists should be trained in their media outlets, on the job, so that there is immediate reinforcement of learning by its application in practice.
- Owners, managers and editors should be included in the training package, so that they fully understand the new practices the journalists are adopting, and they fully understand the benefits to themselves and the media outlet of the new practices.
- Where necessary, adequate business and financial training is provided for owners and managers to improve the financial sustainability of the media outlet, and ensure journalists are paid.
- If necessary, and if ethically possible, medium-term financial support is provided for the media outlet, particularly targeted at adequate remuneration for journalists.

Discussion phone-in programmes

A discussion phone-in programme is one in which there is either an individual or a panel of people in the radio or television station studio. Normally, the programme's presenter will chair the discussion. Listeners or viewers are invited to call with questions or comments, or send them by text, email or via social media, to an individual or all members of the panel, which they are supposed to answer. The presenter can challenge them for not answering a question. Topics can either be chosen by callers, or the presenter can set an agenda.

Station equipment and organization

Discussion phone-in programmes require a device which allows phone calls to be received and fed into the mixing desk, to be recorded or broadcast live, and enough microphones for each panel member. Some stations use a delay device, so that a live discussion is delayed by a few seconds before transmission. This is used so that, in the case of a caller or other participant saying something that should not be broadcast, the broadcast can be temporarily halted.

Some stations employ staff to screen calls before they are put through to the studio guests, opening their phone lines some time before the broadcast starts, so that there is a queue of screened callers ready when the programme starts. Screening is used to ensure that callers have genuine and interesting questions, that they are not repeating a question another caller is asking, that they are in a fit state to go on air (they are not drunk, for example), and that they are not going to abuse or defame anyone or any group, or indulge in hate speech.

In some stations, there will be a producer in the studio cubicle, monitoring the broadcast and in communication with the presenter through headphones or an earpiece. This is so that there is a double check on what is said. For example, if someone involved says something defamatory on air and the presenter does not notice, the producer can alert the presenter and a retraction can be asked for from the participant who said the words.

A live broadcast needs to be carefully timed to ensure that, if there is an agenda of topics, they are all covered, and that the programme ends at the allotted time. If there is a producer, then he or she will be responsible for the timing; otherwise, it will be done by the presenter.

These programmes need careful preparation and handling, and *Module J8: Producing a live phone-in discussion programme*, in Section 6, provides training agendas and materials.

How these programmes can help empower local communities

By allowing ordinary people to speak directly to politicians or others with power in a public forum, phone-in discussions give opportunities for communities to hold those with power to account. Of course, politicians can refuse to take part but, if the programme is scheduled regularly, it becomes more and more difficult for a politician to refuse, as that could begin to look suspicious – as if the individual has something to hide from public scrutiny.

As individual members of a community get more used to posing questions and hearing others posing questions, then their confidence and self-efficacy can increase, which in itself can be an empowering process. They can also begin to feel more engaged with the political process.

Making phone-ins effective

Most of the requirements for making effective phone-in discussion programmes are covered in the training module mentioned above.

One key issue is the make-up of the panel, if there is one. There needs to be a range of experience and opinion among the panel, if possible broadly representative of the range of opinion in the community.

Risks

There are countries in the world where to try to hold those with power to account brings substantial risk, either to the individuals concerned or to the broadcasting station itself. These risks may not be obvious, especially to an international organization. On the other hand, self-censorship is also a great risk to journalism. This means that a risk assessment should be carried out to ensure that, on the one hand, no one involved in the programmes is being put at serious risk, while, on the other hand, the organization is not being over-cautious, and limiting its journalism for no real reason.

Investigative journalism

This is a kind of journalism that does not cover the main range of news. The main range of news is visible and obvious: political statements, accidents, new factories opening and so on. Investigative journalism tries to bring the hidden to light, especially when whatever is hidden has been deliberately hidden for some reason. Often, this will be corruption, crime or hidden agendas. A hidden agenda might be where a politician is making decisions based on motives other than those stated, for example.

How this can help to empower communities

By uncovering errors or wrongdoing which have affected or are affecting a community, investigative journalism can open up the opportunity for the community to do something itself to rectify the problem, or for the community to get someone else – someone in power, for example – to do something to rectify the problem. For example, suppose there is a situation where communities in a difficult-to-access region are not getting boreholes dug to provide clean water. There is a project to provide boreholes, but the implementing agency is not installing them, while reporting to the donor who is paying them that they are. If a journalist or a team of journalists can obtain copies of the reports being given to the donor, and compare what is written in them with the reality on the ground, then the donor can take action to get the boreholes installed, and whatever other action they may want to take.

How to make investigative journalism effective

There is a training plan and a set of materials in *Module J9: Investigative journalism*, in Section 6.

During a similar training, a team of two journalists in Somalia found a story about corruption in the building of camps for displaced people near Bossaso, a port used at that time by people displaced by conflict in South Somalia trying to get to Yemen. The building of the camps was funded by UN organizations and international NGOs.

The overall case that this team put together focused on the discrepancies in standards between a camp built by one Somali organization in comparison with a camp built by another. As is shown here, there had been earlier research into this case, which had been unable to come to a conclusion.

Camp X, built by Agency 1, was built and equipped to a significantly lower standard than Camp Y, built by Agency 2, on similar budgets.

These points were confirmed by two sources:

- In Camp X the shelters were not adequate for living in, and only 10 per cent of residents were in proper tents. By comparison, 80 per cent of Camp Y residents were in proper tents. In fact, the residents of Camp X were given sticks and plastic sheeting, and had to build their own shelters.
- In Camp X there was one toilet per ten families, as against one toilet per two families in Camp Y.

- In Camp X, water could only be obtained from a well, while in Camp Y there was a distribution network of taps providing water.
- In Camp X there was no health point, and no health campaign. In Camp Y, there was a health point with a stock of medicines and medical staff and they ran sanitation and health campaigns in the camp.

A local businessman the team had tracked down said that Agency 1 was one of two NGOs who asked for receipts to show inflated amounts. The example he gave was a receipt (which had been seen by the journalists) for $35,000, when, in fact, the goods had cost $15,000. This corroborated earlier research findings that, when valued, the goods bought by Agency 1 were worth significantly less than the agency claimed it had paid, and it showed that Agency 1 looked like the instigator of a fraud.

The charge that an interview based on this investigation would have put to Agency 1, therefore, was that it had spent far less on Camp X than it had claimed, and less than Agency 2 had spent on Camp Y, and that this looked like deliberate fraud.

Risks

Again, there are countries in the world where investigating what those with power are doing secretly brings substantial risk, either to the individuals concerned or to the broadcasting station itself. Again, these risks may not be obvious, especially to an international organization. As already said, to veer towards self-censorship is also unhelpful. Again, this means that a risk assessment should be carried out to ensure that, on the one hand, no one involved in the programmes is being put at serious risk, while, on the other hand, the organization is not being over-cautious, and limiting its journalism for no real reason.

Training agendas and materials

Suggested agendas and materials for training in topics relevant to this chapter can be found in Section 6:

Module J7: News for a community station
Module J8: Producing a live phone-in discussion programme
Module J9: Investigative journalism

Engaging an audience in human rights and political processes

Engaging an audience in human rights

This chapter is about helping populations understand and engage with the whole concept of human rights and the nature of individual rights, rather than training journalists in how to report on violations of human rights.

In 2010 and 2011, there was a BBC Media Action project in Somalia called *Nolosha iyo Qaanunka* (*Life and Law*). The context for this project was the writing of a new draft constitution for Somalia. This was necessary because the existing government, known as the Transitional Federal Government, had been set up in 2004, and was only ever intended as an interim measure. It was part of a very long process of trying to bring peace to Somalia. A new constitution was needed to establish a permanent government. There had been a civil war in parts of Somalia since 1991. The north-west region, calling itself Somaliland, and the north-east region, called Puntland, had both achieved a level of peace and had functioning governments. However, the south central region was still at war, with large areas of the region under the control of the Islamist group Al Shabab, which aligned itself with Al Qaida. In fact, the Transitional Federal Government only controlled a part of the country's capital, Mogadishu, and no other territory. There was substantial international impetus behind the new constitution-making process, and the hope was that a new constitution would contribute to a successful peace process.

The Consultation Draft Constitution, as the new constitution for Somalia was then called, put considerable weight on human rights. Not only did it include many of the articles of the UDHR, it also set up a Human Rights Commission to enforce these rights. In general, it went far beyond any previous Somali constitution in this area.

Among the population, however, any understanding of the concept of human rights or of the individual rights themselves was extremely limited. Outside of the Republic of Somaliland, in the north east, which had declared itself independent, no one in the country, unless they had lived abroad, had ever lived under a rights-based system of government, and there was routine and widespread violation of rights.

Even in Somaliland, which had a functioning, democratic government, some rights were routinely violated. Freedom of movement, for example, was very restricted in the south by warlord-controlled checkpoints. In Somaliland, and elsewhere, the free movement of the extensive nomadic population was being increasingly restricted by the enclosure of land for agriculture.

Clearly, this was a very challenging context for trying to engage the population in an understanding of human rights.

A participatory format

Just to broadcast the rights, even with an explanation, would have been very abstract and remote. So, a format was devised that would link individual rights with listeners' life experience. Discussions of individual rights were recorded in small groups. In a group there would be someone who could explain the right to two or three other people, who would be ordinary Somalis, but chosen because the right under discussion would have particular relevance to their lives. The discussion was led by a journalist.

The rights specialist explained the right, and there was discussion to clarify its meaning for the other members of the group. The journalist then interviewed the other members of the group, on the impact that this particular right would have on their lives if it was introduced and enforced.

Two examples of how this format worked are given here.

Example 1: On the right to freedom of expression

The article in the draft constitution said,

1. A person has the right to express their opinions and to impart information and ideas in any way.
2. A person has the right to seek and to receive ideas.
3. A person has the right to express their artistic creativity, and to academic freedom and freedom of scientific research.

One member of the discussion panel had been chosen because he was from an unidentified place where there was no freedom of expression. (Most listeners would assume he lived somewhere under the control of Al Shabab.) When the right was explained to the panel, they all quickly understood it, but were astonished at the scope of expression the right would guarantee, and were pleased with the idea. However, the third Member of the panel, from the place where there was no freedom of expression, reflected that it would be great to have freedom of expression but questioned whether the constitution would ever come to where he lived.

Example 2: On environmental rights

The article in the draft constitution said,

1. A person has the right to an environment that is not harmful to their health or well-being.
2. A person has the right to have the environment protected from pollution and other damage.
3. Everyone has the right to have the natural resources of the nation protected from unsustainable exploitation.

The panel gathered by the journalist for this right consisted of an elder from a village where the environment has been badly affected by charcoal production, a local journalist concerned with the environment, the head of a local environmental NGO, Horn Relief, and a man who cuts down trees and burns the wood for charcoal. (Northern Somalia is an arid environment. The uncontrolled and extensive cutting down of trees for the production of charcoal leaves the land very vulnerable to wind and water erosion.)

The village elder welcomed the idea of the right but the charcoal burner was dismissive, and clearly did not expect that the constitution would be enforced.

The journalist widened the discussion by asking the head of Horn Relief what was happening in the sea. She reported that waste dumped by passing ships was severely damaging the offshore reef, which is a breeding ground for fish, the implication being that the fishing industry was under threat. She went on to say that international shipping was free to do this because of the lack of action by the government, which was unaccountable. Hence the importance of the draft constitution, so linking the constitution to the realities of the fishing industry.

Assembling this panel to discuss this right meant that the article of the draft constitution on this right was discussed in a lively, conflicting discussion thoroughly grounded in the realities of life for Somalis, bringing human rights and, in fact, the whole constitution into a perspective in which listeners could engage with it.[1]

This simple format appeared to work well to bring the concept of rights and individual rights into a sphere where people with no experience of a rights-based system and little understanding of the concept of rights could engage with them.

Engaging an audience in a political process

In 2016, BBC Media Action published a paper called *Inspiring Political Participation, Lessons from the Media*,[2] which looked at the practices and outcomes of governance projects it had carried out with funding from the UK Department of International Development, in twelve countries, since 2011. The paper drew up some key guidelines for what makes successful programming in this field, based on research with some 23,000 respondents.

The key guidelines can be summarized as follows:

- Understand that information, on its own, is not enough, and there needs to be discussion.
- Provide role models of political participation.
- Ensure there is balance of diverse opinions, for constructive dialogue.
- Be adaptable to changing media and political landscapes.
- Facilitate audience participation and two-way communication, through a variety of channels.
- Accept that any change towards political participation is a long-term process.

Most of the projects referred to in this paper involved panel discussion programmes in front of a live audience, who could also ask members of the panel questions.

Nolosha iyo Qaanunka, the Somali project already discussed in this chapter, also aimed at promoting political participation. The programmes were also in a very different format from those discussed in this paper. However, the paper's findings for what makes a successful governance project corresponded closely with the practices that had been carried out in *Nolosha iyo Qaanunka.*

Adaptability to the political situation

This is one of the key guidance points in the BBC Media Action paper. It is worth looking at *Nolosha iyo Qaanunka* as an example of that adaptability, given the extreme demands the situation created. This is given as an example of analysing what a project is trying to do, and how it developed a format to try to meet those demands.

The context

Nolosha iyo Qaanunka was a part of a wider United Nations Development Programme (UNDP) project. The overall project's aim was not only to inform the audience about the new Consultation Draft Constitution (CDC) for Somalia, but to encourage feedback from the audience on it, with a view to its revision. This feedback would then be passed back to the government and to the body that had originally developed the CDC, the Independent Federal Constitution Commission. What was being asked for was for members of the public to take part in a public consultation exercise on the draft constitution. That is political participation.

It has already been said that this was a challenging situation with regard to addressing the human rights elements of the draft constitution. There were further challenges. The CDC was a document of 179 articles, set out in sixteen chapters. It covered issues of citizenship, individual's fundamental rights, issues of property rights, the environment, how the democracy would function, the structure of the republic, the parliamentary system and the parliament, the presidency, the judiciary, public finances and peace and security. Most of these were concepts with which the people of Somalia were almost entirely unfamiliar. As said, large areas of the country had had no government since 1991.

The gulf between the aspiration and the situation

To give some examples of what this meant in terms of people's engagement with the CDC. There were six articles on citizenship, when, for most people in Somalia, no government means no citizens. Most of the population had never had rights. Property rights had been extensively violated, and continued to be. Somalia, as a whole, had only fleetingly had democratic government at any time in its history. For most, there was no judiciary and there was no peace and no security.

Furthermore, there had never been a public consultation exercise, outside of Somaliland.

Looking at participation from a behaviour change approach

When a project is making broadcast programmes to help an audience engage with a political process, it is useful to follow some elements of the behaviour change communication approach. (This approach is discussed fully in Section 5 of this book.) So, to try to bridge the gulf between the political aspiration of public participation and the reality on the ground, *Nolosha iyo Qaanunka* took some elements of a behaviour change approach. (This is also hinted at in the BBC Media Action paper, in the key guidance to show role models of political participation.)

It should be noted that this means that any such project needs a robust editorial process to ensure that this approach does not move into political manipulation of an audience.

(However, having a structured behaviour change element would probably not be the case, for example, in a transitional justice project which is reporting on a trial, unless, perhaps, there is an explicit parallel peace and reconciliation process going on, in which the population are being encouraged to participate at a national or local level.)

In following a partly behaviour change approach, a first step in a political engagement project is, through research, to identify the key barriers to political engagement among different parts of the audience.

In the example of *Nolosha iyo Qaanunka*, the project developed a profile of the audience. In this case, a huge international effort, coordinated by UNDP, and other organizations, particularly the US-based National Democratic Institute for International Affairs, had done a great deal of research. A workshop was organized that brought together organizations that had carried out research and individuals who had close knowledge of the understanding and attitudes of the Somali people.

The profile revealed that there were more factors widening the gulf between many members of the audience and the draft constitution and the constitutional process.

The profile showed that a majority had never heard of the draft constitution or the process. Of those who had heard of them, some were opposed to the draft constitution, because they believed it to be a foreign imposition, because they thought it was opposed to their interests, or because they associated it with the government. Some had no interest in the process; others thought that peace needed to be established before there could be a constitution-making process; and yet others thought that the constitution would not change anything.

It is important, after a profile of the audience has been drawn up, that it is kept in mind what the project is aiming to achieve when identifying barriers. In this case, opposition to the draft constitution, for whatever reason, was not a barrier, as the programmes were to encourage participation in the process, not to encourage support for the draft constitution.

What this profile also showed is that the project's programmes had to be hybrids, that is, delivering information though straightforward journalism for the majority who knew nothing about the draft constitution and the consultation process, and a behaviour change approach to encourage participation.

The next stage in the development of a behaviour change element is to determine the major steps in terms of knowledge, attitude and behaviour. A change in behaviour is normally only going to happen in these major steps: a change of knowledge, leading to a change of attitude and then to a change of behaviour. (See Chapter 2 for a full discussion of this process.)

In the example of *Nolosha iyo Qaanunka,* these major stages would be:

- a change of knowledge: to learn about and understand there is a consultation process on the draft constitution, how the process works and what it aims to achieve
- a change of attitude: to develop an attitude of wanting to participate in the consultation process
- a change of behaviour: to go from non-participation to participation

Behaviour change usually requires that an audience are taken through the process of change step by step. So, breaking these major steps down into smaller steps might look like this:

- to understand what the process is, how it works and how their voices will be heard
- to understand why there is a public consultation process
- to understand why they are being asked to participate and have a right to shape the constitution
- to understand that this is different from previous constitution-making processes, in giving them this right
- to hear the case for and against whether their participation will make a difference
- to understand what their participation is and what makes the constitution special and gives it legitimacy
- to understand what they can do to participate

These steps would probably need to be broken down further, to make each of them small enough for broadcast. (See Chapter 30 for a full discussion of how this is done.)

Choosing a format

The choice of a programme's format will depend partly on the nature of the political process within which the programmes are trying to encourage participation.

In the case of *Nolosha iyo Qaanunka,* the audience needed to receive information on different strands in parallel, in order to make sense of the process they were being asked to participate in. For example, they needed to learn about the constitution at the same time as learning about the consultation process, since neither made sense without an understanding of the other. For that reason, a magazine format of different broad topic strands running together was chosen, developed in the way described in Chapter 21, on distance learning.

The strands developed included the following:

- what a constitution is, that is the nature of a constitution and what one does, with examples, especially of constitutions which have been part of a peace process

- participation, that is taking listeners through the fact that there is a consultation process, how it works and how listeners could participate in it
- audience opinion, that is a strand of opinion, based on audience research, that is put forward for listeners to discuss, such as 'We need peace before a constitution'
- the draft constitution and human rights, that is participatory discussions of articles in the draft constitution
- the big issues, that is information and conflicting views on major questions over the draft constitution, like 'Is the draft constitution compliant with Shari'ah law?'

Participants in the programmes

For the behaviour change element of the programmes to work, there needs to be plenty of voices of people from the viewing or listening audience. This has a twofold purpose. The first is so that issues are raised in discussion at a level the audience are familiar with, and the second is to provide viewers or listeners with role models of participation. Such participation could be in the small panel format described earlier in this chapter, in phone-in programmes, or in larger discussion formats.

Discussion promotes understanding

Discussion is vital in programmes like these. If an issue is discussed between people who are from the viewing or listening audience and someone who is well informed on the issue, then the people who are from the audience can ask questions – questions which reflect the knowledge levels in the audience – until they understand the issue. When they understand it, there is a good chance that most in the audience will have been taken with them through the discussion, and understand, too. A well-chosen panel of participants can also represent the range of opinion among the audience, and so different members of the audience can hear their opinions being expressed, and through that they can identify with and get access to the debate.

Discussion promotes discussion among the audience

A second vital function of discussion in the programmes is that it is likely to promote discussion among the audience after the programmes. This matters because talk helps to internalize learning but, also, evidence suggests social attitudes or social norms are changed through discussion. So, the three stages of behaviour change can happen. The change in knowledge comes from the programme contents and, especially, discussion items, and the change in attitude from discussions between audience members, leading to behaviour change, and participation in whatever political process the project is about. (For a full account of the role of discussion in learning see Chapter 2, and in behaviour change see Chapters 26 and 28.)

In the example project, BBC Media Action's *Nolosha iyo Qaanunka* (*Life and Law*), which ran from 2010 to 2011, during the public consultation period for a new draft constitution for Somalia, there were two discussion slots.

One was the discussion slot on the human rights articles of the draft constitution, which is explored at the beginning of this chapter. In the programmes, the panels of listeners who were chosen to take part usually included one who knew nothing about the draft constitution, one who was opposed to it, and one who was positive about it. In this way, the make-up of the panels reflected the broad positions of audience members. What the panels also provided was role models of ordinary people, whatever their opinions of the draft constitution, participating in the process. Role models are essential in behaviour change communication. (For a full discussion of role models, see Chapter 26.)

That discussion slot was at the detailed level of the draft constitution, the individual article level. The second discussion slot was at the 'big theme' level. These big themes were both those in the draft constitution and those about the draft constitution. The big themes within the draft constitution were compliance with Shari'ah law, human rights, gender, federalism and land and property. The big themes about the draft constitution were, for example, there is no need for a constitution when we have the Quran, the draft constitution is a foreign imposition and the constitution is the only available route to peace versus we need peace before a new constitution.

For this slot, one of these big themes was chosen and two well-informed speakers gave the case for and against the proposition. Listeners were invited to call in with their responses. (The project used a missed-call system; that is, callers phoned the number broadcast and ended the call before it connected, but the number was recorded, and project staff phoned back to record a short interview. This process saved callers the cost of their call.) This process, on its own, was showing listeners role models of participation.

Lessons learnt

Ultimately, the demands made on *Nolosha iyo Qaanunka*, by the political situation – the mismatch between the aims of the overall project and the situation on the ground, the sheer complexity of the draft constitution, and the failure by the international community to get the various governments in the country to engage with the process – probably rendered it unsuccessful.

However, it is important to try and fail, as long as there is learning from the failure. Discussing *Nolosha iyo Qaanunka* at length in this chapter is an effort to learn from it.

A final key lesson is, when participation in a very large political project, as the draft constitution was, is offered, it is vital to assess how far the success of your organization's effort will depend on the decisions of others, over which you have no control. (This issue is discussed in Chapters 23 and 24.) A concomitant to that assessment is to assess how far, and in what ways, any failure might do harm to the audience. In this case, as discussed in Chapter 23, could harm have been done in increasing cynicism about political participation?

Training agendas and materials

Suggested agendas and materials for training in topics relevant to this chapter can be found in Section 6:

Module J8: Producing a live phone-in discussion programme
Module J9: Investigative journalism
Module J10: The production of factual programmes for behaviour change

Section Five

Communication for behaviour and social change

An overview of communication for change

The capacity of the media to influence behaviour change has been recognized for many years, particularly in stirring up violence against selected groups, as, for example, Julius Streicher achieved with his newspaper *Der Stürmer*, in the mid-1930s in Nazi Germany, stirring up hatred against Jews. Using media to influence behaviour in a constructive way began in earnest in the 1970s, and now communication for behaviour and social change is a very widespread use of communication in development. More recently, techniques developed in the 1970s have been blended with theories of behaviour and social change to produce highly organized methodologies like the US government's Centers for Disease Control and Prevention's *Modelling and Reinforcement to Combat HIV* (MARCH).

A brief history

Before the 1970s, there had been attempts to use drama to promote change, but successful behaviour change drama really started in 1977. In that year Miguel Sabido, a vice-president at *Televisa*, a large television company in Mexico, began to produce telenovelas aimed at creating behaviour change. (A telenovela is a long-running, episode-by-episode drama.) He is credited with inventing the transitional character. A transitional character is one who starts off displaying behaviour that is the opposite to the one the drama is promoting but which, over time, changes that behaviour, thus role-modelling behaviour change for viewers or listeners to follow.

As has been mentioned in Chapter 1, one of these telenovelas, *Acompáñame*, was aimed at changing behaviour regarding family-planning practices, and it had a remarkable impact. According to Population Media Center, among other impacts attributed to the programme, the number of women going to family-planning facilities went up by 33 per cent in 1977, the first year of broadcast. By comparison, in the previous year there had been a small decline in attendances. Contraceptive sales went up by 23 per cent in the same year. Again, by way of comparison, there had been a much smaller increase in the previous year. Most tellingly, from 1977 to 1986 Mexico's population growth dropped by 34 per cent, and a USAID speaker attributed much of the credit to the *Televisa* behaviour change telenovelas, which had been on during that time.[1]

Another early example of a soap opera seeking behaviour change, this time on radio and in Africa, was *Twende na Wakati (Let's Go with the Times)*, in Tanzania. The serial drama had been produced by PCI-Media Impact and broadcast on the national radio station. It aimed at changing behaviour related to HIV and family planning. It made use of the transitional character concept. Among a number of results suggesting positive impact, the number of people going to family-planning clinics for the first time increased by 50 per cent in the first six months of the drama being on air in 1993, while in an area where the drama was not heard, the number of people going to family planning clinics for the first time stayed at much the same level throughout 1993 and 1994.[2]

More or less in parallel with *Twende na Wakati, Soul City* was launched in South Africa in 1994 and is still on air in 2019. At its core a television drama, the project also uses radio and print materials, and social mobilization activities on the ground. It has a wide brief covering the whole range of health issues as well as social issues, including housing and land, violence and employment.

Strengthening the theoretical base

Esta de Fossard's book *How to Write a Radio Serial Drama for Social Development* was published in 1996 by Johns Hopkins University, while MARCH was developed by Centers for Disease Control in 2000–2.

These last two combined Sabido's methodology with theories of social change. The term 'modelling' refers to the use of role-model characters in the dramas, and reinforcement refers to on-the-ground activities, like travelling theatre groups, and support from other people.

The approach that this book takes is based on the MARCH methodology.

Serial dramas for behaviour and social change have been used to address many different areas of behaviour. Miguel Sabido himself produced telenovelas addressing: registering for literacy classes and adult education; parenting; women's role in society and the family; and silence on the subject of street children.[3] *Beled Taki Hou Taki (Your Home Is Yours)*, a radio serial drama in what is now South Sudan, made by Free Voice, was aimed at changing behaviour among returning refugees in 2008 and 2009. The international NGO La Benevolencija uses radio serial dramas in Rwanda, Burundi and the Democratic Republic of Congo, among other countries, to change behaviour to break the cycle of violence, by promoting, for example, 'active bystandership', that is, encouraging witnesses to violence to intervene rather than simply observe.

Both *Beled Taki Hou Taki* and the La Benevolencija dramas used or use the Fossard methodology. The MARCH methodology has been used to address issues other than HIV. For example, it was used in two BBC Media Action radio serial dramas on mother and baby health in South Sudan, starting in 2012, and Somalia from 2011 to 2013. It was also used by the organization Girl Effect, with funding from private sources and the UK government's Department for International Development, in dramas promoting the empowerment of adolescent girls in Ethiopia, Rwanda and Malawi.

Some behaviour change projects are part of a wider project, where there are different elements that are mutually supporting and reinforcing. For example, starting in 2012 BBC Media Action in South Sudan has been broadcasting *Our School*, a factual radio programme trying to bring about behaviour change that will keep more girls going to school for longer. The broadcasts are part of the much wider *Girls Education South Sudan* project, which includes a cash-transfer scheme, which helps families with the costs of keeping their girls going to school, and provides grants to schools to improve facilities for girls and teacher training.

Individual change and social change

The methodologies discussed are based largely on the understanding that much behaviour and social change is normally a gradual, step-by-step process, and are based on role modelling, using either characters in a serial drama or real people in factual programmes to model the behaviour change sought. (Some organizations talk about messages for bringing about behaviour change, but the argument against messaging has already been made in Chapter 2.)

Behavioural scientists are careful to distinguish between behaviour change and social change. They say that both are necessary to sustain new, healthy and constructive behaviours in a given population, and can be targets for communication. The distinction is that behaviour change is an individual process, while social change is a wider change in norms, attitudes and practices at societal level.

It is a basic tenet of many behaviour change approaches that people's behaviour is influenced by the attitudes and practices of people around them and what is considered 'normal' for their group. Thus sustainable individual behaviour change needs accompanying change in social norms. This is the MARCH approach, which argues that, while individual behaviour change may be carried out by someone on their own, it is unlikely to be sustained without supportive change in attitudes among those around the individual. Whatever slight difference there may be, both approaches require that communication is designed to bring about both behaviour change and social change.

While it might be possible for an individual to change their behaviour alone, and without talking to anyone else about it, that cannot be true for changing social norms. For a social norm to change among a group of people, there must be communication about it. People need to talk about it. In other words, and reflecting the role of talk in learning, stimulating talk among the audience is crucial for facilitating social change in support of behaviour change, and thus for making the change sustainable. (For the role of talk in learning, see Chapter 2 and *Module J1: An exploration of how people learn* in Section 6.)

Key concepts in behaviour change communication

The duration of a change

Changing behaviour can be a complicated process, because so many factors can be involved. While some change can happen overnight, normally it is a gradual process over time. In general, the more deep-seated the behaviour, the longer change can take.

For some behaviour changes to occur, the individual needs to challenge parts of their identity. In some cultures, for example, a man gains status from having multiple sexual partners and there is an admiring name for such men, so that behaviour is part of their identity. However, that behaviour is clearly putting themselves and their partners at risk of HIV infection. To change to less risky behaviour involves challenging that named identity, and identity can be very deep-seated. Many serial dramas attempting to combat HIV try to challenge perceptions and self-perception of what a 'real man' is. Such change is likely to take a long time. In one MARCH drama in Zambia, *Gama Cuulu*, the scriptwriters developed a storyline showing a male character changing his HIV-risk behaviour by reducing the number of sexual partners he had. The writing team allotted two years for the achievement of the changes.

New knowledge and skills precede change

A further key concept in behaviour change communication is that there are precursor changes to taking action. These include increasing knowledge and, often, developing skills; changing attitudes and beliefs, especially relating to the risk of existing behaviours and weighing up the consequences of new behaviours.

Change of behaviour is very unlikely to occur for an individual without new knowledge, particularly of the risks on the one hand and of the benefits on the other. It is also unlikely if the individual is not able to relate that knowledge to him- or herself. To put it another way, if someone does not know the benefits of changing their behaviour, and the risks of not changing their behaviour, then no change is likely to happen. Similarly, if someone knows about those benefits and risks, but cannot see that they are relevant to themselves, then, again, no change is likely to happen.

A change of behaviour also often requires the acquisition of skills. Learning how to negotiate with others to allow change to happen is a communication skill that is often necessary. For example, a young mother-to-be may need to negotiate with her mother-in-law over what happens to the baby immediately after birth, to ensure it is not given water, which, in many countries, can put the baby's life at risk.

A step-by-step approach

Change is easier if people are shown small steps they can take towards it, rather than being expected to make one huge leap. This is partly a matter of self-confidence. It can take a great deal of confidence to make a big change, especially if it is one that is not fully understood or supported by others. Taking things step by step means that the achievement of one step can build self-confidence for taking the next, and so on.

Role models are central

Self-efficacy, that is, an individual's belief that they can make the change asked for, is held to be a very important factor in successful behaviour change, particularly in overcoming any setback. Clearly, if an individual understands the risks and benefits, and sees they are relevant to themselves, but does not believe they can make the change, again, change is unlikely to happen. So, behaviour change communication focuses on building that belief.

If, in factual programmes, audience members hear or see people like themselves who have already made the change, or are in the process of making the change, then that is likely to build their belief that they can, too. In a drama, a fictional character, who is like themselves, going through the process of change, is likely to have a similar impact.

Role models can be powerful learning tools, motivating others and showing, in detail, how change can be achieved: how problems can be overcome, where to seek support, or how to negotiate, for example.

Competing for an audience

Behaviour change communication needs to be highly engaging, competing effectively for audiences with other broadcasting. If someone is not listening or viewing, they will not change.

Behaviour change communication needs, particularly, to attract and engage listeners who do not agree with the changes it is trying to bring about. This is for a number of reasons.

The people who do not agree with the programmes' intentions are the people who the programmes need to influence the most. It is for this reason that the key characters in serial dramas for behaviour change start off by displaying the behaviour that is furthest from the behaviour the project is promoting. The intention is that audience members who themselves behave that way will identify with those characters. As those characters change, those audience members will, it is hoped, be taken on the same journey of change. Through the role models, they will learn the risks of no change and the benefits of change, see the skills needed to make change, and build the self-efficacy to achieve change.

Conflict to provoke discussion

As has already been noted, discussion of the issues raised in the programmes is an important part of learning and bringing about social change. Clearly, factual programmes or dramas that only present one side of an argument are not going to promote discussion. So, factual programmes for behaviour change need to present both sides of any case, views that support the aims of the programmes and views that are opposed, and they should be left, as they stand, for the audience to discuss them. In a drama, there needs to be conflict between characters, again, promoting discussion in the audience.

As has been said in Chapter 2, learning does not take place when people listen, but in discussion after listening. It has been standard practice in education, for a long time, to encourage talk as it is an essential part of learning: it is when people internalize knowledge. There is strong evidence that getting the audience to discuss issues raised in programmes enormously increases the impact. For example, a research finding from a campaign in Indonesia called *Involving Husbands in Safe Motherhood* was:

Husbands who talked to someone about becoming an alert husband were ten times more likely to say that they gained new knowledge compared to men who did not engage in interpersonal communication.[4]

Culture is everything

Behaviour change communication projects should pay close attention to the culture in which they are operating, as culture is enormously influential on the behaviour of individuals. If there is a cultural practice that is, for example, putting the health of individuals at risk, then a behaviour change project may wish to challenge the culture to reduce or eliminate the risk.

However, rather than confronting a culture head-on, it is better to research whether there is a culturally acceptable alternative available. As discussed in Chapter 2, in some parts of South Sudan, there is a strongly held practice that involves giving a baby a piece of food when it is seven days old. This is very risky, as it may well expose the child to a diarrhoeal infection.

Discussion with a group of people from the culture revealed how strongly the practice is held. If a child is born outside South Sudan, and does not go through the ceremony, then, if they visit South Sudan, they need to go through it, even if they are adult. On the basis of this, one of the group suggested that, in the drama the project was making, the ceremony could be shown to be postponed until the baby was six months old, when it would be weaned onto solid food anyway. The group agreed that this would be a culturally acceptable alternative, in the light of the new knowledge about the risk to the baby's health.

Using accurate terminology

When a team is involved in a behaviour and social change communication project, it is important to use accurate and precise terminology. For example, in a health project, it is better to refer to behaviour that puts health at risk as 'risky', whether it is hygiene practices in baby care, or HIV; or if, say, the topic is smoking, then smoking can be described as 'unhealthy', while someone trying to give up smoking can be described as moving towards 'healthier' behaviour. These terms are better than describing behaviour as 'negative' or 'positive'.

The reason this matters is that terms like negative and positive can acquire other connotations. This is especially a concern in dramas, though it does apply to factual programmes as well. A character seen as negative in terms of the particular behaviour concerned can quickly be seen by writers and producers as more widely negative. The character can acquire morally questionable characteristics, or even social and economic ones. However, a character seen by writers as positive can acquire more morally upright characteristics and can even become economically more successful.

Yet there is no necessary link between more healthy behaviour, for example, and either moral rectitude or economic success. A smoker can be a generous giver to charity or volunteer to care for old people, while someone who has given up smoking can, in the moral sphere, be selfish and exploitative. A character who continues to put themselves and others at risk of HIV infection can run a successful business, while a character who has learned to protect him-/herself from HIV can be a business failure.

This is not to say that a character who continues to put themselves and others at risk should not be seen to face the health consequences of that behaviour. Of course, putting others unknowingly at risk has a moral dimension, but a drama or factual series should not suggest that behaviour change leads to moral or economic status outside the immediate sphere of the behaviour. A key measure to help prevent this creep – which may well be unconscious on the part of the writers – is to be precise and consistent in the terminology used in the project.

Choosing a format

The advantages of drama

The strengths of a drama are that storylines can be shaped at will to take characters on convincing journeys of change, so that viewers or listeners can follow, over a realistic time scale (which can be months or years), a character role model going through a process of change. (Such a thing is theoretically possible in a factual series, and how it could be done is discussed below.)

Drama can create emotional engagement between audience members and characters, which is, again, very much harder in factual programmes. Research by BBC Media Action has shown this is very valuable in promoting behaviour change.[5]

A drama can show the tragic consequences of not changing behaviour, sometimes graphically, even to the point of a character dying, and that, too, can have a real impact. To include such a thing in a factual programme would be unethical and exploitative, even if real interviewees could be found.

It is much easier to create dilemmas for promoting discussion among the audience in fiction, than in factual programmes.

A huge advantage that drama has over factual programmes is that, since it is entirely made up, a drama never runs the risk – as there can be in factual programmes – of not being able to find interviewees with the experience and knowledge needed for a particular topic. For example, behaviour change projects are often keen to find interviewees who are, in the jargon, positive deviants, that is, people who have made the change the project is trying to achieve, before the project started. Such interviewees can be very difficult to find.

A disadvantage of drama

There is one area where drama can be weaker than factual programming, unless written by a very skilled team. In a drama, it takes considerable skill to convey factual information, say, on hygiene or how HIV is transmitted, without the dialogue sounding forced and artificial. It can also be difficult to have discussion of the issues the drama is about, within the drama, unless that discussion takes place in a context of conflict;

otherwise, such discussions can make a drama less compelling. It is achieving this convincingly that takes skill.

The advantages of factual programmes

The great strength of factual programmes for behaviour change for some in the audience will be that they feature real people – people like the listening or viewing audience – talking about their efforts at change and their successes. It will include opposing opinions – again, those of people like themselves – about fears on the behaviour change being discussed, and on the need for the change and the wisdom of changing. It will include listeners or viewers asking questions they themselves want answers to, and receiving those answers. It will be a series of programmes they can dip in and out of, without losing the thread, as they might if they dipped out of a drama.

The disadvantages of factual programmes

The great weakness is that factual programmes cannot easily take their audiences on a long, immersive journey of change, in the way that a drama can with a role-modelling character. Factual programmes are, by necessity, more piecemeal, with issues being covered in many different interviews with many different people.

It could be possible to find a potential changer who is interested in changing behaviour, and to team that person up with an appropriate advisor. The advisor sets a small target for each programme, moving the potential changer towards behaviour change and, in each programme, there is a discussion as to how the potential changer dealt with the last target. This would mean a long-term story of change. However, such a strategy would be fraught with risk. There is a high chance of the potential changer dropping out, or failing to change, which could have a negative impact on any viewer or listener who is following them as a role model.

A further challenge that factual programming for behaviour change can present is that it takes a relatively high level of journalistic skill and commitment to find the right interviewees and record their stories in a way that is helpful to the audience.

A type of factual programme that is used quite often in broadcasting for behaviour change projects is the discussion programme. However, a purely discussion programme cannot provide the role models needed, and so there does have to be some journalistic input. Often, discussion programmes are used alongside a behaviour change drama, and the necessary content for the discussion to consider comes from the drama.

There is a fuller discussion of formats for communication for development in Chapter 6.

Serial drama for change: The why and how

Why use drama?

The rationale for using serial drama on radio or television to try to change behaviour and social norms is based on a number of factors, including attracting the widest possible audience, the value of role models, the impact of emotional engagement, the centrality of social interaction to behaviour change, drama's capacity to handle sensitive issues and, in some circumstances, its ability to vividly show the possible consequences of unchanged behaviour. In addition, there is its demonstrable success in some projects.

The widest possible audience

If a communication for development project is to maximize its impact, and it is trying to influence individuals across the population, it needs to attract a large audience. To do that means having a highly engaging product, especially in a crowded media market. Drama is very popular. For example, the viewing figures for the first half of January 2017, for one popular television channel in the UK, show that the top eight most watched broadcasts were all dramas. If, therefore, drama can deliver development outcomes, it is an obvious choice.

Role models

As is discussed in Chapter 26, role models are important factors, both in motivating individuals to change and in showing how change can be brought about. Most behaviour change dramas are based on the concept of the transitional character, that is, a role-model character who starts off behaving in a way that is opposite to the behaviour the drama is promoting, and who, over time, changes to engaging in the new behaviour the drama is promoting. The intention is that members of the audience who behave in the same way at the start will identify with the transitional character and subsequently follow the character's example and gradually change their behaviour. This is the major mechanism by which such dramas operate. However, the transitional character also shows the audience how the behaviour change can be achieved, the steps that need to be taken, the setbacks that may occur, the skills that need to be acquired and so on.

Emotional engagement

There is research which suggests that the audience's emotional engagement with characters in a drama can be an important factor in their achievement of behaviour change. In 2012 and 2013, BBC Media Action ran a behaviour change communication project in Somalia called *Tiraarka Qoyska*. Each weekly broadcast consisted of an episode of a radio serial drama followed by a discussion programme covering some of the issues raised in the drama. The project was designed to change behaviour in hygiene and feeding practices to try to reduce mortality among babies up to six months old. Research shows that behaviours were changed but that, of the two elements in the broadcasts, the drama was recalled by listeners as the most influential:

> the research found no link between issues most recalled from the magazine programme and improved health indicators among listeners. This may suggest that emotional engagement with the drama motivated listeners to rethink common misconceptions that inform practices.[1]

This quote highlights the value of drama against factual broadcasting in this field.

Social interaction

Again, as is discussed in Chapter 26, behaviour change methodologies hold that behaviour change cannot be sustained in isolation, and that there need to be changes in social attitudes (called norms in the vocabulary of behavioural science) in the community around someone changing their behaviour. However, most behaviour change involves social interaction, and drama is excellent at portraying social interactions. This often works to show a transitional character changing social interactions in order to achieve behaviour change, thus modelling for the audience the negotiations that are needed for behaviour change to happen.

Sensitive issues

Behaviour change communication often has to deal with sensitive issues, often having to break taboos. Certainly in the past, for example, communication attempting to change behaviour to reduce risks of HIV infection has needed to discuss issues which, in some cultures, were not talked about. Drama, often through humour, has managed to bring these topics into the open, even though they are highly sensitive.

Actions and consequences

Because it is fictional, drama is uniquely able to show serious consequences of a failure to change behaviour. In the BBC Media Action drama in Somalia – part of *Tiraarka Qoyska* – discussed above, characters died as a consequence of unhealthy behaviour. The research showed that two stories, in which babies died, had a particularly strong impact on behaviour change outcomes (see above).[2]

In the MARCH methodology, there is the concept of the contrast model. At the beginning of a behaviour change storyline, the transitional character and another character are very similar and behave in much the same way. As the storyline progresses, the transitional character embarks on a journey of behaviour change, while the other character does not. While, ultimately, the transitional character enjoys the benefits of behaviour change, the other character suffers the consequences of not changing.

For example, in 2006 and 2007, there was a storyline in a MARCH drama in Zambia in which two young women were friends and both were involved in transactional sex. One, the transitional character, gives up transactional sex and takes an HIV test, which shows she is HIV positive. She is prescribed anti-retroviral drugs, which, at that time, required patients to adhere to a regime of healthier living, being careful with diet and alcohol and other lifestyle features. Over a long period, the transitional character adopts healthy living, and goes on to live a healthy life. In contrast, the other character does not even get herself tested, and, in the end, suffers badly and dies. Clearly, no other broadcasting format could do this. (These two storylines are discussed in detail later in this chapter.)

Conclusion

These points show the main aspects of the rationale for using serial drama which follows an organized methodology in attempts to bring about behaviour change.

An introduction to MARCH methodology

What is set out in this section is the methodology of the MARCH project, created by Centers for Disease Control and Prevention in 2000–2, seen from a practitioner's point of view. For a full theoretical discussion of the project, see *Modeling and Reinforcement to Combat HIV: The MARCH Approach to Behavior Change*, in the *American Journal of Public Health*, June 2001.[3] This article explains the theory and research the methodology described here is based on.

On the issue of which medium to use for a MARCH project, MARCH principles can be used to develop any appropriate narrative form on any medium that can carry education and entertainment. MARCH has been applied to videogames and episodic print formats like comic books. However, radio has been used for many MARCH projects because it has been the most common form of mass media in the countries in question, and among the chosen target audiences. (Of course, a radio drama can be distributed as a podcast, with the advantage that registered listeners will get all the episodes automatically, in the right order, to be listened to whenever wanted.) However, all the stages of development would be equally applicable to television drama, and the two media only diverge at the scriptwriting stage.

MARCH dramas need to be original, engaging and compelling. If they are not, they are unlikely to attract and keep an audience, and so will fail.

Identifying need

The start of the development of a MARCH drama is the identification of behaviour change objectives. Any MARCH project has identified an overall large need among its target population and has identified behaviour change as the most appropriate method for reducing that need. Originally, the need the project was designed to meet was the reduction in the impact of HIV on populations. Since then, the same methodology has been used, for example, to try to reduce infant mortality and to improve the life chances of girls. Within that large need, specific, more targeted needs are identified. In the case of improving girls' life chances, these more specific targets might be: to persuade violent fathers to stop being violent and to appreciate time with their daughters, to persuade parents to let their daughters socialize more with less focus on academic studies, to show girls how solidarity among themselves can reduce risks.

The identification of the overall need is likely to arise from UN agency or government statistics, and the more specific needs come from research into knowledge, attitudes and behaviour among the target population.

Developing transitional characters

At the heart of a MARCH drama is a set of transitional characters, who model behaviour change over different periods of time. Each of the more specific needs becomes a behaviour change objective for one of these transitional characters. Each transitional character is invented and developed to model the process of changing their behaviour to achieve one of these objectives. The drama consists of a number of transitional characters' storylines, each showing the character on a journey of change, and running in parallel with one another.

Through these storylines, MARCH dramas work by showing the audience why they need to change, what they need to change, how they can make those changes, and the possible consequences of failing to change. In other words, they are dramas in which characters perform actions, or fail to act, and face the consequences of their action or inaction.

Delivering knowledge

Knowledge is important, of course. If people do not know that their current behaviour is either putting themselves and others at risk or actually causing harm, or is limiting their life chances, they are unlikely to change that behaviour. However, what MARCH dramas do not do is deliver messages. Messages alone are rarely enough, partly because knowledge alone is rarely enough. (See Chapter 2 for a fuller discussion of the effectiveness of messaging.)

Where MARCH dramas do deliver knowledge, they do it in dramatic contexts, in emotionally engaging scenes, as it is in those circumstances that people absorb knowledge. (This issue is discussed in the rationale section of this chapter, above.) People rarely absorb knowledge from dry information: they need to be engaged with the situation in which the knowledge is given, and they need to be prompted to discuss the information. If this happens, audience are more likely to truly understand the relevance of the information to them and absorb it sufficiently for it to move them towards changing their behaviour. Discussion is best prompted by characters facing personal and important dilemmas that are left unresolved, so that listeners will talk about what the character should do.

A key principle that is shared between MARCH methodology and modern drama is that of 'Show, don't tell'. In MARCH, characters are shown going through a process of change. They are shown, for example, learning and using the skills they need to communicate effectively, rather than what they are doing being described. Similarly, in modern drama, events are shown in action, rather than described.

Barriers and facilitators

Identification

In order that the journeys of change in a MARCH drama are based in reality, the methodology involves identifying factors that influence the specific behaviours that will be modelled in the drama. Those factors that hinder behaviour change can be called barriers, and those which support the process of behaviour change can be called facilitators. Their identification is important because, essentially, the storylines show the transitional characters overcoming barriers and making use of facilitators to achieve their behaviour change objective.

Classification of barriers and facilitators

Barriers and facilitators are identified from the formative research, or from a summary of the research, and are classified into three groups: personal, social and environmental. (See Figure 27.1.)

Classification is useful for designing the drama, partly to understand better how the barriers and facilitators function, but also to help determine where they will come into play in the storyline and how they can be shown supporting or hindering characters in their journeys of change in the drama.

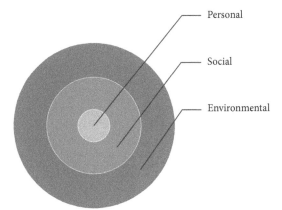

Figure 27.1 *A diagram of the three classifications of barriers and facilitators used in MARCH behaviour change methodology*

Personal barriers and facilitators

Personal barriers are, in effect, barriers that are in the individual's head, their level of education, and their individual characteristics. They will vary from situation to situation and culture to culture but, in general terms, they include:

- a lack of knowledge of the issues involved, and of what is beneficial behaviour and what is not
- misconceptions about the outcomes of different behaviour
- a lack of skills, like negotiation, seeking information and planning ahead
- a failure to perceive the relevance of any information, that is, I do not see that information about particular behaviour applies to me
- a failure to perceive risk, that is, I do not see my behaviour as being some kind of risk to me, nor that changing it would reduce or remove that risk
- a failure to understand outcomes, that is, what are the consequences, either beneficial or not, of a particular behaviour likely to be, or, what are the rewards or punishments of different behaviours likely to be?
- a lack of self-efficacy, that is, no confidence in one's ability to perform a certain action or behaviour, which is prioritized in MARCH methodology, because it is thought to be a major barrier, and one of the functions of the role-modelling characters is to help overcome it

Personal facilitators are the opposite of these:

- accurate knowledge of the issues
- few or no misconceptions
- possession of the relevant skills
- a perception that the information available is relevant
- an accurate perception of risk, and an appreciation of how a change of behaviour will reduce or remove that risk
- positive expectations of the outcomes of behaviour change
- strong self-efficacy

Social barriers and facilitators

These are those influences that come from an individual's immediate social circle, that is, family and friends and acquaintances, as well as the social norms that surround them.

Again, social barriers and facilitators will be culturally specific but, in general, barriers can include:

- a lack of accurate knowledge among strong influencers
- social attitudes that are misconceived
- role models who reinforce behaviour that is not beneficial

Social facilitators would be the opposite of these.

Environmental barriers and facilitators

Environmental barriers are those which are completely external and which, generally, an individual cannot control or have an effect on, so that they have to get round them, rather than overcoming them.

Environmental barriers can be physical things, like the lack of physical facilities that support behaviour change by providing benefits for it.

Environmental barriers can be economic:

- the lack of a market for whatever the character makes or grows
- a weak economy
- personal poverty
- the lack of availability of credit

Environmental barriers can be legal:

- discriminatory laws
- a lack of enforcement of law, like anti-corruption law
- a lack of any legal framework
- a lack of accessible means of obtaining legal redress

Conversely, environmental facilitators could be:

- physical like the presence of a health facility
- economic like a strong economic environment
- legal like supportive laws which are enforced

The stages of change

The stages of change come from a theory of behaviour change developed to understand how people stop smoking.[4] In this theory, five stages of behaviour change are identified. In the MARCH approach a transitional character may go through all five stages, depending on what stage the formative research suggests the majority of the target audience are at. So, for example, at the beginning of the drama a character may be shown already thinking about a change to his or her behaviour, such as a man thinking of stopping disciplining his family through violence.

The stages of change are a crucial tool for building storylines. (See Figure 27.2.)

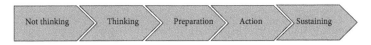

Figure 27.2 *A diagram showing the five stages of change used in the MARCH behaviour change methodology*

The five stages are:

1. *Pre-contemplation (Not thinking)* when the character is not thinking about their behaviour, or is in denial about their behaviour
2. *Contemplation (Thinking)* when the character begins to think about their behaviour
3. *Preparation* when the character is actively taking steps towards a change in their behaviour
4. *Action* when the character is changing their behaviour
5. *Maintenance (Sustaining)* when the character is keeping up the changed behaviour

Setbacks

Few human enterprises ever run smoothly, and all kinds of obstacles get in the way of what people aspire to do: unexpected consequences of actions; a loss of self-belief; events; the interventions of other people. So, a realistic drama should

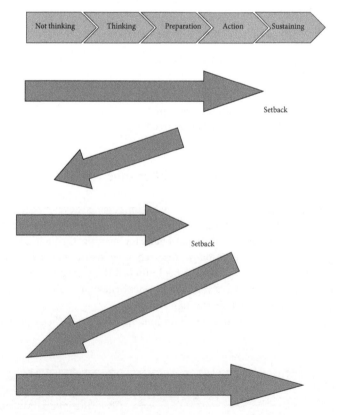

Figure 27.3 *A diagram showing how setbacks in a process of behaviour change can take an individual backwards through the stages of change*

show its characters encountering obstacles that push them back in their journey of change, and then show them resuming their efforts to change, even if that takes a long time.

Such obstacles are, for the purposes of MARCH drama, called setbacks (Figure 27.3). As a transitional character works their way through the stages of change, a setback will push them backwards, so that they go back to a stage of change they have already been through once. The size of the setback determines how many stages the character goes back. A very severe setback could take a character from the action stage as far back as the pre-contemplation stage. The character needs to start from that point and work their way through the stages of change all over again.

A key tool: The behaviour change trajectory chart

In MARCH methodology, a number of tools were developed to assist scriptwriters and producers in the process of designing and tracking the storylines, and integrating the findings of the formative research. This permitted the storylines to be aligned with the stages of change and include appropriate personal, social and environmental barriers and facilitators.

A key tool is the behaviour change trajectory chart (see Table 27.1). It is a graph, and one is completed for each transitional character. The vertical axis sets out the stages of change, from not thinking at the bottom to sustained change at the top. The horizontal axis is the story timeline, divided into episodes, weeks or months, depending on the intended length of the storyline. The horizontal axis is also annotated with key events that will occur during the story.

The notes following the chart identify the barriers and facilitators operating in each event, supported by a piece of the formative research to explain how the barrier or facilitator was identified. Some of the events may be directly associated with the behaviour the character is changing, while others will be important climactic points that drive the drama. For each event the writer has to decide what stage their character is at and place a dot on the chart. A line is drawn to connect the dots, which shows the character's progression up through the stages, and back down again at a setback, then the recovery and rise up through the stages again, and back down again at another setback, and so on. By visualizing the trajectory, it is easy to see how difficult the storyline has made the achievement of the behaviour change. The aim is usually to make the achievement as authentic as possible.

This chart and the accompanying notes are from an HIV drama in Southern Province, Zambia. It plots the two-year journey of change of a character called Munyati. At the start of the drama, he was a 'Tonga Bull', that is, a man who gained social status from having multiple sexual partners. He was a vegetable trader, buying in the village where he lived, and selling in a nearby town. He was married to Mangalita, and, at the same time, he maintained a sexual relationship with his first girlfriend, Kasimbi. Mangalita lived in the village, Kasimbi in the town. Munyati and Kasimbi had a child, who lives with Kasimbi. Munyati also had a girlfriend in the village, Mukabanji. He had casual sexual encounters with several other women.

Table 27.1 A two-year behaviour change trajectory chart

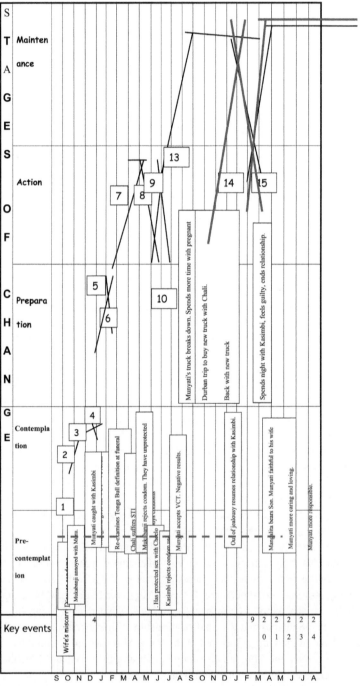

An example behaviour change trajectory chart

This is a chart produced by the team in Zambia. The only additions are explanations of acronyms.

Character: Munyati
Behaviour Change Objective: Be faithful to one sexual partner in knowledge of HIV status.

KEY

- NB. The dash line shows Munyati's trajectory on faithfulness.

1. SOCIAL BARRIER – After poverty, frustration in marriage is the main determinant of the high prevalence of risky sexual behaviour, including concurrent and multiple partner relationships. (Formative assessment, 2005) Munyati needs a son, Mangalita has miscarried.
2. SOCIAL FACILITATOR – Positive advice from close friends increases risk perception. Chali encourages Munyati to use condoms. Advice from elders/ leaders is taken seriously. Haampango urges Munyati to be more focused.
3. SOCIAL FACILITATOR – Frustration from a girlfriend helps men concentrate on their wives. Mukabanji is annoyed with Munyati upon hearing from Mangalita that he has girlfriends in town.
4. SOCIAL BARRIER – Women are not expected to commit adultery, whereas men committing adultery are viewed as both acceptable and inevitable (Grey Literature Review, 2005). Munyati caught committing adultery with Kasimbi. At the council of elders, he is acquitted.
5. SOCIAL FACILITATOR – Disclosure of a negative status by a spouse is likely to encourage partners to access voluntary counselling and testing (VCT) services. Mangalita goes for VCT and discloses to Munyati that she is negative.
6. SETBACK/PERSONAL BARRIER – Without counselling first, people are likely to refuse to go for the HIV test. Munyati rejects VCT as encouraged by Mangalita, thinking it's an accusation that he is HIV positive.
7. SOCIAL FACILITATOR:
   a. Married men with an extra-marital partner use condoms with their spouse (Zambia Sexual Behaviour Surveys, 2000). Munyati accepts the use of condoms with wife.
   b. Seeing negative consequences resulting from risky sexual behaviour in one's peers instils a sense of responsibility, or acts as a deterrent to others. Chali suffers a sexually transmitted infection (STI). Munyati buys condoms.
8. SETBACK/SOCIAL BARRIER – Despite perceiving themselves to be at risk for HIV/AIDS, many people do not do anything to protect themselves against HIV/

AIDS. (Grey Literature Review, 2005). Mukabanji rejects condom use, Munyati has unprotected sex with her.

9. PERSONAL FACILITATOR – Most men and women perceive that they themselves are at risk of contracting HIV/AIDS (Grey Literature Review, 2005). Munyati refuses to have unprotected sex with a sex worker Cheelo.

10. SOCIAL BARRIER – There is a discrepancy between the high levels of knowledge and risk perception and the prevailing risky behaviour and practices in the community (Formative Assessment, 2005). Kasimbi, a teacher, rejects condom usage.

11. SOCIAL FACILITATOR/ENVIRONMENTAL FACILITATOR – People are now more willing to get tested for HIV/AIDS (Formative Assessment, 2005). Munyati has developed a measure of self-efficacy and accepts VCT at Galaba clinic.

12. SETBACK – Men find it difficult to end a relationship with a lady they have a child with. Out of jealousy, Munyati resumes relationship with Kasimbi.

13. PERSONAL FACILITATOR – Most men and women perceive a clear relationship between the presence of concurrent and multiple partner relationships and the spread of HIV/AIDS (Formative assessment, 2005). Feeling guilty, Munyati dumps Kasimbi.

For each transition, the writers then have to draw on the research to identify suitable factors that precipitate the character through and between the stages, and these can be written onto the chart. Though many of the barriers and facilitators act in all the stages of change, the different types of factor will be emphasized in different stages.

Classes of barriers and facilitators in stages of change

In general, certain personal factors are more likely to be important in the early stages of change, as knowledge is acquired and attitudes change to motivate the transitional character. The change from not thinking to thinking is clearly something that happens in the character's head, and may be caused by a key emotional event that helps a character become aware of the risks they are taking or the relevance of information to their own situation.

Self-efficacy, however, tends to come into play slightly later in the preparation stage, as the character learns from secondary characters who are managing to achieve the desired behaviour, and starts gaining skills to attempt the new behaviour. The weighing-up of possible consequences is likely to happen at thinking and preparation stages.

Social factors are likely to operate in all of the stages of change. For example, something happening to someone in the transitional character's social circle is often a strong motivating factor to start the process of change, while sustaining the change, once it has been achieved, can depend on social support. Social influences such as gender norms or peer pressure may hinder change.

Environmental barriers are more likely to operate in the preparation and action stages, as the character comes up against them in trying to change.

Characters

Supporting characters

The function of supporting characters

For each transitional character there will be a network of supporting characters, who:

- help to expose the personal barriers and facilitators
- are the social barriers and facilitators
- are the route through which the environmental barriers and facilitators operate
- are contrast models (see below)

Different characters can perform one, two or all three of these functions.

Interlinked character networks

Each network of a transitional character and their supporting characters does not exist in isolation. There will be cross-linking between the networks, so that transitional characters can, themselves, be supporting characters for other transitional characters, and supporting characters can be in different transitional characters' networks. Doing this gives the audience a much better sense that there is an interlinked community.

In addition, in radio drama especially, it is a good idea to keep down the number of characters, as it is difficult for the listener to follow the drama if there are too many characters. The MARCH drama aiming to reduce newborn mortality in Somalia, which has been referred to earlier, had eighteen characters, of whom six were transitional.

Function does not define a character

It is important to note that, just because a supporting character is a barrier to a transitional character's change, that does not necessarily make them a bad or negative character. Equally, a supporting character who is a facilitator is not necessarily good or positive. Indeed, a supporting character who is a barrier to one transitional character can, at the same time, be a facilitator to another transitional character.

The contrast model

One particular kind of supporting character is the contrast model. A contrast model starts off from the same point as the transitional character they are contrasting with.

For example, in one MARCH drama in Zambia, two 19-year-old girls share a flat, and both participate in casual transactional sex.

The transitional character is Mapenzi, who is HIV positive. Her behaviour change objective is to maintain her medication regime, and live healthily by avoiding alcohol, eating well, and avoiding unprotected sex.

The contrast model is Cheelo, whose HIV status is unknown. She does not get HIV-tested, drinks alcohol excessively and has frequent, unprotected transactional sex.

Mapenzi goes on a process of behaviour change. After a lot of struggling, she achieves her behaviour change objective. She marries an HIV positive man, and they start a business together.

Cheelo maintains the same behaviour as before. Eventually, she gets ill, and her sex work income ends. She is evicted. She gets pregnant. The baby is born prematurely and soon dies. Shortly afterwards, Cheelo dies.

Although the contrast model is a characteristic of MARCH dramas, not all MARCH dramas have them.

Transitional characters

A different character for different sections of the audience

Typically, there will be between four and ten transitional characters going through their storylines in parallel with one another at any one time in a serial drama.

Often, different transitional characters represent different parts of the audience, because the different behaviour change objectives will be aimed at different parts of the audience.

For example, in a drama trying to reduce infant mortality, if the formative research shows that older women have strong influence over what happens to a baby immediately after birth, then a behaviour change objective of early initiation of breastfeeding might be targeted at older women, and the transitional character will be an older woman. However, since the mother provides breastfeeding, a behaviour change objective of maintaining exclusive breastfeeding for the first six months will be aimed at young mothers, and the transitional character will be a young mother.

Transitional character storyline duration

The different transitional characters' storylines will not all be the same length. There are two factors on which production teams need to base their decisions on the lengths of the different storylines.

The first of these are any constraints on the choice because of the events in the storyline. For example, in a drama aiming to reduce infant mortality, one storyline had the behaviour change objective of exclusive breastfeeding for the first six months. This drama, referenced several times already, was called *Dareemo*, made by BBC Media Action in Somalia. In the storyline, one transitional character gave birth in the first episode of the drama but that baby died within a few weeks, which prompted the character to find out why, and so embark on a journey of behaviour change.

A few months later, the character became pregnant again and, as there is a convention in such dramas that events take the time they would in reality, she gave birth nine months later. By the time of the second baby's birth, the character had to have completed the behaviour change, so that the new baby would be exclusively breastfed from birth. So, in this case, the timeline was 13 months, dictated entirely by the events in the story.

Where there are no such constraints, the production team need to make an assessment of how long the required behaviour change is going to take, on the basis that the harder it is, with more difficult barriers to overcome, the longer it is going to take. In MARCH dramas, storylines can vary between about six weeks long and two years. (For a fuller discussion of the factors influencing storyline durations, see Chapter 26.)

The ending of a transitional character's storyline

Once a transitional character has reached the behaviour change objective, that storyline ends and the character will usually stay in the drama, but not as a transitional character, just as a supporting character. A new transitional character with a new behaviour change objective and a new storyline will take over. This character will usually be an existing supporting character, though, very occasionally, an entirely new character will be brought into the drama. This is not a part of MARCH's stated methodology but something that has happened in practice.

Developing characters for a MARCH drama

This is a summary of one way characters can be created. This process is not entirely part of MARCH methodology, but has been developed in practice. A full training plan for the development of a MARCH drama, including character development, is in two training modules in Section 6:

Module D2: An introduction to the MARCH methodology for behaviour and social change serial dramas, and its application.
Module D3: Scriptwriting a serial drama for behaviour change.

Developing a transitional character

This development starts with the behaviour change objective and the formative research. From the formative research, barriers, facilitators and potential setbacks associated with the behaviour change objective are identified and classified.

A transitional character profile form can then be used to fill out the character. (See Table 27.2.)

Table 27.2 A transitional character profile form

Transitional character name:
Behaviour change objective:
Target audience segment:

Age	
Gender	
Origins	
Why they are in the location	
Level of education	
Wealth	
Occupation	
Level of influence in the family	
Level of influence in the community	
Family	
Other social contacts	
Personal barriers	
Social barriers	
Environmental barriers	
Personal facilitators	
Social facilitators	
Environmental facilitators	
Setbacks	

(This form is also in *Module D2: An introduction to the MARCH methodology for behaviour and social change serial dramas,* in Section 6.)

There are a number of entries in the profile about status and levels of influence, because a character's status within their family and in the community is likely to have a substantial impact on how easy it is for them to change their behaviour. A character with lower status is probably going to find it more difficult, as higher status individuals may have some level of control over the lower status character's behaviour. How a character has gained the status they have may also be a significant factor. If a character's relatively high status comes from the behaviour that needs to be changed, it is likely they will find it harder to change the behaviour as it risks losing status.

The origins of a character may be important if the target audience is made up of a number of different cultures, or is spread across different regions. It is usually helpful in gaining an audience across those cultures or regions to have characters who are representative of the cultures or regions. There may also be an issue of status. If the character has come from a different place to where the drama is set, that may affect their relationships and influence in the family and community.

The reason why the character has come to live in the drama's location may also affect their social status. If, for example, they are there because they have arrived by marriage, they may have a different status than if they have been displaced by conflict from their place of origin.

A character with a low level of wealth is likely to find behaviour change more difficult, as poverty is likely to throw up more environmental barriers.

A transitional character's occupation needs to be chosen with care. It can, for example, be chosen to be a powerful barrier to change.

Developing a supporting character network

The module in Section 6, *Module D2: An introduction to the MARCH methodology for behaviour and social change serial dramas, and its application,* takes a writing team through the process of developing a supporting character network for each transitional character. The network is based on creating characters who represent the barriers and facilitators in the transitional character's profile in the different ways set out earlier in this chapter. The family and other social contacts box in the transitional character profile form helps writers work out the transitional character's social network, and how different characters act as barriers or facilitators.

Each character can embody or represent more than one barrier or facilitator, and the barriers and facilitators can be embodied or represented in more than one supporting character. The network should embody or represent all of the barriers and facilitators identified for the transitional character.

There is a supporting character profile form in that module, which is a simpler version of the transitional character profile form.

Normally, once networks have been developed for each transitional character, they are reviewed together to see where supporting characters from different networks can be merged, and where transitional characters can be supporting characters in another network. This is to keep the number of characters to a minimum. *Module D2* takes teams through this process.

Developing and writing a serial drama for change

This chapter is based heavily on my experience of the development of a number of serial dramas, and in the training of writing teams for those dramas.

An approach to writing good drama

Any behaviour change drama needs to be engaging and compelling, as it can only attract an audience if it is. There are certain characteristics that are crucial to compelling drama, and have been shown to be effective in attracting audiences to serial dramas.

Conflict

The first of these is conflict, which should lie at the heart of a drama, including comic drama.

The storylines should be driven by conflict and, ideally, every scene should be built round conflict.

Dramatic conflict does not necessarily mean violence or even shouting. One definition might be that dramatic conflict arises when the different characters are all trying to achieve different goals, and their paths to those goals collide. So a drama is a continuous struggle for control between characters, as it is only through control that each can achieve what they want. The conflict can also be internal when a character wrestles with his or her own conflicting needs and emotions.

Conflict is necessary because, without it, a scene would just be two pleasant individuals having a chat. It is only necessary to look at almost any classic drama to see the importance of conflict. In *Module D3: Scriptwriting a serial drama for behaviour change* in Section 6, there is a simple training exercise that demonstrates why conflict is vital for drama.

There are also two technical reasons for the value of conflict in drama, and these are that it is much easier to write conflict and it is much easier to act conflict.

Dramatic action

Dramatic action is equally vital to a compelling drama, so everything that happens between characters in a drama should be action, that is, characters should be doing something, not just talking about something. Something should happen in each scene, so that scenes have outcomes, and the audience is carried through a scene knowing there is going to be an outcome, but not knowing what it is going to be.

For example, a scene in which two characters are discussing whether an NGO should come to their village to vaccinate children is not in action. A scene in which one character is trying to take their child to be vaccinated and another character is trying to stop them, so that the outcome is either that the child is vaccinated or is not vaccinated, is in action.

What this means is that the cases for and against vaccination are expressed in conflict and in actions, and there is an outcome that the audience can have a stake in. This is very different from the kind of health drama that is sometimes produced, in which a health worker character explains the merits of vaccination to a passive, listening character. Having this argument in a scene based on conflict and action offers the audience a level of emotional engagement. As has been discussed, there is evidence that emotional engagement helps audiences remember, and motivates them to discuss and potentially act. If, in this scenario, the vaccination of the child is prevented, say, by physical force, and later in the drama the child dies of the disease they were to have been vaccinated against, then the serial is a drama of actions and consequences, and not one of explanations.

Setting the cases in a situation of conflict also means that the scene may well promote discussion among the audience. The benefits of this kind of discussion are covered in Chapters 2 and 26.

If the idea that every scene should be in dramatic action is accepted, it means that, ideally, scenes should never have one character debating something with another, or one character explaining an issue to another, or one character describing something to another.

In *Module D3: Scriptwriting a serial drama for behaviour change* in Section 6, there is an exercise that demonstrates the value of dramatic action.

Dramatic tension

Dramatic tension is a device that helps to keep an audience engaged. It is created by the writer withholding information from the audience, letting them know just enough to understand what is happening but no more. The cliffhanger often used in soap operas at the end to an episode – in which something decisive is about to happen but the action is stopped just before it does – is an example of this, but dramatic tension can be used anywhere in a drama. For example, if a girl is talking to a baby, and she is in a hurry, getting ready to take the baby somewhere, but the audience does not know where, the audience is more likely to be attentive because they want to know where the girl is going to go, and why she is in a hurry, and, more, what her relationship with the baby is.

Conclusion: Conflict, action and tension

These three dramatic devices – conflict, action and tension – should inform every stage in the development and writing of a serial drama. If they are not used to inform the construction of storylines, it will be very difficult to build them in at the synopsis or dialogue writing stages.

Cultural sensitivity

In the development of a serial drama for behaviour and social change, there is a strong need for cultural sensitivity and, again, this is something that needs to be present from the start of the storylining process. Serial drama, or soap opera, is based very much on the concept of naturalism, which is a Western intellectual concept. Not all audiences will appreciate it, or even understand it. For some, for example, the telling of several stories in parallel with each other is simply baffling. Those designing and developing this kind of drama need to be fully aware of local drama or storytelling traditions.

A sequence for the development and writing of a behaviour change serial drama

This chapter sets out one way of developing and writing a serial drama following the methodology developed for the MARCH project, though the steps it sets out would be applicable to any serial drama based on role modelling.

(In *Module D3: Scriptwriting a serial drama for behaviour change*, in Section 6, there are detailed notes on training a team in preparing and writing an audio drama, though much of it is applicable to a visual drama.)

There are a number of clear steps in the development and writing of a serial drama for behaviour and social change, most of which would be applicable equally to a television or a radio drama.

This sequence assumes that a research team has carried out formative research and that behaviour change objectives have been decided.

1 Barriers and facilitators

These are identified from the formative research and classified. From them the transitional characters and, for each, a network of supporting characters are developed (as discussed in Chapter 27).

2 Streamlining the networks

The transitional characters and the networks of supporting characters are shared among the whole team, to identify where there are similar characters who could be combined, and where one transitional character can be a supporting character to another transitional character. The purpose of this step is to reduce the number of characters to a minimum, which is easier to manage and is easier for the audience to follow (as discussed in Chapter 27).

Once the whole cast of characters has been decided, the supporting character profiles are completed, and the details of family and social circle are added to the transitional character profiles (as discussed in Chapter 27).

3 A universe is developed

Conventionally, a single fictional location – called a universe – is created for the setting of a serial drama. This has the advantage that all the characters can plausibly meet up with each other. Sometimes, though, it is a split location, perhaps between rural and urban, or between city slum and city suburban, for example, but with connections made by one or more of the transitional characters.

In a behaviour change drama, the universe is often designed to make the achievement of the transitional characters' behaviour change objectives as difficult as possible. The design should be guided by all the environmental barriers and facilitators that appear in the transitional characters' profiles. In a drama in Somalia, for example, the home of a young mother modelling behaviour change in hygiene practices was placed as far away as possible from the well.

The first decision, though, again using information from the character profiles – including origins and occupations – is to decide where in the country the universe is to be set. While the universe is fictional, it can be set in a recognisable region. Again, the region should be chosen on the basis of being one that offers the toughest environmental barriers to the transitional characters' behaviour change.

Normally, there is both a map and a written description of the universe, so that writers are consistent in where characters live and work in relation to each other.

Once the universe has been finalized, there may be implications for the character profiles, which may, therefore, need revision.

4 Storyline durations

The length of each transitional character's journey of behaviour change should be decided at this point (see Chapter 27).

5 Long storyline development

These are the sequences of events that take each transitional character from their starting point of not thinking to their achievement of their behaviour change objective. One way of starting this is to work out some key events in the whole sequence first. These can be the overcoming of a barrier which takes the character from one stage of change (see Chapter 27) to the next, and the setbacks, with events which, again, take the character from one stage to the next after a setback. This is likely to give about ten key events. Once they are in place, the whole storyline can be developed. At this stage, the description of each event is only going to be two or three sentences, and the events are not episode by episode. One important point is that the story should be driven by conflict and events should be in dramatic action.

The events in each storyline are normally numbered.

6 Storyline coordination

Once all the transitional character long storylines have been developed, there needs to be some kind of mechanism to bring them together into a coherent serial drama. One way of doing this is to develop a character timelines chart, which also includes other influences on events.

Typically, this is a table, with the vertical axis setting out the episodes and their transmission dates, while the horizontal axis sets out a series of columns for real, external events that need to be reflected in the drama, the season, and then a column for each of the transitional characters (see Table 28.1).

Table 28.1 A sample character timeline chart

Ep	TX date	Events	Season	TC 1	TC 2	TC 3	TC 4	TC 5	TC 6
15	04/10/12	Eid-al-Udha	Rainy	8	20	17	10	9	6
16	11/10/12		Rainy	9			11		7
17	18/10/12		Rainy	10 Thinking	21	18		10	

In this example, the Ep column is the episode number, TX date means the transmission date, the Events column lists pre-determined external events, like festivals and holidays (it is important to know the season when the episode is transmitted, as that needs to be reflected both in what the characters are doing and the sound or visuals). Then there is a column for each transitional character, in which the numbers are for the events in their long storylines. The episode in which they move from one stage of change to another is marked, as in this example, when character 1 moves into the thinking stage in Episode 17, in event number 10 of his storyline.

When the format of the chart has been set out, it is best to identify the transitional character (TC1) who has most interactions in his or her storyline with other transitional characters. The events in that character's storyline are plotted in one column of the chart, allowing for the fact that there will be gaps between some events in the storyline, and they need to be allowed for in the plotting on the chart.

The points where the other transitional characters have interactions with that anchor character are then plotted in their columns in the chart, also allowing for when interactions between other transitional characters occur. The anchor character's timeline is not fixed, and it may be necessary to adjust the anchor character's timeline. If, for example, the gap between interactions between, say, transitional character 3 (TC3) and the anchor is too close to allow for events that have to happen in TC3's storyline, then the anchor timeline needs to be lengthened at that point so that the events in TC3's timeline can happen in proper time.

This is a process of juggling events in different storylines until they all fit together. This will, inevitably, lead to gaps in storylines. These gaps need to be filled with more detail of how the character goes from one event in their transitional story to the next. This will normally be done at the detailed storylining stage.

This process sets out the episodes in which the key events for each transitional character have to happen, over the lifetime of their behaviour change journeys, so creating the fundamental structure of the serial drama.

7 The detailed storylining

This is usually carried out by the whole production team working together, often with other members of the project team, including research and management. This can be all done at the beginning, before the drama starts being broadcast. However, detailed storylining is a very large piece of work and, often, only a relatively short period is done in detail, perhaps three months. The drama can start being broadcast, and then detailed storylining can be done at intervals, again of perhaps three months, during the lifetime of the drama.

In this process, using the long storylines, the character timelines and the character profiles, the project team produce an episode-by-episode and scene-by-scene storyline. It is important to ensure that no storyline is left unrepresented for more than one episode. Scene descriptions are more detailed, but describe only the setting and the conflict and action at the heart of the scene. Typically, scene descriptions will be about five sentences. If, at this stage, scene descriptions are too detailed, the dramatic point of the scene can easily be lost.

Each storyline point is annotated with details of the barriers or facilitators that are operating in the scene.

An editorial review process of the detailed storylines is very useful, perhaps involving a behaviour change specialist, a drama specialist and cultural experts. If the project has a Technical Advisory Committee, detailed storylines would be sent to the members for comment. Experienced writing teams can make mistakes, even to the point of putting audiences off behaviour change rather than encouraging them to pursue it.

8 Episode structuring

This is simply the process of deciding the order of the scenes in each episode. Conventionally, scenes in one episode are normally in chronological order through the course of one day. This arrangement makes the passage of time less jarring than if the action jumps to another day in the same episode. However, it is important that the final scene of an episode ends with a dilemma, if at all possible, and that there is a cycling of storylines, so that successive episodes each end with a scene from a different storyline.

Ending each episode with a dilemma has two functions. One is to encourage the audience to watch or listen to the next episode to find out what the solution of the dilemma is. The other, more important, reason is to encourage members of the audience to talk to each other about the drama. This is because there is evidence that talking to each other encourages the change of social norms (as discussed in Chapter 26).

Conventionally, if one episode ends on a dilemma or a cliffhanger, there will be a scene in the following episode that shows what the outcome of the dilemma or cliffhanger was, but this is not necessarily the case. If there had been a dilemma, normally, at some point in the following episode the character concerned will be seen pursuing one of the options that had been available. Again, though, this may not be the case. If there had been a cliffhanger, like a chase, for example, there might be a scene of the family of the person who was being chased looking for him or her, or, in mourning for him or her, or celebrating a miraculous escape. This shows the audience that time has passed, and it does not matter how much, between the episodes. This device gives a sense that the drama is happening in real time. If the action just continues where it left off a week earlier, that is likely to highlight the artificiality of the drama.

9 Scene synopses development

Synopses are usually developed by writers working on their own, after the detailed storylines have been finalized. There are two different ways of organizing a writing team. One way is for each writer to write a complete episode, so that one writer will develop the synopses and write the dialogue for every scene in one episode. The other is for the writers to write the scenes for different storylines. One writer develops the synopses and writes the dialogues for all of the scenes in transitional character 1's storyline, while another does the same for transitional character 2's storyline, and so on.

The advantage of the second arrangement is that there is more likely to be consistency of speech style and characterization throughout each storyline. It is probably also a more efficient way of proceeding, as each writer will be focusing on one or two storylines, and is less likely to need to look back at what has recently happened in the storyline before writing new scenes.

The development of synopses is the point when the basic storyline point is turned into a drama scene. The advantage of including a synopsis stage in a writing process is that it gives everyone involved the chance to focus on the structure of the scene, and, for the writer, the chance to concentrate on the structure and technical aspects of a scene, without having to also concentrate on writing good dialogue at the same time.

The synopsis should contain everything that happens in the scene, and all of the technical details that will make it work on whichever medium being used. The synopsis for the last scene in each episode should show how the scene is going to end with, at least, a cliffhanger, or, preferably, a dilemma for a transitional character.

A very useful tool for writers to use when they are developing synopses is visualization, even when writing for radio. If the writer imagines the setting, where the characters are, how they move, and, crucially, other factors that could affect how the scene works – for example, if, in reality, there would be other people who could overhear a confidential dialogue – then it can hugely improve the quality of the writing.

A synopsis is typically one-half to two-thirds of a page long.

There is normally an editorial review process for synopses, though less elaborate than the one for the detailed storylines. It is good practice for writers to swap completed synopses for internal review, before they go forward to a more formal review process.

10 Writing the dialogue

For many writers, a key principle of writing dialogue involves the management of exposition. Exposition is background information that is needed for the audience to understand a scene. This might be past events that have got the characters into the situation they are currently in, for example, or, in radio drama, it might be explaining factors in the scene's setting that affect, or are going to affect, the characters.

Long sections of exposition can slow down the action of a drama, and it is important to keep it to a minimum. As writers write the dialogue, they should consider if the exposition they are putting in is absolutely essential to the audience's understanding of the scene. It is also useful to remember that withholding some information is crucial in creating dramatic tension. Some writers talk of the weaponizing of exposition. Given that drama is driven by conflict, by struggle between characters, the idea is that any exposition that needs to be in a scene is used by one character or another as a weapon in that struggle. Doing this avoids chunks of undramatic description or explanation in a script.

Special considerations in writing drama for radio or podcast

Audio is obviously a limited medium of expression for drama. In behaviour change drama, it is being used to take characters on sometimes complicated and always difficult journeys of change. Furthermore, the radio drama is being asked to take substantial numbers of listeners on those journeys with the characters. To have this impact, the drama has to be emotionally engaging; that is, it has to work well as drama, and to do that, it needs to follow the dictum of 'Show don't tell.' In other words, the drama demonstrates; it does not lecture.

These audio dramas are dramas of actions and consequences. In this kind of drama, each character's beliefs are conveyed in actions, not explanations. The grandmother's belief that colostrum is bad for the baby comes over in her preventing the mother feeding the newborn baby, and making the mother express and discard the colostrum instead, or the grandmother's belief that the baby should be given water comes over in her giving the baby water while the mother is at work.

Using all means available for communicating an audio drama

Writing drama for audio is a demanding task, and writers need to use the few means of communication available in radio drama to the maximum.

Those means are:

- voices speaking dialogue
- sound effects
- the movement of actors around the microphone
- sometimes, music

The writer is responsible for the creative use of all of these.

The implementation is the responsibility of the production team and the cast but it is the writer who puts all these elements into the script in the most effective way they can. As will be discussed later, if, for example, the writer has not thought through how the actors are going to move, it is very difficult for the production team and the cast to make movement work.

Dialogue

In terms of the dialogue, it is much easier for the listener to follow the drama if, at the beginning of each scene, the writer takes some straightforward measures. In general, people are not as good at recognizing voices as they are at recognizing faces, and writers cannot rely on listeners knowing who the characters in a scene are by recognizing the voices alone. It is, therefore, very helpful for an audience if, in the first 30 seconds of a scene, subtly, the dialogue tells the listener:

- who the characters in the scene are, that is, their names and the relationship between them
- where the scene is taking place
- when the scene is taking place, if it matters to the meaning of the scene
- what is happening

Of course, there will be occasions when the writer does not want the listener to know this information for reasons of dramatic tension or comedy. There is an exercise to help writing teams explore subtle ways of doing this in *Module D3: Scriptwriting a serial drama for behaviour change*, in Section 6.

When character profiles are developed, it helps listeners recognize which character is which if the characters are given subtly different speech styles and styles of presenting themselves. This does not mean going into the realms of caricature, or giving characters catch phrases. This information should be in the character profiles, and writers need to check the character's profile and make the speech style fit the profile.

Sound effects

Since behaviour change dramas try to present themselves as reflecting the realities of their audiences' lives, they are normally in the naturalistic style of the soap opera. If such a drama is to be credible, then sound effects are an essential component. (A behaviour change drama does not need to be in this style, and the choice needs to be based on cultural acceptability, as said earlier.)

Sound effects are sounds that are added to a scene to lend a sense of realism. When a drama has been recorded in a studio, there will usually be background sounds added, often called atmosphere or atmos, to give the listener a sense of the location. This might be an exterior sound or, say, the sound of a radio, to suggest a domestic interior. Then there are sound effects that suggest to the audience something which is happening in the scene, like the sound of a character's activity, or something that is present in the scene, like a baby.

It is normally the writer's responsibility to write in sound effects cues, usually shortened to FX or SFX. It is important, when writing sound effects cues, for the writer to keep in mind that audiences often cannot identify a sound effect without help. So, it is usually necessary for the writer to subtly tell the listener what the sound is, in the dialogue. For example, if the listener hears a rustle of paper, but the action is actually unwrapping a package, then the dialogue needs to refer to a package in some way.

Sometimes, radio drama is recorded on location, which will usually mean no background sound effects need to be added, as the location will have been chosen for its sound.

Movement round the microphone

In audio drama, having the actors moving in relation to the microphone can add significantly to the listener's understanding.

This kind of movement can be used for three things:

- to help the listener understand the story
- to help the listener understand the conflict, which is often manifested as a struggle for control between the characters
- to help the listener understand the characters' emotions, to raise the audiences' level of emotional engagement

There are two reasons why the writer has significant responsibility in developing the use of movement in a script. The first is that movement is a means of expression, and it needs to work in complete conjunction with the other means of expression, especially the dialogue. Therefore, it works best if it is conceived as part of a whole. The second is much more mechanical. In order for the actors' movements to be heard, the actors need to be speaking as they move.

(Note: the use of the sound of footsteps for this purpose is inadvisable. The natural footsteps of actors often cannot be heard, especially on a low-quality radio or mobile phone. Most recording studios are carpeted, to reduce reverberation, which makes footsteps virtually silent. Even where a studio has different floor surfaces available, which is rare, footsteps are quiet, because the microphone is normally nearly 2 metres above the floor. Adding sound effect footsteps in post-production, by mixing pre-recorded footsteps, is very time consuming and difficult to get right.)

In addition, where movement is being used to improve the understanding of the conflict, it is precisely the combination of the words and the movement that makes it effective. So, sufficient dialogue needs to be written to allow the actor to make the complete move while speaking all the time. Of course, it is the writer who needs to produce that dialogue.

The writer's task is different depending on whether the drama is being recorded in stereo or mono. (There is a discussion of the relative merits of each in the next chapter.) When recording is in stereo, the writer needs to work out which sides the characters are going to be, and whether they enter and leave the scene on the same side, or cross the stereo and leave on the opposite side to that from which they entered. In mono, the movements are simply towards the microphone and away from it.

Movement to help the listener understand the story

When movement is being used to help the listener understand the story, or understand events, then it is simply the actor moving towards the microphone when they come into the scene, and away from it as they leave the scene.

Movement to help the listener understand the conflict

The conflict in a drama is often represented in a struggle for control between characters in a scene. The sense of the struggle can be reinforced for the listener by the use of movement. The listener can get a sense of who is in control by how close they are to the microphone. For example, when character A is in control, that character is closest to the microphone, but if character B is beginning to take over control, that character can move closer to the microphone, while character A retreats from it.

This is not automatically the case, and there are times when a character can assert their control by moving away from the microphone and leaving the scene, for example. If character B has won control, that character can show they are dismissing character A by walking away. It is the combination of the movement and the words that is effective.

Movement to help the listener understand the characters' emotions

Movement to help the listener understand the emotion in a scene usually involves small movements close up to the microphone. It is important that the movement is towards or away from the microphone, not towards or away from the other actor, as that would not be audible. This kind of movement is usually worked out between the producer/director and the actors during rehearsal. This is partly because the moves are small, so that dialogue does not need to be provided to cover them, and partly because of the difficulty a writer would have in trying to visualize them. It is simply easier to try the movement out with the actors.

Music

Music is often used in behaviour change serial dramas, and the choice and uses made of it are often the responsibility of the writing team. Usually it is music that would be made by people in the target audience, such as church music or music played at a village dance. This helps strengthen cultural affinity and, more important, it helps to make the audience feel the drama is relevant to people like themselves. Recognizing that the behaviour change being shown is relevant to themselves is a vital early step towards behaviour change. As long as a member of the audience thinks that what the drama is saying is only relevant to other people, they will not even begin to consider changing their behaviour.

What follows from this is that the choice of any music should be determined by the culture and preferences of the target audience, and it may not be traditional music.

For example, the UK-based charity Girl Effect's project, with the aim of empowering target audiences of adolescent girls, bases its radio serial dramas – in Ethiopia, Rwanda and Malawi – round the formation of a band, who sing and play contemporary pop music rooted in the current music industry of whichever country the drama is set in.

Script format

When the writing team are at the dialogue stage, the scripts should be in the different industry standard formats used in radio and television. There are several software packages available that will automatically put a script into the appropriate format. These formats have been developed over time to best fit the production practices of different media. They have certain features in common.

They leave a lot of space on the page, partly because it makes the dialogue easier to read, but also because notes and amendments often need to be written on the script, without getting in the way of reading the dialogue. They clearly distinguish between different parts of the script with different functions. For example, in a radio script, sound effect instructions will be all in upper case, while dialogue will be in standard format. Cues are numbered, usually starting a new sequence on each page. This is so that it is quick and easy for a producer/director and the cast and crew to navigate the script. For example, if the producer/director wants to retake part of a scene, he or she can just say that the retake is from cue 6 on page 12 to cue 3 on page 13.

Training agendas and materials

Suggested agendas and materials for training in topics relevant to this chapter can be found in Section 6:

Module D1: A selection workshop for a serial drama project
Module D2: An introduction to the MARCH methodology for behaviour and social change serial dramas, and its application
Module D3: Scriptwriting a serial drama for behaviour change

Production and post-production for a serial drama

This chapter is written on the assumption that there will be a team of writers, at least one producer, an audio technician and a production assistant working on the drama. However, there are circumstances where financial constraints do not allow for such a team, and it may be that the producer/director also takes on the role of the audio technician, and even of the production assistant as well. This is not the most efficient way of producing a drama, and is almost certainly going to lead to poorer quality, so projects should aim for winning the funding for a complete team, if at all possible.

The production of a serial drama for behaviour and social change is not significantly different from the production of any serial drama for broadcast. This chapter sets out the process, step by step.

It concentrates on drama production for audio, as the medium which is still important for communication with the most in need. For television production, there are several handbooks, such as *The TV Studio Production Handbook* by Lucy Brown and Lyndsay Duthie.[1]

Facilities for recording and mixing drama

Usually drama requires some specialized facilities, though it can be recorded entirely with portable recording equipment using different locations to give authentic acoustics. However, it is important to compare the relative costs of taking casts to different locations, the time taken for this, and the danger of extraneous noise which cannot be controlled, with the cost of creating or hiring a studio with the required equipment.

Mono or stereo?

However, a first consideration is whether to record the drama in mono or stereo. Where listeners can hear stereo, it has considerable advantages for drama, as listeners can hear the characters moving across the stereo 'picture', giving an extra dimension to the drama.

However, stereo poses some production issues. A decision between mono and stereo should be based on what proportion of the audience can properly listen in stereo. (Some radios have two speakers for stereo, but the two are so close together that it is hard to hear any stereo effect.) In most development contexts, it is likely that the proportion will be low, and, if this is the case, it is not worth taking on the extra work and risk that stereo poses.

Stereo demands more work than mono because the writer needs to work out left and right positioning and movement, instead of just towards and away from the microphone. Also the producer needs to direct and monitor the recording in left and right instead of just towards the microphone and away from it as well.

Further, in mono, if an omnidirectional microphone is used, actors can stand all round the microphone in a circle, whereas, for stereo recording, the space available is much more limited. At best, it is two segments of the circle, offering half as much space for the actors and, often, only one segment, offering a quarter of the space. If there are several actors in a scene, this can mean they are working in a congested space, which can cause recording problems that take time to resolve.

There is also the risk, in stereo recording, of a phenomenon called phase reverse or phase cancellation. In effect, instead of the left and right legs of the stereo augmenting each other, they cancel each other out. This usually cannot be heard when listening in stereo but, when listening in mono, it can result in the drama being completely silent.

The difficulty is that, during production, if everything is monitored in stereo, the production team can be completely unaware that there is a problem, and it will not be detected until the episode is broadcast and listeners in mono can hear nothing.

The solution is, when recording and mixing, to occasionally switch the monitoring to mono. This, of course, takes up time and, if the problem is detected, it needs to be sorted out, taking up yet more time.

Figure 29.1 *A very basic studio for recording audio drama*

Recording in a studio

Drama is normally recorded around one microphone, and Figure 29.1 shows a fairly basic recording studio for a development context, set up for drama. There are two microphones, but they are each in a different acoustic, and only one would be used at any given time, not both. Sound deadening is provided by heavy curtains all round the walls, and the studio is divided into different recording areas by locally made acoustic screens.

These are panels filled with padding, with one hard wooden side and a soft fabric side. In the picture, they are arranged with the hard surfaces facing the microphone on the left: this produces a more echoey acoustic, for example, for a kitchen.

The microphone on the right is between the curtaining and the soft side of a screen, so that it will be in a much less echoey acoustic: suitable, for example, for scenes set in a bedroom, or even for scenes set outdoors, where there is no echo. The small door is a sound effect.

The use of a single microphone allows for easy movement by the actors, and for very straightforward recording. It also means actors can communicate with each other non-verbally.

Recording outside

Where there is not too much background sound, scenes set outside can be recorded outside, as shown in Figure 29.2. In this case, a directional microphone is being used, that is, a microphone which only picks up sound in front of it, not all around. In this case, it directed away from a nearby road so that it does not pick up the sound of traffic.

Figure 29.2 *A scene from a Somali radio drama being recorded outdoors*

The only additional equipment needed for recording outside are long cables for the microphone and for a pair of headphones. The producer can either listen in the studio cubicle, while a floor manager organizes the actors outside, following the producer's instructions over headphones, or the producer can be outside with the cast, listening to the performances on headphones connected to the mixing desk in the cubicle.

The sound effects library

A key resource for audio drama is the sound effects library. Normally, there will be two. One will be an electronic library of pre-recorded sound effects, and the other will be the practical effects cupboard. Practical effects are those made at the same time as the actors are recorded. They might range from unopened drink cans, which will only be opened during recording, to a large tub full of earth and a mattock, for digging scenes.

In most development contexts, sound effects need to be specially recorded for the drama, so that they are specific to the country or region. While sound effects can be bought in developed countries, appropriate ones for development contexts are rarely available for purchase.

Background sounds need to be recorded for different seasons, so that the drama reflects the reality of listeners' lives. All exterior effects need to match the nature of the drama's universe, so, for example, if the drama is in a rural area all sound effects should be recorded well away from traffic noise. All backgrounds should be recorded for at least 20 minutes, so that it is not necessary to use exactly the same section over and over again. If exactly the same few minutes of a background is used, listeners can begin to notice.

Figure 29.3 *Recording sound effects of a truck in rural Zambia. The truck and driver were hired for an hour to record a range of effects*

Over time, the collection of pre-recorded sound effects will become large. The effects, therefore, have to be stored in a well-organized library of different folders on a hard drive, so that they can be quickly and easily retrieved for use in the drama. File names for effects tracks should be as precise as possible, giving the location, the time of day, season and detail of the sounds in the effect: for example, *Countryside outside of a town, 6 am, rainy season: birdsong, cock crowing, goats passing.*

The maintenance of the library would normally be the work of the audio technician, though the producer should also have an up-to-date copy so that he or she can audition sound effects in advance of recording and mixing.

Small practical effects should be kept in a lockable cupboard, while larger ones, like effects doors (see Figure 29.1), should be kept in the studio.

An acoustic universe

Before any production begins, the production and writing teams together should work out the characteristic sound of each of the main locations in the drama. The decisions should be recorded in the narrative description of the universe. The components of the characteristic background need to tell the audience the location background (rural or urban, for example) and the economic situation of the characters who appear in this location. The components will be the following.

- The background sound effects, which will change throughout the year as seasons change, but will reflect, for example, the construction of the house. If it is made of corrugated iron, it will sound very different from a house built of thatch and mud brick, or built of tiles and fired bricks or built of concrete.
- The acoustic, that is the level of echo in the location. An echoey acoustic, as might be heard in a large building, like a church, or one with very hard surfaces, like metal, is usually called a 'live' acoustic, while one where there is no echo, as in an exterior, for example, is called a 'dead' acoustic.
- Any characteristic sound effects that are associated with the inhabitants or users of the location. For example, a Somali frankincense preparation and packing factory will have a live acoustic, the characteristic sounds of frankincense preparation, and the traditional singing of the workers as they prepare the frankincense. In contrast, a South Sudanese *tukul*, a small house built of mud brick with a thatched roof, will have a much deader acoustic, with a rural background heard from outside, with little activity sounds apart from cleaning, as most work and food preparation will be done outside.

The decisions on acoustics will depend on the resources available. If the studio is big enough, and is equipped with acoustic screens, then different interior acoustics can be established in it. (See Figure 29.1.)

In summary, in an average studio in a development context, there are three options.

- A 'live' interior, which is echoey: this is created by turning three or more of the screens so that their hard sides are facing the microphone. Actors also need to be positioned so that they are facing towards the microphone and opposite a hard surface.
- A 'dead' interior, which is not echoey: this is created by turning the screens so that their soft sides are facing the microphone. This is often the best exterior acoustic available, too.
- An exterior: this is created by using the microphone outside the studio, where that is possible and there is not too much distinctive sound in the background, and can be used for any scene set outside.

In a well-resourced project, a number of different acoustics can be set up in a compound, for example, or a set of actual locations can be researched and chosen, one for each setting that regularly appears in the drama, and the project takes the cast to those locations to record.

However, in many development contexts a choice of acoustics is an unachievable luxury and all scenes are recorded in the same studio space.

More echoey acoustics can be added electronically but, unfortunately, if a studio has quite a live acoustic, that cannot be removed from a recording. If space is limited, it is therefore better to make the studio acoustic as dead as possible.

The cast

Once scripts are written and technical facilities organized, the first stage of production is the casting and, if necessary, the training of actors.

Managing a cast

To have a good cast who consistently attend rehearsals and recordings is extremely important for a serial drama, but, in development contexts, casts can create serious problems. If only one actor in a scene does not turn up for rehearsal and recording, it is very difficult to do a reasonable recording of the scene, as it is difficult to add a single voice separately at a later date. In many countries in the Global South there are no professional actors, so most members of a cast will have other jobs, and acting is unlikely to be their main source of income. This circumstance can create serious scheduling problems. Where there is political or economic instability, casts can be very unreliable.

Motivating and involving a cast in a project is very important, and a project should make sure that the actors fully understand what the drama is trying to achieve, and its potential impact. Favourable audience responses and evidence of impact can be important factors, and communicating them to the cast is likely to be helpful. Some serial dramas organize road shows, taking members of the cast to, say, rural areas to perform in front of live audiences and to get in touch with those audiences to help them understand the importance of the drama.

Contracts and pay

At the same time, research should be carried out for, and careful consideration given to, contractual and remuneration arrangements with the cast, so that there is an obligation for them to attend regularly and that rates of pay are properly competitive with other jobs that are available to them.

In many countries, this may not be a problem at all, but a project needs to find out if there is a potential problem almost before doing anything else.

Casting

Casting is usually carried out by the producer/director with advice from the writers, who will have insights into the characters. For audio, a major casting consideration is for the voices chosen to be as distinctive from each other as possible.

A basic auditioning process will involve actors being given the profile of the character they are being considered for, and scripts in which the character has a significant role in the dialogue.

The actors need to be given sufficient time to prepare and ask questions about the character, then be asked to perform.

The producer/director will then them through the direction process given below, and the actor performs again.

Actors are judged on their ability to bring the character to life, and their ability to take direction.

Stages of production

What is set out here is a suggested sequence of the key stages of the production process, what is involved in each stage, and who is responsible for each stage.

Everyone involved in the production, including the audio technician, should read the script carefully and, if necessary, clarify issues with the writers well in advance of recording.

Sound effects preparation

The production team and technician identify effects in the script that are not in the library, and which need to be recorded, and they identify those effects that will be best recorded with the speech, that is, the practical or spot effects. These will be, for example, crowd effects to be made by the cast, door effects, and work effects, like cleaning and digging. The technician identifies which of these are in the practical effects library and which are not.

The technician records the new effects needed, and acquires new practical effects needed. The new recorded effects are edited and are filed in the library. All practical effects need to be stored in the effects cupboard, which should be kept locked.

The technician works out which practical effects can be done by the cast, and which will need to be done by the production assistant. All practical effects need to be rehearsed in the studio or outside by the technician and production assistant before the cast arrives, to ensure that they can be recorded quickly and efficiently when the cast are present.

Acoustics

In this stage of preparation, the production team work out which acoustic to use for each scene in the script, although if an acoustic universe (see above) has been created, most decisions on the acoustics will have been made. The only ones remaining at this stage will be where there is a new setting that has not featured before.

Rehearsal and recording schedule

The production team and production assistant draw up a schedule for rehearsing and recording the episode, well in advance of the recording.

The production assistant uses this schedule to call the cast needed, and to ensure they are at the studio at the time required.

Producer/director's preparation

The producer/director who is going to direct the session should read the script thoroughly, so that they understand it completely. If there are parts they do not understand, they need to check with the relevant writer.

Preparing for cuts

The producer/director needs to be well prepared to make cuts in case an episode is too long. It is risky to wait to decide what to cut after recording and mixing, as desirable edits may not work, because of the way an actor speaks, because of actors speaking over each other, or because a practical effect is going on behind the speech. It is much better for the producer/director, in consultation with the writing team, to find, before recording, sections of the script of different durations that can be cut, if necessary.

This means that, during recording, a cut version of a scene or speech can be recorded, which can be edited in to replace the full-length version, if needed. Having a number of different possible cuts gives different options, depending on how much material needs to be taken out. The cuts should be worked out with the writers, so that nothing that is vital to the drama's behaviour change impact is cut.

Planning for effective performances

From looking at the scene outlines or synopses, the producer/director should find out what barriers and facilitators are working in the scene, if any, so that they can ensure that the performances show these factors in action.

The producer/director's main task is to get the most effective performances from the cast. One simple way of doing this is for the producer/director to ask a set of questions designed to help the actor understand their character better, and the situation the character is in. Getting actors to think about these issues can help to improve performances, not least because it helps them understand the subtext.

The producer/director's questions should include the following.

- What is your character trying to achieve?
- How is your character trying to achieve what they want?
- Where is the conflict or struggle for control in the scene?
- How has your character got into the situation they are in the scene, that is, what has happened in the past?
- Which character ends up in control?

As an example, this is a scene from a radio serial drama in western Zambia, designed to combat HIV. The characters are: Wamulume, a transitional character with a behaviour change objective of reducing the number of his sexual partners and being faithful to his wife; Wamulume's wife, Namakau; Munu (15 years old), Wamulume's son by another woman, Mutale; and Wamulume's and Namakau's daughter, Saboi (14 years old).

The background situation is that Wamulume has recently ended his long-time affair with Mutale and he has taken custody of Munu from her. Munu has been brought up in town but Wamulume lives in a small village. Until Munu's arrival, Saboi had grown up as the only child but, now, all of Wamulume's attention is on Munu, and he gives very little attention to Saboi. Munu is not happy living in the village.

It is the period of the huge River Zambesi flood, and the village is an island in the flood.

In the scene, Wamulume has just brought a boat load of maize from the town, and Namakau tells Munu to unload the boat and take the maize sacks to the kitchen. Munu refuses, claiming that, as a boy from town, he is not used to carrying heavy loads. Wamulume agrees with him and tells Saboi to carry the maize. She does so but the sacks are heavy and she asks why she and Munu cannot share the work. Wamulume dismisses the question and takes Munu off to teach him hunting.

The answers the actors playing these four characters should give to the producer/director's questions might be as follows.

What is your character trying to achieve?

- Wamulume wants Munu to stay because it helps him avoid the temptation of Mutale as he no longer has to visit her to see his son.
- Namakau wants to see her child being treated in the same way as another woman's child.
- Saboi wants to be held in the regard she used to be, not be demeaned in front of Munu, and to win her father's affection back.
- Munu wants to exploit his father's favouritism for all it is worth.

How is your character is trying to achieve what they want?

- Wamulume by exercising his dominance of the family.
- Namakau by exercising parental authority.

- Saboi by showing reasonableness and compromise.
- Munu, by being stubbornly defiant, in the confidence that he has power over his father.

Where is the conflict or struggle for control in the scene?

- It is largely between Munu and Namakau.

How has your character got into the situation they are in the scene, that is, what has happened in the past?

- Wamulume by his desire to avoid risking HIV, and to keep his son with him.
- Namakau by maintaining her traditional role as a submissive wife.
- Saboi by the unwelcome arrival of Munu, her father's switch of affection and her mother's powerlessness against her husband.
- Munu by having a decision on where he lives imposed on him.

Which character ends up in control?

- Munu

A particular problem with radio acting is that actors read their scripts, instead of learning their lines as they would if they were working in a visual medium. Sometimes, actors sound as if they are reading, and they need to be helped to sound as if they are speaking naturally. The process for doing this is often known as 'lifting the words off the page'.

This direction system has been shown to be effective at solving this problem.

Visualization

The producer/director should visualize each scene, so that they can take into account any factor that would be affecting the events, and can direct the actors' performances accordingly.

In visualizing this example scene, the maize sacks are inside a dugout canoe drawn up onto the land. It is only a short distance to the kitchen, as the boat has been positioned by Wamulume to be as close as possible, so the distances that characters are moving for most of the scene are short, while Wamulume's and Munu's exit together at the end of the scene is much longer, as they walk off to go hunting. It also means that the maize sacks need to be heaved up over the canoe's side.

Therefore, the end of the scene could be Wamulume and Munu chatting and having a laugh as they go off into the distance, while, close up, Saboi is making noises to show her effort as she heaves a sack up and out of the canoe, and she breathes heavily as she carries it away. Still breathing heavily, she returns, and heaves out another sack, giving a sharp image of the contrasting outcomes of the scene for the two children.

Actors' preparation

The head writer and production assistant should make sure that the cast are given the script well in advance of rehearsal and recording, so that they have the time to become thoroughly familiar with it. Actors need to read the script aloud to themselves a number of times. Over time, they should become familiar with the questions the producer/director will ask (see above), and have answers ready.

Rehearsal

A rehearsal process for an audio drama usually has two stages: the first outside the studio or recording area to develop spoken performances, and the second in the studio or recording area to combine the spoken performances with movements and any practical sound effects.

The rehearsal should be organized and led by the producer/director, and the writer should also be present for clarification or for minor changes to make a script clearer or easier to perform.

There are many different ways of rehearsing and directing a drama. One method, which it is best to avoid, is the producer/director demonstrating to actors how to perform the script. It is likely to lead to the actors engaging superficially with the script, and not developing a performance based on a thorough understanding of the character. It is also a waste of the creative resource of the actors. Engaged actors can bring different understanding and insights. Performances based on a thorough understanding of the character and situation are always going to be better than those based on a superficial imitation of someone else's ideas.

The method suggested above is just one that has proved successful in development contexts.

The development of spoken performances

This will normally start with a read-through. The actors are seated and read the script aloud. This has a number of functions. It can allow the producer/director and writer to identify difficulties in the script that need minor changes, and the actors to seek clarifications of meaning. It gives the producer/director the opportunity to assess the performances and to decide on the level of rehearsal and direction needed.

Unless performances are very good at this stage, the producer/director should ask each of the cast the set of questions set out above, to help them understand their character. (Over time, as actors get more used to this approach, and as they understand their character better, this should become a routine and fairly quick process.)

Once the cast have understood what their character is struggling to achieve in a scene, it is useful for the producer/director to identify the level of desire in each of the characters for whatever it is they want to achieve. This is often done on a scale of 1 to 10, with 1 being a low level of desire, and 10 being a very high level of desire.

Depending on the time available for rehearsal, the producer/director can try the scene out several times, each time giving the actors different levels of desire.

So, perhaps, in the first try-out, the producer/director tells actor A that the character has a level of desire of 8, and actor B, a level of 2. Then, perhaps, actor A is given a level of 1 and actor B a level of 7. On the basis of what the director hears in each of these try-outs, they then tell the actors the levels of characters' desire they want to hear in the final performance.

If there is less time, the producer/director needs to have in mind in advance what the levels of the characters' desire are, and asks each actor what they think the level of desire is in their character, and why. If there is a large discrepancy between the level the actor thinks and the level the producer/director thinks, they can argue it out but, ultimately, it should be the producer/director's choice.

Going back to the example scene from the western Zambian drama, the levels of desire and why they are at that level could be as follows:

- Wamulume has a level of 10 because, ultimately, his life is at stake.
- Namakau has a level of 5, because she is uncertain, torn between her desire to assert herself over Munu for Saboi's sake, and her desire to be a traditionally good wife.
- Saboi has a level of 2, because she finds herself in a completely new situation. She is uncertain about what to do, so she has doubts about any course of action she chooses, and cannot have a strong desire for any of them.
- Munu has a level of 10, because he is in a new situation and wants to assert himself. He knows he is in a position of power, for the first time in his life.

It should be understood that these levels of desire are what the characters feel and are self-justifications. They are not in any sense an objective justification for what they are doing. In this instance, Wamulume is not justified in his insensitivity towards, especially, Saboi, but also towards Namakau, however much he may feel he is.

The producer/director leads the actors in rehearsing the script until they are satisfied with the performances and, the following in particular.

- No actor sounds as if they are reading.
- Each performance matches the levels of characters' desire the producer/director has asked for.
- The meaning of the scene is clear.

This may appear a cumbersome rehearsal process for episodes of a soap opera, but, over time, it will become second nature to everyone involved and will be quick.

Page turns

If the cast, or any member of the cast, is new to radio drama, it will be necessary to decide how page-turns are going to be made, and to practise. This is because the microphone can pick up the sound of a page-turn very easily and, if a page-turn is done while someone is speaking, it cannot be edited out. So disciplined script handling is important to avoid a lot of retakes. (See below for details of retakes and editing.)

There are two different ways of handling page-turns. In the first, the whole cast in a scene wait until the last line on the page has been performed, and then all turn their pages at the same time, with the first line on the next page not performed until all the turns have been completed and there is silence. If this is done properly, the noise of the page-turns can easily be edited out.

The other method, which is a little more risky but avoids breaks in the performance, is that each actor, when they have finished performing all their lines on a page, turns away from the microphone and, very carefully, turns the page as quietly as possible, not turning back towards the microphone until the page-turn is complete.

Adding the dimensions of positioning and movement, and of practical effects

In the studio or, if outside, in the recording area, the producer/director leads the cast in a walk-through of the scene. The producer/director positions the actors in what they think are the right distances from the microphone. Any actor who needs a practical effect is given it, and rehearses its use, or, if it is determined that the actor cannot use it, another person, usually the production assistant, is positioned to use the effect in conjunction with the actor.

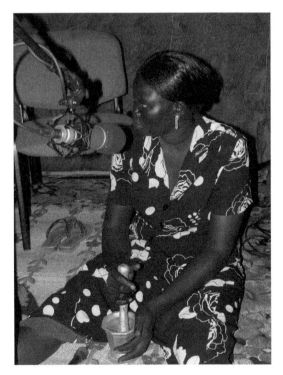

Figure 29.4 *Recording a practical effect of grinding coffee at the same time as the voice, in South Sudan. Traditionally, coffee shop owners sing as they grind the coffee*

The producer/director identifies each point in the script where a move is needed, and the actors make those moves, with the producer/director estimating their ending position for each move. The actors note down their starting and ending points on their scripts. It is also useful if some kind of marker can be used to mark the starting and ending points on the floor or on the ground.

If the scene is an intimate one, then the producer/director and the actors work out where small moves to help the audience understand the emotion of the scene are made and how close they need to get to the microphone. These will be small moves of leaning in towards the microphone or leaning back, away from the microphone. The moves will not involve moving the feet. It is important to understand that when characters are getting closer to each other, the actors move towards the microphone, not towards each other.

The producer/director then listens to the scene in the cubicle, with the actors performing the moves, and with the practical FX. Having listened to the scene, the producer/director adjusts the distances from the microphone, judging them by what they hear through the monitoring speakers. Ultimately, all movements in a radio drama should be judged by how they sound, not by how they look.

During these rehearsals in the studio or recording space, the producer/director and the audio technician need to pay attention to:

- the script being followed as written
- the balance of voices
- distortion (the sound is distorted by the actor being too close to the microphone or too loud)
- the audibility of practical effects, and that they sound natural, and not exaggerated
- the audibility of the movement
- the script handling and that it is properly disciplined

Recording

Once the producer/director is satisfied with the performances, and the technician is satisfied with the technical quality, then the scene can be recorded. (Though, often, everything is recorded, in case a rehearsal turns out to be the best performance.)

Again, during recording, the producer/director and technician need to pay attention to:

- the script being followed as written
- the balance of voices
- distortion
- the audibility of practical effects, and that they sound natural, and not exaggerated
- the audibility of the movement
- the script handling and that it is properly disciplined
- actors stumbling over their words or misreading their lines, or getting the wrong intonation or pronunciation
- unexpected noise

If something goes wrong during recording, for example, there is a script noise, a voice distorts, or anything else needs attention, the usual practice is to stop the performance. If there is a problem that needs attention – say, if a voice is too quiet or too loud – it is sorted out by the producer/director. If, for example, an actor gets a pronunciation wrong, the producer/director will stop the performance, give the correct pronunciation, tell the actor where to start from again, and restart. If it is simply a script noise, or some other one-off event, the producer/director will explain the problem to the cast, and ask them to go back to the beginning of the affected speech, and start the performance again from that point. The affected section is later edited out. This process is usually called retaking, and the newly started recording is called a retake.

In the case of an actor stumbling over their words or misreading, actors should be trained to automatically go back to the beginning of the speech, and record it again. However, sometimes actors do not notice an error and just carry on reading the script. If this happens, the producer/director needs to stop the performance and ask the actor to do a retake, telling them where to start from.

The reason for going back several words, or even lines, is that people have a tendency to overemphasize when correcting themselves, so that, if the retake is on the affected word, it will not edit properly because of the overemphasis.

If the producer/director is not satisfied with the performance of a scene, or thinks it could be done better, they need to talk to the cast, explaining what they want to be improved, and the whole scene is retaken. This can happen several times. It is good practice not to erase the different recordings of the scene, because, sometimes, the best performance can be achieved by editing together sections of the scene from different recordings.

Whenever there is a retake, either of a few lines or of an entire scene, the producer/director should make a note on the script, as this can save considerable time in the editing. If, for example, there are five takes of a line, and the producer/director knows that the only acceptable one is the last, then, in the editing, the producer/director can tell the technician. If the producer/director is editing the material themselves, they can see from the script that there are five takes and can look on the audio display on the computer for the fifth, and edit out the first four without listening to them.

After a scene has been recorded, if there is a cut option, then the section of the scene with the cut in it should be recorded before moving on to the next scene. This is partly because the cast needed will still be present, and partly because the way the scene was performed will be fresh in the actors' minds, and so the section with the cut in it is more likely to match the original recording.

Editing

After an episode has been recorded, the recording needs to be edited, which, with modern audio software, is a relatively simple task, though it does need to be undertaken with care. Poor editing can lead to edits the listener can hear, either, for example, because the edits are too abrupt, or because they have been done inaccurately, causing clicks. To avoid these problems, after each edit the cursor should be taken back to a few words before the edit, and the recording played from there, so that the edit can be heard, and any problem can be corrected.

Editing is needed to take out retakes, and any other extraneous material. Also if, for example, the scenes have not been recorded in the order they will be broadcast, for scheduling reasons, they need to be put in the correct order.

When the recorded material is being edited, it is the responsibility of the producer/ director to decide on the best take of each scene to use in the final broadcast, so all takes should be listened to, unless the producer/director has noted on the script which one was the best at the time of recording.

When the episode edit has been completed, the duration of the episode should be noted, and, if cuts are needed, they are done before the mix. However, it does need to be remembered that the mix may introduce background fades at the beginning and end of scenes, which will affect the duration.

Mixing

The mix is when any background or other effects not recorded with the voices are added, along with any music. It is the responsibility of the producer/director, but is usually done by the audio technician under the instructions of the producer/director.

Background sound effects and music need to be mixed with care, with particular attention paid to ensuring the complete audibility of the speech. If there is any doubt, then it is essential to favour the speech over the effects and music.

After production

Once an episode has been completed, it should be listened to by the whole team, to make sure there is no material in it that should not be there, like retakes which have not been edited out, and also to check it conforms to the script, and sections have not been taken out by accident.

The Character Bible

The Character Bible is a record of what happens to each character in the drama, and it needs to be updated after every episode has been recorded, because the final broadcast version might be different from the script, because of cuts for duration.

The purpose of the Character Bible is to make it quick and easy for a writer to research a character before writing a scene that includes that character. The writer can see who the character has met before, and what they have done in previous episodes, without having to search through the scripts.

The Character Bible is organized into sections for each character, and each section starts with the complete character profile. There is then a table for the character, which just lists which episodes and which scenes the character has been in, with a list of the other characters in the scene, and a very brief explanation of what the character did.

The format of the character bible should be designed so that it is quick and easy to update.

Updating should take place after each episode has been recorded and edited, in case parts of the original script have been cut, changing what happens in the scene.

(See Table 29.1 for a possible format.)

Character name:

Table 29.1 A possible page layout for a drama's character bible

Episode number	Scene number	Other characters in the scene	A one sentence description of what the character does

Training agendas and materials

Suggested agendas and materials for training in topics relevant to this chapter can be found in Section 6:

Module D4: Production team and technician training for drama

Factual programmes for change: The why and how

Some elements of MARCH methodology can be used in factual programmes to promote behaviour change, particularly in the use of role models and the identification and use of barriers and facilitators.

The advantages and disadvantages of factual programmes compared with drama have been set out in Chapters 6 and 26. In brief, factual programmes for behaviour change are likely to cost less than drama, they allow greater audience participation and they are better at giving some kinds of information. Against that, they are less emotionally engaging, they describe and explain rather than show change in action, and they cannot show the full, possible consequences of a failure to change.

Some audiences prefer factual programmes to drama, and a communication needs assessment would show this preference, if it exists.

Methodology

Behaviour and social change communication methodology should be the central focus of the production of this kind of factual programme. It is not an add-on to conventional production techniques and processes. (See Chapter 27 and *Module D2: An introduction to the MARCH methodology for behaviour and social change serial dramas, and its application*, in Section 6.)

This means that behaviour and social change communication methodology affects every level of programme-making: developing a curriculum, the choice of interviewees, the conduct of interviews, editing recorded material, and the programme presentation.

Often, a factual series will run alongside a drama, so that they are mutually reinforcing, with the factual series providing most of the information and participatory element.

Format

Typically, a factual behaviour change programme will use a magazine format, with a number of topic strands running in parallel throughout the series, with each strand addressing one behaviour change objective. There will be one item for each strand in each programme.

For a behaviour change series on mother and baby health, for example, the first month's programming could be set out in a grid. (See Table 30.1.)

Table 30.1 An example grid for developing the breakdown of topics for a factual behaviour change series

Week number:		1	2	3	4
Strand 1	**Ante-natal care (ANC)**	Why ANC is good for the baby	Why ANC is good for the baby	Why ANC is good for the mother	Why ANC is good for the mother
Strand 2	**Safe birth (health facility vs home)**	Advantages of facility birth for baby	Advantages of facility birth for baby	Risks of facility delivery	Risks of facility delivery
Strand 3	**Newborn care**	Proper care can save baby's life	What is proper care?	What is proper care?	Why proper care matters
Strand 4	**Exclusive breastfeeding (bf)**	Advantages for the baby of bf in 1st hour	Advantages for the baby of bf in 1st hour	No water for the baby in 1st hour	No water for the baby in 1st hour
Strand 5	**Maternal aftercare**	Lack of care risks life	Risks to mother and baby	Danger signs	Danger signs
Audience-led	**Answers to audience questions**	Answers to audience questions	Answers to audience questions	Answers to audience questions	Answers to audience questions
	Audience opinions	Audience opinions	Audience opinions	Audience opinions	Audience opinions

As discussed in Chapter 21, the rationale of using a magazine format is that different sections of the programme will engage different parts of the audience, and each programme will contain a range of different voices.

Identifying target audiences

Each item in each programme will contain people from the audience, carefully chosen to address the different sections among the target audience. So, in the example, there would be young mothers, young mothers-to-be and older women who have had or expect to have a role in managing their daughter's or their daughter-in-law's pregnancy and care of the newborn baby. All should be talking about their first-hand experience of, again to follow the example, their first visit to ante-natal care, the consequences of a lack of care for a mother after she gave birth, or the different outcomes for babies of exclusive breastfeeding and of giving water to a baby under six months old.

Some interviews will be with medical personnel, usually midwives, who speak in ways the audience can readily understand, focusing largely on their personal professional experience. The focus should be on personal stories to engage the listener or viewer. The items should be in a range of formats, including one-to-one interviews, multi-voiced packages and studio discussions.

Strand duration and structure

The duration of a particular strand will be decided by realistic assessment of how long the behaviour change is likely to take. (See Chapter 27.)

The structure of a strand should be based on the formative research, and the barriers and facilitators identified from it, so that items tackle the barriers to behaviour change and capitalize on facilitators. The overall structure of a strand should follow these stages:

1. Getting the attention of the audience to the importance of the strand's topic.
2. Offering the knowledge required for change, and, if necessary, the skills required for change to happen.
3. Addressing attitudes to change.
4. Showing the practical steps needed to bring about behaviour change.

An outline of the curriculum process

A curriculum needs to be developed for each strand, and is a list of topics broken down into a programme-by-programme structure of individual programme items. (See Chapter 21.)

Each item in each programme needs to be a small enough piece of information to be conveyed in between 3 and 7 minutes, depending on the format of the item.

The curriculum is needed so that the steps to achieving the behaviour change objectives:

• can be understood by the audience
• follow a step-by-step structure towards behaviour change
• follow the structure of knowledge, attitude, behaviour
• show people overcoming or avoiding barriers, and using facilitators

The process by which audience members can overcome the barriers and use the facilitators is then broken down into a series of small steps, under the headings of knowledge and skills, attitudes and practical steps, by the production team, using their cultural and social knowledge, and calling in external expertise where needed.

Those steps then become the programme items. Often, there will be more than one item on each step, to reinforce the learning. (See below.)

Building a behaviour change curriculum in detail

A behaviour change curriculum starts with deciding behaviour change objectives, that is, what behaviours is the project trying to address. These usually come from an analysis of the formative research and are usually subject to negotiation between the project management and the donors.

Once behaviour change objectives have been established, it is often the case that the information in the formative research is summarized by a project manager – for example, with the objectives set out, and pieces of information from the research relevant to each listed under each one, and broken down into barriers and facilitators. If this is done, the production team can work from this document rather than from the raw research. If not, the team will need to identify and classify the barriers and facilitators themselves from the research. (See Chapter 27 for this process.)

The curriculum breakdown

A curriculum breakdown is a list of programme item topics, which is created from:

- the information in the analysis of the formative research to identify barriers and facilitators
- the production team's cultural knowledge

The production team works through the barriers and facilitators, listing each under the relevant heading of knowledge, attitude or behaviour. The team then works through the barriers and facilitators, breaking down each into smaller programme items, and these items take the audience through tackling a barrier or using a facilitator step by step.

Working out the steps

If using the curriculum grid set out in Chapter 21, the team insert the items under the programme numbers, in an order that represents a step-by-step series towards the overall behaviour change, covering knowledge issues first, then attitude issues and finally, practical issues of behaviour change.

It is also better to look at personal factors first (knowledge or a lack of knowledge is always personal, anyway), then social (again, attitudes are often socially established) and then environmental. (See Chapter 27 for the sequencing of the different classes of change factors.)

It will normally be necessary to repeat the topics of items several times, but each time taking the item of information from different angles and in different formats.

A good way of ordering the items in a strand is to deal with several barriers and their equivalent facilitators in parallel, so that an item on barrier A could be in programme 1, an item on barrier B in programme 2, and on barrier C in programme 3, returning to barrier A in programme 4 and repeating the pattern.

Once the curriculum is complete for all the behaviour change objectives for a specified time, probably not less than six months then, programme by programme, the items can be developed using the factual package development grid set out in Chapter 7 and in *Module J2: A selection workshop procedure for factual communication*, in Section 6.

At the production level

The choice of interviewees

Choosing appropriate interviewees is, of course, vital to the success of the series in helping members of the audience change their behaviour.

Overwhelmingly, interviewees will be people with whom the audience can identify, that is, people like themselves. These interviewees will be:

- role models for the audience, that is, people who either have achieved some of the steps towards the behaviour change in question, or are in the process of trying to achieve them, and who can explain why and how they have either achieved some change or are trying to change
- people whose beliefs, attitudes and behaviour are opposed to the behaviour change the programmes are promoting, so that listeners who think the same way will keep listening, and this will promote discussion among the audience

In most behaviour change communication projects, research should identify those key people in the community who have a role in the particular behaviour change that the project is addressing. For example, in a project on mother and baby health, these target audiences might be:

- young mothers-to-be, who are the key target for behaviour change
- other people who either have influence over the mother's behaviour, or directly affect the treatment of the mother and baby, who might be older women, often relatives of the mother and traditional midwives, or husbands

Where experts are interviewed, they need to be people who can communicate effectively with the audience.

It is very important to include voices representing different parts of the audience – and they should be both male and female – as routes to behaviour and social change for different sections can be significantly different, and different members of the audience will identify with different voices.

Taking all these considerations into account, in the example project trying to reduce mortality rates among babies less than six months old, under the behaviour change objective of the need for breastfeeding to be exclusive for the first six months, there could be the following programme items:

- a package on why water should not be given to a baby under 6 months old
- a package on why food of any kind should not be given to a baby under 6 months old
- a package on the way breast milk meets all the nutritional needs of the baby
- a role-model young mother's interview on why she switched to exclusive breastfeeding

- a role-model young mother talking about her struggle to understand why breastfeeding needs to be exclusive
- a discussion between a traditional midwife and a qualified health worker on feeding practices for young babies
- a series of step-by-step interviews as a young mother-to-be learns why breastfeeding needs to be exclusive
- a young mother-to-be interviewed about her dilemma over exclusively breastfeeding or not, as she is getting different advice from different people
- an older woman listens to advice from both sides on what she should tell her daughter about breastfeeding
- a question and answer session, as a qualified health worker answers queries from a small group of young husbands on why breastfeeding needs to be exclusive
- a question and answer session, as a qualified health worker answers queries from a small group of grandmothers on why breastfeeding needs to be exclusive

Interviewing

As discussed in Chapter 1 on producing programmes for development projects, of the six standard journalistic questions – What? Where? When? Who? Why? How? – the last two are the lowest priority in normal journalism, whereas in behaviour change programming, they are the highest priority. This is because listeners need to understand these points, rather than where and when the events happened. This is not topical news.

The nature of the programmes, in summary

Because of the ways people learn and change, factual behaviour change programmes have these characteristics.

- The programmes follow a curriculum of small steps towards behaviour change, over a long period of time.
- The curriculum is organized so that it deals with change of knowledge first, then change of attitude and, finally, change of behaviour, and it addresses tackling barriers and using facilitators.
- The programmes include interviews with people like their listeners, and do not rely on experts.
- Interviewees are, most often, role models, ordinary people who are going through a process of behaviour change, or people who have been through a successful process of behaviour change.
- Interviewees will also be people whose beliefs, attitudes and behaviour are opposed to what the programmes are promoting, so that listeners who think and believe the same way – the people the programmes most need to change – are engaged and can be taken through a process of change.

- The programmes will promote discussion between opposing views among listeners as they try to get people talking to each other about the topics they are covering.
- Interviews will often be personal stories so that listeners are engaged.
- Experts need to be people who can speak in ways that ordinary people can understand.
- Out of the six standard journalistic questions – What? Where? When? Who? How? and Why? – interviews will concentrate on the last two, the How? and the Why?, that is, how the interviewee did something and why they did it.

Training agendas and materials

Suggested agendas and materials for training in topics relevant to this chapter can be found in Section 6:

Module J1: An exploration of how people learn
Module J2: A selection workshop procedure for factual communication
Module J8: Producing a live phone-in discussion programme
Module J10: The production of factual programmes for behaviour change
Module D2: An introduction to the MARCH methodology for behaviour and social change serial dramas, and its application

Section Six

Training plans and materials

Journalism

Notes on training

If participants are being trained in a language which is not their first, it will probably be helpful to put basic information and exercise instructions on PowerPoint slides, if facilities exist for it, or on printed handouts, so that they can both hear and read them.

Training Part 1

Journalism

Module J1: An exploration of how people learn
Module J2: A selection workshop procedure for factual communication
Module J3: Presentation training
Module J4: Humanitarian communication
Module J5: Training for child journalists
Module J6: Creativity in writing for children
Module J7: News for a community station
Module J8: Producing a live phone-in discussion programme
Module J9: Investigative journalism
Module J10: The production of factual programmes for behaviour change

Module J1: An exploration of how people learn

Course objectives

For participants to:

- understand the mechanisms by which people learn most effectively
- understand how those mechanisms can be used in communication for development
- explore practical applications of those mechanisms in communication

Materials

Copies of all of the following handouts for each participant and the facilitator, or as PowerPoint slides. If PowerPoint is used, the facilitator needs to make sure there are also paper copies for any handouts which need to be completed by participants.

Handout J1.1: How people learn

Questions to ask

1. What has been the best learning experience you have ever had? That is:
   when something was difficult, but you still mastered it
   or
   when you learned something particularly quickly
   or
   when you learned something that has been especially useful to you
2. Tell me how the learning process worked.
   Was this formal teaching in an institution, like a school, or informal learning from a contact – a friend or member of your family?
   Who was the teacher or where was the teaching coming from?
   What materials or equipment were used?
   What prompted you to undertake this learning?
   Talk me through the process from beginning to end.
   How long did it take?
   What made this learning experience the best you have had?

Handout J1.2: An aide-memoire to the theory

- Research shows that learning does not come directly from programmes but from discussion prompted by the programmes
- Without discussion, there will be little learning and little change
- Some kinds of broadcasting do not promote much discussion:
  where there is no tension or problem presented
  where a message is very clearly driven home
  where everything is obvious and formulaic
  where there is a predictable, neat ending with every issue sorted out
  programming which lectures
- Broadcasting which *does* promote discussion will usually have some of these characteristics:
  subtlety
  challenge and disturbance
  real problems and tension
  people who the audience have empathy with, very often people like themselves
  unresolved endings
  unexpected endings, or endings which are expected but have a twist

Equipment

Flipchart
Laptop and projector, if available

Agenda, training session 1: An exercise exploring how people learn

This first exercise helps participants understand some of the basic key concepts needed for effective communication for development and question some assumptions they may have. It does this by drawing on their own experience. It also serves as a training needs assessment (TNA) for the facilitator, because it will reveal what the participants already know about some of the concepts.

1. The facilitator gives out or presents *Handout J1.1: How people learn*, and talks the participants through it.
2. The participants work in pairs. In each pair, partner A asks partner B these questions and makes notes on the answers, then partner B questions partner A.
3. In a plenary session, each partner A reports back on their partner B's learning experience, and then each partner B reports back on their partner A's learning experience.
   a) As the reporting back goes on the facilitator takes notes on each report back, focusing on examples of:
      - learning step by step
      - learning by doing
      - the role of talk in the learning
      - the involvement of role models, in motivating the learning and in showing how whatever is being learned can be done
      - learning purely from being told, without any subsequent discussion or activity
   b) After each report back, the facilitator checks with the partner being reported on that the report was accurate, and can seek clarification of the involvement of any of the above elements in the learning process.
4. In summing up, the facilitator draws out where these elements were involved in the reported learning experiences:
   - learning step by step
   - learning by doing
   - the role of talk in the learning
   - the involvement of role models, in motivating the learning and in showing how whatever is being learned can be done

The facilitator explains how many of the reported experiences involved each of these elements, and how many involved:
   - learning purely from being told, without any subsequent discussion or activity

It is likely that the first four elements will feature in significant numbers of the reported experiences, while it is likely that the last will feature in very few indeed.

Agenda, training session 2: Working out the implications for making communication material

This exercise is designed to engage participants in applying the findings of the first exercise into production.

1. The facilitator summarizes the situation that, if it is accepted that learning is most effective when it is based on a step-by-step approach, when it uses learning by doing, encourages talk among the audiences and involves the use of role models, then there are implications for the nature of broadcast programmes or communication distributed through mobile technology or social media.
2. Group work: The whole group is divided into four, and each group is given the task of devising strategies to make use of one of the identified communication elements, either in factual programmes or in a serial drama, depending on the nature of the project. That is, Group 1 has to devise a strategy for using a step-by-step approach, etc.
   - using a step-by-step approach
   - learning by doing
   - encouraging talk among the audiences
   - involving the use of role models
3. In plenary, groups report back, and the whole team evaluates each strategy, based on likely effectiveness and practicability. If a group's strategy is deemed ineffective or impractical, the whole team devises a replacement strategy.

The whole team considers if any improvements can be made to any of the strategies.

Agenda, training session 3: An exercise in practical application

1. The team are divided into the four groups again. Each group is allocated:
   - a specific section of the target audience
   - one of the devised strategies (preferably, one the group was not originally involved in developing, so that each participant gets the widest possible experience in working in detail on the key concepts)
   - a topic the project is intended to address
   Each group develops a factual programme item or a drama storyline – depending on the nature of the project – using their given strategy, on their given topic and aimed at their given audience sector.
2. Each group presents their work to the whole team, who evaluate it for likely effectiveness and practicability. They suggest adjustments where needed.
   Ideally, the work produced in this training will be used in the production of the communication material.
3. Round up and clarifications: The facilitator uses *Handout J1.2: An aide-memoire to the theory*, either printed or on a PowerPoint slide, to sum up the training and to clarify any points not understood by participants. (This handout includes many ideas which have emerged from this training in the past.)

Module J2: A selection workshop procedure for factual communication

This is a selection workshop for a team of reporters for factual programme making. This outline is based on training for radio, and it is appropriate for a selection process for television or social media as well, as it tests candidates on the selection criteria, but using a simpler technology than video.

Course objectives

For participants to:

- be given the opportunity to display the criteria set out in Handout J2.1 (below)

Materials

Copies of all of the following handouts for each participant and the facilitator, or as PowerPoint slides. If PowerPoint is used, the facilitator needs to make sure there are also paper copies for any handouts which need to be completed by participants.

Handout J2.1: The selection criteria

- A willingness and ability to learn: in journalism and production skills
- The application of journalism and production skills learned in the workshop
- Effective participation in the training sessions
- Ability to work alone and meet a deadline
- A willingness and ability to give and receive constructive criticism
- A good grasp of the principles of behaviour change communication and an ability to explain them clearly and persuasively

Candidates will be assessed against these criteria by their performance in individual and teamwork tasks.

Table J2.2 A factual package development grid

Strand	Topic
1. What is the identified need that this package is helping to meet?	
2. What change can the audience make to meet this need?	
3. Which part of the audience needs to make this change?	

Strand	Topic
4. What kind of change does the target audience need? A change of knowledge, attitude or behaviour?	
5. Does the target audience have access to the resources to make this change?	Yes/No: If the answer is No, stop and research a different change. If the answer is Yes, explain the answer.
6. List the points of information the audience need to make this change.	Against each point, or set of points, list who the information would best come from.

Table J2.3 An example completed factual package development grid

Strand: Increasing personal income	Topic: Better hygiene is better marketing
1. What is the identified need that this package is helping to meet?	*For better marketing to increase sales*
2. What change can the audience make to meet this need?	*Learn how improved hygiene is better marketing in food and drink businesses*
3. Which part of the audience needs to make this change?	*Owners of very small food and drink businesses*
4. What kind of change does the target audience need? A change of knowledge, attitude or behaviour?	*Knowledge*
5. Does the target audience have access to the resources to make this change?	Yes/No: *Yes* If the answer is No, stop and research a different change. If the answer is Yes, explain the answer. *Since the change is one of knowledge, the only material resource needed is an access to the broadcast material*

6. List the points of information the audience need to make this change.
a) Taking the example of the milk business:
  i. Plastic jerrycans are not hygienic containers for transporting milk, as they cannot be adequately cleaned, and are a deterrent to customers
  ii. Milk containers, like metal churns, which can be thoroughly cleaned and which are visible to customers, improve sales
b) Examples from other food and drink businesses of simple changes for visibly better hygiene which improves sales
	Against each point, or set of points, list who the information would best come from.
	A street milk seller who witnesses how dirty the inside of a plastic jerrycan is, even after it has been cleaned, when it has been opened up by the journalist or a hygienist
	A street milk seller who has changed from using plastic jerrycans to metal churns or traditional containers.
	An informed customer whose choices of where to shop are based on hygiene standards

Equipment

Flipchart
Laptop and projector
Audio recording equipment
One or more laptops with audio editing software

Agenda, training session 1: An exercise exploring how people learn

1. Facilitator's introduction to the project and the workshop: The facilitator explains the aim of the workshop, which is to select a specified number of people to be the reporting team for a factual programme series for communication for development.
2. *Handout J2.1: The selection criteria* is presented or distributed, with discussion for clarification.

Session is then as for *Module J1: An exploration of how people learn, Session 1*

Agenda, training session 2: Identifying needed change

1. The participants are each given a copy of *Table J2.2: A factual package development grid*. The facilitator takes the group through it, using information from Chapters 2 and 7, if necessary.

    To reinforce the explanation, the facilitator may want to use *Table J2.3: An example completed factual package development grid*, asking different participants to explain how the process goes from one step to the next, in this example. (The context for this example is that it is part of a project on fighting poverty by increasing incomes, in this case, among milk sellers in Somalia. One barrier to maximizing income is poor hygiene in transporting milk, which limits prices buyers are prepared to pay. The problem is the use of plastic jerrycans, which are impossible to clean properly.)
2. Each participant is given one need among the target audience which has been identified by formative research for the project this workshop is part of. Candidates are asked to complete Boxes 2 and 5 in the grid:
    - identifying the change needed to meet the need
    - whether the target population have the material resources to make the change
3. In plenary, each presents their analysis, and the rest of the group assess if the thinking is right.
    Candidates revise their analyses in the light of the comments.
    Candidates will be marked on:
    - their grasp of the basics of a needs and change analysis
    - their ability and attitude in giving constructive criticism
    - their ability to apply constructive criticism to their work

Agenda, training session 3: Identifying information needs, sources and questions

1. Candidates identify the information the target population will need and where that information can be found from a single voice, and complete the relevant grid boxes.
2. Formulating questions: If necessary, the facilitator leads a training session using role play to explore how to structure questions.
    Candidates draft questions.
3. In plenary, each presents the analysis and the questions.
    The group make their comments on the suitability of the questions.
    Candidates revise questions on the basis of comments made.

4. Recorder training and practice: the training will depend on the type of recorder, but needs to address microphone positioning and audio level.
   Candidates will be marked on:
   - their grasp of the basics of information and sources
   - their ability and attitude in giving constructive criticism
   - their ability to apply constructive criticism to their work
   - their technical capacity with a recorder

Agenda, training session 4: Setting up interviews and interviewing

1. The facilitator takes the group through the process of researching and finding appropriate interviewees.
   Each candidate presents their choice and their justification for it to the facilitator, who has the opportunity to correct any errors, while giving marks on the basis of the original choice.
2. Interview rehearsals: In pairs, candidates rehearse introducing themselves and asking their questions, while their partner improvises responses.
3. Conducting interviews: Candidates record their interviews.
   Candidates will be marked on:
   - their grasp of the basics of finding interviewees
   - their teamwork in rehearsing interviews

Agenda, training session 5: Editing, technical, editorial and ethical

1. The facilitator provides basic training in using the digital editing software to make inaudible edits, and to remove errors, repetitions and stumbles.
   The facilitator may want to set a limit on the final length of the interviews after editing, so that candidates have to make considered editorial decisions.
   The facilitator should also set out basic ethical issues involved in editing, particularly that the interviewee's meaning cannot be changed.
2. Candidates edit their interviews.
   Candidates will be marked on:
   - their demonstrated grasp of technically accurate editing
   - the quality of their editorial and ethical judgements

Agenda, training session 6: Completing packages

1. The facilitator provides basic training in journalism for voice. Candidates draft scripts for an introduction and conclusion to their interview.
2. Presentation: Candidates receive basic training in presenting on a microphone.
   Candidates rehearse with a partner and then record and edit their presentations.
3. Digital assembly: Candidates receive training in assembling a basic audio package.
   Candidates assemble and finalize their packages.
4. The packages are played to the group and assessors.
   Group comments are invited.

Candidates will be marked on:
- the editorial learning demonstrated in the complete package, covering the editorial quality of the interviewing and the writing
- the technical quality of the package, in recording, editing and presentation
- the teamworking shown in rehearsals

Module J3: Presentation training

Course objectives

For participants to:

- become more fluent and natural when presenting on a microphone

Materials

Set of four scripted items, either real or made up, that the participants are going to need to present. For a humanitarian station, for example, these might be: some personal messages; important information to save lives, limit disease and injury, and limit risk; a family reunification appeal.

A training needs assessment (TNA) for presentation that has been carried out during the recruitment process or during actual broadcasting. The training needs assessment should identify one or two major issues in each individual's presentation that need to be addressed – such as too many pauses or 'ums' and 'ers', or non-natural rhythm.

Equipment

Audio recording equipment

Agenda, training session 1: Basic presentation training

Note: This training agenda would be for a humanitarian or community station which broadcasts a lot of music, with presentation interspersed between songs, but the technique can be adapted to different contexts.

1. Each participant is given the set of scripted items, and given time to read them through once, and then asked to add an introduction of themselves and any other improvised comments they would like to make.
2. Each participant then presents the items, and is recorded. The facilitator notes down each time that the issues needing addressing occur, for example, writing a '1' each time there is an 'um' or an 'er', if that is the issue.
   The facilitator highlights to each participant the specific issues that need to be addressed, and each is asked to read a sentence more slowly and without committing the highlighted error.

3. The facilitator emphasizes the need for preparation and practice.
   Each participant is given 2.5 minutes (the approximate length of a song) to practise reading aloud one item, with any additional, improvised material, taking care to avoid the highlighted presentation problem.
   Each participant is given a further 2.5 minutes to prepare another item, and so on until all four items have been practised.
4. Each participant reads all four items, they are recorded, and, again, the facilitator notes down each time the highlighted issue occurs.
   The facilitator tells each participant how many times the highlighted issue occurred in the first reading, and how many in the second. (There should be a substantial improvement.)
   For each participant, the first and second recordings are played and compared.
5. The facilitator sums up. Presenters should rehearse, aloud, the next item they are going to read, while the song preceding it is playing, paying attention to avoiding the highlighted issue.
6. Presenters should be monitored over the next week for sustained improvement.

Module J4: Humanitarian communication

This is a possible plan for a fast basic training in humanitarian communication, for a team who already have basic journalism and radio, television or social media skills, as might be needed in urgently setting up a humanitarian communication operation, such as a radio station, or for training the existing staff of a local station.

Course objectives

For participants to:

- understand what communication can do in a humanitarian crisis
- understand the priorities for communication in a humanitarian crisis
- be able to address those priorities through broadcasting

Materials

Copies of all of the following handouts for each participant and the facilitator, or as PowerPoint slides. If PowerPoint is used, the facilitator needs to make sure there are also paper copies for any handouts which need to be completed by participants.

Note: Handout J4.1 will need to be prepared for the training from the most recent needs assessment of the target audience, and Handout J4.2 will need editing to match the situation the station is in and the phase of the crisis.

Handout J4.1: A report on the assessed information and communication needs of the affected population

Handout J4.2: The potential for communication to meet the needs of affected populations in a humanitarian response

To help save lives, and reduce injuries and ill health among the affected population, by providing information on:

- preparation for leaving
- avoiding dangers (for example, in conflict, landmines and unexploded ordnance, after a natural disaster, avoiding unsafe structures)
- maintaining health in changed circumstances, through individual and collective action
- safe routes and where and when shelter or shelter materials, food and clean water are available

To provide psychosocial help for the affected population by:

- helping the population feel safe, connected, calm and hopeful; with the above information on keeping safe, testimony of shared, positive experience, respite entertainment and music
- helping to provide access to social and emotional support by helping to reunite families and establish or re-establish social networks, and providing advice on maintaining family relationships in changed conditions

To help to provide practical change and psychosocial support by helping to enable affected communities to help themselves, individually and collectively, by:

- providing accurate information so that affected individuals and communities can make informed decisions about their lives
- providing role models, advice and skills training for rebuilding livelihoods
- providing support to collective action by providing role models and advice
- providing support to collective action by understanding and promoting the technical, social, economic and political skills among the affected population, helping to put those with skills in touch with those who need them

(This handout draws on the WHO's *Psychological First Aid: Guide for Field Workers.*[i])

Handout J4.3: A humanitarian programme format:

1. Menu (45 seconds): a list of the items in the programme, illustrated with one or two short clips of between ten and fifteen seconds each to make the programme sound very inviting for a range of listeners
2. Psychosocial support (2 minutes) for affected population
3. News for affected communities (3 minutes): Reliable, up-to-date information that is of practical use to the affected population
4. Main topic (4–6 minutes): A one-to-one interview with an official, on a problem that members of the affected community have raised
5. Entertainment (3–4 minutes): A brief period of respite for the audience, either a song, a piece of comedy, a one-off story reading or a serial reading

6. A choice out of health (practical information on maintaining health in new circumstances); family reunification; shelter; or rebuilding livelihoods, depending on the priorities identified in the previous exercise

Equipment

Flipcharts: one for each group of four participants, and one for the facilitator
Laptop and projector

Agenda, training session 1: What can communication do to help in a humanitarian crisis?

1. Training needs assessment (TNA)
   If the team are part of the affected population, the facilitator asks:

   > Has communication, especially broadcasting, done anything to help you and your families in this crisis, and, if so, what?

   If the answer is that communication has not played a role so far in the crisis, the facilitator asks:

   > Could communication have done anything to help you and your families in this crisis, and, if so, what?

   Then the facilitator widens the discussion with the group, by asking for their ideas of what the role of a communication operation, like a radio station, in a humanitarian crisis could be.
   Depending on the level of understanding and thinking, the course may need to be tailored to those levels, leaving out sections on topics the group already understand.
2. Exploring what communication can do in a humanitarian crisis
   The facilitator presents or gives out *Handout J4.1:* A report based on the needs assessment.
   The participants work in small groups. From the report and, if they are part of the affected population, drawing on their own experience, groups work out, and write on their flipchart:
   - which of the identified needs they think communication can meet, or help to meet
   - how communication can help to meet each of these needs
3. In plenary, each group present their answers and the rest of the team:
   - ask questions for clarification
   - discuss whether the ideas put forward are feasible, with the facilitator adding comments
   As this exercise proceeds, the facilitator draws up a list of the needs that the team think communication can meet, on a flipchart or other display device.
4. The facilitator gives out an appropriately edited version of *Handout J4.2: The potential for communication to meet the needs of affected populations in a humanitarian response*, or displays it as a PowerPoint slide.

Drawing on the work they have done so far, and looking at the handout, groups prioritize the different roles communication can perform to best meet the affected population's needs, as set out in the needs assessment report (Handout J4.1).

The prioritization is based on:

- how far each role addresses an identified need
- the urgency of the need for each role at the present phase of the humanitarian response

5. In plenary: Groups present their priorities and explain their reasoning
Collectively, the team decide the five roles that have the highest current priority.

Agenda, training session 2: Making humanitarian broadcast material

This training is set out for the items to be in a single magazine programme. However, the items could each stand alone within the mix of music, messages and other information on a dedicated humanitarian station.

In this session the team will first collectively work on research for Slot 4, the Main Topic, and then work in groups; each group has to make one or more of the items for a magazine programme, following this format.

1. The facilitator introduces the exercise, with the format (Handout J4.3) either distributed as a handout or displayed as a PowerPoint slide, and can elaborate on the slots using the notes provided in Chapter 17.
Research for the main topic: The team, working individually or in pairs, are to prepare interviews and then go out and record them with a selection of the affected population. The selection should reflect a balance of different groups within that population, including a balance of men and women, and of different age ranges, to find out what issues are currently concerning them and which they would like to ask the responsible authority or agency about.
The format of the interview is to ask what issue or issues are concerning the interviewee.
(This training assumes that members of the team are experienced in recording interviews for broadcast.)
Individuals or pairs develop questions that will bring out the details of the concerns and stories of the interviewees.
2. Individuals or pairs go out to record up to six interviews each.
3. Individuals or pairs report back, listing the broad topics raised by members of the affected population, and a consolidated list is compiled, grouping the topics under the responsible authority or agency.
The team decide, from the consolidated list, on one or two topics to pursue, based on the number of people who have raised them, the significance of the impact of the issue on the affected population and the priorities the team chose in Session 1.
4. Depending on their experience and the previous training the team have received, it may be necessary to do the following exercise to remind them of the need for balance.
The facilitator takes one of the topics chosen by the team and asks the team how they would report the story.

An experienced and/or well-trained team will say they need to 'get the other side'; that is, they need to produce a balanced story between the complainants and the authority or agency complained about.

The team discuss and/or research how they are going to find the right person to interview in the authority or agency.

This matter is now put on hold, temporarily, as the facilitator returns to the exercise programme format.

5. Members of the team either choose the item they want to produce or are allocated an item by the facilitator, including the Main Topic, as just researched.

From this point, the individuals or groups making each item follow the development and production procedure as set out in Chapter 7 on producing programmes for development contexts.

Module J5: Training for child journalists

This course is ambitious and not all children will be able to handle all of it, so the facilitator will need to assess how far along it the group being trained are going to be able to go. It may be, for example, that the children are only taught the first section, on interviewing, and that the subsequent work of editing and assembling into a package is done by an adult reporter.

Any adult working with children should be given a code of conduct based on what is discussed in Chapter 18 of this book, or the project organization's own code of conduct on working with children, or any legal code of conduct on working with children in force in the country where the work is being done.

An organization also needs to ensure it is complying with any legal requirements concerning working with children which are in force in the country where the work is being done. For example, many countries require a criminal records check before an individual is allowed to work with children.

Course objectives

For participants to be able to:

- come up with story ideas and choose interviewees
- record interviews and edit them
- write and present a linking script
- make a simple package

Materials

PowerPoint slides 1 to 11:

1. What do journalists do?
2. Where do you think the stories come from, and who finds them?

3. Are the stories journalists tell true or made up?
4. How can a journalist know if a story is true or not?
5. What do journalists do?:
    *   find stories
    *   find people who can tell the story or who can tell part of the story
    *   check the story is true
    *   tell the story
6. What we will be doing:
    *   finding out how to find stories
    *   finding out how to ask questions
    *   finding out how to record people
    *   finding out how to tell the story on radio
7. Interview topic: The most important experience they have had in the last year.
8. Journalists choose topics they want to cover; they don't just report what happens to come their way.
9. Audio editing:
    *   to take out stumbles and hesitations
    *   to cut the interview to the time allowed
    *   to choose the parts of the interview that will be most engaging for the audience
10. The rules of editing
    *   a journalist must not change the meaning, by, for example, taking out a negative
11. Writing a script
    *   what the audience needs to know at the beginning
    *   what they need to know to understand the second interview
    *   how the interviews are connected
    *   what the audience are going to take away from the conclusion

Copies of all of the following handouts for each participant and the facilitator, or as PowerPoint slides. If PowerPoint is used, the facilitator needs to make sure there are also paper copies for any handouts which need to be completed by participants.

Handout J5.1: A reminder for young reporters

Choosing your interviewees

*   The most important decision you make about an interview is who you interview.
*   Be adventurous in your choices: Think up the best person or the best organization that suits your needs; don't just choose people you happen to know, or who are easy to find.
*   Be practical in your choice and make sure it is possible and safe to interview them.
*   Make sure that your interviewees speak in a way your audience will like and understand.
*   If you can, talk to your interviewees on the phone before you record, to make sure they are what you want.
*   Always try to set up an interview in advance. It is very frustrating to turn up and find that the person isn't there, or can't talk to you.

Preparing your questions

- Think carefully about your questions; you usually only get one chance to ask them.
- Make sure your questions are open, not closed; that is, they invite your interviewee to explain and not just answer yes or no.
- Think about what this speaker is going to contribute to your piece, and make sure your questions will get all the answers you need.
- Practise your questions, so that, even if they're written down, you don't sound as if you're reading.

Recording

- If you are using a separate microphone, loop the cable round your hand, to stop cable rattle.
- Use headphones to make sure that the recording is good quality.
- Do a test run before you start recording, using the level meter to make sure both voices are about as loud as each other.
- Hold the microphone closer to the quieter person, and farther away from the louder one.
- It is usually better to hold the microphone still, in between the two people, rather than moving it towards one person and then the other.
- When you're asking questions, if you make a mistake, stop and re-record the question.

The interview

- Always take a trusted adult with you.
- Check you have all the equipment you need, including batteries, and make sure it all works before you go to your interview.
- Turn up on time.
- Be polite.
- Control the situation: Sit yourself and your interviewee in positions where you can record comfortably, and get good sound quality.
- Don't let your interviewee put you in any kind of danger.
- Don't let yourself be bullied or patronized. Have confidence in your questions and work through them carefully.
- If an answer needs more exploring, ask extra questions.

Audio editing

- Before editing on a computer, back up or make a copy of your original interview, in case editing goes wrong.
- Once you've loaded all you want, listen through to it and
  edit out retaken questions
  select the sections you want

- You may find it easier to edit by a process of elimination, taking out the worst bits first, then the next worse and so on.
- Remember that you must not change the meaning of what the interviewee said or misrepresent the interviewee in your editing.

Making a package

- Write the script by deciding what the audience needs to know at the beginning, and then what they need to know to understand the second interview and how the interviews are connected and what the audience are going to take away from the conclusion.
- Remember you must be fair to your interviewees in your script and must be objective; do not give your own opinion.

Equipment

One flipchart
Laptop and projector
Audio recorders, one between each two participants
Laptops with audio editing software

Agenda, training session 1: Training needs assessment

Note: During this session, it is important that the facilitator hears responses from all the group; otherwise, they could get a distorted idea of the level of understanding.

Needs assessment discussion

1. The facilitator discusses what members of the group watch on television, listen to on radio or look at online (depending on the media they have access to).
2. If any watch or listen to the news, the facilitator discusses what kind of news stories they are interested in: local, national, international? About children?
3. The facilitator asks if any members can tell a recent news story they have seen, heard or read. If they can, this can be a reference point for later stages of the day's training, and the facilitator can use it to illustrate certain points.

Introductory discussion: What journalists do

1. The facilitator writes on the flipchart or puts up PowerPoint slide 1:

   What do journalists do?

   The facilitator writes on the flipchart key phrases as and when they come up: Tell stories, give information, etc.

2. The facilitator writes on the flipchart or puts up PowerPoint slide 2:

   Where do you think the stories come from and who finds them?

If members of the group told stories they had seen or heard in the needs assessment session, the facilitator could put the question: How do you think those stories got on to the television/radio/online?

The facilitator writes on the flipchart key phrases as and when they come up:

Find stories, find people who can tell the story

3. The facilitator writes on the flipchart or puts up PowerPoint slide 3:

Are the stories journalists tell true or made up?

It is hoped the answer 'true' will come up.
The facilitator emphasizes how important it is that the stories are true.

4. The facilitator writes on the flipchart or puts up PowerPoint slide 4:

How can a journalist know if a story is true or not?

The facilitator writes on the flipchart key phrases as and when they come up:

eyewitness, more than one person, they see evidence, from someone they trust

5. The facilitator has on an already written flipchart page or on a PowerPoint slide 5:

What do journalists do?
find stories
find people who can tell the story or who can tell part of the story
check the story is true
tell the story

6. The facilitator has on an already written flipchart page or on PowerPoint slide 6:

What we will be doing:
finding out how to find stories
finding out how to ask questions
finding out how to record people
finding out how to tell the story on radio

Agenda, training session 2: Interviewing and recording

Interviewing
1. In pairs, one has two minutes to find out as much as they can about their partner, and then reports back to the whole group. The facilitator checks the report-back is accurate.
Partners swap roles and repeat the process.
2. The facilitator chooses one of the group, or himself or herself, to sit at the front facing the rest of the group. That person will role-play a famous sports star.
The facilitator discusses with the group what kind of sports star this person is.
The facilitator writes on the flipchart that the interview is about what happened, when the 'sports star' was growing up and what made him or her become a sports star.

The in-role person needs to think up a story, while the rest of the group discuss what sort of questions will get the most out of the story for children like themselves.

The facilitator tries out the interview with whole group asking questions

One of the group tries to tell the story, based on the answers to the questions.

The facilitator leads a discussion if this is the whole story and how interesting it is.

Discussion as to whether the best questions were asked, and what other questions could have got a better story, with prompting by the facilitator.

Introduction to recording equipment

3. Each pair is given a recorder.
   The facilitator demonstrates how it works.
   Pairs try to record each other.
4. In pairs, one interviews the other on why they are on this course. The facilitator brainstorms question ideas first; individuals write the questions they are going to ask their partner.
   Each pair records one interview.
5. The interviews are played back and there is discussion on the choice of questions, and whether they produced an informative interview.
   If there is time, partners swap roles, and repeat the process.

Technical training in correct use of recorders and doing retakes

6. The facilitator demonstrates the problems of recordings that are too loud – distortion – or too quiet – inaudibility.
   The facilitator demonstrates how to position the microphone between the interviewer and interviewee, so that it is closer to the quieter person and farther away from the louder person.
   The facilitator shows the importance of recording somewhere fairly quiet.
7. In pairs, one is witness to a dramatic event (the facilitator could suggest a car accident), and the other is a reporter trying to find out exactly what happened.
   The facilitator monitors whether each pair is recording at a good level, and corrects if not.
8. The facilitator introduces the idea of retakes for questions – if the reporter hesitates or stumbles while asking a question, he or she should re-record the question. It will probably be necessary to explain that the original question can be taken out by editing, which the group will be doing tomorrow.
   The retake game: The group sit in a circle, with an interviewer and interviewee in the centre.
   The scenario is the same as the one just used above.
   The interview proceeds, but, if the interviewer stumbles or hesitates and does not do a retake, they are out, and they are replaced by the interviewee, and a new interviewee is chosen.
   Each interviewer is timed, with the timings written up on a flipchart sheet. The winner is the interviewer who stays in for the longest time.

9. *The final practice interview: Bringing it all together*

This is an exercise bringing together the journalistic skills covered with the technical skills of level and retaking.

The facilitator has on an already written flipchart page or on PowerPoint slide 7:

> Interview topic: The most important experience they have had in the last year.

In plenary, discuss possible questions to get the best interview.
The facilitator can prompt by asking questions:

> Do we just want to know the events, or do we want more? If so, what?
> What questions are going to get those answers?

Individuals write their questions.
In pairs, one interviews the other and records it, and then they swap round. Each interview is not longer than two minutes.
The interviews are played back and evaluated by the group and the facilitator on how engaging the interview was, whether the questions had been good and on the technical issues of level and retaken questions.

Agenda, training session 3: Interviewing for real

Note: Depending on the ages of the participants and the situation, the facilitator may need to find adults – colleagues or parents – to accompany each pair of children. These adults will need to be briefed on their role, which is to make sure that the children are safe and do not become subject to bullying or intimidation, and that they need to allow the children to do the work without their interference.

1. The facilitator uses a handout or PowerPoint slide 8:

   > Journalists choose topics they want to cover; they don't just report what happens to come their way

   The facilitator goes on to explain to the participants why they are in a good position to choose topics for the audience the project has in mind. For example, they are children themselves, in the same situation as the audience, etc.
2. The facilitator introduces the activity for the day. In pairs, each pair is going to choose a topic for an interview, based on what they think will interest an audience like themselves. They will then decide who would be the best person or kind of person to interview. As far as possible, this should be someone they do not already know.
3. Each pair chooses their topic and interviewee.
4. In plenary, each pair explains their topic and their choice of interviewee.
   The group discuss the suitability of the choice – is it someone who will have something useful and interesting to say to their intended audience – and how each interviewee might be found.
   Each pair prepares their questions and rehearses asking them, with one of the pair role-playing the interviewee.
5. Each pair contacts potential interviewees, either by phone or by visiting.
6. Each pair goes out to find their interviewee and record their interview.

Agenda, training session 4: Audio editing

Ideally, each pair should have a laptop loaded with audio editing software.

1. The facilitator introduces the idea of editing audio, on the flipchart or PowerPoint slide 9:
   Audio editing:
   > to take out stumbles and hesitations
   > to cut the interview to the allotted time
   > to choose the parts of the interview that will be most engaging for the intended audience
2. The facilitator demonstrates how audio is loaded on to a laptop.
   Each pair loads their interview.
3. The facilitator demonstrates how to cut questions that include stumbles or hesitations and which have been retaken.
   Each pair edits out retaken questions from their interview.
4. The facilitator sets a time limit on the length of the interviews.
   The facilitator discusses with the group the selection of the least interesting parts, probably using one of the interviews as an example to focus the discussion.
5. The facilitator discusses the rules of editing, on the flipchart or PowerPoint slide 10:
   The rules of editing:

   > A journalist must not change the meaning, by, for example, taking out a negative.

   Pairs edit their interviews to time
6. Once all editing is done, the group listen to each edited interview and discuss:
   > the interest of the piece
   > the technical quality of the recording
   > the technical quality of the editing

Agenda, training session 5: Balancing interviewees

1. The facilitator introduces the ideas of different points of view and balance. There are two ways this might be done:

   > The facilitator shows the participants a balanced piece of journalism or a balanced discussion from television, radio or a news website.

   > The facilitator asks the participants what they think about a current topic, knowing that there will be different points of view among the group.

2. In plenary, the facilitator follows either of these by asking the participants to identify the different points of view, either in the news extract or in their own discussion.
   The facilitator relates the issue of balance to the interviews each pair recorded in Session 4.

They ask each pair what different point of view they need to balance the interview they recorded. Other participants are asked for their suggestions.

5. Each pair chooses a second interviewee and repeat the processes carried out in Session 4, to produce a second edited interview.

Agenda, training session 6: Writing and recording a script to make a package

1. The facilitator introduces the day's task, which is that each pair of participants is going to write a script consisting of three parts: an introduction to the package, a link between the two interviews and a conclusion.
2. The facilitator discusses two key ethical principles in writing scripts, which are fairness and objectivity.
3. They then go on to discuss with the group what information needs to be in each section of the script, writing them down on the flipchart or using PowerPoint slide 11: Writing a script:
    what the audience needs to know at the beginning
    what they need to know to understand the second interview
    how the interviews are connected
    what the audience are going to take away from the conclusion
4. Pairs draft their script, and the scripts are discussed either in plenary or just with the facilitator.
    Pairs record their scripts.
5. The facilitator demonstrates how to assemble the elements of the package in the editing software.
    Pairs of participants assemble their packages.
    All packages are played back, and the group evaluate each for editorial and technical quality.
6. The facilitator gives out and discusses *Handout J5.1: A reminder for young reporters.*

Module J6: Creativity in writing for children

For adults to write and produce educational programming for children, especially when resources are limited, requires high levels of creativity. This course is designed to help writers and producers think outside the normal limits to come up with imaginative programming that will engage children.

Creativity does not mean elaboration and complex effects, and can mean very simple ideas.

Course objectives

For participants to:

- understand the mass media's obligations under the UN Convention on the Rights of the Child
- break out of conventional thinking in writing for children

- understand the nature and role of interactivity in programming for children
- understand the roles of creativity and interactivity in delivering a formal curriculum
- in groups, to create and produce a television or radio programme for children and involving children, and based on interactivity

Preparation

This module involves working with children, as participants in programmes and as an audience evaluating programmes made by the course participants.

All participants should be given a code of conduct based on what is discussed in Chapter 18 of this book, or the project organization's own code of conduct on working with children or any legal code of conduct on working with children in force in the country where the work is being done.

An organization also needs to ensure it is complying with any legal requirements concerning working with children which are in force in the country where the work is being done. For example, many countries require a criminal records check before an individual is allowed to work with children.

Two small groups of children, up to four per group of participants, should be recruited, and all permissions gained for them to work with the project, and any provisions required by law in the country are put in place. One group will be participants in the programmes to be made during the course, and the other will evaluate the completed programmes.

Materials

Copies of the UN Convention on the Rights of the Child (UNCRC), one for each participant

Four radio or television education programmes for children – if possible, covering science, maths, and language – which:

- show children as active learners engaged in practical activities
- include drama or animation that conforms to the characteristics described in Chapter 22, especially in encouraging interactivity

There is a great deal of this material on YouTube.
Copies of the local school curriculum for one particular age group

Equipment

Flipcharts: One for each group of four participants, and one for the facilitator

Facilities

Adequate production facilities for the number of groups of four to rehearse, record, edit and mix their programmes on whatever medium the project is using, in one-and-a-half days.

Participants

The course participants will be mainly writers or producers who have media experience, including some who know how to record television or radio material. There should also be a number of experienced teachers who are familiar with the local curricula. These participants could have been recruited by a project as educational advisers, on a full-time or part-time basis.

All participants should be familiar with the Articles of the UNCRC before the course starts.

Agenda, training session 1: Creativity with the UNCRC

1. Introductions of facilitator/s and participants take place, and include relevant experience.
   The participants are organized into groups of about four each, with at least one teacher participant in each group.
2. The facilitator asks the participants to read three of the Articles from *The UN Convention on the Rights of the Child:*
   - Article 12 on the right to self-expression
   - Article 17 on the obligations of mass media to children
   - Article 28 on the right to education
   The facilitator poses the question: 'What are the implications of these articles for an educational project (that is making media material for use in schools) or a distance learning project for children?'
   Each group discuss the question and write up their list of implications on their flipchart.
3. In plenary, each list is considered and a complete list of implications agreed by all is written up.
4. Ways of teaching children their rights: This exercise is designed to promote originality and creativity.
   The facilitator organizes for each group to choose a different article of the UNCRC, but the other groups do not know which article each has chosen. The choices can be any of the Articles, not just the three already discussed.
   Each group's task is to discuss possibilities for a gripping story that will teach children of a specified age about the group's chosen article of the Convention, and follows the implications of Articles 12, 17 and 28 of the UNCRC which the participants listed earlier.
5. Groups are given a specified period to work out the possibilities for their story.
6. Each group is asked to write four different possible opening lines for their story and to write them up on their flipchart
   Once the task is finished, they are asked to write four more.
7. In plenary, each group present their possible opening lines. The whole group choose what they consider to be the *riskiest* of each group's eight lines.
   Each group then write their story, starting with the chosen first line.
8. Scripts are written, read out and discussed, based on the following criteria:
   - Is it a story likely to engage children?
   - Can the other groups work out which Convention Article the story is about?

When all participants know which Article the story is about, they read that Article and consider a third question.

• Does the story teach fully what the Article says?

Later in the course, in Session 5, these stories are read to an audience of children. The children, on a voting basis, rank the stories from best to worst.

The children are asked what they thought each of the stories was teaching them.

Note: The aim of the next part of the course is for each group to develop a television or radio programme on a topic in the science curriculum, which would encourage children to actively participate and be creative.

The output from this session will be a presentation script for the programme and the structures for a series of activity slots.

In Session 3, groups will do the same, but on topics from the language section of the curriculum. At the end of Session 3, each group will decide which of its two proposed programmes it wants to actually produce.

In Session 4 of this training module, groups will work with a group of children to produce their chosen programme, either on science or their language one. They will record the children taking part in the structured activity slots needed for their chosen programme. Each group will then record the presentation script of their chosen programme and edit the relevant recorded activity slots. Each group's recorded script and edited activity slots will be assembled into a complete programme, so that each group will have a complete programme to be played to, and evaluated by an audience of children in Session 5.

Agenda, training session 2: Building a science programme round interactivity

1. Looking at the different levels of interactivity discussed in Chapter 22, the participants discuss which they think will be possible, given the circumstances of the children the project is aiming to educate. In particular, they need to consider whether stopping the programme at intervals throughout it will be feasible.

2. The facilitator plays some examples of good programmes for children, which have the characteristics as described in the materials list for this module.
   The facilitator helps the participants tease out and list on a flipchart the characteristics that make these programmes good in encouraging children's participation and interactivity.

3. In groups of about four, the participants look at the science section of the relevant school curriculum.
   Each group chooses a different topic in the science curriculum, and a section of it that can be handled in one television or radio programme.
   Looking again at the levels of interactivity listed in Chapter 22, groups work out what interactions they would want children to participate in, if they were watching or listening to the programme, which would help them understand the science topic being covered. For example, if the topic is the water cycle, is there an experiment that children in the target group could do? (Given the circumstances that they are in.) They should aim for as many interactions, at each level, as possible.

4. In plenary, each group presents their choice of topic, what, specifically, their programme is going to be about and their proposed interactions.
    Other groups comment on the feasibility and suitability of the proposed interactions.
    Groups revise their proposals according to the discussion.
5. Groups develop a programme synopsis that will deliver the interactions proposed. The synopsis should include:
    *   who will be in the programme
    *   the key events in the programme
    *   how the programme will be presented, and how the interactions will be explained to the audience
    If the programme is to be on radio, particular attention needs to be paid to how a practical activity, such as an experiment, can be effectively communicated to the audience.
6. In plenary, each group presents their synopsis to the rest of the participants. Each is discussed in terms of coherence, which means looking at whether:
    *   the proposed personnel and events will provide the information the children in the audience would need to carry out the proposed interactions
    *   the proposed presentation strategy is going to communicate to the target audience the information in the best way possible
    *   if the programme is going to be on radio, the presentation strategy is going to enable the listening children to carry out the intended activities
    *   the proposed programme complies with the Convention on the Rights of the Child, as set out in the implications written during Session 1.
    Groups revise their synopses in the light of the plenary review.
7. Groups write a structure for the activities in the programme. This involves deciding what materials the children taking part will need, the instructions they will give to the children for the activity or activities and how to ensure there are no risks for the children. Groups will also script the presentation needed, including all instructions for audience interaction.

Agenda, training session 3: Building a language programme round interactivity

1. This session is largely identical to Session 2, except that the topics for programmes will come from the language section of the local curriculum.
    The only difference is that, when looking again at the levels of interactivity in Part 3 of the session, groups may want to consider drama as an activity. For example, if the topic is verbs, is there a creative way of demonstrating it in drama?
2. If a group chooses to use drama, then, in Part 7 of the session, they will script the drama rather than structuring activities.
3. After developing their language programme structure, groups choose which of the two programmes they have developed – science or language – they are going to produce. The facilitator needs to ensure that half of the programmes chosen are on science and half on language.

4. Groups work out the resources they will need to produce their programme and source them. They also source sufficient materials for a class of children, which will be four times the number of groups, to be able to carry out the interactive activities their programme sets, or to perform in the drama their programme includes.

Agenda, training session 4: Recording with children

The first group of children who have been recruited to participate in the programmes to be made attend this session. They are allocated to the different groups of course participants.

1. If a group of participants has included a structured activity in their programme, they give the children the materials and instructions for the activity and record the children trying to do the activity. Adult intervention should be kept to an absolute minimum, to allow the children to find their own solutions to any problems they face. This may well involve recording far more material than will be in the final programme.
   If a group has written a drama, they need to rehearse it and and then record it, with the children taking part.
2. If a programme requires children to present it, then they need to be rehearsed and recorded.
   The children leave when the recordings involving them have been completed.
3. The participant groups record any adult presentation needed and then edit and mix their programmes.
4. Each group writes a chart, which lists the interactions expected while children watch or listen to their programme, and has the numbers 0 to 5 after each expected interaction. These charts will be used by all the participants to record their observations of children's reactions to the programmes in Session 5. Zero will mean there was no response from the children, while 5 will represent full and committed interaction.

Agenda, training session 5: Evaluation by children

The second group of children who have been recruited to watch or listen to the programmes, and to respond to them, attend this session.

Each group of participants in the training will nominate a teacher participant from a different group to lead the children in any organized interaction expected, while the children watch or listen to the group's programme.

1. The stories written in Session 1, on children's rights, are read to the children.
   The children, on a voting basis, rank the stories from best to worst.
   The children are asked what they thought each of the stories was teaching them.

2. The programmes produced yesterday are played to the children. By observation, the participants record the levels of interaction achieved by each programme on the chart provided by the group that produced each programme.
   For each programme, after all interactive activities have been completed by the children, the teacher participant leading them will ask what they have learned from the programme.
3. In plenary, after the children have left, there will be a detailed evaluation of each programme, which will consider:
   - the relative success of each of the interactions, based on the observations recorded by the participants and the facilitator
   - the overall success of the programme based on observed learning among the children, and the children's own reporting of learning
4. In plenary, there will be an evaluation of the stories written in Session 1, in the light of the children's responses.
5. After the evaluation of each programme and story, the facilitator will draw up a list of lessons learned.
6. The facilitator will draw up a report recording the outcomes of the evaluations on each programme and story, recording the lessons learned, for distribution to all staff involved in the project.

Module J7: News for a community station

Course objectives

For participants to:

- produce engaging local news which will build an audience by meeting their information and communication needs
- understand the role of a community station in empowering the community
- produce journalism which fits within that role

Materials

Note: Handout J7.2: News priorities will need to be edited and adapted to local circumstances.
Audience research results for the station
The radio station's statement of principles
Copies of all of the following handouts for each participant and the facilitator, or as PowerPoint slides. If PowerPoint is used, the facilitator needs to make sure there are also paper copies for any handouts which need to be completed by participants.

Table J7.1 Decisions on output for a community station

Which factors will matter most when decisions are made on what should be broadcast on your radio station?

Put a number next to each factor in order of your priorities, with 1 as the highest priority and 12 as the lowest.

Factor	Priority
What interests the journalist	
What interests the editor	
The cost	
What interests the listener	
What the listener should be interested in	
What local government wants to say to the listeners	
News that is free on the internet	
Music that can be downloaded for free	
Information that is good for the community	
What NGOs want the station to broadcast	
What the community's religious leaders want the station to broadcast	
What is safe to broadcast	

Handout J7.2: News priorities

The following news stories are all fictional.

1. Choose five of the stories which you think your station would choose to put in a daily bulletin.
2. Put them in the order you think your station would put them, that is, with the most important first and the least important last.

   The stories:

   - A United Nation's plane crashes at a nearby airport, with five people slightly hurt
   - Mosquito nets distributed in the community by an INGO
   - A national politician visits a nearby town
   - Local woman pelts husband with his own empty beer bottles
   - Political change in Western countries reduces international development aid money
   - A local women's cooperative opens a craft shop in a nearby town
   - A McDonald's restaurant opens in a nearby town
   - Rainy season is late
   - Training held for local journalists on election coverage
   - New local hospital opens
   - Three die of a mysterious infection in a nearby children's hospital
   - Local chief 'guilty of corruption'

Handout J7.3: Sources

Who is a good source
A journalist needs to get as close to the story as possible, that is find the people directly involved, or people who actually saw the event or events. If you are talking to someone who was told of the events by someone else, there will be inaccuracies, and that person will not be a believable or reliable source.

Listen to your source
Even if someone claims to have seen an event, it may not be true. If what they say has little detail, then it is likely they are not telling the truth.

Checking your source
You should always try to have two, independent sources, making sure that they are genuinely independent, and that one did not get the story from the other. If you cannot get two, then you need to make a judgement on whether your one source is trustworthy.

Who said what?
It's important to make clear who said what. If you have two sources, and they said different things, then it is all right to say that, as long as you are clear about who said what.

Eyewitnesses
Eyewitnesses can be very good sources, giving your listeners a real sense of what happened. However, even they cannot be relied on completely, and you will need to get other sources as well. Always try to find out where they were, and how near the events.

Say who your source is
Always try to get the name of a source and, if it matters, what their job is, so that listeners can understand what attitude they are likely to have to the events of the story.

Handout J7.4: Creating a news bulletin running order

- Make sure the order you run stories, reports and packages reflects what your audience want.
- Put the strongest item at the beginning, as your main headline.
- Spread the most interesting and engaging stories throughout the bulletin, so that you keep your audience listening.
- Choose and arrange items for variety of tone and format.
- Mix up long and short items.
- In a long bulletin, you may well want to say, 'Still to come…' at intervals, telling the audience the most interesting items coming up in the rest of the bulletin.
- It is common to end a bulletin with a light story.

Equipment

Flipchart
Laptop and projector
Laptops for use by participants, equipped with word processor and audio editing software
Portable recorders and headphones

Participants

This is a training plan for completely inexperienced journalists at a new community radio station. It focuses on producing a community news bulletin. For more sophisticated programme production, see Chapter 7 on producing factual programmes.

This training covers the special considerations in broadcasting on a community radio station. It does not cover standard radio journalism training, such as the six standard questions, as material for this is widely available. For this course, participants will need to know the six standard questions.

Agenda, training session 1: Putting principles into practice

Each participant has a copy of the stated principles of the station.
1. The facilitator uses a flipchart or presentation software to display a series of questions.
    a. What is community radio for, in comparison with other media outlets available in the area?
       Agreed responses are written on a flipchart sheet.
    b. What does the station have to do, based on the principles, that is different from other media available?
       Agreed responses are written on a flipchart sheet.
    c. What are the strengths and weaknesses of community radio in comparison with other media outlets available in the area?
       Two lists of agreed responses are written on two flipchart sheets.
    d. What does the station have to do to build on its strengths and to minimize its weaknesses, while still keeping to its principles?
    Agreed responses are written on a flipchart sheet.
2. Outside of the training, these responses need to be written up as a guiding charter for the station's journalists. It may need to be presented to, and agreed by, the management committee.

Agenda, training session 2: The audience

If there is audience research, each member of the team should have a copy, to use it to try to answer the facilitator's questions. If not, they will need to use their knowledge of the community.

1. The facilitator displays and asks this question: What do you know about your audience?

2. The facilitator displays and asks the following questions.
   a. How diverse is the audience? Are there different sections?
   b. Can you try to define your whole audience or the different sections of it, by:
      - age
      - gender
      - location
      - language
      - wealth
      - occupation
      - interests
      - political opinion
      - religion
      - level of education

   If there are different sections of the audience, which there almost certainly will be, the answers to this list can be written on a different flipchart sheet for each section.

Agenda, training session 3: Choosing what is news

1. The facilitator points out there are lots of stories in the world and in the community, and displays and asks the following question.
   On what basis do you choose your news stories?
2. Each participant is given a copy of *Table J7.1: Decisions on output*. Each fills it in. The facilitator leads a discussion on decisions made, and asks how far do they fit the station's principles?
   The participants and facilitator draw up a list of three agreed priority factors.
3. The facilitator displays and asks: How does a team choose which stories to cover? Each participant is given a copy of *Handout J7.2: News priorities* (a facilitator may want to adapt the stories to be more appropriate locally).
   Each participant makes their choice of five stories, and the one which would be the main story.
   Each participant reports back, and explains their reasons for the choices made.
4. For each list, in plenary, the team consider these questions:
   a. According to the stations principles, do the choices fit?
   b. Do the choices match the listener profiles worked out yesterday?
   c. Do the choices play to the station's strengths and minimize its weaknesses?
   Collectively, the team draw up a list of the five stories and the main story, which best answer the above questions.

Agenda, training session 4: Technical recording training

The exact nature of this session will depend on the type of recorder available. Broadly, the session should cover:
- the necessity of using headphones
- recording at the right level

- getting a balance of voices
- taking account of and compensating for any background sound

Agenda, training session 5: Finding stories and recording interviews

1. The facilitator explains that, over the coming days, the team are going to produce a 10-minute news bulletin for the station. This will involve:
   - finding stories
   - interviewing
   - applying the principles and ethics of journalism
   - writing and producing stories for the bulletin
   - assembling the bulletin
2. The facilitator displays and asks the following question:
   Where can news come from?
   Participants suggest organizations, places and other sources for news stories.
   They are written up, and should finish up with a list something like this:
   - police
   - court
   - market
   - wherever people talk
   - local organizations
   - local government
   - arts/cultural venues
   - weddings
   - funerals
   - hospitals
   - religious establishment

   The facilitator asks: When they find a story, what information about it do they want to get? (This is a revision exercise on the six basic journalism questions, which the team should have been taught.)
3. The facilitator allocates specific places for participants to go to find local stories. Individually or in pairs, participants go out to find possible leads or whole stories, with recorders and notebooks. The facilitator explains that they are to record interviews, if they find a good story and if it is possible to interview someone.
   On the participants' return, the facilitator displays the following questions.
   a. According to the stations principles, does the story fit?
   b. Does the story match the listener profiles worked out yesterday?
   c. Does the story play to the station's strengths and minimize its weaknesses?
   Each participant or pair report back on what they have found and where. The whole team looks at each story in turn, and answer the above questions.
   In addition, the team consider if each is:
   - a complete story
   - a lead

4. All participants are given *Handout J7.3: Sources*, and the facilitator goes through it to make sure everyone understands it.

   Each story or lead is judged against the criteria of who is a good source to decide whether each participant has found a good source?

   Collectively, the team decide which stories can be followed up and which need further checking.

5. From the stories and leads chosen for follow-up, the team discuss how each one might best be followed up to make a complete story.

   In particular, they discuss how balance can be achieved in the story.

   Individuals or pairs go out to follow up. Others go out to find new stories.

   Those who have followed up report back what they have found.

   There is discussion if what has been found is sufficient or not. If not, there is further discussion of what is still needed.

   New stories are considered against the criteria set out above.

Agenda, training session 6: Audio editing training

The facilitator discusses the ethics of editing; otherwise, the exact nature of this session will depend on the software being used.

   Participants edit their material.

Agenda, training session 7: Writing stories and reports

The team are trained in

- writing a news story
- writing a report
- writing for radio

They then proceed with choosing a format and writing.

Agenda, training session 8: Assembling the bulletin

All participants are given *Handout J7.4: Creating a news bulletin running order*, and the facilitator goes through it to make sure everyone understands it.

Once all of the stories are edited, written and recorded, then the team and facilitator need to discuss and choose the main story.

The other stories are judged to be stronger or weaker, and the strong are interspersed with the weaker.

A menu of the whole bulletin is written to go at the beginning.

The bulletin is recorded.

Agenda, training session 9: Reviewing the bulletin

The bulletin is reviewed by the management committee and a cross-section of listeners.

Module J8: Producing a live phone-in discussion programme

Course objectives

For participants to:

- learn the mechanics of producing a live discussion and phone-in
- see the value of such programmes for allowing communities a public voice

Materials

Copies of all of the following handouts for each participant and the facilitator, or as PowerPoint slides. If PowerPoint is used, the facilitator needs to make sure there are also paper copies for any handouts which need to be completed by participants.

Handout J8.1: Choosing panel guests

In making their choice of guests, the team need to make sure that:
- the guests are editorially appropriate
- they represent a balance of points of view, knowledge and experience
- they are easily understandable

Handout J8.2: A back-timing table example

This is a simple example of a back-timing table. The format is an overall topic that has been chosen and broken into four sub-topics. Listeners or viewers phone in with questions or comments. The panel respond.

By listing the end times, then any delays earlier in the programme do not make a difference. The following end times still need to be met.

The programme starts at 14.30 ends at 15.30.

Topic	End time
Presenter introduction of the panel and topic	14.35
Sub-topic 1 ends	14.50
Sub-topic 2 ends	15.02
Sub-topic 3 ends	15.14
Sub-topic 4 ends	15.26
Closing anno	15.30

Handout J8.3: Live programme presenter's preparation checklist

- Know the topic, with a brief understanding of each guest's knowledge, experience and viewpoint on it.
- Have a seating plan.
- Know guests' correct names.
- Know the time available, and, if needed, have a back-timing plan.

Handout J8.4: Live programme presenter's tasks before going live

- Introduce guests to each other.
- Explain the studio equipment to the guests.
- Explain to guests the discussion is live.
- Explain the rules to the guests.
- Explain the time available.
- Brief the guests on the topic and which aspects of it you want to discuss.

Handout J8.5: Live programme rules for guests

It is very useful to have a list of simple rules to ask guests who are in the studio for a live discussion to follow.
- Switch off all mobile phones (on silent is not enough, as some mobiles make signals which can be picked up and broadcast by the studio equipment).
- Do not talk over each other, and allow other speakers time to speak.
- Show respect to other guest/s, without insults or swearing.
- Speak 'through the chair'; that is, address all comments to the presenter, not the other guest/s.
- Do not move about.
- Avoid movement that makes noises; remove any jewellery that makes noise.
- Speak into the microphone, and keep the set distance from it.
- Keep to the topic.
- Use language that is appropriate for the audience, avoiding foreign words.
- Avoid making defamatory comments about anyone.

Handout J8.6: Presenter's checklist of tasks during a live discussion

- Introduce topic and guests.
- Explain any absence: If a point of view that should be represented is not represented, explain why (for example: the guest refused to take part, illness, etc.).
- Explain the format and invite phone calls.
- Identify guests whenever they speak.
- Keep making eye contact with guests.
- Maintain balance and impartiality.
- If a guest makes defamatory remarks, ask them to withdraw them, and dissociate the radio station from the remarks.
- Recap the discussion occasionally.
- Allow guests to have drinks.
- Be patient and calm, and avoid getting into arguments.
- End the discussion with thanks.

Handout J8.7: Presenter's control of a phone-in

There are some things that a presenter should do to help a phone-in run smoothly, and avoid problems.
- Each caller should be told they are live on air.
- Establish each caller's name and where they live.

- Help callers who are struggling to get to the point they want to make, by summarizing what the presenter thinks is the point they are trying to make.
- Keep calls brief, and end them politely but firmly if the caller is rambling.

Handout J8.8: Cutting callers off

It is sometimes necessary to cut off a caller abruptly. Callers' behaviour that justifies this includes:
- swearing
- defamation
- evidence of drunkenness or drug use
- rudeness
- hate speech or threat of violence
- failure to get on to the topic, even after being asked
- failure to switch off own radio when asked to

Equipment

Flipchart stand and flipcharts
Laptop and projector (or use print materials)

Facilities

Either a room large enough to house a panel and an audience, suitably microphoned, and equipped to receive and broadcast calls, or a studio large enough to house a panel only, and equipped to receive and broadcast calls.

Agenda, training session 1: Choosing a topic and studio guests

1. Participants are asked to suggest topics for a programme, showing how it meets an identified need among the audience. The topics are listed on the flipchart.
   As a group, the participants choose one topic on the basis that it is the most pressing need or the most empowering topic for the audience, or, at least, for part of the audience.
2. The facilitator takes the participants through *Handout J8.1: Choosing panel guests*, answering questions and making clarifications. Participants suggest what range of knowledge, experience and opinion the programme will need. These suggestions are written on the flipchart, and a shortlist agreed.
   In small groups, participants are given the task of researching and finding one panel guest per group, coming back to the session with a shortlist of possibilities. (The groups need to make it clear, when they approach someone to be on the panel, that, at this stage, it is for a training session and not a broadcast programme.)

Agenda, training session 2: Chairing a live discussion and phone-in

Careful planning is essential for any successful live broadcast, but it is especially important for phone-ins, and when dealing with potentially controversial issues, as the team might be.

1. If the intended programme is long, say, an hour, the station may want to divide it into sections, taking a different sub-topic of the overall topic in each section. If this is the case, the first step for the facilitator is to help the participants in breaking down the overall topic into smaller topics, for both the discussion and the phone-in, and decide how long the team want to spend on each of these sub-topics.

   They should work out how much time to allocate to each sub-topic, based on its importance and complexity.

   It is also important, at this stage, for the participants to decide how they want to introduce each sub-topic. They might, for example, start a discussion among the panel, perhaps prompted by a question from the presenter, and then invite callers to phone in.

2. If the programme is to be divided into sections, then it is important to use back-timing, so that every sub-topic is covered, and given adequate time. Back timing is part of the planning process, and it gives the presenter an easy guide to what he or she should be doing at each stage during a live broadcast.

   The facilitator hands out or presents *Handout J8.2: A back timing table example*, and then takes the participants through the following stages, building on the work already done.

   The team have their list of the items they want in the discussion and phone-in, and the times they want to allocate to each.

   a. The facilitator asks the participants to work out the real ending time for the phone-in, taking into account advertising breaks or a news bulletin, which need to be within the programme's allotted time.

   b. The facilitator gets the participants into pair, and using the handout, shows the team how to draw up a simple table, working backwards from that time, first deducting the amount of time allocated to the last item, and working out what time the item before it needs to end.

   c. From there, the facilitator shows the participants how to work backwards to determine the actual time each item has to end.

   d. One pair explain the timings they have worked out. If any other pairs do not agree, the whole group examine the workings out of the different pairs, to find out who is right, and why.

3. Now the participants have a chosen topic, broken down into sub-topics with a back timing table, if needed. The facilitator introduces the next stage, which is looking at the role of the presenter.

   The facilitator asks the participants what kind of knowledge and information the presenter needs to have before the programme starts. Answers are written on a flipchart.

   The facilitator gives out or presents *Handout J8.3: Live programme presenter's preparation checklist.*

   Participants compare it with their list of the presenter's needed knowledge and information, and add or take away items from each list to create a consolidated list for themselves. The facilitator can ask the participants to judge if the list is simple and practical and suitable for daily use. If necessary, the list can be simplified.

4. The facilitator then asks what a presenter needs to do once the guests have arrived, before they all go live on air. Once again, participants suggest ideas, which are written on a flipchart, and then they eliminate those they do not think necessary. The facilitator gives out or presents *Handout J8.4: Live programme presenter's tasks before going live.* Participants compare it with their list of the presenter's tasks, and add or take away items from each list to create a consolidated list for themselves. The facilitator can ask the participants to judge if the list is simple and practical, and suitable for daily use. If necessary, the list can be simplified.

5. Next, the facilitator picks out one item on the list: Rules for guests. The same procedure is followed. Participants suggest ideas for rules which will:
   • help keep the discussion understandable and interesting for the audience
   • help keep the discussion reasonably calm
   • avoid irritations for the audience
   • avoid the broadcaster breaking the law

   These ideas are listed on a flipchart, and then edited. The facilitator gives out or presents *Handout J8.5: Live programme rules for guests.* Once again, the participants' list of rules for guests and the handout list are consolidated into a practical list.

6. The facilitator explains that, having looked at preparation, the training is moving on to what the presenter has to do in handling a discussion during broadcast. (This section of the session does not cover the issue of handling callers. That is covered in the next section.)

   Participants make suggestions for what a presenter needs to do during a live discussion programme. The suggestions are written on a flipchart, and the list is edited.

   The facilitator gives out or presents *Handout J8.6: Presenter's checklist of tasks during a live discussion.* Once again, the participants' list and the handout list are consolidated into a practical list of responsibilities.

7. It is always best, if it is technically possible, to have a producer in the studio or control room who takes all calls, and has a brief conversation with all callers before putting them on air. The purpose of this is to screen callers to try to ensure they are genuine callers who have something to say on the topic, and not people calling for no reason, or to disrupt or insult.

   However, this is not always possible, and so, it is necessary to have a list of measures for a presenter to follow when they are handling a phone-in in which the callers are not being screened by someone else before they are on air:
   • to try to reduce the risk of a caller causing a problem on air
   • to keep the programme as interesting as possible for the audience

   This part of the training follows the same pattern as the last few: Ideas on how to avoid problems during a phone-in are suggested by participants, written down on a flipchart and the list edited.

   The facilitator gives out or presents *Handout J8.7: Presenter's control of a phone-in.* Once again, the participants' list and the handout list are consolidated into a practical list of measures.

8. The facilitator explains that, sometimes it is necessary to end a call immediately, even in the middle of a sentence, because of something the caller does. Once again, the participants are asked to come up with ideas of the kinds of behaviour that could make this measure necessary. The list is written on a flipchart and edited.

   The facilitator gives out or presents *Handout J8.8: Cutting callers off*. As before, the list in the handout and the participants' list are consolidated, to become a practical list of behaviours which justify the rapid ending of a call.

   All of the checklists produced in this training session should be refined after a rehearsal programme (see below), and after actual live broadcasts, to make sure they are exactly right for the culture and ethos of the station.

Agenda, training session 3: Running live discussion and phone-ins

There is a lot of information here for presenters to absorb, and it is essential to give them at least one opportunity to try running a mocked-up discussion and phone-in before they have to do it live on air.

If possible, get genuine guests, who need, of course, to be told that they are taking part in a training exercise (see Session 1 of this training plan). Otherwise, members of the team can play the parts of the studio guests, while the remainder of the participants and other station staff, if possible, play the callers. Some of these callers should be allocated roles displaying behaviour which is in the list of behaviours that demand rapid ending of a call, to see if the trainee presenter ends the call, and, if they do, how they do it.

The participants should be given handouts of the lists of rules and checklists the presenter is supposed to be following.

Together, the participants and guests, if there are any, run through a mock discussion and phone-in and, at the end of it, they discuss the trainee presenter's performance against the various sets of rules and checklists given in this module's handouts.

Module J9: Investigative journalism

This module takes a facilitator, step by step, through the process of teaching investigative journalism. It gives the information needed to discuss with the participants at each stage, and a series of activities that will lead them through their first investigation.

Course objectives

For participants to:

- understand what investigative journalism is
- learn the skills of investigative journalism
- carry out a genuine investigation into an individual or organization

Legal considerations

The facilitator needs to understand the legal framework for journalists in the country they are in, researching media and defamation laws, and seeking legal advice.

The facilitator needs to carry out a training needs assessment on legal issues. If that reveals all or some participants do not understand the legal framework, then training needs to be supplied.

Participants, if they do not already know it, need to understand that some people will try to use the law to silence journalists.

Because of possible consequences, it is essential for the facilitator to keep journalists' editors and managers informed, when participants are doing investigations.

Materials

Copies of all of the following handouts for each participant and the facilitator, or as PowerPoint slides. If PowerPoint is used, the facilitator needs to make sure there are also paper copies for any handouts which need to be completed by participants.

Handout J9.1: What is investigative journalism?

Investigative journalism is journalism which:
- investigates on behalf of its audience or a section of its audience
- exposes wrongdoing or incompetence that affects others
- is sceptical and challenging
- follows leads
- assembles its case and tests it rigorously
- is willing to stop following an investigation if the evidence is not strong enough, even if a lot of work has been done

Handout J9.2: The role of the investigative journalist

- To find stories to investigate
- To find leads and contacts and to follow them through
- To be sceptical until the truth is proved – sceptical of accusers and those who are accused
- To test all evidence
- To carefully construct his or her cases, to make them as clear as possible
- To be fully aware of the law, as it applies to defamation

Handout J9.3: Finding a story to investigate

Ideas or stories can come from many sources:
- the journalist's own observation, which can be physical, for example, they see something questionable or, say, from their scepticism about political statements
- other media, including social media, may provide names of groups campaigning against corruption, for example
- members of the public
- people involved who are disgruntled or concerned and bring a journalist the story
- the public can be invited to contact a long-running investigative series with issues

Handout J9.4: Finding interviewees

Types of interviewee:
- interviewees directly affected by the issue (those deprived of resources by the corruption, for example)
- insiders, or former insiders, in the organization you are investigating
- people doing a similar job to the one you are investigating, so that how they are proceeding and their results can be compared
- experts who can explain the context, the scale and the wider consequences of the issue

Routes for finding interviewees
Even more than is the case in normal journalism, getting to the person who is finally interviewed may take several stages.
- The original source will often be a good lead.
- Domestic pressure groups and international agencies will often have a database of experts who will talk about particular issues.
- Searches on networking sites like Linkedin can find individuals useful to the investigation.
- Other media may provide the names of concerned groups.
- Internet research will often find organizations who can help.

Handout J9.5: Gathering other evidence

Interviewees are likely to be the most useful source of evidence but other kinds of evidence may often be needed.

Public documents

- government reports on, say, NGO performance or the environment
- reports by authoritative organizations, like concerned NGOs
- publicly available statistical evidence
- comparative physical evidence
- publicly available financial information ('Follow the money' remains key in investigative journalism.)

Private documents

Private documents are much harder to obtain, and you need to be sure that their use does not break any laws. You are most likely to get them from someone inside an organization.
- Bank statements can reveal individual payments or receipts, or patterns of payments.
- Letters and e-mails can be extremely revealing.
An organization's internal documents can reveal much more than their public ones, and it often makes interesting reading to compare the two.

Handout J9.6: Assembling your case

When you are putting your investigation together, you need to do the following.
- Make the issue and its significance clear.
- Set out your evidence clearly and without confusion – make sure your words cannot be misinterpreted.
- Make sure what you say in your script is fully supported by the evidence you present.
- Keep your script to the facts and avoid emotional description.
- Make sure you are not in danger of making unsubstantiated allegations against anyone.
- Allow all the relevant points of view adequate coverage.
- If you are covering crime, make sure you are not prejudicing any future trial, or are in danger of contempt of court.

When drawing conclusions consider the following points.
- It is easy to either exaggerate or oversimplify in an investigative conclusion.
- Make sure the evidence supports the conclusions you draw.
- You may want to end your piece by simply setting out one point of view against another, leaving your audience to draw their own conclusions, but still be careful of defamation by implication.

Equipment

Flipchart
Laptop and projector (or use print materials)

Agenda, training session 1: Training needs assessment

1. The facilitator asks participants what they think the characteristics of investigative journalism are, and writes them up on a flip chart, making sure that all of the participants have a chance to offer their ideas. This is to make sure the assessment is valid for all of the participants.
   If the responses largely correspond with what is listed in *Handout J9.1: What is investigative journalism?*, then there is no need to use that handout, and the facilitator can move straight on to the next question. If there are significant mismatches or gaps in the participants' list, then the facilitator gives out or presents *Handout J9.1: What is investigative journalism?* The facilitator goes through the handout with the participants for clarification and, perhaps, expansion through examples.
2. The facilitator then asks, based on the characteristics listed, what the role of the investigative journalist is. Again, making sure all participants take part. The responses are written up.
   If the responses largely correspond with what is listed in *Handout J9.2: The role of the investigative journalist*, then there is no need to use that handout, and the facilitator can move straight on to finding stories. If there are significant mismatches or gaps in the participants' list, then the facilitator gives out or

presents *Handout J9.2: The role of the investigative journalist*. The facilitator goes through the handout with the participants for clarification and, perhaps, expansion through examples.

Agenda, training session 2: Finding a story

1. The facilitator gives out or presents *Handout J9.3: Finding a story to investigate*. In pairs, participants think up or find three possible investigations.
   Each pair presents their ideas, and the other participants consider them against these criteria:
   Investigations take time and effort, so an editor wants to be reasonably sure that any that journalists propose have some chance of success.
   There may be a lot of reasons why an investigation is not worth pursuing. The following are some examples.
   - A closer look shows there is no problem to investigate.
   - It will be impossible to find enough evidence.
   - The investigation would be of no interest to the audience.
   - There is a risk of a journalist putting themselves and, perhaps, colleagues, in danger if they follow the investigation.

   On the basis of these points, participants agree which proposed stories should be followed up and which should be rejected. Participants carry out initial research on those that are chosen for following up, to assess whether they can be pursued further.

2. The facilitator explains that the key to deciding if an investigation is worth following up is whether a journalist can find two completely independent sources who both suggest there is something to investigate.
   So, the journalist needs to check at least one completely different source from the original, who could either suggest there is a story or offer sufficient evidence that there is not that the journalist cancels it.
   The facilitator can suggest where a second source might be found:
   - further physical observation
   - the organization that you are investigating
   - some other concerned organization (perhaps a local authority, other customers, a government department)

   Each pair of participants searches for a second source, and then present their findings to the whole group. The group consider which of the stories now appear to be the most worth investigating, and make decisions accordingly, with the guidance of the facilitator.

3. The facilitator gives out or presents *Handout J9.4: Finding interviewees*, and talks it through for clarification and expansion.
   Pairs are asked to list the evidence they need to pursue their investigation further, and where they are going to look for it.
   Pairs report back to the whole group, and there is a discussion on the feasibility of what each pair is proposing to do, and suggestions for better evidence and/or where to look for it.

4. Pairs follow their proposed and modified course to find interviewees, develop questions and conduct interviews.

   Depending on the experience of the participants, the facilitator may want pairs to report back and discuss what they are planning to do at each stage, either just with the facilitator or with the whole group.

5. The facilitator gives out or presents *Handout J9.5: Gathering other evidence*, and goes through it for clarification.

   On the point about comparative physical evidence, the facilitator might want to give the example that, in the investigation discussed in Chapter 24, comparing Camp X with Camp Y was crucial evidence.

   As a whole group, participants discuss, for each pair, whether they might find evidence to strengthen their case from any of the sources listed in the handout. If they think they might, then pairs need to go and do the research, returning with further evidence they have found.

6. The facilitator explains that any evidence or interview from a source needs to be tested or corroborated, and leads a discussion on how that can be done. They write up the suggestions on a flipchart. If the following ideas do not come up, the facilitator adds them to the list:

   • corroboration from sources entirely independent from the first source and offering first-hand evidence – for example, a number of independent eye-witnesses

   • corroboration from documentary evidence

   Pairs assemble their evidence and corroboration. They present it to the whole group and the participants test it.

   If the participants are not satisfied that the corroboration is strong enough, pairs do further research and re-present the corroboration for further discussion.

7. The facilitator may want to give out *Handout J9.6: Assembling your case*, to serve as an aide-memoire while participants assemble their cases.

   Pairs assemble their case and put it, with its conclusion, to the whole group to check if it is convincing.

8. The facilitator explains that it is important for the individual or organization that has been investigated to have the right of reply. This can be done in a challenging interview following the broadcast of the investigation.

   Either the facilitator or a participant should take the role of the individual or the spokesperson of the organization. (The person taking this role will need time to study the investigation and prepare their responses.)

   After each role-play interview, the whole group discuss how well the investigating team handled the interview, and draw up a list of strategies for dealing with such an interview.

9. The facilitator asks the group what should be said after an investigation has been broadcast if the individual or organization that has been investigated refuses to be interviewed.

   The group, guided by the facilitator, should work out a form of words to be used.

Module J10: The production of factual programmes for behaviour change

This course is a model for a kind of training which is different from the previous journalism modules. It is designed to get a small production team started in all aspects of the production process, including working out the allocation of production tasks among the team, an overall workplan and individual workplans, with deadlines. It is, therefore, a model which could be applied to any of the previous courses if this is the situation in which the course is being held.

Course objectives

For participants to:

- become skilled in making behaviour change magazine programmes
- develop a format for the planned magazine programmes
- produce one pilot programme under the leadership of the facilitator
- produce a second programme led by the team leader, under the supervision of the facilitator
- work out a production timetable and individual workplan
- plan a behaviour change curriculum for 1 year

Materials

Copies of the project's behaviour change objectives, one for each participant
Copies of the project formative research or a summary of it, one for each participant
Copies of all of the following handouts for each participant and the facilitator, or as PowerPoint slides. If PowerPoint is used, the facilitator needs to make sure there are also paper copies for any handouts which need to be completed by participants.

Handout J10.1: Knowledge, attitude, behaviour

This is an illustrative example from a project for reducing mortality among babies under six months old.

   If this is in a programme strand with the behaviour change objective of exclusive breastfeeding for the first six months, in some cultures, a barrier could be:

   The myth that the breast cannot deliver milk for three or four days after birth.

Knowledge

The breast can deliver milk as soon as the baby is born.
The breast responds to the stimulus of the baby sucking.
Encouraging the mother that milk will come actually helps it to come.

Attitude

Mothers need to believe they will produce milk from the start.
Older women and birth attendants need to believe this.
Husbands need to believe this.

Behaviour

The mother needs to ask for the baby and initiate breastfeeding as soon as possible.

Older women and birth attendants present need to give the mother confidence that she can produce milk.

The husband needs to give the mother confidence that she can produce milk.

This is only an illustrative example, and, usually, there will be far more items than there are here.

Handout J10.2: Finding contributors

Finding the right contributors for behaviour and social change factual programmes is essential, and a team needs to spend time and effort on it. Often, the best experts for programmes like these are people who are like the target audiences, and who are in the process of, or have managed to make, the behaviour changes the project is trying to promote. However, it is often not easy to find such interviewees because the requirements of interviews in this kind of programme can be very specific, and the kind of interviewees being sought are not necessarily very visible.

Production teams may find the following advice useful.

The reporter

Reporters need to:
- give themselves plenty of time to find contributors
- use the phone and online research, if available, as much as possible
- have the questions set out and a clear, short explanation of the purpose of the programmes before they call potential contributors
- have a clear brief on what they want the contributor to do
- keep at the task
- not to accept the first person they talk to, until they have heard others

When a reporter phones a potential contributor, they should:
- not to accept the first person they talk to, until they have heard others
- ask for their experience and expertise
- ask them to say exactly how they would answer the questions

The interviewee

They are not the interviewee needed, if:
- they cannot answer fully

- they use jargon, acronyms or complicated language
- they are boring

They are the interviewee needed, if:
- they can give clear and full answers
- they use simple, jargon-free language
- they are engaging

Using the phone

Reporters need to use all the means of communication they have available to find leads and interviewees. They should not be afraid to use the phone. An email or Facebook post can be ignored, but it is much harder to ignore a personal call. Trying to find the right interviewee can require considerable persistence. It can take days of continuous effort.

1. The reporter researches on the internet and makes a list of all the likely contacts they can think of: colleagues, relatives, friends, other journalists, professionals in the relevant field.
2. The reporter contacts each of them, asking if they know a possible interviewee.
3. If the contact does not offer a lead, the reporter asks for any further contact they might have who might have a lead.
4. The reporter follows any lead offered, but does not stop making contacts while having to wait for a possible lead to call back, or if there is no answer from a lead.
5. The reporter keeps going until the right interviewee is found.
6. A reporter may well need to record more than one interview for each item, so that you can choose the best.

Going to gathering places

A useful technique for a reporter to find personal interviewees is to think of places such people might go – for example, particular shops or facilities they might use.

The reporter needs to handle the task of talking to whoever runs the location/the shopkeeper carefully. It is important that they know what the reporter is doing, and they might be able to help.

Professional contributors

Most behaviour and social change factual programmes need, at least, some professionals in the appropriate field, of different kinds. However, just because someone is a professional does not mean they are going to be a good interviewee.

Reporters need to:
- choose professional interviewees with great care
- test them out, as described above

To keep professional interviewees on a level that audiences can understand, it can be advisable to keep them in touch with reality.

A simple way of doing that is to try to get them to illustrate their points with good, real-life examples from their own experience.

A slightly more difficult approach is to record actuality. That is, the reporter records the professional as they do their work, explaining what they are doing as they are doing it.

However, when doing this, a reporter must:

- make sure the balance between the voice and the background sound is right, so that the voice can be clearly understood
- make sure that his or her questions are recorded at the right level
- not create any kind of additional risk to anyone, for example, if recording appears to be distracting the interviewee as they work, then it should stop until they have finished the work.

Handout J10.3: An aide-memoire on the principles of behaviour and social change factual programming

Behaviour change communication is different from normal broadcasting because it is based on careful research on how people learn and how people change.

How people learn

People very rarely learn just from being told something. They learn in two ways:
- by discussion with other people
- by doing

How people change

- Change almost always takes time and it is usually a gradual process.
- People usually change in a three-stage process: A change of knowledge, a change of attitude and a change of behaviour.
- Change is easier if people are given small steps to take rather than being expected to make one huge leap.
- People often change because they are following a role model.

Behaviour change programmes need to attract and engage listeners, and particularly listeners who do not agree with the changes the programmes are trying to make. This is because of the following reasons.
- If someone is not listening, they will not change.
- The people who do not agree with the programmes' intentions are the people who the programmes need to influence the most.

The nature of the programmes

Because of the ways people learn and change, behaviour change programmes are different from other programmes.

- They try to get people talking to each other about the topics they are covering.
- They follow a curriculum of small steps towards behaviour change, over a long time.
- The curriculum is organized so that it deals with change of knowledge first, then change of attitude and, finally, change of behaviour.
- They include interviews with people like their listeners, and do not rely on experts. They rarely have interviews with voices from government.
- Interviewees are most often role models: Ordinary people who are going through a process of behaviour change or people who have been through a successful process of behaviour change.
- Some interviewees should be people whose beliefs, attitudes and behaviour are opposed to what the programmes are promoting, so that listeners who think and believe the same way – the people the programmes most need to change – are engaged and can be taken through a process of change.
- The programmes will promote discussion between opposing views among listeners.
- Interviews will often be personal stories so that listeners are engaged.
- Experts need to be people who can speak in ways that ordinary people can understand.
- Actuality is valuable in this kind of programming.
- Out of the six standard journalistic questions – What? Where? When? Who? How? and Why? – interviews will concentrate on the last two, How? and Why? That is, how did the interviewee do something and why did he or she do it?

Equipment

Flipchart
Laptops for each member of the team

Participants

This is a training course for a small production team who already have allocated jobs within an organization and assigned to a specific project, including a production team leader. It assumes the team are already experienced in programme production but not in behaviour change communication.

Agenda, training session 1: Training needs assessment

The facilitator asks each participant to explain the parts of their CV that they think is relevant to the project.

The facilitator asks different participants to talk through different stages of the programme production process.

The facilitator asks each participant to set up and record an interview on a topic relevant to the programmes to be produced.

The purpose of these tasks is to assess each participant's understanding of the programme production process and their journalistic skills.

Agenda, training session 2: The nature of behaviour change

1. The facilitator explains that this is an exercise, done in pairs, in which each participant identifies a behaviour change they have made in their own lives, and explains to their partner:
   - why it happened
   - how it happened
   - how long it took
   - the influence of other people's opinions and behaviour on that change
   - factors that inhibited the process of change (barriers)
   - factors that helped the process of change (facilitators)

   Pairs change roles, so that both partners describe their behaviour change.
   Each participant explains their partner's story of change.
2. As each story of behaviour change is told, the facilitator writes up key factors as they are raised in the different stories:
   - motivations
   - length of time
   - barriers
   - facilitators
3. After each story a brief discussion is held on what prompted and influenced the behaviour change, and the facilitator notes down key elements on a flipchart. (This chart can then be used to show examples of what starts behaviour change, of barriers and of facilitators, when the training covers those topics.)
   The intended outcomes of this exercise are:
   - to show that behaviour change is something that we all undergo, and not just something that happens to our audiences
   - to explore, in real-life examples, how behaviour change works and what influences it

Agenda, training session 3: Module J1: An exploration of how people learn

This session uses the whole of Module J1.

Agenda, training session 4: Creating a behaviour change curriculum

1. The facilitator introduces the idea of a curriculum – a structured sequence of learning – which is created by breaking down large issues into smaller items, each lasting between four and seven minutes of broadcast time. The process has three stages:
   - breaking large topics in the formative research summary into small items
   - classifying them under knowledge, attitude and behaviour
   - putting them into a step-by-step progressive order of audience understanding
2. The facilitator discusses one of the project's behaviour change objectives with the team to ensure it is fully understood.
3. The facilitator reintroduces the idea of the barrier, a factor that inhibits or even currently prevents progress towards a behaviour change objective. The facilitator may

refer back to the introductory exercise of personal behaviour change experiences, and pick out barriers to some of those changes, to illustrate what they are.

Barriers can be, among other things:

- a lack of knowledge
- a mistaken belief
- an unhelpful attitude, like fatalism
- a lack of access to resources

Looking at the formative research summary, the facilitator asks the team, as a whole, to identify factors that are barriers to the achievement of the behaviour change objective just discussed.

The barriers are listed on a flipchart.

4. The facilitator (the person leading the training) re-introduces the idea of the facilitator (a beneficial factor in behaviour change) and, again, may refer to any identified during the personal behaviour change experience exercise, to illustrate what they are.

   Facilitators can be among other things:

   - knowledge
   - a well-founded belief
   - a helpful attitude, like a strong desire for an outcome this behaviour change can bring
   - access to resources

   Looking at the formative research summary, the facilitator asks the team, as a whole, to identify factors that are facilitators for the achievement of the behaviour change objective just discussed.

   The facilitators are listed on a flipchart.

5. Each participant is asked to take one barrier and to break down the process of overcoming it into small steps, each of which can be handled in a short programme item, and including the relevant facilitators.

   In plenary, each participant presents their list of items, and the facilitator and group discuss whether each step:

   - moves towards overcoming the barrier
   - is small enough to be handled in a single programme item

   If necessary, participants revise their items.

6. The facilitator introduces the concept of knowledge, attitude and behaviour, and there is a discussion on why knowledge items need to come before items on attitude, and why both come before items on behaviour.

   The facilitator may wish to use *Handout J10.1: Knowledge, attitude, behaviour* as an illustrative example.

   Participants list their items under the headings of knowledge, attitude, behaviour. In plenary, the facilitator and group discuss if each participant has categorized their items correctly.

   If necessary, participants revise their lists.

7. The facilitator takes one example set of programme items, and takes the group through the process of putting a sample of them into progressive order, putting knowledge items first, then attitude and then behaviour, but also putting the items in order within each category.

Again, participants present their lists, and there is discussion about whether the programme items are in the right order. Any revision needed is carried out. These steps are repeated for all of the barriers for all of the behaviour change objectives, so that the curriculum is completed, for six months or so, either in the training or at a later date.

Agenda, training session 5: Developing a programme format

The choice of item formats

It may well be that an editor, senior producer or consultant will decide which item formats will be used for each strand of the programme. However, if there is no one experienced in making magazine programmes, and if there is time, here is an alternative approach.

1. The facilitator takes the team through the process of working out what information needs to be in one particular item that has been chosen from the lists worked out earlier in the training, either by completing a factual package development grid, as set out in Chapter 7, or by using some other method.
2. The participants then look at the item formats described in Chapter 7, and each member chooses a different one.
   Supported by the facilitator, each team member makes a programme item based on the developed factual package development grid, using the format they have chosen.
3. The items are produced and played to the whole team, followed by a discussion of the strengths and weaknesses of each of the formats used.

The programme format

1. The facilitator discusses the format set out in Chapter 7, which is appropriate for a behaviour and social change programme, if wanted, with one slight variation. The impact of the programmes is likely to be stronger if the last item in each programme is edited in such a way that it ends with the main interviewee's story unfinished or, better still, with the main interviewee facing a dilemma.
2. The facilitator can ask what purpose a dilemma might serve. They can elicit that the purpose of this strategy is to encourage members of the audience to talk to each other about what that interviewee's choices are or what they think that person will do. As has been discussed before, audience members talking to each other is a powerful learning tool and helps to shift social norms to create a more supportive context for behaviour change.

Agenda, training session 6: Production of programme items

Once the decisions on the format are made, the participants can be allocated different items to make and can go through the production process: completing a factual package development grid (see Chapter 7), which is reviewed in plenary and revised as necessary; researching and finding the contributors needed; devising questions for the interviews, which, again, will be discussed in plenary and revised as necessary and recording interviews.

1. **Using a factual package development grid**
   If the participants are not familiar with using a development grid, the facilitator can use Sessions 2 and 3 of *Module J2: A selection workshop procedure for factual communication*, along with *Table J2.2: A factual package development grid* and *Table J2.3: An example completed factual package development grid*. (These two items are also in Chapter 7.)

2. **Finding contributors**
   The facilitator may want to use *Handout J10.2: Finding contributors*, and go through it with the participants, taking them through the process it sets out, in practice. This should help them deal with the particular demands of this kind of programme-making.

3. **Starting and ending lines for items**
   The facilitator introduces the concept of the 'hook', a line which will encourage the audience to pay attention to the item. A hook sets up a mystery or a tension, which will be explained or resolved in the item. Preferably, it will be a line from one of the interviews but, if not, the reporter's script needs to provide it.
   A closing line for one item should try to set up a dilemma or leave the story unresolved, as discussed above. Additionally, the facilitator can point out that the presenter can reinforce the impact of the dilemma, perhaps with a question.
   The facilitator asks the team, as they listen to the interviews, to try to identify potential hook lines and dilemma-setting lines or to identify points where the interview could be stopped, in order to create an unresolved ending.
   The main interview for each item is played. After each, there is discussion on potential hooks and endings.
   Each participant edits their material, including editing to establish the agreed opening and closing lines.
   Each participant writes their item presentation script, to be reviewed by the facilitator and redrafted, as necessary.
   The item presentation script is recorded and the item is assembled.
   In plenary, all items are listened to or watched, and reviewed, followed by revision as necessary.

4. **Choosing menu clips**
   In plenary, potential menu clips are chosen, following the procedure set out in Chapter 7, if guidance is required, and a final choice is made. Reporters copy the chosen menu clips and give them to the presenter.

5. **The presenter script**
   The presenter writes the script, which is presented and reviewed in plenary, with revision as needed.
   The presenter records the script.

6. The programme is assembled.

Agenda, training session 7: Programme review

1. The production team and others in the project organization listen to or watch the programme. Where necessary, transcripts are provided to any who cannot understand the language used in the programme.

   Before the programme is played, the facilitator highlights four questions:

   > Does the programme fulfil the project intentions?
   > Will it attract the target audiences?
   > Will it hold the target audiences?
   > Will it promote discussion?

   After the programme has been played, the review group discuss these questions.
2. If problems are identified, discussion can follow these questions:

   > Why and how did the problem arise?
   > What needs to be done to put the programme right?
   > What needs to be done to avoid the problem in the future?

Agenda, training session 8: Review of the production process

1. The production team and the facilitator, together with the project management team, look back at the process by which the programme has been produced, with a particular focus on teamworking.

   If problems are identified, ways of avoiding them in future are discussed and decided on.
2. The facilitator works with the team to develop a production schedule and individual workplans. Looking back at the production process for the programme just made, the facilitator takes the team through the production process to draw up a timetable and responsibilities for future production. The reason for following this procedure is so that the production schedule reflects the realities of production.

   This session should identify:

   - the steps that need to be taken
   - the order in which the steps need to be taken
   - the deadlines for programmes to be completed, and working backwards, the deadlines for each step to be completed
   - which team member is going to be responsible for which programme items

   From this analysis, a realistic production schedule is drawn up.

   Using that schedule, individual members of the team draw up their own workplans for coming programmes.
3. A second programme can now be made by the team, with members of the team taking their proper roles, so that the process will be led by the team leader. The facilitator will take a hands-off, supervisory role, intervening only when necessary.

   Before the team start work on the second programme, the facilitator may want to go through *Handout J10.3: An aide-memoire on the principles of behaviour and social change factual programming*, with them.

Drama

Training Part 2

Module D1: A selection workshop for a serial drama project
Module D2: An introduction to the MARCH methodology for behaviour and social change serial dramas, and its application
Module D3: Scriptwriting a serial drama for behaviour change
Module D4: Production team and technician training for drama

Module D1: A selection workshop procedure for a serial drama project

This is a selection workshop for a team of writers and production staff for a serial drama. This outline is based on training for radio. It is appropriate for a selection process for television or social media as well, as it tests candidates on the selection criteria, but using a simpler technology than video.

Course objectives

For participants to:

- be given the opportunity to display the criteria set out in Handout D1.1 (below)

Materials

A topic for a single scene which is relevant to the project's drama

The three scenarios needed for Module D3 Session 1

Copies of all of the following handouts for each participant and the facilitator, or as PowerPoint slides. If PowerPoint is used, the facilitator needs to make sure there are also paper copies for any handouts which need to be completed by participants.

Handout D1.1: Selection criteria

- An ability to write entertaining and engaging drama, which improves over the period of the workshop

- A growing understanding of the principles of behaviour and social change drama, shown over the period of the workshop
- A strong aptitude for working in a team
- An ability and willingness to learn
- A strong aptitude for giving and receiving constructive criticism
- An ability to concentrate on the task in hand for prolonged periods
- An understanding of the values of the project and the organization running it
- An objective approach to the aims and content of the drama

Handout J1.1: How people learn

Handout J1.2: An aide-memoire to the theory

One of the drama's behaviour change objectives, with the associated barriers and facilitators and the relevant target audience
Table D2.1: Transitional character profile form
Handout D3.1: Possible definitions of dramatic conflict and dramatic action

Equipment

Flipcharts
Laptop and projector, if available
Laptops/tablets for participants

Agenda, training session 1: The selection criteria

1. The facilitator makes the introductions, and explains the aim of the workshop, which is to select a specified number of people to be the scriptwriting team for a serial drama aiming at behaviour and social change.
2. The facilitator gives out or displays on PowerPoint *Handout D1.1: Selection criteria* and discusses it for clarification. They give an explanation of the workshop structure and marking system, which is that candidates will be taught aspects of drama writing and will be marked on the work they produce. They will also be marked on how they conduct themselves in the workshop, especially in terms of teamwork and constructive criticism.

Agenda, training session 2: A theory of how people learn and its application in drama

1. The facilitator takes the candidates though *Module J1: An exploration of how people learn*.
2. The facilitator sets an individual writing task: Candidates are asked to write a scene on a specific topic in the drama, which will promote discussion among the audience.
   Candidates will be marked on:
   - their teamwork in the exercises
   - their demonstrated grasp of the day's learning

Agenda, training session 3: The basics of drama: conflict, action

1. The facilitator takes the candidates through *Module D3: Scriptwriting a serial drama for behaviour change, Session 1 – the basics of good drama writing*
2. Each candidate writes the synopsis of a scene on a specific topic in the drama. Each candidate displays or reads their synopsis out and the group discuss if there is conflict and if the scene is in action. If there is not, the group discuss how it can be changed so that there is.
   The facilitator gives a reminder of the need for constructive criticism.
3. Individual writing task: To write the scene they've written the synopsis for.
   Each displays or reads their scene out and the group discuss if the dialogue shows the conflict and action.
   If it does not, the group discuss how it be can be changed so that it does.
   Candidates will be marked on:
   • their grasp of the basics of drama and their ability to put them into practice
   • their ability and attitude in giving constructive criticism
   • their ability to apply constructive criticism to their work

Agenda, training session 3: Specialist considerations in writing drama for the medium being used

1. The facilitator explains the overall intention of this session is:
   • to look at the challenges of writing for either radio, television or social media
   • to look at solutions practically
   • to try writing a scene that will be effective in the medium being used
2. This could involve a pair repeatedly improvising a scene until it meets the criteria needed for effectively communicating it in the medium being used. The facilitator draws out – or, if the drama is on radio, uses the guidance given in Chapter 28 – the key issues that need to be addressed for the different media.
3. Individual writing task: Candidates revise the scene written in Session 2 to take account of the special needs of the media being used.
   Candidates will be marked on:
   • their grasp of the basics of drama and their ability to put them into practice
   • their grasp of the requirements of the medium being used

Agenda, training session 4: Writing collaboratively

1. The facilitator explains the overall intentions of session are:
   • to look at the need for collaborative writing
   • to see how it can work in practice
   • to evaluate individuals in their approach to collaborative writing
2. A practical exercise: In pairs, candidates swap the dialogues they revised in Session 3, and each reads the other's.
   Pairs discuss each script, agree changes and list changes each writer is going to make. Proposed changes should be on the basis of what has been taught already to make it better drama and more appropriate for the medium.

3. Each rewrites their dialogue incorporating agreed changes.
   Candidates will be marked on:
   - their grasp of what has been taught so far, as shown in their own revisions in Session 3, and in their suggestions for the revision of their partner's script
   - their ability and attitude in giving and receiving constructive criticism
   - their teamwork

Agenda, training session 5: Character development

1. The facilitator takes the candidates through Module D2, training session 3: Developing a transitional character.
2. Candidates work in groups of four. Each group is given a behaviour change objective and a set of barriers and facilitators, and information on the target audience for this character.
3. Each group develops a character profile, and presents it to the whole group, explaining their decisions.
   Candidates will be marked on:
   - their teamwork
   - their creative input into the character development sessions

Agenda, training session 6: Selection

After the final marks have been added up, the names of the successful candidates for the writing team are announced.

Module D2: An introduction to the MARCH methodology for behaviour and social change serial dramas, and its application

Course objectives

For participants to:

- understand the nature of behaviour change
- understand MARCH methodology
- be able to apply it in the development of a serial drama

Materials

Copies of the formative research or of a summary of the formative research
   A PowerPoint presentation summarizing MARCH methodology:

1. *MARCH* stands for *Modelling and Reinforcement to Combat HIV*, devised by the Centers for Disease Control in 2000.
   Since then, it has been used for other subjects than just HIV.

2. The project's behaviour change objectives.
3. MARCH dramas do not tell people what to do through messages. They show what to do through role modelling.
4. The role models are the transitional characters, and there is one transitional character for each behaviour change objective.
5. The drama consists of a number of transitional characters' storylines which run in parallel as each character struggles to achieve behaviour change.
6. MARCH dramas work by showing the audience why they need to change, what they need to change and how they can make those changes.
7. A key principle, which is shared between MARCH methodology and modern drama, is that of 'Show, don't tell'.
8. MARCH dramas deliver knowledge in dramatic contexts, in emotionally engaging scenes, which helps people absorb it.
9. MARCH dramas encourage audiences to talk, so as to help retention of learning and to bring about social change.
10. Social norm change is change in attitudes among the people around someone changing their behaviour. Social change seems to be necessary to sustain behaviour change.
11. So that a MARCH drama is based in reality, factors that get in the way of behaviour change, called barriers, and factors that help towards behaviour change, called facilitators, are identified from the formative research.
12. Barriers and facilitators are classified as:
    • personal
    • social
    • environmental
13. Personal factors are in the character's head or come from their individual characteristics: barriers are a lack of self-confidence, a feeling that they cannot make the change, or a lack of knowledge or skills.
14. Social factors are in the transitional character's immediate social circle: relationships and norms.
15. Environmental factors are those which the transitional character cannot control: like facilities, culture and the law.
16. The stages of change: there are five stages of behaviour change, and each transitional character may go through all five, or, say, start when they are already thinking about changing their behaviour or end when they have achieved the change, but have not yet sustained it.
17. Stage 1: Pre-contemplation – when the character is not thinking about his or her behaviour.
    Stage 2: Contemplation – when the character begins to think about his or her behaviour.
    Stage 3: Preparation – when the character is actively thinking about how to change his or her behaviour.
    Stage 4: Action – when the character is doing things to change his or her behaviour.
    Stage 5: Maintenance – when the character is sustaining the changed behaviour.

18. Setbacks: as a transitional character works their way through the stages of change, a setback will push them backwards, so that they go back to a stage of change they have already been through.
19. Supporting characters: for each transitional character there will be a network of supporting characters.
20. Supporting characters either:
    - help to expose the personal barriers and facilitators
    - are the social barriers and facilitators
    - are the route through which the environmental barriers and facilitators operate
    - are contrast models
21. Transitional characters can be supporting characters for other transitional characters, and supporting characters can be in different transitional characters' networks.
22. Often, different transitional characters represent different parts of the audience.
23. Different transitional characters' storylines will not all be the same length.
24. Once a transitional character has reached the behaviour change objective, that character tries to sustain their changed behaviour and either becomes a supporting character or starts on a new journey of behaviour change, or is written out of the drama after being shown sustaining the behaviour change for a period of time.

If the drama is continuing, usually a new transitional character with a new behaviour change objective takes over.

Materials

Copies of all of the following handouts for each participant and the facilitator, or as PowerPoint slides. If PowerPoint is used, the facilitator needs to make sure there are also paper copies for any handouts which need to be completed by participants.

Table D2.1 Transitional character profile form

Transitional character name:	
Behaviour change objective:	
Target audience segment:	
Age	
Gender	
Origins	
Why they are in the location	
Level of education	
Wealth	

Occupation	
Level of influence in the family	
Level of influence in the community	
Family	
Other social contacts	
Personal barriers	
Social barriers	
Environmental barriers	
Personal facilitators	
Social facilitators	
Environmental facilitators	
Setbacks	

Table D2.2 Supporting character profile form

Supporting character name:	
In these transitional characters' networks: 1. 2. 3.	

Age	
Gender	
Origins	
Why they are in the location	
Level of education	
Wealth	
Occupation	
Level of influence in the family	
Level of influence in the community	
Family	
Other social contacts	
Role in transitional character 1's network	Barrier/Facilitator (delete as needed) Details:
Role in transitional character 2's network	Barrier/Facilitator (delete as needed) Details:
Role in transitional character 3's network	Barrier/Facilitator (delete as needed) Details:

Equipment

A computer and projector
A flipchart and markers
Laptops for all participants

Agenda, training session 1: Personal experience of behaviour change

1. The facilitator makes the introductions and explains the purposes of the session:
   - exploring when participants have undergone behaviour change and the factors that influenced it, or inhibited it
   - the influence of other people's opinions and behaviour on that change
2. In pairs, each participant tells the other about a behaviour change that they have made.

Partners report back to the whole group.
After each, there is a brief discussion on what prompted and influenced the behaviour change.
Notes are made on a flipchart, to draw out where these accounts reflect characteristics of MARCH methodology.

Agenda, training session 2: Presentation on MARCH methodology

The facilitator goes through the PowerPoint presentation summarizing MARCH methodology. For each slide, the facilitator enlarges on the points made, based on the content of Chapters 27 and 28.

Agenda, training session 3: Developing a transitional character

If possible, it will be valuable to have one or more of the research team present.
    Participants work in groups of up to four.
    The first stage of this session may not be necessary if the researchers have already allocated barriers and facilitators to the specific behaviour change objectives the drama is dealing with.

1. Each group take one behaviour change objective with the intended target segment of the audience.
   From the summary of the formative research, each group identifies the barriers, facilitators and potential setbacks associated with their behaviour change objective.
   Groups classify the barriers and facilitators as personal, social or environmental.
   In plenary, groups present their classified lists of barriers and facilitators.
   The whole group review each list, judging if the selected barriers and facilitators are appropriate for the behaviour change objective, and if the classifications are correct.
   Groups revise their lists as necessary.

2. The facilitator takes the participants through *Table D2.1: Transitional character profile form*, explaining why each box is there, and what needs to be written in each one.

Notes for facilitators on the transitional character profile form

Overall

A character's status within their family and in the community is likely to have a substantial impact on how easy it is for them to change their behaviour. A character with lower status is probably going to find it more difficult, as higher status individuals may have some level of control over the lower status character's behaviour.

How a character has gained the status they have may also be a significant factor. If a character's relatively high status comes from the behaviour that needs to be changed, it is likely they will find it harder to change the behaviour as it risks losing status.

It is for these reasons that a number of entries in the profile are about status and levels of influence.

Origins

If the target audience is made up of a number of different cultures, or is spread across different regions, it is usually helpful in gaining an audience across those cultures or regions to have characters who are representative of the cultures or regions.

If the character has come from a different place to where the drama is set, that may affect their relationships and influence in the family and community.

Why they are in the location

The reason why the character has come to live in the drama's location may affect their social status. If, for example, they are there because they have arrived by marriage, they may have a different status than if they have been displaced by conflict from their place of origin.

Wealth

A character with a low level of wealth is likely to find behaviour change more difficult, as poverty is likely to throw up more environmental barriers.

Occupation

In radio drama it is a good idea for the team to choose occupations that have an associated characteristic sound, partly because it lends additional richness to the drama's soundscape and partly because it makes it easier for listeners to identify characters quickly.

Family and other social contacts

At this stage, these two boxes cannot be completed. They need to be completed once the transitional character's network of supporting characters has been worked out.

3. Groups develop their transitional character using the character profile form.
   In general, the characteristics they choose should make the achievement of the behaviour change objective as difficult as possible. This will be an initial effort, as the profile is likely to be modified as other elements of the drama, particularly the universe, are developed.
4. In plenary, groups present their character profiles, explaining their thinking. The whole group reviews each profile, particularly assessing whether the character is likely to be appealing to the intended target audience segment and whether the profile is consistent.

Groups revise their profiles as necessary.

Agenda, training session 4: Developing a supporting character network

1. The facilitator should remind the participants of Slide 20 in the PowerPoint presentation summarizing MARCH methodology, on the functions of supporting characters. Supporting characters either:
   • help to expose the personal barriers and facilitators
   • are the social barriers and facilitators
   • are the route through which the environmental barriers and facilitators operate
   • are contrast models
2. The facilitator sets the groups the task of developing a network of supporting characters for the transitional character they have just developed. The network, at this stage, should be no more than eight characters. Each character can embody more than one barrier or facilitator, and the barriers and facilitators can be embodied in more than one supporting character. The network should embody all of the barriers and facilitators identified for the transitional character, in the functions shown above.
   At this stage, it is the network that is being developed, so individual supporting character profile forms do not need to be completed.
3. In plenary, each group presents the network it has developed, outlining the relationship each supporting character has with the transitional character.
   The whole group reviews each network, particularly assessing whether it represents all of the barriers and facilitators identified, and whether it looks as if it might contribute to a compelling drama.
4. The whole group looks at all of the networks and work out where supporting characters from different networks can be merged, including where transitional characters can be supporting characters in another network. This is to keep the number of characters to a minimum.
5. Once the whole character list has been agreed, the facilitator takes the participants through *Table D2.2: Supporting character profile form*.
   The groups add the details of family and social circle to the transitional character profiles.

Training Module D3: Scriptwriting a serial drama for behaviour change

This is a suggested training course for a serial drama scriptwriting team, though for some sessions the writing team can be joined by other individuals or groups, as suggested for each session.

The training outline is based on the assumption that the writing team will already have completed *Training Module D2: An introduction to the MARCH methodology for behaviour and social change serial dramas, and its application.*

The course and materials are for writing audio drama, but can be readily adapted to visual media.

Course objectives

For participants to:

- be able to develop a universe for the drama, which poses significant barriers for the transitional characters in the achievement of their behaviour change objectives
- be able to develop engaging and entertaining long transitional character storylines, following MARCH methodology
- be able to develop engaging and entertaining episode-by-episode storylines, exploiting fully the characteristics of conflict, action, tension and 'Show, don't tell'
- be able to write engaging and entertaining dialogue, at the same time exploiting to the full the resources offered by the medium the project is using for dramatic impact

Materials

Copies of all of the character profiles
A map of the region or country the project is taking place in, displayed where all participants can see it.
The universe map (once it has been produced)
Figure 27.2 A diagram showing the five stages of change used in the MARCH behaviour change methodology (see Chapter 27).
Long storylines (when completed)
Character timelines chart (when completed)
Examples of audio drama scenes demonstrating movement around the microphone

Scenarios prepared by the facilitator

The facilitator needs to have prepared three scenarios for a pair of participants to improvise. The scenarios should reflect a key theme of the drama the team are being trained to write.

The three scenarios will be the following.

1. A scenario with no conflict or action. One character is explaining or describing something to the other, who understands and agrees with what is being explained or described.

If the team are being trained to write a health drama, this could be one mother of a young baby explaining to another that she has a leaflet announcing that, sometime soon, an NGO is visiting where they live to vaccinate children against the major childhood life-threatening diseases. The mother who has read the leaflet gives a brief summary of what it says, and the two agree that the NGO visit is a good thing.

2. A scenario in which there is conflict, but no action. The characters argue, in principle, but nothing happens.

Following the example, the mother in the first scenario who was being told about the forthcoming but unspecified NGO vaccination visit is with her husband. She says she thinks it will be a good thing, in principle, to get their new baby vaccinated. The husband disagrees, in principle, arguing against vaccination. He may cite whatever is the current and most compelling case being circulated in society against vaccination. The facilitator does not need to explain the case to be made on either side. The point is just to demonstrate dramatic conflict.

3. A scenario which is in action and in which there is conflict. One character is trying to do something concrete, and the other is trying to stop them, because they believe that what the first character is trying to do is wrong in some way.

Following the example, it is close to the end of the last day of the NGO doing vaccinations. The mother is taking the baby out of the door to get it vaccinated. The husband tries to stop her, because he disagrees with vaccination. The scene has to end with the baby being taken to be vaccinated or not.

A selection of recordings of possible background sounds which are hard to distinguish.

Practical sound effects (for the suggested scenario, these will be a piece of wood, some nails and a hammer).

Copies of all of the following handouts for each participant and the facilitator, or as PowerPoint slides. If PowerPoint is used, the facilitator needs to make sure there are also paper copies for any handouts which need to be completed by participants.

Handout D3.1: Possible definitions of dramatic conflict and dramatic action

Dramatic conflict

The basis of all good drama is conflict. Storylines should be driven by conflict, and each scene should have conflict.
- Conflict does not always mean violence or even shouting.
- Conflict arises when the different characters are trying to achieve different goals and they struggle with one another to achieve their goals.

Dramatic action

Everything that happens between characters in a drama should be action; that is, characters should be doing something, not just talking about something.

For example, a scene in which two characters are discussing whether an NGO should come to their village to vaccinate children is not in action. A scene in which one character is trying to take their child to be vaccinated, and another character is trying to stop them, is in action.

Action means the scene has an outcome. Audiences are more likely to pay attention if they know there is going to be an outcome to a scene but do not know what it is going to be.

Table D3.1 A character timeline chart

Ep	TX date	Events	Season	TC 1	TC 2	TC 3	TC 4	TC 5	TC 6

The Ep column is the episode number. TX date means the transmission date. The Events column lists pre-determined external events, like festivals and holidays. Season means the season, as it affects weather and activities. TC is transitional character, and each box will contain the numbers of events in their long storylines. The episode in which they move from one stage of change to another is noted here.

Handout D3.2: Annotated scene description example

(Please note that this is a fictional example for an illustrative purpose only.)

This is a sample scene description from a drama promoting behaviour change with regard to HIV, in the storyline of Kayama. He is a transitional character who is HIV positive but has not revealed his status. His behaviour change objective is to achieve healthy living, including revealing his HIV status and adhering to medication.

The annotated scene description might be like this.

Kayama is in Shek's Bar, with Mubita and Libongani. They are celebrating Mubita's very successful sale of cattle. Mubita pressures Kayama to have another whisky. Kayama refuses but Mubita and Libongani tell him that this is an important occasion; Mubita is paying and it looks bad for Kayama to refuse. Unable to explain why he should not drink too much, Kayama accepts the whisky.

Social barrier: 42 per cent of HIV+ interviewees cited alcohol as a cause for people on anti-retroviral therapy to miss their medication (Project formative research, 2016).

Handout D3.3: A definition of visualization

Visualization is picturing the place where the scene is happening, what the characters are doing and what they might have with them, trying to identify every detail.

Handout D3.4: Writing a scene synopsis

A scene synopsis should include:
- the scene's location
- the characters in the scene
- the activities any of the characters are doing at the beginning or during the scene (perhaps their work, cooking, cleaning, etc. bearing in mind the season)
- the sound effects that will be used in the scene, and where they will be used, again, bearing in mind the season
- a detailed description of what happens in the scene as the conflict and action are played out
- where the characters are in relation to the microphone at the beginning of the scene
- how the characters will move throughout the scene, and how these moves are intended to help the audience to understand what is happening in the scene

When working out a scene it is important to remember that a scene does not need to start with the characters meeting and greeting each other, nor end with them parting.

Handout D3.5: Writing for audio drama

As you listen to each version of the same scene, fill in the answers to these questions as fully as you can.

Version 1

Dialogue Does the dialogue sound natural and believable? Yes/No

Who?

What are the people in the scene called? _____

What is the relationship between them? _____
(e.g. mother and daughter)

Where?

Where is the scene taking place? _____
(Be specific: if it's in a home, whose home?)

When?

At what time of day is the scene taking place? _____

Version 2

Dialogue Does the dialogue sound natural and believable? Yes/No

Who?

What are the people in the scene called? _____

What is the relationship between them? _____
(e.g. mother and daughter)

Where?

Where is the scene taking place?   _____
(Be specific: if it's in a home, whose home?)

When?

At what time of day is the scene taking place?   _____

Version 3

Dialogue Does the dialogue sound natural and believable? Yes/No

Who?

What are the people in the scene called?   _____

What is the relationship between them?   _____
(e.g. mother and daughter)

Where?

Where is the scene taking place?   _____
(Be specific: if it's in a home, whose home?)

When?

At what time of day is the scene taking place?   _____

Version 4

Dialogue Does the dialogue sound natural and believable? Yes/No

Who?

What are the people in the scene called?   _____

What is the relationship between them?   _____
(e.g. mother and daughter)

Where?

Where is the scene taking place?   _____
(Be specific: if it's in a home, whose home?)

When?

At what time of day is the scene taking place?   _____

Handout D3.6: Sound effects

In audio drama, sound effects help to build the audience's belief in the drama, as they help it to sound more realistic.

Sound effects are either mixed after the voices have been recorded, when they are called pre-recorded effects, or recorded at the same time as the voices, when they are called practical effects.

Sound effects are of two types: background sounds and sounds of activities.

Background sounds

When voices are recorded in a studio, there is no sound with them, because studios are soundproof.

However, people are virtually never in silence, there is almost always sound in the background and so, depending on what the location of a scene is supposed to be, an appropriate background sound is added.

Activities sounds

When people are doing things, those activities almost always make a noise. For the drama to have credibility, those sounds need to be heard as the character is doing whatever the activity is.

These effects are often made by the actors, so that, for example, when a character is digging, the speech is in time with the sound effect.

It is the writer's responsibility to work out what sounds should be heard at different times in the scenes, and to write the instructions into the script.

Sound effects instructions usually look like this:

1. FX: BUSY STREET BACKGROUND

However, humans are poor at sound recognition, and, in most cases, unless a sound is very distinctive, they will not instantly recognize what a sound effect is. Dialogue should, therefore, contain subtle hints of what any sound effect is:

1. FX: BUSY STREET BACKGROUND
2. CATERINA   Where are all these people going?

Handout D3.7: 'Talk as you walk' in audio drama

So that listeners can hear the characters in the drama moving, the actors need to be speaking as they move towards or away from the microphone.

Footsteps are not a good solution. Natural footsteps can rarely be heard, and adding pre-recorded footsteps in post-production is a very fiddly and time-consuming task, because if one character's footsteps can be heard, then all characters' footsteps need to be audible.

When writers put movement instructions into the script, they need to provide lines for the actor to speak as they move, and the lines need to be long enough for the actor to speak all the time they are moving.

If the approach to the microphone an actor is going to make is quite long, a few words will not be enough. For example:

1. FX   HOSPITAL BACKGROUND
2. ANGELO   (Approaching the mic) Good morning.

An actor could only take one or two steps while saying, 'Good morning'. So, more words need to be in the script to allow for a longer approach:

1. FX   HOSPITAL BACKGROUND
2. ANGELO   (Approaching the mic) Good morning. Am I in the right place for an X-ray?

Handout D3.8: Dramatic tension and weaponizing exposition

Dramatic tension

- Dramatic tension is created by withholding information from the listener, letting them know just enough to understand but no more.
- It keeps listeners listening, because of the sense of mystery.

Weaponizing exposition

- Exposition is a character explaining what has happened in the past that has led to the present situation, or describing the present situation, for the benefit of the audience.
- Exposition should be kept to a minimum, as it holds up the action.
- Wherever possible, exposition should be turned into a weapon by one of the characters to help them win the conflict.

Handout D3.9: Evaluation criteria

The scenes are assessed against the following criteria.
- Are they entertaining, engaging drama?
- Is there conflict?
- Is the scene in action?
- Is there dramatic tension?
- Does the who, where, when, what is happening work?
- Is there good use of movement clearly set out in the script?
- Is exposition weaponized?
- Are there appropriate sound effects?

Equipment

Flipcharts for each pair of the drama writing team
Different coloured markers
Audio equipment with a small, low-quality loudspeaker
A microphone, not connected, on a stand, or something representing a microphone, which does not need to be able to record

Agenda, training session 1: The basics of good drama

Participants

Writing team
1. The facilitator can conduct a training needs assessment by simply asking the participants what they think are the characteristics of a good drama. On the basis of the responses, the facilitator may decide there is no need for the session, or decide there is a need for the session.
2. If the facilitator decides that a session on dramatic conflict and dramatic action is necessary, without explaining what the session is going to be about, the facilitator asks for two volunteers who will act out a scene.

The facilitator gives the volunteers the first scenario, as described above, in the Materials section, without letting the rest of the group hear. It may be necessary to emphasize that there should be no conflict, as participants sometimes introduce conflict. The volunteers are given a few minutes to prepare and then they perform the scene.

3. A different pair of volunteers is chosen, and the process repeated with the second scenario, which has conflict in it.

   The facilitator discusses with the participants which of the two scenarios was the most engaging. Almost always, participants say the second.

4. Another pair follow the process improvising the third scenario, which has conflict and is in action.

   The facilitator discusses with the participants which scenario was the most engaging. Almost always, groups rate the last as the most engaging and the second as more engaging than the first. The facilitator leads a discussion on what the third one had that the second did not, and what the second one had that the first did not.

5. The facilitator teases out the conclusion that the second had conflict and the third had conflict and action. The facilitator gives a definition of each and emphasizes their central role in drama of any kind. They may want to use *Handout D3.1: Possible definitions of dramatic conflict and dramatic action*, above, or display it.

Agenda, training session 2: The development of a universe

Participants

Writing team

1. The facilitator explains what a drama's universe is: the place or places that all the characters live in.

   The aim of the session is to produce a map and a written description of the universe for the drama that the team are going to write, so that writers are consistent in where characters live and work in relation to each other.

   The facilitator highlights that, in a behaviour change drama, the universe is often designed to make the achievement of the transitional characters' behaviour change objectives as difficult as possible. This is so that the environmental barriers faced in real life by people in the worst situations are addressed.

   In some cases, the location and type of the universe are obvious and there is no reason to follow the process set out here, or even part of it.

2. From the character profiles, the participants read out where the different characters come from, and those locations are listed on a flipchart.

   Using the map of the region or country, the facilitator leads a discussion on where in the country people from those different backgrounds could live together. The options are listed on a flipchart.

3. The facilitator asks the participants to identify all the environmental barriers and facilitators offered by the physical universe, that is, physical things like facilities or the lack of them, but not the law or culture. These are noted on a flipchart.

   The facilitator leads a discussion looking at the options for location already written, to identify which of them, if any, present the physical environmental barriers and facilitators listed. Any that would not are crossed out.

4. The participants are asked to identify the occupations of the transitional characters, which are listed, and there is discussion on which of the listed locations would house those different occupations. Any that would not are crossed out.

5. A final choice of location is made on the basis of the one that would offer the toughest environmental barriers to the transitional characters' behaviour change. If no location can offer the mix of characters with different origins, their physical environmental barriers and facilitators, and their occupations, then adjustments need to be made to the details of the character profiles so that a credible location can be identified.

6. Working in pairs, the participants identify what kind of a place the universe would be, taking into account all the factors so far discussed, and construct a case for their choice. Depending on the region or country, the options might be a village, an urban area of a town, a slum area of a big city or a displacement camp. It might be a split location, perhaps between rural and urban, or between city slum and city suburban, for example, but with connections made by one or more of the transitional characters.

    Each pair presents their proposal and their justification for it.

    If pairs come up with different proposals, then there is discussion and either a choice is made of one proposal or a combination of one or more of the proposals put forward.

7. With the location and the type of place decided, working in plenary and, again, taking into account the factors considered so far, the participants discuss and decide on the characteristics of the universe, and they are written on a flipchart or, preferably, recorded on a laptop by a scribe. These characteristics need to be credible to the type of place and its location. Characteristics might be some or all of the following:

    • the governance of the place, now taking into account the other, non-physical environmental barriers and facilitators

    • the availability of special facilities relevant to the topic of the drama, like hospitals, specialist clubs or agricultural resources and advice, the distance to them and the available transport

    • the facilities immediately available for daily life, like shops, water supply, latrines, waste disposal, schools, economic opportunities, social spaces and religious places

    • the problems the location presents, like threats to health or lack of security

    • size of the population

    • the dominant economic features

    • the dominant cultural features, including people like traditional healers or fortune tellers, cultural events, customs or rituals

    • the nature of dwellings

    Outside the training, these points will serve to create a narrative description that will be readily available to all of the writing team over the lifetime of the drama, alongside the universe map.

8. The facilitator or one of the participants will draft a map on a flipchart sheet, or on a computer, using drawing software, from the participants' suggestions.

The process should start with locating key physical features, like roads and rivers, and then key facilities for daily life, like banks, shops and markets, transport facilities, water supply, social and religious places and schools.

9. The next step is placing the living and occupational places of the transitional characters, making sure that the locations pose a mix of authentic barriers and facilitators to their behaviour change, for example, the presence of risk settings, such as bars, as well as supportive facilities, such as a clinic. It is often the practice for the universe to be designed to make the transitional characters' behaviour change as difficult as possible, by including environmental barriers which are hard to overcome. This is so that the characters' situations represent the worst possible case.

10. Once these are in place, the living and occupational locations of the supporting characters are put in place, again with an authentic mix of infrastructure-related

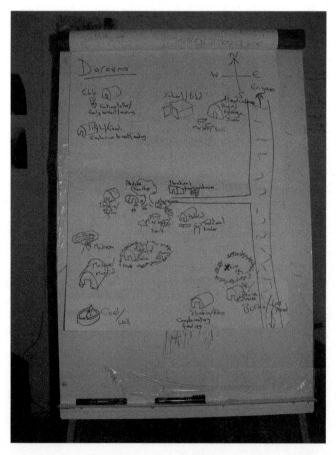

Figure D3.1 *The original draft universe map for a MARCH drama in Somalia. Normally, the working version is developed from the draft by a professional artist. The British Broadcasting Corporation (BBC), 2012*

barriers and facilitators. It may be, for example, that a supporting character, who is an important facilitator for a transitional character, lives somewhere inaccessible to the transitional character.

At this stage, the character profiles may need adjustment to ensure that they form a coherent whole with the universe.

11. Outside the training, the universe map can be professionally drawn, faithfully representing the flipchart or the computer-drawn draft.

Agenda, training session 3: The development of long storylines

Participants

Writing team
Production team
Research team
Cultural and technical advisors
Note: While this outline suggests that the participants work in pairs, the facilitator may prefer to run all the sessions as whole group. This gives the facilitator greater control over the development of the storylines, and more opportunities for intervening if the group get stuck for ideas.

1. The facilitator introduces the concept of the long storylines. Each long storyline is the sequence of events that takes a transitional character from not even thinking about their behaviour through all the stages of change to the achievement of the behaviour change objective.

   Working in pairs, each pair of participants is allocated one or more of the transitional characters, and their task is to work out the duration of each long storyline for those characters.

   In doing this, they need to take into consideration the following:
   - any events that have a fixed timescale – for example, if the character needs to conceive and give birth during the behaviour change trajectory, that is nine months
   - if the change has to happen within a set time because of external factors
   - how difficult the behaviour change is going to be

   If there are many barriers, or if the barriers are going to be very difficult to overcome, the storyline is going to be long. For example, if one of the barriers is the character's own identity, that is going to be difficult to overcome. If the character has little influence in their family and community, that is going to lengthen the storyline.

   Pairs need to work out the duration and put together their case for that duration, with key points listed on a flipchart sheet.

2. Each pair presents their proposed duration and their supporting case. The whole group discuss the case, based on the following questions.
   - Have the pair taken into account all the factors affecting the duration?
   - Have they correctly judged the difficulty of making the change?

The whole group decide on the duration of each long storyline.

3. The facilitator introduces the concept of the key storyline events, which are the events that take the transitional character from one stage of change to the next. These events are likely to be the overcoming of a barrier. The first one, which takes the character from not thinking to thinking, could be an accidental event, but after that they need to be acts of will on the character's part, and not accidents or events led by another character.

4. The facilitator introduces the concept of the setback. This is a one-off event that deters the transitional character from their behaviour change and makes them drop back through the stages of change. If a setback is severe enough, it can even take the character right back to the beginning.

   The task for each pair is twofold.

   The first part is to develop two or three setbacks for their transitional character, working out how many stages of change each one takes the character back.

   The second part is to develop key events that take the character from each stage of change to the next, both initially and after each setback. Each event should have conflict and be in action. Event descriptions should be two or three sentences.

5. In plenary, each pair presents the sequence of key events and setbacks in chronological order. The rest of the participants judge the events on the basis of the following criteria.

   • Are all the key events acts of will on the part of the transitional character?
   • Are they all overcoming a barrier?
   • Are the setbacks appropriate to the character and the behaviour change?
   • Has the severity of the setbacks been judged correctly?
   • Are the key events significant enough to take the character from one stage of change to the next?
   • Do the key events make sense in the order they are in?
   • Do the key events have conflict and are they in action?

   Depending on the answers to all these questions, pairs revise their setbacks and key events.

6. The facilitator asks each pair to work out how many episodes their character's long storyline is going to take, and then to work out, approximately, in which episode each of their key storyline events is going to take place. Pairs need to allow for time taken in the character recovering from setbacks. (These figures will not be exact because at a later stage, the storylines need to be coordinated with each other.)

7. The facilitator introduces the concept of the driving conflict or conflicts. These are ongoing conflicts between their transitional character and other characters, which drive the storyline. They will come from the relationships between the transitional character and different characters in their network of supporting characters. There could be different conflicts at different stages of the storyline.

   Pairs look at the character profiles of the transitional character and the characters in the supporting network, and develop a set of driving conflicts. The conflicts should relate to the behaviour change objective of the transitional character. For each conflict, they need to work out:

- what each character is trying to achieve that brings them into conflict (in one or two storylines, the team may want tragic events that set off the conflict)
- which other characters are involved in the conflict, why they are and how they are
- how the conflict manifests itself in action and in the emotions of the characters

In plenary, pairs present their ideas for driving conflicts. The other participants judge the presented conflicts on their credibility and propose alternative ideas for any thought not to be credible.

8. The facilitator sets up the next task, which is for each pair to work out the events that will happen in their character's storyline between the start of the drama and the key event that takes the character into the thinking stage. Events should be driven by the driving conflicts. The number of events should be roughly the same as the number of episodes, as previously worked out.

    In plenary, each pair presents their initial storyline events. The whole group assess them on the following criteria.

    - Do they tell a coherent story?
    - Are they driven by conflict?
    - Does each event have conflict and is it in action?
    - Are the events the basis for compelling drama?

    Pairs revise their storyline events as necessary.

    This training sequence is repeated for each series of events as each transitional character goes from one stage of change to the next, including those after setbacks.

    In this way, all the transitional characters' long storylines are developed.

9. The facilitator introduces *Table D3.1: A character timeline chart*. This exercise is best carried out using a computer, as it is extremely fiddly and difficult to do on a flipchart. The purpose of this chart is discussed in Chapter 28. The intention is that the table will be extended with additional rows.

    Pairs are asked to count the number of events in their character's long storyline in which the character interacts with another transitional character. The events in the storyline of the transitional character with the most interactions with other transitional characters are plotted in one column of the chart.

    A second long storyline is plotted in a column, and events are moved up or down the column so that the events when the two characters meet are in the right place in both of the storylines. This does not mean the order of events is changed but simply that gaps are put into the storylines.

    A third storyline is plotted, and all of the columns are adjusted so that interactions between the third character and Character 1 correspond, and with Character 2 correspond. This is repeated until all the transitional character storylines are on the chart, and all scenes between transitional characters correspond.

    Where there are gaps in the timeline, that is, episodes that do not have scenes for some of the transitional characters, the relevant pairs devise new scenes to fit.

Agenda, training session 4: Episode-by-episode storylining

Participants

Writing team
Production team
Research team
Cultural and technical advisers

1. The facilitator sets out the aim of the session: To produce three months' episode-by-episode storylines.
   In the same pairs as in previous sessions, each pair looks at the season that Episode 1 is to be broadcast in, and work out how it may affect the occupational and other activities of the transitional character and their supporting characters. Pairs look at any real external events that may be happening at the time Episode 1 is broadcast, or that are coming up in the weeks following Episode 1, to work out if any of the characters will be involved in the event or in preparation for it. These might be religious events or national celebrations, for example.
2. In plenary, pairs present their work, and the whole group are asked to make suggestions for how seasonal and external event effects might affect where scenes are set, and how the effects can be shown in the scenes in Episode 1. These suggestions are recorded by the pair whose work is under discussion.
   Pairs develop the scenes for their transitional character for Episode 1, as allocated in the character timelines, working in this new information.
3. Using the character profiles, pairs then annotate each of their transitional character's scenes in Episode 1 with information on the barriers and/or facilitators that are operating in the scene, including citing the source of the information.
   The facilitator may wish to give an example, using *Handout D3.2: Annotated scene description example* printed or on a presentation slide.
4. These further developed descriptions of the scenes are copied from the long storylines to a new document: the episode-by-episode storyline. The whole group work out which scene looks the most appropriate to end with a dilemma, or at least a cliffhanger. That scene is selected as the last in the episode. If scenes need to take place at particular times of the day, they are put in chronological order. Otherwise, scenes are organized so that adjacent scenes are contrasting, with, say, a lively scene following a more sedate one.
5. The pattern of this session is repeated for all the episodes the project wishes to develop at this stage, producing a long document of the combined storylines, episode by episode. The facilitator needs to point out that the final scenes of episodes need to be in a cycle, so that, over a number of episodes, all the transitional character storylines have an episode-ending dilemma scene.

Agenda, training session 5: The role of positioning and movement in audio drama

It is appropriate, at this stage, to explore the use of movement around the microphone in audio drama, since it is introduced in the scene synopsis, which is the next stage of writing. (There is a full discussion of movement in Chapter 28.)

1. If possible, the facilitator should play some sample audio drama scenes which show movement in use.
   From these the facilitator can bring out the different functions movement has in helping the listener understand:
   - the story, that is, what is happening, by showing, for example, a character coming into or leaving a scene, or moving as they do their work
   - the struggle for control between characters, by, for example, one slowly approaching the microphone as they gain more control, while the other character retreats from it, as they lose control
   - the emotion in a scene, when, for example, two characters show their affection for each other by both moving closer to the microphone
   If such audio examples are not available, the facilitator could devise three scenarios related to the drama the writers are being trained for:
   - one in which one character is arriving home after some time away, and approaches the microphone as they enter the house
   - one in which, somehow, a character who starts the scene in control of the situation gradually loses control to another character
   - a couple have had a row, but are getting over it and are trying to get back on good terms with each other
   Different participants improvise these scenarios, and the facilitator then records the improvisations, first without movement, and then introducing appropriate movement.
2. Participants can then listen to the recordings and judge if the movement helps the listener understand, in the three cases: what is happening, the struggle for control and the emotion.

Agenda, training session 6: Scene synopsis development

Participants

Writing team
Given that the writing team is going to be smaller than the group that has been in the training up to this point, the tasks in this and following sessions might need to be individual, rather than in pairs.

1. The facilitator introduces the session with an explanation of what a scene synopsis is and the reasons for writing them. This is the stage when the writers work out the details of a scene and describe the scene as a narrative. A synopsis will normally be about half a page long. The stage is needed because it is easier to work out the structure and shape of a scene in a narrative than it is to go straight to the dialogue, and it is easier to review synopses than dialogues.
2. The next step – visualization – only needs to be done if the project is a radio drama, as a television drama will have a storyboard to accompany the synopsis. The facilitator asks three volunteers to improvise a scene set in a hospital. Two of the characters are teenage girls who are good friends. One of them is in a hospital ward being treated for injuries. The other is visiting her. The injured girl's mother

is with them. The mother starts to tell the visitor that her daughter got injured in an accident. The daughter angrily interrupts and tells her mother that the friend already knows that that is not true, and that she was injured by her father's violence. She says she wants to go to the police and wants her friend to go with her. The mother does not want the police involved, because she is terrified of the impact on the family, if the father goes to prison.

The facilitator gives the three a few minutes to work out the scene.

They perform the scene.

3. If the scene is performed with the mother constantly asking her daughter to keep her voice down or not to talk about the violence when other patients might hear, then the facilitator can say that it is a well-visualized scene, and go on to discuss visualization, skipping the next step.

   If the scene is performed at a normal conversational level, and no reference is made to their conversation being overheard, then the facilitator asks the group to visualize the scene. If they do not realize that there are other people close by, the facilitator asks what is all round these three characters. (The answer is a lot of beds with patients in them, and visitors around them.)

   The facilitator can ask the three who performed the scene to try it out again, this time taking account of the visualization.

   Once done, the facilitator can discuss the differences in the scenes, which illustrates how important visualization can be. For some scenes, though, it will not make any difference.

4. The facilitator gives out *Handout D3.3: A definition of visualization* and discusses it for clarification.

   In the same pairs, each pair takes a scene from Episode 1 that they are going to write and visualizes it, taking note of what they discover from the exercise and working out how they think what they have found will affect the scene.

   Pairs present what they have found from the visualization exercise. The whole group assesses whether the findings are accurate, and whether the proposal on how they will affect the scene is appropriate.

   Pairs revise their findings as necessary.

5. The facilitator introduces the concept of a scene synopsis for a radio drama and what needs to be in it, using *Handout D3.4: Writing a scene synopsis*.

   Following these guidelines, pairs draft a synopsis of the scene from Episode 1 that they have already visualized. The synopsis should include the seasonal and external event effects already identified, and any findings from the visualization.

6. Pairs present their draft synopses.

   The whole group reviews each synopsis against these criteria.
   - It includes everything the storyline requires, the seasonal and external event effects and anything the visualization found.
   - It has conflict and is in action, in line with the storyline description.
   - The scene will spend more time exploiting the conflict than in small talk and setting up.

   After the review, pairs revise synopses as necessary.

Agenda, training session 7: Dialogue writing for radio

Participants

Writing team

This session explores techniques for writers to get over the information, in the first thirty seconds of a scene, that listeners to radio drama need in order to understand the scene. This is: who the characters are and the relationship between them; where the scene is taking place; if it is important, the time of day, and what is happening between the characters.

1. Without explaining what the exercise is for, the facilitator briefs two volunteers on a short scene they are going to improvise. One is the mother, the other a son or daughter. The scene is the son or daughter arriving home after being away for several months. As soon as the character arrives, they sense something is wrong but they do not know what. The pair are only going to improvise the first thirty seconds or so of the scene.
   The facilitator asks the pair to go out of the room to prepare their scene.
2. While they are doing that, the facilitator gets all the other participants to turn their chairs round, so that the pair will be acting their scene to everyone else's backs. The participants are told not to turn round to look at the scene.
   They are each given a copy of *Handout D3.5: Writing for radio drama*. The facilitator should highlight the first question, about the dialogue sounding natural. This is very important as, sometimes, writers use artificial language to get the information across.
3. The facilitator calls in the pair who are going to improvise the scene, and they perform for about thirty seconds. The other participants complete the Version 1 section of the form. The facilitator leads a discussion on what the audience could and could not understand. If the audience did not understand all the information asked for, the facilitator asks the improvising pair to go out of the room again to try to revise the scene so that all the information is there.
4. They return and perform the scene again, and the audience record their reactions in the Version 2 section of the handout.
   This procedure is repeated until the scene contains all of the information and is in natural language.
5. The facilitator discusses which techniques the improvising pair used to get the information across without sounding artificial. The facilitator then leads on to asking the participants what other techniques could work. (This is a cultural issue. In some cultures, it is normal, for example, for people to use each other's names in conversation, while in other cultures, that sounds artificial. In many cultures, endearments are a useful way of showing a relationship. However, while some cultures have endearments which are very specific about relationships, like, 'my daughter', others do not. So, endearments are not always going to work.)
6. Pairs or individuals are given the task of writing the first 30 seconds of their scene for Episode 1.

One by one the openings of Episode 1 scenes are read out, and assessed by the other participants, on the same criteria as in the earlier exercise.

Pairs or individuals revise their scene openings as necessary.

Agenda, training session 8: Sound effects and movement instructions for audio drama scripts

Participants

Writing team
Audio engineer

Equipment

Audio equipment with a small, low-quality loudspeaker

A microphone, not connected, on a stand, or something representing a microphone, which does not need to be able to record

A piece of wood, some nails and a hammer

1. The facilitator introduces the topic of sound effects and plays a pair of background effects which are similar, using a small, low-quality loudspeaker. There is a discussion on what the sounds are.

   If the participants cannot identify the sounds correctly, the point has been made that listeners need prompts in the dialogue which subtly tell the listener what the sound is.

   If they can identify the sounds, then the facilitator can discuss where and how the audience will be listening to the drama. Some of the examples will be in places with high background sounds. So the facilitator can pose the question of whether a listener in such a place will be able to make out what the sounds are.

2. This is a suggestion for an improvisation showing the value of recording practical effects with the voices. The facilitator can use any practical effects and devise a scenario using them. If the training can be conducted outside, digging with a mattock would be a good alternative, for example.

   The facilitator asks two volunteers to improvise a scene, without practical effects, so it will just be the dialogue. The improvisers should not attempt to make any sound effects. One character is a householder, the other, a carpenter who has come to do some repairs. The carpenter is in a hurry because they have another job to get to. The householder is very fussy and keeps warning the carpenter to be careful and not to rush.

   The pair then perform the same scene again but, this time, the carpenter character uses wood, nails and a hammer.

   After the second improvisation, the facilitator asks the participants if it would be better to record the scene without sound effects and mix the effects later, or to record the scene with the actors using practical effects.

   The facilitator hands out or presents *Handout D3.6: Sound effects*, and discusses it with the participants.

4. The facilitator reminds the participants that their scripts need to include movement instructions, and introduces the concept of 'Talk as you walk'. The facilitator may illustrate the point by setting up a microphone, or a substitute for one, in the training room and showing that, for example, just saying 'Good morning' is not enough for a character to come into a scene and get to the microphone.
The facilitator hands out or presents *Handout D3.7: 'Talk as you walk' in audio drama*, and discusses it with the participants.

5. Pairs or individuals continue the script they have written the opening for, and draft their whole scene, following their synopsis, and including sound effect and movement instructions, and taking account of the need for 'Talk as you walk'.

6. Scripts are circulated and participants judge whether:
   - the backgrounds suggested are appropriate
   - the sound effect references in the dialogue are both useful and subtle
   - the practical effects proposed are appropriate and practical
   - the movement instructions are clear
   - enough dialogue has been written for 'Talk as you walk'

Agenda, training session 9: Dramatic tension and weaponizing exposition

Participants

Writing team

Materials

Copies of all drafted scripts for each participant

1. When the participants' scripts have been drafted, the facilitator introduces the idea of dramatic tension, giving out or presenting, if necessary, *Handout D3.8: Dramatic tension and weaponizing exposition*.

2. Each writer looks at their own script to see if there is any information about what is happening or about to happen that could be withheld until later in the scene, or even held over to a later scene or episode.

3. The group as a whole look at and discuss each script in turn, with the writer proposing their ideas about information that could be withheld. Agreement is reached on each script.
   Writers of the relevant scripts take the information out.

4. The facilitator introduces the idea of weaponizing exposition, using *Handout D3.8: Dramatic tension and weaponizing exposition*.

5. Each writer looks at their own script to see if there is any exposition which could be turned into a weapon in the conflict, and how it could be.

6. Again, led by each writer in turn, the whole group looks at all of the scripts to see if there is any exposition that could be made into weapons for any of the characters to use in their conflict with the others.
   Writers of the relevant scripts revise their scripts.

Agenda, training session 10: Final evaluation and revision

Participants

Writing team
Other project personnel not so far involved in the writing, and able to understand the language the scripts are written in

Materials

Paper copies of scripts for the number of characters in each script

Equipment

A recording studio, or portable recorders
    Any practical sound effects required
    Audio playback equipment

1. The facilitator introduces the final revision.
   Each writer is asked to gather the cast they need, using other members of the writing team and bringing in other project staff, as needed.
2. Each script is rehearsed by its cast, directed by the writer, and recorded, including movement and practical sound effects. (A schedule of rehearsals and recording will probably need to be drawn up.)
3. Copies of the scripts can be distributed for reading, though it is better if they are evaluated as audio drama.
   The evaluation group are assembled, including the writing team and other project staff, as appropriate.
   The facilitator distributes or presents *Handout D3.9: Evaluation criteria*, discussing each criterion in turn to ensure they are all understood.
4. After each scene is played, it is evaluated by the group against the criteria in *Handout D3.9: Evaluation criteria*.
   As each scene is reviewed, writers take notes and later revise the scripts.
   In most projects there will be an editorial process that the finished scripts will need to go through, followed by further revision, before recording with the cast.

Module D4: Production team and technician training for drama

Participants

Writing team
Production team
Audio technician
Cast

Materials

Episode script
Character timeline chart
Universe map and description
Character profiles
Copies of all of the following handouts for each participant and the facilitator, or as PowerPoint slides. If PowerPoint is used, the facilitator needs to make sure there are also paper copies for any handouts which need to be completed by participants.

Handout D4.1: Assessing FX in a script

When reading a script to assess the FX needs, ask these questions.
- Are there any effects instructions missing; that is, are there points in the script where an effect is needed but it is not written down?
- Are any of the characters eating or drinking in any of the scenes?
- Are any of the effects instructions unclear and, if so, what additional information is needed?
- For the background effects, what time of day is the scene taking place, and will that make any difference to the effect needed?

And follow this instruction.
- For each effect, participants should note down if they think the effect should be practical or pre-recorded, and be able to explain why.

Practical effects should be used:
- if there is an activity that will affect how the actor speaks, or that will affect the performance in some other way
- if the effect needs to be precisely timed to the speech

Practical effects should not be used if their use in the studio would be risky in some way.

Handout D4.2: An aide-memoire for the effects gatherer

Background effects need to be recorded for a period of at least twenty minutes.
Effects are recorded at voice level.
Effects that may be used in different scenes with different backgrounds should be recorded in the quietest background available. This allows for the effect – for example, of a vehicle recorded from outside the vehicle – to be used in a rural setting, with an added countryside background, or in an urban setting, with a busy street background.

Handout D4.3: An aide-memoire for actors

Your words should sound as if you have just thought them. How can this be achieved?
1. Read your script – out loud – over and over again.
2. Find the conflict.

First, work out what your character is trying to achieve in the scene.

Then, work out what the other characters are trying to achieve in the scene. The conflict is where what your character is trying to achieve collides with what the others are trying to achieve, and it is not, usually, argument and shouting.

3. Work out how your character is trying to win. (Is it by bullying? Persuasion? Charm? Whining? Threats? Flattery?)
4. Work out where the conflict or struggle for control is in the scene.
5. Work out how your character got into the situation they are in in the scene; that is, what has happened in the past?
6. Work out which character ends up in control. That is, which character gets what they want?

Agenda, training session 1: Constructing the acoustic universe for audio drama

This session will depend on the availability of different acoustics for the production. If the only acoustic available is one studio, which is too small for different acoustics to be constructed inside it, then the session is not needed. (See Chapter 29 for creating different acoustics in a studio.)

1. The facilitator should lead the writing and production teams in exploring the acoustic options available:
   - Is there a studio available which is big enough for different acoustics to be created in it?
   - Is there an outside space that could be used for recording?
   - Are there different locations with different acoustics that could be used, and is this option financially viable?

   If the only available recording space is a studio that is too small to house different acoustics, this session will not be necessary.

   However, if different acoustics are available, then the session is necessary.
2. The production and writing teams, led by the facilitator, look at all the key locations on the drama's universe map, and work out what the appropriate acoustic would be for each. This can be done by taking the following steps:
   - working out if the main activities carried out in each location would be done outdoors or indoors
   - if indoors, working out in what kind of building the activities would be carried out
3. The facilitator explains that the acoustic of the building; that is how much echo there is will depend on its size and the materials it is made of.
   - Larger spaces will be more echoey than small ones.
   - Spaces made of hard materials, like tiles, brick, stone, concrete or metal, will be more echoey.

- Spaces made of softer materials, like mud brick, wood and thatch, will be less echoey.
- Interiors with a lot of soft surfaces, like furnishings, carpets and curtains, will be less echoey than those with harder surfaces.

The facilitator, the writing and production teams decide on the level of echo for each interior location in the drama.

4. When the team have worked out the acoustics for each location, outside of the training, the facilitator and the audio technician can work out which arrangement of acoustic screens will be used for each, or will find appropriate locations for each.

Agenda, training session 2: Gathering sound effects

Participants

Writing team
Production team
Audio technician

In this session, the facilitator takes the writing and production teams through the typical process of sound effects gathering, by looking at one episode. The writing team will not normally be involved in gathering effects but, if they participate in the training, it is likely to help them refine their effects instructions, by helping them understand better the information needed to gather accurate effects.

1. Looking at the character timelines, the participants consider the season the episode will be broadcast in, and whether the effects can be satisfactorily recorded immediately. If not, the group need to work out when it will be possible.
2. The facilitator explains that effects-gathering starts with a careful reading of the script and gives out or presents *Handout D4.1: Assessing FX in a script.*
3. With *Handout D4.1: Assessing FX in a script* in front of them, participants work alone to read the script, answer the questions and follow the instructions.
4. The facilitator leads a discussion with the whole group, going through each question in turn, and decisions are made on each.
   In the case of eating or drinking, the facilitator explains that actors will need to eat or drink if the scene is going to sound believable. If any character is eating or drinking, exactly what sounds are needed? Does a fizzy drink can or bottle need to be opened, for example?
5. When the decisions have been made, the group consider two further questions on each effect.

Pre-recorded effects

Will pre-recording be necessary, or will the background when the voices are recorded be sufficient?
   Where and how can the effect be recorded?

Practical effects, including eating and drinking

Where and how can the effect be obtained?

6. The facilitator presents the effects gatherer with a copy of *Handout D4.2: An aide-memoire for the effects gatherer* and makes any clarifications needed.

   Outside the training, arrangements for recording and obtaining effects are put in place and carried out.

Agenda, training session 3: A rehearsal process with actors

Participants

Writing team
Production team, including the producer/director
Cast needed for one scene in the episode being used (who join the Session at point 4.)

Materials

Episode script
Character timeline chart
Universe map and description
Character profiles

Equipment

Studio or exterior recording equipment

1. The facilitator introduces the concept of visualization, as described in *Training Module D3, training session 6: Scene synopsis development* and *Handout D3.3: A definition of visualization*. The facilitator explains that visualization is important in an audio drama. The writers should have already visualized the scenes as part of the writing process. The producer/director needs to visualize scenes.

   If the producer/director visualizes each scene, they can work out if there are any factors that would affect how a scene should be performed. It might be something about the situation or about the characters.

2. The production team, including the producer/director, are asked to take the first scene in the episode and to visualize it. They explain their visualization, and the writers compare it with theirs. If there are differences, they are discussed and resolved.

   The group then discuss how the visualization might affect the performance of the scene, and the producer/director takes notes.

   The group then work through all the scenes in the episode, repeating the process each time.

3. The facilitator introduces the idea of characters' levels of desire, rated on a scale of 1 to 10. Taking the scene they are planning to rehearse in the training, the

facilitator asks each of the group to work out a level of desire for each of the characters in the scene, and a reason for choosing that level. (See Chapter 29 for a full discussion of levels of desire.)

Once all have finished, the facilitator asks the producer/director for their answers, and then, asks the others in the group if they agree with the level and the reasons. If any of them do not, then there is a discussion until agreement is reached. The producer/director notes the agreed levels and reasons.

4. The cast of one of the episode's scenes are introduced to the session.
   Under the guidance of the facilitator, the producer/director organizes and runs a read-through of the scene in question, and afterwards asks the cast if they fully understand what their characters are saying.

5. The producer/director asks each actor in turn the following questions.
   What is your character trying to achieve in the scene?
   How is he or she trying to achieve it?
   Where is the conflict or struggle for control in the scene, if there is any?
   How is your character trying to achieve what they want?
   How has each character got into the situation they are in the scene, that is what has happened in the past?
   Which character ends up in control in the scene?

   If an actor cannot answer the questions, the producer/director asks the whole cast, and, if there are still no answers, or the answers are wrong, the producer/director will, eventually, have to say what answers they have worked out.
   The producer/director gets the cast to run through the scene again.
   The facilitator asks the whole group if the performance was better than the first read-through, and, if it was, in what ways.

6. The producer/director asks each actor how much their character wants whatever it is they are trying to achieve in the scene. The level of desire is rated on a scale of 1 to 10, with 1 being a very low level of desire and 10 being very high. The director also asks each actor why they chose the level they have said.
   If any of the levels or reasons are sharply different from those the group agreed earlier in the session, there is discussion until agreement can be reached, unless the actor's reasoning is simply wrong.
   The producer/director gets the cast to run through the scene again, asking the actors for performances that match the stated level of desire.
   After the performance, the facilitator asks if there was further improvement or not, and whether the actors' performances matched the levels of desire agreed. If any did not, then the producer/director needs to discuss with the cast and the training participants how the actors' performances can match better.
   The scene is run through again.

7. The next part of the session should be held in a studio, or outside, around a microphone, with everything set up to record.
   The facilitator explains and demonstrates the concept of 'Talk as you walk' to the actors. (See *Module D3, Session 8: Sound effects and movement instructions for audio drama scripts* and *Handout D3.7: 'Talk as you walk' in audio drama*.)

The producer/director positions the cast for the beginning of the scene, and then walks them through their moves. Going into the cubicle, the producer/director asks the cast to do the scene with all the moves.

The facilitator asks the group if, from what they heard, the moves were correct or not. The producer/director makes adjustments accordingly.

The scene is performed and recorded.

The group assess the performance and, if needed, the scene is re-recorded.

8. Once a satisfactory performance has been recorded, the facilitator reinforces the key points of the rehearsal training session.

Outside of this training, the facilitator supports the producer/director in training the rest of the cast, following the procedure set out here.

Glossary

The field of communication for development has a large number of technical and jargon terms, and this section of the book will explain the meaning of as many as possible of them, based on interviews with a range of individuals in the field.

The definitions given here are specific to this and related fields, and many terms will have different meanings outside of this field.

It is also true that the same term can appear to identify different concepts to different people. The term 'social change' appears to describe two different concepts, depending on who is using the term, while, for some organizations, 'social change' and 'behaviour change' seem to be virtually interchangeable. At the same time, individuals and organizations – even different sections of the same organization – use different terms for what appear to be the same concept. So, for example, while the US Centers for Disease Control uses the term 'reinforcement' for activities on the ground that are co-ordinated with broadcasts, BBC Media Action tends to use the term 'social mobilization' for the same kind of activity. This section of the book will attempt to unravel these issues of terminology, clarifying where there are different meanings for the same term, and where different terms are used for the same concept, across the field.

Table 1 Alternative terms in communication for development currently in use

Term used in this book	Alternative terms
Communicating with communities	Beneficiary communication
	Community engagement
	Communication for humanitarian action
	Humanitarian communication
	Closely related terms
	Accountability to affected populations (AAP)
Global South	Developing countries
Reinforcement	Social mobilization
	On-the-ground activities
	Closely related term
	Learning activities
Participation	Two-way communication
	Communication as development
	Interactivity

Table 2 Similar terms in communication for development that have more than one meaning

Term as used in this book	Alternative meanings
Communication for development The whole field of using two-way communication – including media and all kinds of face-to-face communication – to facilitate people's participation on their own development. This includes humanitarian communication in crises.	Media for development 1) The same meaning as communication for development 2) One-way communication, from the broadcaster to an audience 3) A part of the wider field of communication for development, using media only
Term as used in this book Social change Changes in social norms – particularly in shared attitudes – that help individual behaviour change to be sustained	**Alternative meanings** Communication for social change Using communication to help marginalized, ignored and vulnerable groups have a public voice for empowerment
Term used in this book Media for development As above	**Alternative meanings** Media development 1) The very specific activity of journalism training 2) Wide-ranging support – legal, economic and professional – for an independent and diverse media sector, in particular for it to hold power to account

Table 3 Specialist terms in broadcasting, international development, humanitarian action and training which may be used in communication for development

Accountability	The duty of a humanitarian or development organization to justify its actions to other organization and individuals, and to respond to feedback
Accountability to affected populations	The duty of humanitarian organizations to respond effectively to feedback they receive from communities and individuals they are trying to help
Acoustic	(Adjective) To do with sound (Noun) In broadcast drama, the level of echo in a performance space. A 'live' acoustic has a lot of echo, a 'dead' acoustic has no echo. The acoustic heard in a scene should match where the scene is set. For example, a scene set outdoors should have no echo.
Acoustic screen	In audio drama, a screen made to alter the acoustic of a performance space. It has a hard side, to increase the echo, and a soft side, to reduce the echo.
Action	In behaviour change theory, when an individual is actively behaving in a new way or stopping behaving in the way they were in the past.

Actuality	The recording of something happening. For example a market trader shouting out their prices or a teacher teaching in a school.
Aide-memoire	Usually a document which contains reminders of how to do something. Often a follow-up to training, to remind participants of the training.
Airtime	1) The time when a broadcasting station is broadcasting. (Often used in the term, 'buying airtime', when development organizations pay local stations to broadcast – or 'air' – their material at an agreed price, time and duration.)
	2) The time available for using a mobile phone. In this meaning, 'buying airtime' refers to paying a service provider to be able to use the phone.
Ambient sound	See background sound.
Audio	Material in sound, to cover radio and podcast.
Back announcement (Back anno)	An announcement made after the end of a broadcast programme, to identify the programme and give credits for the staff. It may also include information to help audience members follow up the programme with practical action.
Background briefing	A journalist asking someone questions for information or opinion, when the answers will not be used directly in any output, but the information or opinion will help to shape the journalist's report.
Background sound	In audio drama, a sound used to paint a picture in the listener's mind to give a sense of place and time.
	In broadcast journalism, the sound in the background of an interview or a report.
Back timing	A process for keeping track of how much time is left in a live programme, to make sure the programme ends at the right time, or for ending a music track at the right time.
Barrier	A factor that hinders or even prevents behaviour change.
Behaviour change	An approach to improving individuals' situations, with regard to health, economic well-being or crime, for example, which encourages individuals to make change for themselves, as the most practicable route to improvement.
Behaviour change methodology	A framework for organizing and structuring theory and evidence to develop an approach which tries to bring about changes in behaviour among a population.
Behaviour change objective	In a drama or other entertainment intended to bring about behaviour change, a particular change which it is hoped the audience will achieve, as they follow a role-model character.
Beneficiary	Someone who is receiving aid from donor organizations. (A term thought to be no longer acceptable, with aid seen as an act of solidarity, not beneficence.)
Big data	Useful information that can be gathered from analysis of multiple electronically stored records, for example, mobile phone companies' records of phone use.

Brief (noun)	The instructions a reporter or producer is given to make a programme item or a complete programme.
Built programme	A broadcast programme which is made up of edited interviews and other items, linked by a presenter reading a written script, usually recorded and not broadcast live.
Cast	The actors who play the different characters in a serial drama.
Casting	The process of choosing the actors to play the different characters in a drama.
Character	A fictional person created by the writer or writers of a drama. (See also transitional character.)
Character Bible	A record of what happens to each character in a serial drama, updated after each episode, to help the writers ensure there is continuity in the drama.
Child-centred	When education or programmes deliver what is in the child's best interests, address children's needs and see the world from a child's perspective, usually including children in the material, and showing them as active, autonomous learners.
Cliffhanger	A device often used in serial dramas, in which an episode ends at a place where the audience were expecting something to happen, but it does not, or, where something happens and the audience does not know what the outcome is. They are left hanging and eager to know what will happen. This hooks them into wanting to watch or listen to the next episode. Cliff hangers can be used in behaviour change drama to encourage audiences to discuss key issues among themselves.
Clip	A short extract from a longer piece of broadcast material, designed to interest the audience in the whole piece, or to show the tone of the whole piece.
Clusters	The grouping of different organizations involved in a humanitarian response to a disaster or conflict according to the work they do (like nutrition or healthcare) to help to coordinate the response.
Communicating with communities	Continuous action by humanitarian organizations to seek out the communities they are trying to help, to listen to them and to respond effectively to what they hear (See Glossary Table 1 for alternative terms.)
Communication needs assessment	An assessment a population's access to the channels of communication and their preferences among those channels (television, mobile phone, etc.) their information and communication needs, and the communication they presently have. It is carried out at the beginning of a project and continuously reviewed.
Community station	Usually a radio station that serves a very limited area, and exists to help meet a specific community's information and social needs, often set up to support the political, social and economic needs of the community.

Constructive criticism	Comments on another worker's material, which is honest but supportive, always giving suggestions for making the material better.
Contact programme	See phone-in programme.
Contemplation	In behaviour change theory, the mental state of someone who needs to change their behaviour, and has started to think about addressing the issue (also known as thinking).
Contributors	People who take part in a broadcast programme, either, for example, as interviewees, members of a discussion panel or participants in a reality programme.
Credit	A spoken or written acknowledgement of an individual's role in or contribution to a piece of communication material.
Cue (In-cue; Out-cue)	1) The first few words (in-cue) of a pre-recorded item in a programme, or the last few words (out-cue). Provided to help the production team correctly identify the item, and for the presenter, when the item is being played, to be alerted to the fact it is about to end, and he or she is going to need to speak. Also known as in-words; out-words.
	2) An instruction in a script where an extra element – for example, a pre-recorded item, sound effect or music – is to be started.
Dead acoustic	In drama, a sound environment in which there is no echo (a dead room is a studio built to have no echo).
Defamation	In journalism, damaging someone's reputation by writing or saying something which is untrue about them.
Demographic	(Adjective) About the structure of a population, for example, the proportion of old to young
	(Noun) One section of a population, e.g. children under eighteen years old.
Digital divide	The division between those individuals and communities who have access to digital communications technology and those who do not, in a given country or region. A lack of access can be caused by a number of factors, including gender, poverty, lack of digital services and deliberate exclusion activities (for example, in some communities, women are intimidated or harassed, to prevent them from accessing online resources).
Disaggregation	The separating out of research data on different groups, in order to identify the different needs, preferences, behaviours of those groups.
Directional microphone	A microphone which can only pick up sound produced in front of it (see also omnidirectional microphone).
Displaced people	A term covering both internally displaced people: those who have fled their homes, but are still in the state they are citizens of; and refugees: those who have fled to a different country.
Distortion	An unpleasant noise produced by audio equipment when a voice or other sound is too loud.

Donor	1) An organization which is distributing aid in a humanitarian crisis
	2) An organization which is funding development projects.
Dramatic action	A vital ingredient of effective drama: what characters in a drama do, rather than what they say, and leading to an outcome.
Dramatic conflict	The struggle among characters in a drama to achieve the outcome they each want
Dramatic tension	The deliberate holding back of information in a drama, to create intrigue and anticipation in the audience.
Duration	The length of time taken by an item in a programme, or for a whole programme.
Edit	1) To cut sections out of recorded material – video or audio – either to make it shorter or clearer or, in drama, to select the best versions, in an effort to improve quality.
	2) To commission and control the content of a piece of media, whether that is a newspaper, broadcast news or material for communication for development.
Exposition	In drama, the giving of information – on a character's past, for example – needed for the audience to understand what is happening and why it is happening.
Facilitator	1) Someone leading participatory training
	2) In behaviour change terminology, something which helps someone to change their behaviour to improve their life.
Factual broadcasting	Broadcasting which uses journalists to research real events, and to conduct interviews with relevant people.
FM	Frequency modulated, a section of the radio wave spectrum which gives high quality but is very limited in its range. Often used by local radio stations.
Format	The standardized structure of a broadcast programme or item in a programme.
Formative research	Research conducted on a project's target population before the project starts.
High production values	In television or radio drama, time and effort gone into making the drama look or sound the best it can.
Host communities or host populations	People who are resident in a locality that displaced people have come to for safety. (Note: See definition of displaced people.)
Humanitarian	An adjective describing work undertaken to assist a population in crisis, caused by conflict or disaster.
Ident or Identifier	The spoken or written name of a broadcasting station, channel or programme, used to remind the audience what they are watching or listening to.
Internally displaced person	Someone who has left their home because of a large-scale disaster or conflict, but who is still within the borders of their home country.

Interview	A journalist asking individuals questions in order to get information or opinion, when the answers are directly used in print, online or broadcast. (This is different from a background briefing.) An interview may be broadcast live or be recorded in some way, for use later.
Institutional knowledge	The collective knowledge an organization gathers, records and organizes, as it learns from doing its work.
International broadcaster	Now that any television or radio station can put itself on the internet, almost all are international, often helping to connect a diaspora with their original country. However, specifically, this term refers to large multi-lingual broadcasters like BBC World, CNN or China Global Television News.
Jingle	A jingle is a short song or piece of music, which acts an identifier for a series, station or, in an advert, a brand.
Link	In broadcasting, a piece of speech or writing, or a symbol which connects one programme item with the next.
Linking script	A script showing the links a presenter needs to read, to hold together the different items in a programme.
Lingua franca	A language adopted by speakers of different native languages within a region or country, to make communication possible among different groups.
Live broadcasting	When the presenter/s and some contributors in a piece of broadcasting are speaking as they are broadcast, and have not been pre-recorded. There may, however, be some pre-recorded contributions.
Local advisory panel	A group of people who can advise a communication for development project on issues of local need and culture.
Magazine programme	A programme made of a series of items in various formats covering different topics, but with one linking theme, often large, like health or livelihoods.
Maintenance	In behaviour change theory, the mental and practical state of someone who has achieved their intended behaviour change, and are keeping to that change (also known as sustaining).
Media landscape	A survey of all of the media operating in a given country or region. It will usually give details of ownership, audience, level of independence and any political affiliation of each media outlet.
Medium Wave	A section of radio frequencies which have long broadcasting range, but of relatively poor quality.
Menu	At the beginning of a magazine programme, a list of the items and topics which are going to be in the programme.
Mix	(Verb) In television and audio drama, adding sound effects and music to the recorded actors' performances.
	(Noun)
	1) The process of adding sounds and music
	2) The final version of a drama, with all sounds added.

Mobile technology	The technology which allows portable electronic systems, devices and networks to communicate. However, it is important to distinguish between the technology of first and second generation mobile phones (1G and 2G), and that of third and fourth generation (3G and 4G). 1G and 2G cannot access the internet and can only use voice calls and SMS to communicate outwards. They can receive radio. 3G and 4G can use the whole range of communication available on the internet.
Mono	When sound is heard through only one channel, so there is no sense of left and right.
Movement	In radio drama, the directed moving of actors around the microphone, to produce effects which help the audience engage with and understand the drama. In mono, only movement towards and away from the microphone can be heard. In stereo, movement to left and right can also be heard.
Nomad	An animal herder who lives a migratory life.
Not thinking	In behaviour change theory, the mental state of someone who is engaged in harmful or risky behaviour, but is not yet thinking about changing it (the technical term is pre-contemplation).
Off air	When a broadcasting station is not broadcasting, or a particular programme series is not currently being broadcast.
Omnidirectional microphone	A microphone which picks up sound produced anywhere around it, so that speakers can stand all round it, and their voices will be equally loud.
On air	When a broadcasting station is broadcasting, or when material is being broadcast at that moment.
Outreach	The effort by a communication for development project to come into face-to-face contact with its audience.
Package	An item in a magazine programme, which contains edited sections of several interviews, usually linked by the journalist.
Participatory training	Training which is based on trainees taking part in learning activities, rather than passively listening to a lecture or watching a Power Point presentation.
Pastoralist	A farmer who keeps animals (Africa and Australia).
Phase reverse	A problem that can arise in a stereo recording, when the two legs cancel each other out; it is hard to detect when listening in stereo, but in mono listening the result can be silence. (Also known as phase cancellation.)
Phone-in programme	A live programme that audience members are invited to call on the phone, or to use text, email or social media, to give information or opinions, or to ask questions. Also known as a contact programme.
Platform	The medium through which material is broadcast or distributed, like television, radio, podcast, social media or other internet channel.

Podcast	An audio programme which is made available for download over the internet. Often users can subscribe to a series and receive new instalments automatically.
Post-production	Work which is carried out to prepare a drama for broadcast, after the actors have been recorded. It will usually include the mix.
Practical effects	In drama, sound effects which are created at the same time as the actors are performing, to make sure they are coordinated with the actors' speech and actions. (Also known as spot effects.)
Pre-contemplation	In behaviour change theory, the mental state of someone who is engaged in harmful or risky behaviour, but is not yet thinking about changing it. (Also known as not thinking.)
Preparation	In behaviour change theory, the mental state of someone who needs to change their behaviour, when they are mentally preparing themselves for the change, and are taking practical steps towards it.
Pre-recorded	A description of audio or televisual programme items or whole programmes which have been recorded for broadcast.
Pre-recorded effects	In drama, sound effects which are recorded separately from the actors' performances and mixed into the drama either as the actors perform or in post-production.
Presenter	The person who speaks directly to the audience in broadcasting, usually linking different items, and sometimes conducting live interviews.
Producer	In television and radio – except for television drama – the person who is hands-on in getting programmes made.
Production team	The group of people who do different jobs to get programmes made.
Programme	A piece of broadcasting which is a self-contained unit of a defined duration, on one topic or on several, linked topics. It has a distinct beginning and end.
Project	A long-term, structured series of activities designed to achieve a specific goal or series of goals.
Protection of civilians site	A site (sometimes called a camp) set up, usually, by the UN, to provide a secure place to live for civilians caught up in conflict.
Psychosocial support	An approach to people affected by disaster or conflict which tries to foster resilience of communities and individuals. It aims at easing resumption of normal life, helping affected people in their convalescence and preventing pathological consequences of potentially traumatic situations.
Public service announcement (PSA)	An announcement broadcast on radio or television which contains important information, on health, for example. Stations are sometimes paid by organizations or governments to broadcast them.
Public service broadcaster	A not-for-profit broadcaster, who, normally, needs to adhere to strict standards of unbiased journalism, to address

	the needs of minority audiences, and to have a strong educational element in their broadcasting.
Rapid-onset disaster	A disaster which happens very suddenly, like an earthquake, typhoon or tsunami.
Reach	The size of the area where a station's signal can be received, and the size and demographic of the audience who can receive it.
Reality programme	A programme which features ordinary people, not media professionals, in different situations and settings. Reality shows often set challenges for participants.
Recorded	A word describing material for broadcast which has been stored on an electronic device.
Refugee	Someone who has left their home because of a large-scale disaster or conflict, who has crossed the borders of their home country, and is now in another country.
Reinforcement	Organized activities on the ground for an audience to take part in, designed to strengthen the impact of broadcast communication.
Report	1) In broadcast media, an item which is presented by a journalist to give factual information. It may be just the journalist or include interviewees as well.
	2) An account from a development organization to a donor, showing project achievements and shortcomings and justifying spending.
Reporter	Journalist.
Retake	During recording – of, for example, an interview or a drama – a re-recording of a section already recorded, because of a mistake or for a production purpose.
Rights-based	An approach to development work which observes and promotes the human rights of its audiences.
Role model	A real person or a fictional character who either already does follow the behaviour a project is promoting or who models the change to that behaviour
Selection workshop	A recruitment process which involves candidates being taken through a series of training sessions. After each session, they are given a task that should demonstrate their learning in the session. Each candidate is marked on their performance of the task.
Self-efficacy	In behaviour change theory, a person's belief that they can make the change required.
Serial drama	A broadcast drama which is in regular episodes, following the same group of characters over a long time. (Also known as soap opera or soap.)
Setback	In behaviour change drama, something that happens which temporarily reverses a transitional character's journey to their behaviour change objective.
Show, don't tell	A writing technique in which the action of a drama is conveyed in what the characters do, rather than what they say.

Slow-onset disaster	A disaster which occurs over a long time, like environmental degradation or the climate crisis.
Soap opera/Soap	A serial drama.
Social media	Interpersonal communication channels which use the internet, like Facebook and Instagram.
Social norms	Attitudes, beliefs and behaviours which are shared and enforced by a community.
Sound effects	Deliberately created sounds used in drama, to give a stronger sense of realism or for comedy.
Spot effects	See practical effects.
Stages of change	A behaviour change theory, which identifies the different mental states a person goes through in changing their behaviour: pre-contemplation (not thinking), contemplation (thinking), preparation, action, maintenance.
Stereo	When sound is heard through two channels, left and right, giving a sense of space and, in drama, side-to-side movement.
Sting	A short piece of music used to punctuate a programme or drama, or to indicate the point where an action is required.
Storyline	A self-contained set of events in a drama, in which a group of characters interact, and which has a distinct beginning and end.
Subtext	In drama, meaning which is not openly expressed by characters, but which is understood by the audience.
Sustaining	In behaviour change theory, the mental and practical state of someone who has achieved their intended behaviour change, and is keeping to that change. (Also known as maintenance.)
Target audience	A particular group which a programme or series is aimed at.
Technical advisory panel	A group who can support a project with advice on both the methodology being used and the topics being covered.
Tension	Holding back information in a factual story to create a sense of anticipation in an audience. (See also, dramatic tension.)
Text	1) A message sent on a mobile device using SMS.
	2) A programme or drama script.
Thinking	In behaviour change theory, the mental state of someone who needs to change their behaviour, and has started to think about addressing the issue (also known as contemplation).
Training needs assessment	An assessment of a group of trainees' existing knowledge, capacity or skill, conducted before or at the beginning of training. It is carried out to ensure that the training is pitched at the right level, and is not teaching either something the group already knows or can do or something too difficult for them to achieve.
Transitional character	In a behaviour change drama, a character who goes through a process of changing his or her behaviour, to act as a role model for the audience.

Transitional justice	Conflict-related trials (often trials for war crimes) which are conducted during a transition from conflict to peace, and seen as contributing to that transition.
Universe	The fictional location created for a serial drama.
Video	1) The technology which allows television to work and for moving visual images to be recorded.
	2) A television film or programme which has been recorded and can be viewed on many different devices.
Voice-over	The spoken accompaniment to a television or film sequence.
Wildtrack	In audio journalism, background sound recorded after an interview for mixing, while editing the material, to mask sharp changes in the background sound.
Words (in-words; out-words)	See cue.

Table 4 Acronyms and abbreviations

AAP	accountability to affected populations
ACAPS	Assessment Capacities Project
ADCAP	Age and Disability Capacity Programme
AET	Africa Educational Trust
ALNAP	Active Learning Network for Accountability and Performance in humanitarian Action
BBC	British Broadcasting Corporation
C4D	Communication for development
CDA	The Collaborative for Development Action, now known as CDA Collaborative Learning Projects
CDAC N	Communicating with Disaster-affected Communities Network
CDC	Centers for Disease Control and Prevention
CDC	Consultation Draft Constitution (for Somalia)
CE	Community engagement
CNN	Cable News Network
CwC	Communicating with communities
DfID	United Kingdom Department for International Development
EC	European Commission
FX	sound effects
GSDRC	Governance and Social Development Resource Centre
HIV	Human Immunodeficiency Virus
HRC	Haitian Red Cross
IASC	Inter-Agency Standing Committee

ICC	International Criminal Court
ICRC	International Committee of the Red Cross
IDP	internally displaced person
IMS	International Media Support
INGO	international non-governmental organization
IOM	International Organisation for Migration
ITU	International Telecommunication Union
MARCH	Modelling and Reinforcement to Combat HIV
MEP	Member of the European Parliament
MIRA	Multi-Cluster/Sector Initial Rapid Assessment
MSF	Médecins Sans Frontières
NGO	non-governmental organization
PFA	Psychological First Aid
PoC	protection of civilians
PSA	public service announcement
SMS	short message service
SOMDEL	Somali Distance Education for Literacy Programme
SPLM	Sudan People's Liberation Movement
STI	sexually transmitted infection
TNA	training needs assessment
TWB	Translators Without Borders
UDHR	Universal Declaration of Human Rights
UNCRC	United Nations Convention on the Rights of the Child
UN	United Nations
UNDP	United Nations Development Programme
UNESCO	United Nations Educational, Scientific and Cultural Organization
UNFPA	United Nations Population Fund
UNHCR	United Nations High Commissioner for Refugees
UNICEF	United Nations Children's Fund
UNMISS	United Nations Mission in South Sudan
UNOCHA	United Nations Office for the Coordination of Humanitarian Affairs
UNRWA	United Nations Relief and Works Agency for Palestine Refugees in the Near East
URD	Groupe Urgence, Réhabilitation, Développement
VCT	voluntary counselling and testing
WASH	water, sanitation and hygiene
WHO	World Health Organisation

Notes

Introduction

1   Thompson Reuters Foundation, 4/2/2015.
2   *Situation Report, Ebola Virus Disease,* World Health Organisation, 2016. (http://apps. who.int/iris/bitstream/10665/208883/1/ebolasitrep_10Jun2016_eng.pdf?ua=1).

Chapter 1

1   *Time to Listen, Hearing People on the Receiving End of International Aid,* Mary B. Anderson, Dayna Brown and Isabella Jean, CDA Collaborative Learning Projects, 2012.
2   Ibid., p. 21.
3   Ibid.
4   Effective Literacy Practice, UNESCO Institute for Lifelong Learning. (http://www. unesco.org/uil/litbase/?menu=4&programme=100).
5   *Research Summary Strengthening Radio Stations' Coverage of Rights, Peace and Governance in Somalia,* Pam Vallance and Rhian Were, BBC Media Action, 2012. (http://downloads.bbc.co.uk/mediaaction/pdf/research_summaries/BBCMA_ research_summary_somalia_radio_stations_NSA_25.pdf).
6   Population Media Center. (https://www.populationmedia.org).
7   *CDAC Network Typhoon Haiyan Learning Review Case Study: Radyo Bakdaw: Accountability and Media in response to Typhoon Haiyan,* CDAC Network, 2014. (http://www.cdacnetwork.org/contentAsset/raw-data/ce68d32e-d9fe-440d-88f9-916faa56a5c2/attached File).
8   *Words of Relief – Ebola Crisis Learning Review,* Translators Without Borders, 2015. (http://translatorswithoutborders.org/wp-content/uploads/2015/10/20150529-Ebola-Learning-Review_FINAL.pdf).
9   *Ann Kite Yo Pale (Let Them Speak),* Imogen Wall and Yves Gerald Chéry, Infoasaid, 2010.
10 *CDAC Network Suite of Common Needs Assessment Tools,* Internews, International Media Support, BBC Media Action, July 2014. (http://www.cdacnetwork.org/tools-and-resources/i/20140721171402-wj4au).
11 *Minimum Standards for Age and Disability Inclusion in Humanitarian Action,* Sarah Collinson, Age and Disability Consortium, 2016.
12 *Ethnologue.* (http://www.ethnologue.com).
13 *Words of Relief – Ebola Crisis Learning Review,* Translators Without Borders, 2015, p. 2. (http://translatorswithoutborders.org/wp-content/uploads/2015/10/20150529-Ebola-Learning-Review_FINAL.pdf).
14 Ibid., p. 4.

Chapter 2

1   'How Obvious Can You Be? Heavy-Handed Messages in EE Material', Doe Mayer, Presented at EE4, 2004.
2   *Tobacco and the Developing World*, Action on Smoking and Health, 2015.
3   *How To Write a Radio Serial Drama for Social Development. A Script Writer's Manual*, Esta de Fossard, Johns Hopkins Center for Communication Programs, 1996.
4   *Can Radio Drama Improve Child Health and Nutrition in Somalia?* BBC Media Action, 2015, p. 6.
5   *Language and Learning*, James Britton, Allen Lane, 1970.
6   Ibid.
7   Ibid., p. 10.
8   'Self-efficacy', Albert Bandura, in V. S. Ramachaudran (ed.), *Encyclopedia of Human Behavior*, New York: Academic Press, vol. 4, pp. 71–81, 1994. (https://www.uky.edu/~eushe2/Bandura/BanEncy.html).

Chapter 3

1   *The Core Humanitarian Standard on Quality and Accountability*, CHS Alliance, Group URD and the Sphere Project, 2014.
2   The Sphere Handbook Humanitarian Charter and Minimum Standards in Humanitarian Response, Sphere Association, fourth edition, Geneva, Switzerland, 2018 (www.spherestandards.org/handbook).
3   *The Good Enough Guide: Impact Measurement and Accountability in Emergencies*, Emergency Capacity Building Project, 2007. (www.oxfam.org.uk/publications).
4   *The Core Humanitarian Standard on Quality and Accountability*, CHS Alliance, Group URD and the Sphere Project, 2014.
5   *Ann Kite Yo Pale (Let Them Speak)*, Imogen Wall and Yves Gerald Chéry, Infoasaid, 2010.
6   *Words of Relief – Ebola Crisis Learning Review*, Translators Without Borders, 2015, p. 2. (http://translatorswithoutborders.org/wp-content/uploads/2015/10/20150529-Ebola-Learning-Review_FINAL.pdf).
7   Ibid, pp. 2–3.
8   *Propaganda and Conflict: Evidence from the Rwandan Genocide*, by David Yanagizawa-Drott, Oxford University Press, 2014.
9   *The Reporters without Borders World Press Freedom Index*, Reporters without Borders. (https://rsf.org/en/ranking/2021).
10 *Can Radio Drama Improve Child Health and Nutrition in Somalia?* BBC Media Action, 2015.

Chapter 6

1   *Haath Se Haath Mila*, BBC World Service Trust, 2003.

Chapter 9

1 *Minimum Standards for Age and Disability Inclusion in Humanitarian Action*, Sarah Collinson, Age and Disability Consortium, 2016.
2 *No Hoodie, No Honey*, UNFPANigeria, 2013. (http://www.comminit.com/hiv-aids-africa/content/no-hoodie-no-honey-social-media-campaign).
3 Ibid.
4 'Empowering local media can make the difference: 5 lessons from the Ebola crisis', Alison Campbell, Devex, 23 April 2015. (https://www.devex.com/news/empowering-local-media-can-make-the-difference-5-lessons-from-the-ebola-crisis-85948).

Section 2

1 *Ann Kite Yo Pale (Let Them Speak)*, Imogen Wall and Yves Gerald Chéry, Infoasaid, 2010.
2 *Words of Relief – Ebola Crisis Learning Review*, Translators Without Borders, 2015.
3 'Empowering local media can make the difference: 5 lessons from the Ebola crisis', Alison Campbell, Devex, 23 April 2015. (https://www.devex.com/news/empowering-local-media-can-make-the-difference-5-lessons-from-the-ebola-crisis-85948).

Chapter 10

1 *Refugees: Emergency Broadcasting Handbook,* John Tuckey, BBC World Service Trust, p. 6.
2 *Do Humanitarian Helplines Help?* Ground Truth Solutions, 28 September 2015.
3 *Psychological First Aid: Guide for Field Workers*, World Health Organisation, 2011.
4 Ibid., p. 4.
5 *The Psychosocial Care and Protection of Children in Emergencies: Teacher Training Manual*, UNICEF, 2009.
6 Ibid., pp. 163–73.
7 *Reality TV for Resilience: Can Reality TV Help Communities to Better Cope with Climate Risks?* BBC Media Action, April 2015. (http://downloads.bbc.co.uk/mediaaction/pdf/bbc-research-summary-reality-tv-for-resilience-april-2015.pdf).
8 Ibid.
9 Ibid.

Chapter 11

1 *Who's Listening? Accountability to Affected People in the Haiyan Response*, Margie Buchanan-Smith, Jonathan Corpus Ong, and Sarah Routley, Plan International, May 2015.
2 Ibid., p. 29.
3 Ibid., p. 47.
4 Ibid., p. 48.
5 Ibid., p. 28.

6　　*CDAC Network Typhoon Haiyan Learning Review Case Study: Radyo Bakdaw: Accountability and Media In response to Typhoon Haiyan*, CDAC Network, 2014. (http://www.cdacnetwork.org/contentAsset/raw-data/ce68d32e-d9fe-440d-88f9-916faa56a5c2/attached File).

7　　http://icai.independent.gov.uk/wp-content/uploads/2014/03/ICAI-Philippines-report-FINAL.pdf.

8　　UNOCHA report. (https://www.humanitarianresponse.info/system/files/documents/files/OCHA%20Typhoon%20Haiyan%20CwC%20Update%20%2313.pdf).

9　　The Drum Beat 687, The Communication Initiative, 6 May 2015.

10　　*Rumour Has It: A Practice Guide to Working with Rumours*, John Bugge, CDAC Network, 2017 (www.cdacnetwork.org/).

Chapter 12

1　　*Cluster Coordination Reference Module*, Inter-Agency Standing Committee, revised July 2015. (https://interagencystandingcommittee.org/system/files/cluster_coordination_reference_module_2015_final.pdf).

2　　*Ann Kite Yo Pale (Let Them Speak)*, Imogen Wall and Yves Gerald Chéry, Infoasaid, 2010, p. 15.

3　　Ibid., p. 18.

4　　Multi-Cluster/Sector Initial Rapid Assessment (MIRA), Inter-Agency Standing Committee, March 2012.

Chapter 13

1　　*Multi-sector Initial Rapid Assessment Guidance,* IASC Inter-agency Standing Committee, revised July 2015, p. 13. (https://interagencystandingcommittee.org/system/files/mira_manual_2015.pdf).

2　　*Humanitarianism in the Network Age*, OCHA, UN Publications, 2013, p. 58.

3　　*Multi-sector Initial Rapid Assessment Guidance,* IASC Inter-agency Standing Committee, revised July 2015. (https://interagencystandingcommittee.org/system/files/mira_manual_2015.pdf).

4　　*Ann Kite Yo Pale (Let Them Speak)*, Imogen Wall and Yves Gerald Chéry, Infoasaid, 2010, pp. 14–16.

5　　*Humanitarianism in the Network Age*, OCHA, UN Publications, 2013, pp. 29, 30. (https://docs.unocha.org/sites/dms/Documents/WEB%20Humanitarianism%20in%20the%20Network%20Age%20vF%20single.pdf).

6　　Ibid., p. 27.

7　　Hirschfeld, D., *Twitter Data Accurately Tracked Haiti Cholera Outbreak.* (http://www.nature.com/news/twitter-data-accurately-tracked-haiti-choleraoutbreak-1.9770).

8　　Bengtsson, L., Lu, X., Thorson, A., Garfield, R. and Von Schreeb, J. (2011). Improved Response to Disasters and Outbreaks by Tracking Population Movements with Mobile Phone Network Data: A Post-Earthquake Geospatial Study in Haiti Data Sheet. (http://www.mobileactive.org/research/improvedresponse-disasters-and-outbreaks-trackingpopulationmovements-mobile-phone-network).

9　　*Humanitarianism in the Network Age*, OCHA, UN Publications, 2013, p. 27 (https://docs.unocha.org/sites/dms/Documents/WEB%20Humanitarianism%20in%20the%20Network%20Age%20vF%20single.pdf).

10   Ibid., p. 34.
11   Ibid., p. 59.
12   *Assessing Information and Communication Needs: A Quick and Easy Guide for Those Working in Humanitarian Response*, CDAC Network, ACAPS, July 2014. (http://www.cdacnetwork.org/tools-and-resources/i/20140721173332-ihw5g).
13   *Words of Relief – Ebola Crisis Learning Review*, Translators Without Borders, 2015.
14   *CDAC Network Suite of Common Needs Assessment Tools*, Internews, International Media Support, BBC Media Action, July 2014. (http://www.cdacnetwork.org/tools-and-resources/i/20140721171402-wj4au).

Chapter 14

1   *Chad Media and Telecoms Landscape Guide* infoasaid, 2012, p. 45.
2   *Chad and the Darfur Refugee Crisis: Internews Humanitarian Information Service 2005–2012*, p. 19.

Chapter 15

1   *Humanitarian Feedback Mechanisms: Research, Evidence and Guidance* ALNAP and CDA (2014), p. 74.
2   *Ann Kite Yo Pale (Let Them Speak)*, Imogen Wall and Yves Gerald Chéry, Infoasaid, 2010.
3   'Haiti Cholera: UN Chief Apologises for First Time over Outbreak', *BBC News website*, 1 December 2016. (http://www.bbc.com/news/world-latin-america-38176288).
4   *Tsunami Evaluation Coalition Joint Evaluation of the International Response to the Indian Ocean Tsunami: Synthesis Report*, 2006, p. 71.
5   *Typhoon Haiyan: Learning Review*, The CDAC Network, November 2014.
6   'Signal FM provides lifeline in Haiti', Wilkinson, T., *Los Angeles Times*, 1 February 2010.
7   Ibid.
8   *Ann Kite Yo Pale (Let them speak)*, Imogen Wall and Yves Gerald Chéry, Infoasaid, 2012.

Chapter 16

1   *Boda Boda Talk Talk – a Bike Delivers Information to Displaced People in South Sudan*, Internews, 26 June 2014. (https://internews.org/our-stories/project-updates/boda-boda-talk-talk).

Chapter 17

1   *Words of Relief: Ebola Crisis Learning Review*, Translators Without Borders, 2015, p. 2. (http://translatorswithoutborders.org/wp-content/uploads/2015/10/20150529-Ebola-Learning-Review_FINAL.pdf).
2   *Time to Listen: Hearing People on the Receiving End of International Aid*, Mary B. Anderson, Dayna Brown, Isabella Jean, CDA Collaborative Learning Projects, 2012.

3   Ibid., pp. 34–5.
4   *Refugees: Emergency Broadcasting Handbook,* BBC World Service Trust/UNHCR, 2004, p. 45.
5   *Age and Disability Inclusion in Humanitarian Action,* Sarah Collinson, Age and Disability Consortium, 2015.
6   *Time to Listen: Hearing People on the Receiving End of International Aid,* Mary B. Anderson, Dayna Brown, Isabella Jean, CDA Collaborative Learning Projects, 2012, p. 24.
7   *Refugees: Emergency Broadcasting Handbook,* John Tuckey, BBC World Service Trust, 2004, p. 19.
8   *Community Engagement to Tackle COVID-19 in the Slums of Mumbai,* Pritha Venkatachalam and Niloufer Memon, The Bridgespan Group, 2020, p. 4. (https://www.bridgespan.org/insights/library/global-development/community-engagement-tackle-covid-19-mumbai-slums).
9   Ibid, pp. 4–5.
10 *On the Front Line Where Crisis Meets Normal,* Liz Carlile, International Institute for Environment and Development, 2020. (https://www.iied.org/covid-19-front-line-where-crisis-meets-normal).
11 *Community Engagement to Tackle COVID-19 in the Slums of Mumbai,* Pritha Venkatachalam and Niloufer Memon, The Bridgespan Group, 2020, pp. 6–7. (https://www.bridgespan.org/insights/library/global-development/community-engagement-tackle-covid-19-mumbai-slums).
12 Ibid., p. 7.
13 Ibid., p. 14.
14 Ibid., p. 8.
15 Ibid.
16 Ibid., p. 12.
17 *Building Inclusive and Resilient Societies in Unpredictable Times,* Sheela Patel, Deon Nel, Slum Dwellers International, 2021. (https://sdinet.org/2021/02/building-inclusive-and-resilient-societies-in-unpredictable-times/).

Chapter 18

1   *The Impact of Conflict on Children,* Graca Machel, United Nations, 1996, p. 10. Chapter 19.
2   *Children of Conflict: Child-headed Households,* BBC World Service. (http://www.bbc.co.uk/worldservice/people/features/childrensrights/childrenofconflict/headed.shtm).
3   *UNHCR Global Trends 2014,* p. 4. (http://www.unhcr.org/556725e69.html)
4   *The Impact of Armed Conflict on Children,* Graca Machel, United Nations, 1996. (http://www.unicef.org/graca/a51-306_en.pdf).
5   *Report of the Special Representative of the Secretary-General for Children and Armed Conflict,* UN, August 2007.
6   'Protections Needed for Children in Nepal', Plan International, 26 April 2016. (https://plan-international.org/press-releases/nepal-earthquake-urgent-need-rebuild-and-repair-schools#).
7   *The Psychosocial Care and Protection of Children in Emergencies: Teacher Training Manual,* UNICEF, 2009. (http://toolkit.ineesite.org/toolkit/INEEcms/uploads/1064/Psychosocial_Care_and_Protection.PDF).

8   Ibid., p. 164.
9   Ibid., p. 168.
10   Ibid., pp. 168–9.
11   Ibid., p. 169.
12   *Pikin To Pikin Tok, a Radio Programme to Support Ebola-affected Children,* Child-to-Child, 2015. (http://www.childtochild.org.uk/projects/pikin-to-pikin-tok-radio-programme/).
13   *The Child-to-Child Resource Book,* Child-to-Child, 2015. (http://www.childtochild.org.uk/news/the-child-to-child-resource-book-activity-sheets/).
14   *Child-to-Child and Children Living in Camps*, ed. Clare Hanbury, Child-to-Child. (http://www.childtochild.org.uk/documents/child-child-children-living-camps/).

Chapter 19

1   'Kurdistan's First Glossy Women's Magazine: A Magazine for All Affected by Crisis', Brigitte Sins, 4 August 2015. (http://www.cdacnetwork.org/i/20150804114316-dz53u).
2   https://www.amnesty.org/en/latest/news/2016/02/syrias-refugee-crisis-in-numbers/.
3   *Time to Listen: Hearing People on the Receiving End of International Aid,* Mary B. Anderson, Dayna Brown and Isabella Jean, CDA Collaborative Learning Projects, 2012, p. 24.
4   *Internews Humanitarian Information Service in Eastern Chad*, Internews, 2013. (https://internews.org/sites/default/files/resources/Internews_Chad_Darfur_2013-03-web.pdf).
5   Ibid., p. 27.
6   *Preventing Conflict between Refugees and Host Communities*, Oliver Walton, Governance and Social development Resource Centre, 19 October 2012.
7   *Daily Express*, 29 April 2015. (http://www.express.co.uk/news/politics/573764/Nigel-Farage-Boat-people-will-bring-half-a-million-ISIS-terrorists-to-Europe).
8   'The Role of Host Communities in North Lebanon', Helen Mackreath, *Forced Migration Review,* September 2014.
9   *Refugees: Emergency Broadcasting Handbook,* John Tuckey, BBC World Service Trust, 2004, p. 3.
10   BBC News. (http://news.bbc.co.uk/1/hi/world/africa/1476225.stm).
11   UNHCR refworld website. (http://www.refworld.org/docid/3b31e167c.html).
12   *Chad, Media and Telecoms Landscape Guide*, Infoasaid, 2012. (http://www.cdacnetwork.org/contentAsset/raw-data/11172b1d-cb97-47c3-829f-5bb8c9a2f37d/attachedFile).
13   *Internews Humanitarian Information Service in Eastern Chad*, Internews, 2013. (https://internews.org/sites/default/files/resources/Internews_Chad_Darfur_2013-03-web.pdf), p. 21.
14   *Internews Humanitarian Information Service in Eastern Chad*, Internews, 2013. (https://internews.org/sites/default/files/resources/Internews_Chad_Darfur_2013-03-web.pdf).
15   Ibid., p. 18.
16   *Chad, Media and Telecoms Landscape Guide*, Infoasaid, 2012, p. 48. (http://www.cdacnetwork.org/contentAsset/raw-data/11172b1d-cb97-47c3-829f-5bb8c9a2f37d/attachedFile).

17 *Internews Humanitarian Information Service in Eastern Chad*, Internews, 2013, p. 12. (https://internews.org/sites/default/files/resources/Internews_Chad_Darfur_2013-03-web.pdf).

18 *Chad, Media and Telecoms Landscape Guide*, Infoasaid, 2012, p. 48. (http://www.cdacnetwork.org/contentAsset/raw-data/11172b1d-cb97-47c3-829f-5bb8c9a2f37d/attachedFile).

19 Ibid., p. 48.

20 Ibid.

21 *Internews Humanitarian Information Service in Eastern Chad*, Internews, 2013. (https://internews.org/sites/default/files/resources/Internews_Chad_Darfur_2013-03-web.pdf) p. 17.

22 Ibid., p. 18.

23 *Chad, Media and Telecoms Landscape Guide*, Infoasaid, 2012, p. 49. (http://www.cdacnetwork.org/contentAsset/raw-data/11172b1d-cb97-47c3-829f-5bb8c9a2f37d/attachedFile).

24 *Refugees: Emergency Broadcasting Handbook*, BBC World Service Trust, 2004, p. 72.

25 *Time to Listen: Hearing People on the Receiving End of International Aid*, Mary B. Anderson, Dayna Brown and Isabella Jean, CDA Collaborative Learning Projects, 2012, p. 24.

26 Ibid., p. 25.

Chapter 20

1 *Mobile Pastoralists and Education: Strategic Options,* Saverio Krätli and Caroline Dyer, 2009, International Institute for Environment and Development (UK), pp. 13–14.

2 *Open and Distance Learning in the Developing World,* Hillary Perraton, 2000, Routledge, Ch. 1.

3 'Open and Distance Learning in the Gobi Desert: Non-formal Education for Nomadic Women', Bernadette Robinson, 1996, *Distance Education: An International Journal,* University of Queensland, Australia, November 1999, p. 9.

4 Ibid., p. 9.

5 *Case Study: Child-centred Educational Radio Project in Kailahun District, Sierra Leone,* David Walker, Bella Tristram, Paola Pereznieto, Tricia Young, United Nations Girls Education Initiative, 2016.

6 Ibid., p. 6.

7 Ibid., p. 7.

8 Ibid., p. 6.

9 Ibid.

10 Ibid.

11 Ibid., p. 4.

12 Ibid., p. 6.

13 Ibid., p. 9.

14 'Open and Distance Learning in the Gobi Desert: Non-formal Education for Nomadic Women', Bernadette Robinson, *Distance Education: An International Journal,* University of Queensland, Australia, November 1999.

15 Ibid., p. 12.

16   Ibid., p. 13.
17   Ibid., p. 16.
18   Ibid., p. 13.
19   Ibid., p. 15.
20   Ibid., p. 13.
21   Ibid., p. 18.
22   Ibid., p. 14.
23   Ibid., p. 13.
24   *SOMDEL Somali Distance Education for Literacy Programme, External Evaluation for Comic Relief,* Dr. Felicity Thomas, July 2006, p. 3.
25   Ibid., p. 9.
26   Ibid., p. 4.
27   'Open and Distance Learning in the Gobi Desert: Non-formal Education for Nomadic Women', Bernadette Robinson, *Distance Education: An International Journal,* University of Queensland, Australia, November 1999.

Chapter 23

1   *Strengthening Radio Stations' Coverage of Rights, Reace and Governance in Somalia,* BBC Media Action 2012. (http://www.bbc.co.uk/mediaaction/publications-and resources/research/summaries/africa/somalia/radio).
2   *The Role of Media in Protection of Human Rights,* G. N. Ray, Press Council of India. (http://www.presscouncil.nic.in/OldWebsite/speechpdf/The%20Role%20of%20 Media%20in%20Protection%20of%20Human%20Rights%20Visakhapatnam.pdf).
3   https://www.hirondelle.org/en/myanmar-en.
4   Ibid.
5   https://www.bbc.co.uk/mediaaction/where-we-work/africa/sierra-leone/charles-taylor.
6   Gordon Hewart, Rex v Sussex Justices, 9 November 1923, quoted in *Oxford Essential Quotations,* ed. Susan Ratcliffe, Oxford University Press, online version, 2016. (http://oxfordreference.com).
7   *Reporting Transitional Justice: A Handbook for Journalists,* Julia Crawford, Janet Anderson, Karen Williams, BBC World Service Trust, International Center for Transitional Justice, 2007, p. 9.
8   *South Sudan Attack: UN to Investigate Juba Compound Raid,* Briana Duggan, CNN, 17 August 2016.
9   *Strengthening Radio Stations' Coverage of Rights, Peace and Governance in Somalia,* BBC Media Action 2012. (http://www.bbc.co.uk/mediaaction/publications-and resources/research/summaries/africa/somalia/radio).
10   *Press Freedom Index.* (https://rsf.org/en/ranking).

Chapter 24

1   *Communication for Empowerment: Developing Media Strategies in Support of Vulnerable Groups,* UNDP, 2006.

2   Communication for Social Change Consortium. (http://www.communicationfor
     socialchange.org/).
3   *How a Partnership in South Sudan Is Making a Difference, One Radio Station at a
     Time*, 2017, Internews. (https://www.internews.org/how-partnership-south-sudan-
     making-difference-one-radio-station-time).
4   *Stories of Community Radio in East Africa: Powerful Change*, Birgitte
     Jallov, Communication for Social Change Consortium. (http://www.
     communicationforsocialchange.org/photogallery.php?id=395).
5   *Local Community Takes Ownership of Radio Stations in South Sudan*, 2013, Internews.
     (https://www.internews.org/our-stories/project-updates/local-community-takes-
     ownership-radio-stations-south-sudan).
6   *Breeze FM Lifting the Spirit of the People.* (http://breezefmchipata.com/?page_
     id=1414).
7   *Research Summary Strengthening Radio Stations' Coverage of Rights, Peace and
     Governance in Somalia*, Pam Vallance and Rhian Were, BBC Media Action, 2012.
     (http://downloads.bbc.co.uk/mediaaction/pdf/research_summaries/BBCMA_
     research_summary_somalia_radio_stations_NSA_25.pdf).

Chapter 25

1   *Nolosha iyo Qaanunka, Programme 20*, BBC World Service Trust, 2010.
2   *Inspiring Political Participation, Lessons from the Media*, Will Taylor, BBC Media
     Action, 2016. (http://downloads.bbc.co.uk/mediaaction/pdf/practicebriefings/
     inspiring-participation.pdf).

Chapter 26

1   Population Media Center. (https://www.populationmedia.org/product/sabido-
     history/).
2   *A Communication Model for the Effects of an Entertainment-Education Soap Opera
     on the Stages of Family Planning Adoption*, Peter W. Vaughan and Everett M. Rogers,
     1996, quoted on the Communication Initiative website. (http://www.comminit.com/
     edutain-africa/content/impact-data-twende-na-wakati).
3   Population Media Center. (https://www.populationmedia.org/product/sabido-
     history/).
4   'Involving Husbands in Safe Motherhood: Effects of the SUAMI SIAGA Campaign in
     Indonesia,' Shefner-Rogers, C. L., Sood, B., *Journal of Health Communication*, May–
     June 2004.
5   *Can Radio Drama Improve Child Health and Nutrition in Somalia?*

Chapter 27

1   *Can Radio Drama Improve Child Health and Nutrition in Somalia?* Shiri Landman
     and Angela Githitho Muriithi, BBC Media Action, 2015, p. 10.

2   Ibid., p. 8.
3   'Modeling and Reinforcement to Combat HIV: The MARCH Approach to Behavior Change', Christine Galavotti, PhD, Katina A. Pappas-DeLuca, MA, and Amy Lansky, PhD, *American Journal of Public Health,* Vol. 91, No. 10, October 2001. p. 1602.
4   *The Stages of Change*, Prochaska et al., 1997. (www.cpe.vt.edu › gttc › presentations).

Chapter 29

1   *The TV Studio Production Handbook*, Lucy Brown and Lyndsay Duthie, I.B. Tauris, 2016.

Section 6

i   *Psychological First Aid: Guide for Field Workers,* World Health Organisation, 2011, p. 4.

Select bibliography

Issues for all communication for development broadcasting projects

Anderson, M. B., D. Brown and I. Jean, *Time to Listen: Hearing People on the Receiving End of International Aid* (CDA Collaborative Learning Projects, 2012).

Biggs, Philippa (ed. And co-author) and Youlia Lozanova (co-author), *The State of Broadband 2017: Broadband Catalyzing Sustainable Development* (ITU, UNESCO, 2017), 3.4 Gender Equality and Gender Digital Divide.

Britton, James, *Language and Learning* (Heinemann Educational Books, 2nd edition, 1993).

Brown, Lucy and Lyndsay Duthie, *The TV Studio Production Handbook* (I.B.Tauris, 2016).

Infoasaid, *Communication Is Aid Animation* (Infoasaid, 2011).

Mayer, Doe, *How Obvious Can You Be? Heavy-handed Messages in EE Material* (EE4, 2004).

McCrum, Sarah and Lotte Hughes, *Interviewing Children: A Guide for Journalists and Others* (Save the Children, 1998).

United Nations, *UN Sustainable Development Goals* (UN, 2015).

Humanitarian communication

ACAPS, *Assessing Information and Communication Needs: A Quick and Easy Guide for Those Working in Humanitarian Response* (CDAC Network, ACAPS, 2014). http://www.cdacnetwork.org/tools-and-resources/i/20140721173332-ihw5g.

Anderson, M. B., D. Brown and I. Jean, *Time to Listen: Hearing People on the Receiving End of International Aid* (CDA Collaborative Learning Projects, 2012).

Andersen, Robin and Purnaka L. De Silva (eds), *The Routledge Companion to Media and Humanitarian Action* (Routledge, 2018).

Buchanan-Smith, Margie, Jonathan Corpus Ong and Sarah Routley, *Who's Listening? Accountability to Affected People in the Haiyan Response* (Plan International, 2015).

Index